Paul Smeyers • Marc Depaepe
Editors

Educational Research: Ethics, Social Justice, and Funding Dynamics

 Springer

Editors
Paul Smeyers
Faculty of Psychology and Educational
Sciences
Ghent University and K.U. Leuven
Belgium

Marc Depaepe
Subfaculteit Psychologie en Pedagogische
Wetenschappen
K.U. Leuven
Belgium

Educational Research
ISBN 978-3-319-73920-5   ISBN 978-3-319-73921-2   (eBook)
https://doi.org/10.1007/978-3-319-73921-2

Library of Congress Control Number: 2018934410

Printed on acid-free paper

This Springer imprint is published by the registered company Springer International Publishing AG part of Springer Nature.
The registered company address is: Gewerbestrasse 11, 6330 Cham, Switzerland

Contents

About the Authors

Jeff Bale is associate professor of language and literacy education at OISE/ University of Toronto. His research interests include political-economic analysis of language education policy and language teacher education. His work has appeared in the *Bilingual Research Journal, Review of Research in Education, Journal of Teacher Education* and *Teachers College Record*. He is coeditor of *Education and Capitalism: Struggles for Learning and Liberation* (Haymarket, 2012) and associate editor of book reviews for the *International Multilingual Research Journal*. He worked for a decade as an ESL and German teacher in urban secondary schools in the United States. Currently, he is the faculty sponsor of a partnership with Downsview Secondary School in the Toronto District School Board, where he collaborates with literacy teachers to prepare mainstream teacher candidates to work with multilingual learners.

David Bridges is professor emeritus of the University of East Anglia (where he previously served as pro-vice-chancellor) and emeritus fellow of St Edmund's College and Homerton College, Cambridge. He writes on philosophy of education (and is an honorary vice-president of the Philosophy of Education Society of Great Britain) but has also directed or codirected a long history of empirically based research projects, with several in international partnerships. He was director of the multidisciplinary Von Hügel Institute in Cambridge and is an elected fellow of the Academy of Social Sciences. A lot of his writing brings together his experience in research leadership, educational policy and philosophical work, as illustrated in the 2017 publication by Springer, *Philosophy in Educational Research: Epistemology, Ethics, Politics and Quality*.

Kathleen Coessens is head of music at Koninklijk Conservatorium Brussel (KCB). She leads CORPoREAL art-research group at Koninklijk Conservatorium Antwerpen and KLAP (knowing and learning in artistic practices) research at KCB. She is a professor at Vrije Universiteit Brussel (VUB) and a member of the research group Centre for Logic and Philosophy of Science (CLPS) (http://www.vub.ac.be/CLWF/home/).

James C. Conroy is vice-principal (internationalization) at the University of Glasgow where he has held the position of professor of religious and philosophical education since 2005. Previously, he was dean of the School of Education (from 2006 to 2010), head of the graduate school and head of the Department of Religious Education. He has held visiting professorial positions in Australia, Brazil, North America and Europe (most recently as EU visiting professor at the University of Warsaw) and has published extensively in the areas of philosophy of education, religion, education and liberal democracy. Jim has served on a number of government committees and has been a director of a number of national and international bodies including Learning and Teaching Scotland. He is a past president of the Association for Moral Education and chair of the Philosophy of Education Society of Great Britain. Currently, he is chair of the *Journal of Moral Education* Trust and chair-elect of the Philosophy of Education Society of Great Britain. In 2012, he was elected a fellow of the Academy of Social Sciences and has held research grants from a range of charities, government bodies and research councils.

Robert A. Davis is professor of religious and cultural education in the University of Glasgow. With a strong background in high school and college teaching, he has taught, written and broadcast widely on areas such as religious education, philosophy of education, history of education and teacher education. He has special interests in childhood studies, catholic education, literary criticism and anthropology, on each of which he has written numerous articles and delivered numerous keynotes. He has co-authored an intellectual biography of the educational reformer Robert Owen and a major study of religious education in British schools, *Does RE Work?* He is the editor of the *Journal of Philosophy of Education*.

Jeroen J. H. Dekker is a full professor of history and theory of education at the University of Groningen. He heads the research programme 'education in culture', is president of the *University of Applied Educational Sciences* (SPO) and is member of the supervisory board of the *Groningen University Fund*. He was a visiting fellow at the European University Institute (Florence), at the European Institute of Columbia University (New York) and at the Max Planck Institute for Human Development (Berlin). A former president of the International Standing Conference for the History of Education (ISCHE), he is co-editor-in-chief of *Paedagogica Historica* and (corresponding) member of the editorial board of *History of Education*, of the editorial board of *Groningen Studies in Cultural Change*, of the advisory board of *Historia y Memoria de la Educación*, of the editorial board of *Pedagogiek* and of the scientific committee of *Annali di storia dell'Educazione e delle Istituzioni Educative*. His publications deal with the social and cultural history of education, childhood and parenting. Among them are *Jeugdzorg in Nederland, 1945–2010* [Youth care in the Netherlands, 1945–2010] (2012), *Educational Ambitions in History* (2010), *Het verlangen naar opvoeden* [From Educational Aspiration to Educational Supervision. Childhood and Education in the Netherlands from the Golden Age until 1900] (2006) and *The Will to Change the Child. Re-education Homes for Children at Risk in Nineteenth Century Western Europe*

(2001), with Frank Simon. He is editor of *Shaping the History of Education? The First 50 Years of Paedagogica Historica* (London and New York: Routledge, 2016) and numerous articles. He is editor of *The Cultural Histories of Education, The Renaissance, 1400–1650* and volume 3 of *The Cultural Histories of Education*, to be published in 2020 by Bloomsbury Publishing.

Marc Depaepe is professor of history of education and history of psychology at K.U. Leuven, campus Kulak (Flanders, Belgium). He was deputy vice-chancellor at K.U. Leuven, responsible for the campuses at Kortrijk (Kulak), Bruges and Ostend between 2013 and 2017. He is co-editor-in-chief of *Paedagogica Historica*, since 2005. He was former secretary (1989–1991) and chairman (1991–1994) of the 'International Standing Conference for the History of Education' (ISCHE). He was former president of the 'Belgian-Dutch Society for the History of Education' (BNVGOO) (1998–2002) and vice-president of the 'Internationale Gesellschaft für Historische und Systematische Schulbuchforschung' (IGHSSF) in Germany (1997–2008). He is member of the board of directors of the International Academy of Education (IAE), since 2012. He has published and co-published abundantly on the history of education. His selected readings, *Between Educationalization and Appropriation*, were published in 2012. In 2015, he was awarded an honorary doctorate at the University of Latvia in Riga.

Lynn Fendler is a professor in the Department of Teacher Education at Michigan State University, USA, where she teaches courses in educational foundations, curriculum theory, philosophy and historiography. She received a master of arts degree in applied English linguistics and a PhD in curriculum and instruction from the University of Wisconsin-Madison. Since 2000, Professor Fendler has been a member of the research community 'Philosophy and History of the Discipline of Education: Evaluation and Evolution of the Criteria for Educational Research'. In 2010–2011, she served as visiting professor in languages, culture, media and identities at the University of Luxembourg. Her research interests include ethics of knowledge, historiography, genealogy, educational research and the philosophy of food. Professor Fendler is the author of *Michel Foucault* in the Bloomsbury [formerly Continuum] Library of Educational Thought, which introduces Foucault's philosophical, genealogical and literary critique to teachers. Her current research projects include studies of non-representational theory, history of the bell curve, humanities-oriented research and the educational problems of aesthetic taste.

Karen François is professor at the Department of Philosophy at Vrije Universiteit Brussel (VUB). She is a member of the research group Centre for Logic and Philosophy of Science (CLPS) (http://www.vub.ac.be/CLWF/home/).

Chris Higgins is associate professor of philosophy of education in the Department of Education Policy, Organization and Leadership at the University of Illinois at Urbana-Champaign, where he serves as editor of *Educational Theory.* A resident associate at Illinois' Center for Advanced Study, he is codirecting a two-year initiative, 'Learning Publics', examining the role of universities, and in particular the arts and humanities, in public life. His book, *The Good Life of Teaching: An Ethics of Professional Practice* (Wiley-Blackwell, 2011), offers one of the first systematic extensions of virtue ethics to questions concerning work and professional identity. His recent and forthcoming publications include 'The Death Spiral of Contemporary Public Higher Education' (*Thresholds in Education*), 'The Public and Private in Education' (Springer *International Handbook of Philosophy of Education*), 'Teaching as a Hermeneutic Calling (*Philosophy of Education*)' and 'Zombie Liberal Education' (*Educational Theory*). He is currently working on three book projects: the first develops a new theory of humanism and liberal learning and offers a critique of the corporatized, vocationalized multiversity; the second is an anti-textbook on professional ethics; the third is an inquiry into the dynamics of the teacher-student relationship.

Ethan Hutt is an assistant professor of teaching and learning, policy and leadership at the University of Maryland, College Park. Hutt earned his PhD and MA at Stanford University. His research focuses on the historical relationship between quantification, education policy and the law. In particular, his work examines the way in which the law has defined the purpose, organization and goals of public education in the United States through the creation of standards and quantitative metrics. He is currently working on his first book—a history of minimum standards in American education—and has published articles on the legal implications of value-added models for administrators and teachers, on the history of grading practices and standardized tests and on accountability in a global context.

Karin Maria Karlics received her PhD from the Department of Information Science and Information Systems at Graz University in Austria in 2011, where she explored information management functions in national economies. She has been a member of the university library team since 2003, focusing on digital libraries, statistics and analytics. She is currently head of the bibliometrics services at the Free University of Bozen-Bolzano in Italy.

Edwin Keiner is a full professor of foundations of education and social pedagogy at the Free University of Bozen-Bolzano, Italy, and currently the vice-dean for teaching at the Faculty of Education. He worked at the Universities of Frankfurt/ Main, Bochum and Erlangen-Nuremberg, Germany. He was the chairperson of the commission on Research on Educational Research and of the section Foundations of Education of the German Educational Research Association for many years and is active in the European Educational Research Association (EERA) as well. He is member of the editorial boards of the *European Educational Research Journal*, the *Paedagogica Historica* and the *Educational Assessment, Evaluation and Accountability*. Among his recent works are: *Unscharfe Grenzen – eine Disziplin im Dialog: Pädagogik, Erziehungswissenschaft, Bildungswissenschaft, Empirische Bildungsforschung* (Glaser, Edith, and Keiner, Edwin [Hrsg.]), Bad Heilbrunn, Klinkhardt, 2015, and *The European Educational Research Association: people,* *practices and policy over the last 20 years* (Honerød Hoveid, Marit; Keiner, Edwin; and Figueiredo, Maria P. [Eds.]), Special Issue, *European Educational Research Journal*, 13 (4), 2014.

Frank Simon is professor emeritus at the University of Ghent (UGent) (Flanders, Belgium). His research deals with history of preschool and primary education in Belgium (education policy, teacher unions, the teaching profession), educational-ization processes, everyday educational practice, classroom and curriculum history, education and cultural heritage, and progressive education.

Paul Smeyers is professor at the University of Ghent and at K.U. Leuven, both in Belgium, and honorary professor at Stellenbosch University (South Africa). He teaches philosophy of education and methodology of the Geisteswissenschaften (qualitative/interpretative research methods). He is the author of numerous articles focusing on Wittgenstein's relevance for philosophy of education, on postmodernism and on issues of the methodology of educational research. He is president of the *International Network of Philosophers of Education* and link convenor for Network 13, Philosophy of Education, *European Educational Research Association*. He is the editor of *Ethics and Education* (Taylor and Francis). Together with Nigel Blake, Richard Smith and Paul Standish he co-authored three books, *Thinking Again*, *Education in an Age of Nihilism* and *The Therapy of Education*, and with Michael Peters and Nick Burbules, *Showing and Doing*. With Marc Depaepe he coedited the series *Educational Research* (Springer, thus far 10 books). Recent publications include a co-authored book with Richard Smith (*Making Sense of Education and Educational Research*, Cambridge University Press, Cambridge, 2014); a collection coedited with David Bridges, Morwenna Griffiths and Nick Burbules (*International Handbook of Interpretation in Educational Research Methods*, 2 vols., Springer, 2015); and a collection he edited for Springer, *International Handbook of Philosophy of Education* (2 vols., to be published in 2018). His latest work focuses anew on Wittgenstein's legacy for philosophy of education. Some of that is included in the collection edited by Michael Peters and Jeff Stickney (*A Companion to Wittgenstein on Education*. Springer, 2017). Attention to Smeyers' contributions in this area is discussed in the foreword (David Bakhurst), the introductory chapter (editors) and a separate chapter by Paul Standish of this collection.

Richard Smith is professor of education at the University of Durham, UK. He was for many years director of the university's undergraduate programmes in combined social sciences and combined arts. He has recently served as vice-chair and chair of the Philosophy of Education Society of Great Britain. He was editor of the *Journal of Philosophy of Education*, 1991–2001, and founding editor of *Ethics and Education*, 2006–2013. In 2014, he served on the United Kingdom's Research Education Framework Panel 25 (Education). His current interests are in the epistemology of educational research, in the moral psychology of self-belief and in virtue epistemology. He is especially interested in aspects of not knowing, in what might be called the quieter qualities such as humility and diffidence and in the place of irony in education. His *Understanding Education and Educational Research*, jointly written with Paul Smeyers (Universities of Ghent and Leuven, Belgium), was published by Cambridge University Press in 2014.

Lynda Stone is the Samuel M. Holton distinguished professor and professor of philosophy of education at the University of North Carolina at Chapel Hill, USA. Stone has been an education professional for over 50 years, publishing internationally and nationally for nearly 30 years. She has edited a dozen volumes, published in over 20 journals and served leadership roles in national and international professional organizations. The chapter in this volume continues her critique of educational research practice particularly in the United States through a return to long time interests in feminist theorizing.

Jean Paul Van Bendegem is professor of logic and philosophy of science at the Department of Philosophy at Vrije Universiteit Brussel (VUB) and at the University of Ghent (UGent). He is the director of the Centre for Logic and Philosophy of Science (CLPS) at VUB (http://www.vub.ac.be/CLWF/home/).

Angelo Van Gorp is professor of history of education at the University of Koblenz-Landau (Campus Landau), Germany. Previously, he was an assistant professor at the Universities of Leuven (2007–2012) and Ghent (2012–2017), Belgium, and a visiting scholar at the University of Birmingham, UK (2009 and 2010), and at the University of Sassari, Italy (2017). His research uses historical perspectives and methods to examine continuities and ruptures in the historical formation of the relationships between schools and communities from the late nineteenth to the early twenty-first centuries. Related to this are current investigations in the histories of progressive schooling, migration and race and the visual representation of schooling and education in documentary film and photography. Van Gorp is coordinator of the International History of Education Doctoral Summer School supported by the Paedagogica Historica Foundation, History of Education Society–UK, International Standing Conference for the History of Education (ISCHE) and the European Educational Research Association (EERA). He is member of the advisory board of *Paedagogica Historica*, of the scientific committee of the *Rivista di Storia dell'Educazione* as well as of the *Storia dell'educazione in Europa* book series and international correspondent of the Voices of War and Peace World War One Engagement Centre, UK. Van Gorp is past vice-president of the Belgian-Dutch Society for the History of Education (BNVGOO) and former link convenor of EERA's (Histories of Education) Network 17.

Inge J. M. Wichgers graduated in interdisciplinary social sciences in 2012 (Utrecht University, BSc) and obtained two master degrees in educational sciences, one of them cum laude, at the University of Groningen in 2014 and 2015. Based on her and L. Hahurij's master thesis, the article 'The Resilience of Recently Graduated and Unemployed Dutch Academics in Coping with the Economic Crisis' was published in volume 13 of the *Journal of Social Science Education*. In 2016–2017, she was co-author of publications on the regulation of children's emotions in the seventeenth century and on school acts in the nineteenth century. In September 2017, she started a PhD project on the impact of high school policy and culture on students' profile and school subject choices in secondary education.

Educational Research: A Tale of Tensions and Constraints

Paul Smeyers and Marc Depaepe

Values unavoidably enter into the conduct of research and the purposes of research. Whose interests have been served by research? Who have been involved as practitioners of research and as subjects of research and who has not? Should educational research be explicitly committed to promoting equality and inclusion? Does this require research to be more aware of the cultural and global contexts of research questions, and what would it mean for research to be more explicitly re-contextualized? What ethical challenges does the conduct of research encounter? Do comparative research rankings impose ethical and social justice constraints? These general issues are then addressed more particularly concerning research funding. Most educational research increasingly requires institutional and financial support. Does funding shape the content of research, and even what counts as research? Does funding shift the efforts of researchers from pure or basic research to more applied research? Does funding encourage the development of large research teams, to the detriment of individual scholars? Who owns the content, results, and data of publicly funded research? Do scholars solicit funding to support research projects, or generate research projects to attract funding? Thus these commonplaces are explored both philosophically and historically, examining the changing sources, patterns, and effects of educational research funding over time.

Do money and ethics go together? Obviously more often than not there is a real tension. This is not different in the area of educational research and, as argued in one of the chapters of this book, universities have always found themselves pressured by

P. Smeyers (✉)
Ghent University, Ghent, Belgium

K.U. Leuven, Leuven, Belgium
e-mail: paul.smeyers@ped.kuleuven.be

M. Depaepe
K.U. Leuven, Kortrijk, Belgium
e-mail: Marc.Depaepe@kuleuven.be

© Springer International Publishing AG, part of Springer Nature 2018
P. Smeyers, M. Depaepe (eds.), *Educational Research: Ethics, Social Justice, and Funding Dynamics*, Educational Research 10,
https://doi.org/10.1007/978-3-319-73921-2_1

1

constraints and opportunities. Similarly, is educational research shaped by the focus of social justice? Again, in most cases it is not, though it can be inspired by the provision of equal opportunities for all, here too it is not a story of only opportunities and challenges but as well of constraints, tensions and pitfalls.

The research community *Philosophy and History of the Discipline of Education* addressed the above questions during the meetings of 2015 (Leuven) and 2016 (Brussels). Both themes, 'Ethics and Social Justice' and 'Funding Dynamics' are part of the focus in the period of 2014–2018 which has as central theme 'Purposes, projects, and practices of educational research'.[1] In this collection one finds first ten chapters dealing with issues of ethics and social justice concerning educational research; these are followed by seven chapters explicitly focusing on funding aspects. It goes without saying that this is neither a systematic nor exhaustive analysis of all the aspects than may be scrutinized. What is offered by philosophers and historians of education is though always partial, yet felt by the research community as extremely important and relevant. What is highlighted in the chapters should in our opinion not only be studied by philosophers and historians but hopefully also by those in the areas of program evaluation, research methods and policy studies. It is offered as an antidote against economistic reductionism, and to strengthen the efforts of colleagues who, granted sometimes to survive, literally buy into unethical practice. Funding is a huge issue in all kinds of research, it is therefore important to examine all aspects of it, such as how the preferences of funding agents themselves have shaped educational research past and present.[2]

The collection opens with a chapter by Davis who argues that recent critiques of the curricular and pedagogical limitations of the Western university model and its various international imitators have focused sharply on the question of knowledge—in particular the supposed privileging in the academy of Eurocentric and 'colonialist' constructions of knowledge at the expense of subaltern or indigenous knowledge repositories and epistemologies. A particular target of this invective has been the modern or so-called 'Humboldtian' research university, condemned for its exclusionary conceptions of knowledge legitimation and its imperial subordination of alternative traditions of wisdom, inquiry, learning and knowledge production. While it is important, however, to recognise the damaging effects of the Western

---

[1] During the 2014 meeting the topic was 'Discourses of change and changes of discourse'; in 2017 attention is given to '(Re)presentation, dissemination and reception'; and in 2018 'Production and acceleration' is focused on. The five themes for this period deal with different aspects of purposes, projects, and practices of educational research.

[2] The research community itself was funded during 15 years by the FWO-Vlaanderen (1999–2013). In the period 2014–2018, meetings could take place thanks to the support of the Philosophy of Education Society of Great Britain, the Vrije Universiteit Brussel, the Free University of Bozen-Bolzano, the Stichting Paedagogica Historica, and the International Network of Philosophers of Education. Though 'output' has in general terms been kept in mind (11 books were published and furthermore several special issues or parts of issues of international journals) the group never felt pressured to publish just for the sake of it or to secure future funding. Instead it is and was thought that addressing a new issue every year this joint academic effort should be made available to the wider scholarly community.

university's complicity with imperial education in all of its hierarchical forms, sustained attention to the careers of the Humboldt brothers and their roles in the shaping of the 'Berlin Curriculum' reveals a much more complex understanding of the modern university at the moment of its incubation. Influenced by their various encounters with indigenous societies, and their wider appreciation of the German tradition, the revolutionary reimagining of university essayed by the Humboldts was in fact much more sympathetic to alternative, marginalised styles of reasoning and synthesising than is commonly acknowledged. The Humboldtian moment may therefore be a much more hopeful one for reflecting upon future directions of the globalised, intercultural academy.

Conroy and Smith analyse the ethical dimensions of the UK's 'Research Excellent Framework' (REF), the latest version of an exercise which assesses the quality of university research in the UK every seven or so years. We find many of the common objections to this exercise unfounded, such as that it is excessively expensive by comparison with alternatives such as various metrics, or that it turns on the subjective judgement of the assessors. However there are grounds for concern about the crude language in which for example all relevant scholarship becomes called 'research', and publications become 'outputs'. The focus on the impact of research, which was a new feature of the most recent exercise, is particularly problematic, creating as it does a tendency to what Aristotle called *alazony,* self-aggrandisement, on the part of academics. We conclude that the REF is a mixed good from an ethical point of view, and that more could be done to mitigate its more unfortunate features.

In the next chapter Dekker and Wichgers claim that researchers increasingly meet ethical dilemmas when doing funded scientific research. In the last few decades, there is a shift in the power balance between funding agencies and researchers which may influence all stages of doing research, such as the formulation of the research subject and question, research methods used, conclusion and publication of results. So funders often specify or suggest a methodological approach and exert pressure to keep the results a secret or re-write reports. Researchers could even have to cope with the seduction of accommodating research results because of possible funding in the future. This could lead to studying non-problems, or, on the contrary, not investigating important but for the funding agency risky subjects. These challenges for researchers were also present in the recent research into historical child abuse in homes and foster families, funded by the Dutch government installed Samson-committee. In the projects funded, researchers had to cope with interests of several institutions and groups, among them the state, also the funding agency of the research. For example, research results showed that sexual abuse was not put on the agenda of the inspectorate, part of the government bureaucracy, while even critical pressure groups and the media only started to report comprehensively on child abuse from the late 1980s. But although the government thus was at the same time funder and subject of the investigations, this possible incompatibility of interests was countered by the autonomy researchers got from the committee itself to develop the whole research project within the given subject and research question. It is a challenge for researchers to resist in such situations possible temptations to conform to interests of others, and to remain critical and independent and so maintain to their academic ethics.

Stone's contribution takes up a contemporary practice in educational research in which an ethics is posited in positionality by the researcher. This is especially prevalent in qualitative social justice research in the USA. Her approach is to present elements of a case, itself out of a classical tradition in ethics. The case has these sections following an opening hypothetical: introduction, research ethics, positionality and social justice, standpoint positionalities, reflexive positionalities, and concluding discussion. Central to the chapter is presentation of roots of positionalities in feminist theorizings that are primarily epistemological and not ethical. On this issue, differences in the two formulations are set out. US research ethics can be reconceived given insights from the chapter.

Coessens, François, and Van Bendegem look at the impact of recent societal approaches of knowledge and science from the perspectives of two rather distant educational domains, mathematics and music. Science's attempt at 'self-understanding' has led to a set of control mechanisms, either generating 'closure'–the scientists' non-involvement in society–or 'economisation', producing patents and other lucrative benefits. While scientometrics became the tool and the rule for measuring the economic impact of science, counter movements, like the slow science movement, citizen science, empowering music-art initiatives and other critical approaches focus on intrinsic and ethical questions of education and knowledge. The examples of mathematics and music education show that a certain evolution of thinking about knowledge and research in terms of quantifiable products is a non-negligible fact that impacts heavily upon the domains of science–mathematics–as well as upon less 'scientific' domains as arts, but that the complexity of human knowledge acquisition and output forces society to consider also other parameters like equality, personal development and participatory processes.

Bale examines competing values evident in research about language education. The chapter begins by focusing on the explicit juxtaposition in language education research between viewing language as a *resource* and language as a *right*. This part of the chapter is historical in that it traces the emergence of resource-oriented discourses to the demise of broad civil rights movements in North America in the late 1970s/early 1980s. He then turns to more recent critiques of language rights within language education research. These critiques are rooted in post-structural approaches to understanding language that, in general, reject rights as tied to a modernist past. Part of the complication in identifying the values within this research is that its authors explicitly frame their research in social-justice terms. The chapter does not seek to question these authors' intentions, but rather to get beyond claims to social justice to clarify for what purposes and on whose behalf we conduct language education research.

Bridges explores the relationship between the epistemological considerations that drive educational research–the 'epistemic' project of the pursuit of truth or at least better understanding–and ethical considerations which function both as a constraint and in some cases as a goal. It is this last claim–that educational research should be primarily driven by, for example, a concern for social justice–that is at the centre of the discussion. The chapter argues that the analysis of a situation or structure as unjust as well as any proposals for the rendering of this situation as more just are both dependant on getting clear about the facts of the case and the likely consequences of doing this rather than that. The epistemic project has to be present alongside any pursuit of justice. Social justice appears however in a different way, as a procedural principle governing the conduct of research, illustrated in, among other sources, MacDonald's model of 'democratic evaluation'. It is argued that a concern to hear the voices of the excluded and the marginalised through educational research is not just an ethical requirement: it is an epistemic requirement if we are to understand things properly. The author then turns to a different set of relations between ethical and epistemological considerations in research, relations rooted in the literature on the ethics of belief i.e., to the set of ethical obligations that bear on what we *should* believe or not, that require us to give careful attention to evidence, to be honest in how we represent evidence and draw conclusions from it–obligations not just to be rational and honest but to express, to make public, what research compels us to believe to be the case, even if it is uncomfortable to do so.

Hutt addresses federally-funded longitudinal datasets, which have become a primary source of information for anyone attempting to describe, evaluate, or influence the American education system. Every year these datasets provide the raw material for thousands of papers and assessments of the system including claims about educational access, attainment, and achievement gaps. Despite their considerable influence in research and policy conversations, there has been little scholarly attention to the historical creation of these datasets, the ideas embedded in them, and the kinds of thinking and ways of seeing the American school system that they enabled. This contribution takes up this issue and examines the way in which early efforts to produce longitudinal information about the operation of America's schools—through Project Talent and the National Longitudinal Study of 1972—shaped the research and the claims that could be made about the American education system. It is argued that these efforts were intimately tied to the ambition to bring systems analysis to bear on questions of school reform—an ambition that created a demand for larger, more precise statistics on school operations—and helped co-construct new ideas about American educational equity and opportunity. While Project Talent reflected the Progressive Era view of educational equity as providing appropriately differentiated schooling, NLS72 represented a new concern for educational inequity as the difference in the aggregated chances of individual students. Though these early efforts failed to deliver on the promise to identify the precise relationship between identifiable school characteristics and school outcomes, they demonstrated the general viability of these techniques and pointed the way toward this new frontier of research. In attending to this history, the author seeks to bring attention to what has become a foundational part of the American educational research infrastructure and the influence that infrastructure has had on education research. In providing new capabilities for researchers and advocates, NLS-72 influenced the kinds of claims—for both good and ill—that would define policy conversations for decades to come—at once bringing into focus a broader picture of national disparities while at the same time obscuring local context and geographic distance. Just as consequentially, the initial survey continues to cast a shadow on American education research through the repetition of initial variables and survey constructs in subsequent decennial surveys (e.g. ELS, HS&B, NELS, etc.)—shaping the way we think about educational success, failure, and inequity in America.

In the next chapter Fendler argues that in educational research that calls itself empirical, the relationship between validity and reliability is that of trade-off: the stronger the bases for validity, the weaker the bases for reliability (and vice versa). Validity and reliability are widely regarded as basic criteria for evaluating research; however, there are ethical implications of the trade-off between the two. The chapter traces a brief history of the concepts, and then describes four ethical issues associated with the validity-reliability trade-off in educational research: bootstrapping, stereotyping, dehumanization, and determinism. The chapter closes by describing emerging trends in social science research that have the potential to displace the validity-reliability trade-off as a central concern for the evaluation of educational research: the introduction of translational sciences, a shift from significance to replicability, a move from inference to Big Data, and the increasing importance of consequential validity.

Action research, Higgins argues, began as an ambitious epistemological and social intervention. As the concept has become reified, packaged for methodology textbooks and professional development workshops, it has degenerated into a cure that may be worse than the disease. The point is not the trivial one that action research, like any practice, sometimes shows up in cheap or corrupt forms. The very idea that action research already exists as a live option is mystifying, distracting us from the deep challenge that action research ultimately represents. Though Joseph Schwab is sometimes credited as a forerunner of action research, it is likely that he would see the new talk of 'the teacher as researcher' as indicative of the very epitomization of which he warned. Dewey's new conception of knowledge, action, and communication—and the vision of the teacher as learner it entails—requires nothing short of a radical rethinking of teaching and inquiry, schooling and teacher education. This essay recalls the promise of action research, exploring its pitfalls, and attempts to get clear on the ongoing challenge it represents.

The chapter by Bridges begins by outlining some of the different ways in which research is funded before focussing on contracted research, which is the model that raises some of the more difficult issues about ownership and commodification. The notion of commodification is itself located in a wider discourse of the knowledge economy, intellectual property and knowledge capitalism. He asks whether it is legitimate in the case of educational research for those purchasing or sponsoring it to claim to be able to do 'what the hell they like' with it, including hiding it from public view. In response it is argued that such proprietorship and commodification threatens three sorts of harm: 'epistemic drift' as a preoccupation with winning contracts and pleasing clients substitutes for the honest pursuit of truth; a failure of systems that hold government and other bodies to account; and a barrier to public access to information and understanding about education, in which they have an important and legitimate interest. This leads to an exploration of the notion that there is something intrinsically wrong, something misplaced and also corrupting about conceiving of educational research as a commodity which can be bought and sold and disposed of as the owner wishes. The idea of research as a gift is explored, and then, as a conversation. Both metaphors point to the difficulty in separating knowledge created under an isolated contract from what preceded it or what follows from it.

Impassioned contemporary critiques of the alleged 'marketisation' of the concept of the institution of the university—now supposedly subject to the inexorable performative logic of neoliberal governmentality—routinely imply, so Davis argues, a preceding period when university education functioned innocent of commercial and financial imperatives. Yet acquaintance with the fiscal history of the European university, from its medieval ecclesial origins to its modern embrace by sophisticated state educational bureaucracies, reveals this impression of innocence to be a myth. From their foundation in the Middle Ages, through the convulsions of Renaissance, Reformation, Enlightenment and Industrialisation, European universities have by necessity been deeply entangled with the operations of money and corporate power. Commonly struggling to maintain a viable resource base, and endemically prey to corruption and misappropriation, universities have been subject to the instrumental patronage of Church, Crown, city and state over many centuries. Stamped by both successes and failures, the pursuit of financial sustainability has produced imaginative collaborations and questionable compacts, the best and worst of which offer valuable lessons for future funding models of European Higher Education.

In the next chapter Smith argues that the primary function of the current obsession with research funding is, like many extensions of neoliberalism into education, largely symbolic: it is symbolic of the hegemony of instrumental thinking and its ambition to expunge all other forms of reason from the academy (which he focuses on here) and other areas of public life. Several brief case-studies illustrate and support his argument. UK academics are increasingly expected to secure external research funding, though often the amounts they must raise are small. Against such insignificant sums the opportunity costs are clear, as academics are distracted from other kinds of research (and teaching). The comparison with Mao Zedong's 'Great Leap Forward' is irresistible: in 1958 every commune in China was required to set up small backyard furnaces to produce steel from scrap metal. Farmers, doctors, teachers and others had to neglect their regular work in order to join in. A second example: many academic research projects that secure substantial external funding actually cost the host university more than the funding brings in. Universities persist in supporting underfunded research because even inadequate external funding has value as 'status capital'. As a symbol of instrumental reason the fixation on funding requires academics to speak the language of the new breed of pro-vice-chancellors and other senior officers who now make their career in management and administration rather than undertaking such tasks for a limited period before returning to their academic work. They speak a new language with the fluency and enthusiasm of converts. Its prominent words–transparency, accountability and performance management, show that the urge to control and discipline the academy is never far away.

   The contribution by Depaepe, Simon, and Van Gorp focuses on the neurologist and educational psychologist Ovide Decroly as a scholarly persona, and deals with the financing of scientific research as well as the financial status of researchers themselves. After all, scientific practice, the production and spread of 'truth', costs money. Decroly barely experienced the evolution from the almost selfless scientist to a scientist who is put under pressure to acquire funds. He rather dedicated himself to the progress of knowledge and renounced money, fame and career opportunities than to capitalize his science into useful output. He rather envisaged a bourgeois lifestyle (science as calling) than that he was formed by the criteria set by grant providers (science as profession). As far as archival documents allow us, Decroly's itinerarium is studies, more or less as an 'independent scholar', simply by looking at the financial means he obtained—one of the necessary conditions for the development and spread of his ideas. Yet, the archival sources are far from complete. On the one hand, many sources have gone lost, and, on the other hand, the preserved (and presumably also expurgated) archive of Decroly cannot answer all of our questions. As a result, the financial picture remains incomplete. However, the sources do give an idea of Decroly's revenues, and his most important financial supporters. In any case, this study offers a corrective for the myth that Decroly—as generous as he may have been—conducted research, only in service of humanity.

   In the following chapter Fendler examines the Bill & Melinda Gates Foundation project, Measures of Effective Teaching [MET]. The chapter synthesizes current research on philanthrocapitalism to highlight some implications of current trends in funding for educational research. The MET project was a massive three-year, $45 million undertaking. It studied six school districts and 3000 teachers in the United States, collected digital video of 13,000 classroom lessons, administered surveys to students, and tracked student scores on two separate tests in efforts to stipulate the parameters of effective teaching. Reports from the MET project publicized research results about how effective teaching might be defined and measured. MET project analyses and conclusions were published in scholarly academic venues, policy briefs, and popular media from 2010 through 2013. Issues of philanthrocapitalism in educational research include the establishment of an incestuous plutocracy, the conduct of educational research in a shadow economy, the promotion of the special interests of private wealthy donors, and shifts in the terms of debate about educational issues for research in the public interest.

   The development of the philosophy of science in the twentieth century has created, François, Coessens, and Van Bendegem argue, a framework where issues concerning funding dynamics can be easily accommodated. The chapter combines the historical-philosophical approach of Thomas Kuhn, with the sociological approach of Robert K. Merton, linking the 'exact' sciences to economy and politics. Out of this came a new domain, namely the study of scientific practices. In this chapter they address why the study of practices is so interesting. The reasons are plentiful. To list some of them: (a) practices have a material aspect, (b) practices are related to learning, (c) practices have a social nature, and (d) practices are easily linked to other practices, e.g., economical practices involving the funding processes. There is an additional reason why practices are interesting: (e) they go together extremely well with '(actor)-network thinking', the locus of these practices. Many such networks are easily identifiable: the scientific network, the technological network, the economic network (including funding networks), the societal network (including the educational network), and (e) the cultural network. Given this theoretical framework, they look at the case of Science, Technology, Engineering and Mathematics (*STEM*) education and its variant Science, Technology, Engineering and Mathematics with Art (*STEAM*) education. Quite some funds are invested in STEM to raise awareness of Science, Technology, Engineering, and Mathematics. Two questions come up immediately: (a) have these initiatives been successful so far and (b) are there alternatives? As to (a) one can only observe that an interesting discussion is going at present and as to (b) what is the alternative to STEM literacy considering that current and prospective jobs require rich STEM literacy—it becomes clear that STEM can benefit from interaction with art and humanities. This brings the authors to the dynamics within the cultural and epistemological domain of art in relation to science. Initiatives as STEAM (STEM with Art) or art-based methods, processes and practices can help develop and transmit science and knowledge as well as provoke innovation. Artistic research is taking more and more part in the big pie of funding dynamics, however in an ambiguous way and with the danger of copying other disciplines practices. Funds even risk to increase a division between artistic research and artistic practice—the last one being funded by the cultural domain and the first one accepted in science funding only if it fulfils the scientific discourse and aims. When real cross-over projects from art to science and vice versa bridge the gap, funding instances often decline to sustain them. Reflection on and implementation of artistic practices in scientific learning and communication would enhance a knowledge practice that considers Pickering's view. Not only for the money. Though we are in it.

In the final chapter Karlics and Keiner argue that universities are highly interested to introduce emerging researchers into new strategies of publishing. Coaching emerging researchers counts as a strategic investment not only into emerging scholars, but also into the universities' reputation and budget. In this context emerging researchers face diverse, even contradicting, tasks, challenges, obligations and commitments, especially when they are working in an intercultural and multilingual academic milieu. Significant problems result, when this cultural and linguistic diversity at the same time is governed by standardised means and criteria, which do not consider such academic milieus. The Free University of Bozen-Bolzano, South Tyrol, Italy, and the field of educational research serve as our experiential background to reflect on the multifaceted paradoxes, challenges and conflicts arising from these problems. Against this background the authors look at different concepts and criteria of research quality and reflect on coaching strategies for emerging researchers and on the ambivalences embedded in and resulting from such strategies. They find significant disadvantages for German speaking scholars in South Tyrol. They suggest to teach and to coach students and researchers to use clever, hybrid strategies of research production, to disenchant the 'scientific' ideals, to learn to walk on the edge between the market according to which one has to sell yourself, and the scholarly and public responsibility according with which one draws one's professional ethics and identity from.

Ethics, Epistemology and the Post-Humboldtian University

Robert A. Davis

The University Ruined or Rebuilt?

The perception that the 'Humboldtian' academy, and the distinctive 'Berlin curriculum' with which it was powerfully associated, is coming to an end is increasingly prominent in contemporary higher educational literature (Kwiek 2009; Zoontjens 2010; Boulton and Lucas 2011; Nybom 2012). Philosophers of education and strategic planners in international higher education generally have for come considerable time grown accustomed to a vigorous critique of the institutions and political programmes that they serve levelled by—especially—the critical pedagogy movement. This critique typically targets the alleged complicity of universities and their various sponsors with the 'neoliberal' forces of global capital (Brown 2015; Khoo et al. 2016). It also attacks trenchantly the resultant 'colonisation' of contemporary higher education by powers inimical to the Enlightenment Humboldtian values and structures of Berlin 1810, through which Europe's tradition of medieval university learning survived the crisis of industrialisation and refurbished itself successfully for the distinctive intellectual and moral tasks of modernity (Chibber 2013). Originally a bastion and custodian of Enlightenment principles of rationality and emancipation, the Humboldtian higher education systems of particularly Europe and North America have become in the postwar period, according to the terms of this bracing assessment, little more than technocratic training laboratories in thrall to the administrative-bureaucratic state and its obeisance before the pervasive and dehumanizing forces of international capitalism—abetting their relentless search for docile labour, boundless consumption and maximum profit (Trifonas and Peters 2005; Brady 2012; Cruickshank 2016; Fulford 2016).

R. A. Davis (✉)
University of Glasgow, Glasgow, Scotland, UK
e-mail: Robert.Davis@Glasgow.ac.uk

© Springer International Publishing AG, part of Springer Nature 2018   11
P. Smeyers, M. Depaepe (eds.), *Educational Research: Ethics, Social Justice, and Funding Dynamics*, Educational Research 10,
https://doi.org/10.1007/978-3-319-73921-2_2

Despite the obvious astringency of its rhetoric, critical pedagogy and its affiliates in other areas of critical theory are not in general fatalistic before this challenging vista of conflicted educational purpose. Indeed, perhaps beginning with the celebrated work of the late Bill Readings (1996) in the mid 1990s, much of the adversarial energy of 'theory' in the last two decades has been concerned with the rescue of higher education from its perceived performative malaise. The prospectus for renewal has taken two principal forms, each of which has accrued much polemical energy from the shifts, turns, crescendos and crashes of late techno-capitalism in the last 25 years.

The first expression of hope for the post-Humboldtian university has harnessed its expectations increasingly confidently to the technological innovations currently overtaking learning at all levels and across all sectors of education. It welcomes the coming of Web 2.0, the advent of digital and handheld technologies, and the rise of autonomous social media and virtual interactivity representative of the leading edge of far-reaching educational experiment (Marshall 2010). Invigorated recently through the stimulus provided by the large-scale and highly ambitious rebuild of the university estate in many developed and developing economies, the proponents of this particular remedy for the contemporary university's problems look to the emerging opportunity of major campus infrastructure redevelopment for a radical reimagining of the organisation and heuristics of the Humboldtian academy (Lepori and Kyvik 2010; Marcus 2016). If their predictions are correct, this will be one in which many of the established patterns of university governance and authority, learning and teaching, assessment and award, will be swept away wholesale by a technologically-enhanced democratisation of study and an empowerment of learners no longer passively disposed before the traditions and hierarchies of university custom (Kirkwood and Price 2014). Epitomised by the supposed obsolescence of 'the lecture' as the emblematic expression of traditional university pedagogy, this revolution will install a replenished culture of maieutic discovery at the heart of university experience and its rebuilt plant and environment. Here transmission will be replaced with enquiry, initiation with contestation, and monologic reverence for the faculties of disinterested reason with emotionally literate and culturally situated engagement, creativity and dialogue (Arvanitakis 2013; Gibbs 2013; Oleson 2014).

The second line of critique is the chief concern of this essay, because it ventures to the heart of the underlying concept of the 'Humboldtian' university, the accompanying 'Berlin curriculum' and its offshoots, as well as the politics and philosophy of twenty-first-century higher education knowledge production on the global stage. The distinctive character of this specific appraisal of the condition of higher education is its unsparing rejection of much that passes for the originary Humboldtian settlement and its influential legacy. Its interrogation extends to university structure, the organisation and transmission of curricular knowledge, the construction of the learner as an historically situated subject, and the implicit, foundational authority of the Enlightenment principles underpinning the orthodox Humboldtian understanding of the university as an institutional locus of research and teaching (Shahjahan and Morgan 2016). It aspires to question all of these principles and assumptions, suggesting daringly that the volatile cultural politics of globalisation now impacting so tempestuously on international higher education is a welcome occasion to problematize the conventional conception of the university, not only in the name of the excluded groups it reportedly does not serve, but in relation to still deeper epistemological and ethical premises of the university as a defining Enlightenment idea itself (Rata 2012; McDonald 2013)

This specific style of critique is here identified with the controversial championing of 'indigenous epistemologies' in the philosophy and practice of education. The reason for this is that indigenous epistemology—or indigenous knowledge—movement is in its radicalism and audacity revealingly representative of the attempt to derive a fully alternative educational paradigm from the current turbulence of globalisation. Establishing to its own satisfaction the credibility and appeal of its new paradigm, it then seeks deliberately to question the overarching conception of the Humboldtian university within it as a favoured model for future patterns and provision of higher education. While in academic parlance the notion of 'indigenous epistemologies' has local frames of application and spans a huge range of cultural and intellectual endeavour, the strategic application of its claims to the 'defamiliarisation' of the university as a site of advanced research and as a community of study has potentially important consequences, stretching well beyond the frequently specific and highly differentiated goals of indigenous epistemology as a disciplinary method in action.

Indigenous Epistemologies

As a defence of a wholly naturalized epistemology, the indigenous epistemology movement, or movements, appraises *all* human epistemological activity as fully natural phenomena to be described, understood, and evaluated from an entirely anthropological and fully *a posteriori* perspective (Ghosh 2010). It therefore both addresses and reframes the complete spectrum of human epistemological activities, ranging from those of vernacular folk and cognitive specialists such as shamans and priests to those of professional philosophical epistemologists, psychologists and laboratory scientists. Indigenous epistemology embraces both local and international epistemological practices, and accordingly at its purest regards so-called 'Western' epistemological preferences as simply one set among a range of diverse, contingent epistemological options advanced by, and hence available to, multiple human agents and communities. In this respect it aims to decentre and 'provincialize' the definitions, objectives, assumptions, approaches, criteria and conclusions of—most especially—the Western scientific worldview (Hall 2001). It almost always pursues this paramount objective in explicitly *ethical* terms, as part of a larger process of social and economic struggle against what it construes as colonial intellectual domination and abjection (Nylander et al. 2013).

Politically speaking, indigenous epistemology strongly rebukes what it unmasks as the double standard embraced by most Western epistemology, exempting itself from the same kind of anthropological scrutiny to which the epistemologies of non-Western or pre-Enlightenment cultures are typically subject at the hands of Western ethnographers. It also therefore repudiates the alleged condescension involved in classic characterizations of the epistemological activities of so-called 'non-Western' actors as simple *ethno*epistemologies, interdependent with the contrasting valorization of the epistemological activities of Western thinkers as a kind of benchmarked 'epistemology proper' dissociated from any local origins or investments. Champions of indigenous epistemology argue that there is an implicit, unexamined dualism commonly expressed in the presumption that thinkers in 'other' cultures practice mere '*ethno*epistemology' or '*ethno*philosophy'. This prejudice then curates and marginalises alternative worldviews as mere anthropological curiosities, deeming their holders unqualified to participate in the West's 'genuinely' philosophical conversation until they become initiated into the mainstream educational practices and authorized styles of rationality most prized by the West—at the institutional apogee of which sits the Humboldtian university and its preferred, executive methods of research and teaching (Scharfstein 2001).

In addition to this, the established scholarly use of the terms 'ethnophilosophy and 'ethnoepistemology' by Western philosophers is unacceptable to the indigenous epistemology movement precisely because it reproduces the conceit that Western philosophy is the normative standard by which all other philosophies and all other contemplative activities of the world's cultures are to be tested and calibrated—leaving Western philosophy *as the only legitimate practice of reason*, rather than as one among many contending and complementary, iterative ethnophilosophical disciplinary paradigms (de Sousa Santos 2015). The more broadly inclusive and centrifugal use of the term 'indigenous epistemology' circumvents this trap, its advocates insist, because it embraces appreciatively (if of course sometimes critically) *every* epistemological activity, be it African, East Asian, European, Circumpolar, Native American, or even pre-Enlightenment. *All* epistemological activities, past and present, can then be understood as instances of indigenous epistemology in this broad categorical sense; and all indigenous epistemologies are legitimate, worthwhile expressions of epistemology in action. From this position of mutual respect, recognition of indigenous epistemology also further supports critical reflection upon the nature, methods, aims, domains and accepted definitions of generic epistemology itself from a broadly anthropological, fully *a posteriori* stance (Phipps 2013).

When actualised in recent discussions of the future of universities across the global landscape of higher education, indigenous epistemology focuses on a range of concerns in teaching and research, linked mostly to questions of authority, admissibility, curriculum, impact, ownership, experience and participation. For the limited purposes of this essay, two of these areas where indigenous epistemology currently seems particularly active will be reviewed: two areas where its proponents claim to have made significant inroads into the shaping of the twenty-first century university thinking. They are:

The critique of the founding 'Humboldtian moment' in the history of European higher education and its collusion with the imperial project

The rejection of the orthodox Western or 'Berlin' curriculum in the name of a new 'epistemological ethic' ontologically attuned to the global environmental and other 'crises of sustainability' confronting education and society at the present time

In each of the two domains, it is possible to take perfectly seriously the urgency and relevance of the questions being raised, but still point to some significant shortcomings in the arguments advanced. It is also possible to reconsider some of the ways in which a Humboldtian or neo-Humboldtian conception of the university might survive the accompanying sceptical scrutiny of indigenous epistemology and indeed respond persuasively to the issues with which the advocates of indigenous epistemology are justifiably preoccupied (Martín-Díaz 2017).

Authority and Subversion in the Humboldtian Moment

Directed at the founding phase of the Humboldtian reform of the European (and by later extension North American) university, the defenders of indigenous epistemology habitually critique the Humboldtian reification of structures of educational thought and practice which they allege privilege and entrench dominant and exclusionary forms of Enlightenment rationality. Hence Wilhelm von Humboldt's (1809/1990) conception of the 'unity' of teaching and research (*Einheit von Lehre und Forschung*) may appear to enshrine a commitment to a collaborative undertaking in which 'the professors are not there for the students, but rather both are there for science (and scholarship)' (Ash 2006). Its enforced 'unity' is, however, already dependent upon privileged versions of rational enquiry and authorized styles of deliberation intrinsically hostile to everything that Enlightenment ideas of educational advancement have pushed into a rejected and repressed obscurantist past or an alien cultural and ethnic pre-rational periphery. The unitary and universalizing trends in Enlightenment constructions of approved knowledge inscribed in the appositely-named 'university' of the Humboldtian imaginary can then be seen as less inclined towards a comprehensive and pluralist approach to all human learning, and more obviously supportive of hegemonic versions of knowledge-production tacitly applied to the maintenance of power by the 'knowledgeable' over the seemingly 'ignorant'. Nan Seuffert (1997) has elaborated a critique of this 'traditional Eurocentric epistemology' which has 'claimed universal applicability across disciplines, cultures and historical periods' (104) through a process of colonial imposition, or what she has termed (echoing Spivak and Said of course) 'epistemic violence' (105).

More extensively, the historian Anne McClintock (1995) has related the same critical paradox to the violent contradictions of European imperialism, reaching one of its several moments of crisis just as the post-Napolenonic Humboldtian reforms were taking root—and as the fragile Westphalian models of national identity and belonging faltered in the face of renewed encounter with the colonial Other. In particular, McClintock highlights a tacit imperial geography of the educated Western mind and its supporting educational institutions which from the late eighteenth century onwards has conflated temporality with global space. Western civilization in this imperial economy is poised at the pinnacle of cultural development, situating other cultures at lower levels of attainment. In a parallel metaphor, time becomes a linear track moving from 'underdeveloped' peoples towards higher 'civilization' and its myriad seemingly monumental achievements in the march of human progress. McClintock cautions that such a temporal construct authorises strategic modes for the internal regulation of education, at all levels, whilst simultaneously structuring, differentiating and subordinating external ethnic and national groups subject to the infantilizing colonial gaze: 'Imperial progress across the space of empire is figured as a journey backward in time to an anachronistic moment of prehistory. Geographical difference across space is figured as historical difference across time' (40).

The logic of this view strengthens imperial and post-imperial attitudes to perceived economic and social progress, which are then concentrated on a white, Euroethnic normative centre and which serve to exonerate prolonged commercial, cultural and even military exploitation of the 'developing' world by the 'post-historical' Western powers. Knowledge in its diverse forms is in this worldview forever classified as a cultural universal, occupying a nonraced and depoliticised space within the diverse ecology of human behaviour and camouflaged as the innocent accompaniment to a progressive Enlightenment humanism ineluctably bound to the paternalist dissemination of 'emancipatory' Western liberal values and economic 'development'. One of the central responses of an indigenous epistemology genuinely attuned to the oppositional potential of its cultural witness is to expose, Tamson Pietsch (2015) has recently suggested, the supremacist assumptions supporting this pervasive prejudice, contesting an account of universilizable knowledge which inflicts epistemic damage on both subaltern, excluded populations *and* on the central idea of the university itself. Such a comprehensive rethink of the purposes of university learning becomes by this light not simply a protest, but an interpellation in the passive performativity of educational competence, subverting the university's metaphors of reception and transmission and reaffirming the agency of multiple indigenous agents involved in the creation and circulation of new and multiple forms of knowledge.

There is much in this potent line of argument with which it is difficult to disagree. The collusion of the early modern institutions of Western education with the scientific racism, possessive individualism, instrumental rationality and the depredations of imperialism is indisputable and well documented. The convergence of the Humboldtian reforms with the last days of Bonaparte's Europe and the imperial redistributions of the Congress of Vienna, lent much new vitality to the European university system and provided an obvious overseas context for the representative taxonomies and axiologies of Enlightenment collecting, classification and appropriation. Nevertheless, it seems unfair to the principles of the Humboldtian reforms to interpret them as exclusively captive in their totality to the advances of the imperial mentality (Worrall 2015).

As Andrea Wulf has very recently pointed out in her *The Invention of Nature: Alexander von Humboldt's New World* (2015), the Grand Tour of the Americas upon which Alexander von Humboldt embarked in 1800, and which he convinced his older brother Wilhelm could be a viable alternative form of tertiary education reproaching the ossified learning of the ancient universities, was itself an 'indigenizing' undertaking. Far from simply imposing prior categories of knowledge collection and categorisation upon the subject Hispanic terrains of Latin America, Humboldt grew increasingly dissatisfied with the armchair theorizing and received opinion of the educational methods in which he had been trained at Frankfurt and Gottingen. Inspired by a knew spirit of inquiry sensitized to local knowledge and cultural wisdom, Humboldt developed entirely novel schemes for recording and explaining the exotic 'unregulated' natural and human histories he encountered on his travels. Indeed, the most serious criticism levelled at him when he returned to Prussia was essentially that he had 'gone native' in his credulous acceptance of indigenous knowledge, concocting fantastical explanatory schemes (eg on 'animal electricity') to reconcile tribal and creole wisdom with European scientific theory. In this regard, Alexander von Humboldt merits the same kind of rehabilitation extended to other enlightened imperial travellers and researchers, such as William Jones, by the likes of Robert Irwin (2006), Ibn Warraq (2007) and Michael Franklin (2011), who see these figures unjustly traduced by the clumsy pressing against them of the catch-all charge of 'Orientalism'. Like Jones in India, Alexander von Humboldt acquired deep respect for the cultures he encountered in South America, seeing in their rich traditions the limitations of Enlightenment rationality and fretful of its ominous, too-easy annexation by the predatory forces of imperial and commercial occupation acted out in the plight of the people among whom he was living and working (Marcone 2013).

Although we would of course be unlikely then to find in the 1810 Humboldtian vision of the reformed European university an educational institution free of imperial taint, or exempt from the gross internal inequalities of its own society (still less its colonial possessions), we do well to read the evidence with some subtlety of mind. Indigenous epistemological criticisms of the immense influence of the 'new' university of Berlin and its several imitators, point particularly accusingly to its elevation of the primacy of 'pure' science (*Bildung durch Wissenschaft*) over hands-on specialised professional training and craft-skill fieldwork (*Ausbildung, Spezialschulmodell*). For some, this is the germ of a development destined to culminate over the course of the next century in the rise of the German academic technocracy: the pure 'We Scholars' attacked by Nietzsche in his 1886 *Beyond Good and Evil* and foreshadowing the corrupted elites responsible for bringing German universities to their darkest nihilistic moment of complicity with state terror. In the 1920s, Berlin University was to host the extremist 'Race Pope', Hans Günther, a eugenicist appointed 'Professor for Racial Science, Racial Biology and Regional Sociology' (Hauschild 1997). Bill Readings' figuration of 'ruins', we do well to remember, was to be grimly and materially realized in the fate of the city Berlin from 1943–1945, uncannily presaged in the melancholy interest of the Third Reich in the so-called 'ruin value' of the overpowering yet strangely despairing monumental buildings with which it refashioned the German capital (Kitchen 2015).

It nevertheless seems clear that from the outset of their schemes—and largely because of the profound educational impact of the Grand Tour rite of passage—the Humboldt brothers sought to understand the conduct of science and scholarship within the reformed university precisely as an open-ended processes of inquiry—'not a finished thing to be found, but something unfinished and perpetually sought after', as Wilhelm described it (Ash 2006, 246). Study at a 'modern' university competing with the hands-on allure of the Grand Tour and its peripatetic learning was therefore for the Humboldts not to be based upon the rediscovery and repetition of things learned in textbooks, but on an approach to pedagogy, and an attitude to skill and to thinking, infinitely broader than—if of course critically inclusive of—the acquisition of specialised knowledge.

The Berlin Curriculum: Ethics and Ontology

Modern suspicion of the so-called 'Berlin Curriculum' and its various post-1810 mutations is commensurate with the wider epistemological anxieties discussed above. In dedicating their reformed university in Berlin to the canons of secular, Enlightened rationality, the Humboldts and their allies endeavoured to refit an older classical curriculum inherited in the first instance from the medieval and Renaissance humanists yet in key respects broken apart by the destructive convulsions of the European Reformation and the Thirty Years War. Europe's uncertain heritage of shrunken, depleted seats of learning already faced by the middle of eighteenth Century a host of civic and confessional rivals offering advanced education to minorities excluded by faith, class, language or regional isolation from the major centres of higher learning (Israel 2002). According to those of their critics fueled in today's climate of controversy by the concerns of indigenous or marginalized epistemologies, Wilhelm von Humboldt redeemed the disintegrating university system, however, by creating a rigid, competitive academic architecture designed to modernize and standardise the idea of the research university and establish its unswerving institutional sovereignty over the production and adjudication of almost all forms human knowledge capital and investigation. For this formidable task, he drew heavily upon Kant's anticlerical disciplinary blueprint from the 1798, *Dispute of the Faculties*, as well as on his 1803 *On Education*. He also relied heavily upon J. G. Fichte's representation of the 'subjects of the higher studies' from his 1807 *Deduced Scheme for an Academy to be Established in Berlin* and his 1808 nationalistic clarion-call, *Addresses to the German Nation*.

For the Kant of *On Education* (1803/2003), university education was intended to accomplish four things (4): first, it must make human beings capable of exerting discipline over their 'animal nature.' Next, it must supply 'culture', immersion in which makes students aware of their own abilities and proclivities within a 'tradition' of thought and learning. Thirdly, it must cultivate refinement and discretion of manners so that students are able to conduct themselves appropriately in society. And finally, university education must provide 'moral training' so that students will learn to choose nothing but good ends—'good ends being those which are necessarily approved by everyone, and which may at the same time be the aim of everyone' (20).

In Fichte's *Deduced Scheme* (1805–1806/1926), '*all scientific material must be comprehended in its organic unity and interpreted in the philosophical spirit…*as the pure form of knowledge' (258). The experience of this unity is to be reached, for Fichte, solely within the confines of the (proposed) university, because only the accumulated pedagogical expertise of the university can supply the proper organization of scientific and philosophical concepts, the correct order in which they should appear, and an understanding of their place in the whole. To realise this ideal, Fichte went still further in proposing that a 'philosophical encyclopedia' be created to structure the curriculum and orient teachers and students towards the Kantian branches of knowledge. Individual subjects were to be treated in accordance with the rational principles of the proposed encyclopedia and all staff were to be required to comprehend and ratify the nature of the overall curriculum by virtue of their own training in philosophy. The encyclopedia, Fichte argued, 'must gradually grow of itself by the interaction of philosophy and the philosophically correct treatment of the particular subjects of science' (194–195). Individual sciences must be guided by a more comprehensive conception of knowledge than that contained in the various sciences themselves—and for Fichte Philosophy is the discipline destined to afford that broader context of understanding and learning within which the separate branches of knowledge can together flourish: 'The spirit of every particular science is a limited spirit', he notes. The 'spirit' of philosophy, by contrast, understands 'first itself and then in itself all other spirits….the artist in a particular science must be above all a philosophical artist, and his particular art is merely a further determination and special application of his general philosophical art' (192–193).

Although Humboldt ultimately rejected Fichte's encyclopedia proposal for his new university, his brilliance was to synthesize Fichte's unified, interdisciplinary curricular concept with Kant's advocacy of a separate 'Philosophical Faculty' for the attainment of educational goals 'that concerns itself with the interests of the sciences, that is, with truth: one in which reason is authorized to speak out publicly. For without a faculty of this kind, the truth would not come to light' (1798/1979, 22). From this combination, the distinctive 'Berlin Curriculum' was formed, enlivening Humboldt's conception of a coherent knowledge-rich *Bildung* in which a perfect resonance might be achieved between the formation of the individual person, the legitimate interests of society and the advance of human civilization from familiar to unfamiliar domains of discovery (Nybom 2007).

In several obvious respects, the imagery of the Humboldtian curriculum does appear to confirm the worst fears of those thinkers and popular pedagogues wary that from its inception the reborn, research-intensive facultised university of the modern era has been predicated upon an exclusionary and totalizing understanding of knowledge inseparable from the institutional power and social cachet of the university itself. Intolerant of difference, hierarchical in governance, elitist in its self-replication, this model of the university and the learning that goes on inside it not only represses rival sources of epistemic authority, it also lacks, despite its declared philosophical investments, the internal capacity to check its own privileges or question seriously its own sources of legitimacy—instead actively *delegitimizing* the knowledge and experience of almost all groups and minorities superfluous to its protected interests.

In many recent expressions of indigenous epistemological protest against this perceived academic ascendancy—including those taken up by sympathizers within the university precinct itself—such criticism has become increasingly *ethical* in character, pointing ominously to the seeming failure of university knowledge-production on the Humboldtian model to deal at all satisfactorily with the contemporary crises of global justice, poverty, displacement and migration, gender and racial oppression and even possibly impending ecological catastrophe (Sillitoe 2010; Nakata et al. 2012;). This ethical turn often proceeds to quite challenging extremes, suggesting that the more recent evasions and silences of the academy in fact disclose longstanding and deep-seated moral failures and inadequacies of Humboldtian university culture. These encompass not only the disasters of the short twentieth Century, but the protracted histories of toxic knowledge production and disordered representation supportive in their various turns of empire, slavery and the rapacious exploitation of the earth's natural and human resources. For educational theorists such as Ronald Barnett (2014) or Peter McLaren (2006) the very idea of the university, indeed, is in this searching analysis simply too bloodstained and too badly marred by histories of discrimination and maltreatment to survive such disclosures in any remotely recognisable form. Inspired by activist readings of Nietzsche, Foucault and Freire, this kind of combative stance demands the epistemological and ethical renunciation of the university in its current (post)Humboldtian guise and its replacement by a renovated humanistic order the precise institutional character of which our own current traumas and limitations prevent us yet from clearly envisioning, but which will be very different from currently dominant ones. It leaves us, instead, with the compensatory but sporadically inspiring glimmer of the Derridean or Levinasian 'University to come', which, these commentators urge, it has now become our moral and educational imperative to create, whatever our position in the prevailing academic system (Anuik and Gillies 2012).

The educational philosopher and ethicist Darcia Narvaez has perhaps gone furthest, in her recent important study of *Neurobiology and the Development of Human Morality: Evolution, Culture and Wisdom* (2014). Here (and elsewhere) Narvaez argues eloquently for a sweeping overhaul of the intellectual and moral priorities of the modern university, which restores the 'paths to moral wisdom' conserved by surviving indigenous cultures everywhere. These same pathways, she claims, are increasingly visible to the academy itself in the scientific confirmation by neuroscience, ethnography and palaeoanthropology of a distinctively human mammalian 'essence' around the demonstrable needs and desires of which all education should be radically reformed to save us from ecological and environmental ruin. Narvaez and other thinkers such as the philosopher Nancy Snow do not seek, as many 'indigenous' commentators and their supporters do, the effective abolition of the university, but they are unrelenting in condemning the errors and arrogance of the Humboldtian-style curriculum of higher learning and its connivance with what they see as the destructive possessive individualism of the modern age. In this analysis the university is less the victim of the intractable forces of neoliberalism and more one of the key crucibles in which its disordered conception of human flourishing is forged (Grosfoguel 2013). This edges, of course, towards a kind of 'ontological' critique in which the university is not only admonished to enlarge its academic compass to include the perspectives and practices of non-Western, non-modern cultures, but where it is fundamentally reproached for intrinsic habits of being, acting, thinking from which it can barely hope to escape (Aman 2015).

It is not of course straightforward to exonerate the 'Humboldtian' university and its organisational and curricular apparatus from many of these charges, even if they may be contested in other ways or, indeed, shown to be overstated or incomplete. It remains important nonetheless to remember that whatever subsequent success it enjoyed as a design for the modernisation of higher education, the much-emulated Humboldtian experiment was in its origins a response to a social and intellectual crisis. Both Alexander and Wilhelm Humboldt reacted against a university culture they felt might indeed be moribund and unfit for purpose in a rapidly modernising and volatile society. Hence while the 'Berlin Curriculum' and its sources may certainly appear in some respects inflexible, *freedom* of teaching and learning (*Lehr- und Lernfreiheit*) also remained central to the Humboldt vision. Wilhelm prized an individual freedom of which he felt Church and state had combined to deprive university students. He therefore argued that students had as much right to choose their instructors and courses of study as professors had to decide what and how they taught. This implied a radical break with any form of set syllabus or monolithic degree programme and opened out student learning to something approaching that same intellectual *eros* that Alexander had experienced in his overseas travels. It also paved the way for advanced individual study and research in the form of the 'postgraduate' degree and ultimately the elective doctorate. Within this overall academic culture, moreover, both Humboldts insisted that every discipline should be subject to scrutiny under the principles of free scientific enquiry, untrammelled by religious or governmental dogma: 'The aim of all scientific work,' Wilhelm concluded, 'is the enlargement of man's character' (1820/1963, 5).

At the very least we can surely argue that the preservation of these principles carries within it today a hospitality to change and a critical receptivity to divergent modes of thinking and learning from out of which a new global conversation on the future of the university and its regimes of knowledge creation might be generated (Sutherland 2014). Should we indeed be moving into yet another revolutionary phase in the history of international higher education, within which many older certainties and ways of working may pass away, and many hitherto silenced voices of the marginalized and the expelled may demand to be heard, then it is at least feasible that the deposits of insight and 'wisdom' established by and through the Humboldtian conception of the modern university may offer us vital resources with which to take our deliberations forward.

References

Aman, R. (2015). The double bind of interculturality and the implications for education. *Journal of Intercultural Studies, 36*(2), 149–165.

Anuik, J., & Gillies, C. L. (2012). Indigenous knowledge in post-secondary educators' practices: Nourishing the learning Spirit. *Canadian Journal of Higher Education/Revue canadienne d'enseignement supérieur, 42*(1), 63–79.

Arvanitakis, J. (2013). Massification and the large lecture theatre: From panic to excitement. *Higher Education, 67*(6), 735–745.

Ash, M. (2006). Bachelor of what, master of whom? The Humboldt myth and historical transformations of higher education in German-speaking Europe and the US. *European Journal of Education, 41*(2), 245–267.

Barnett, R. (2014). Imagining the humanities – Amid the inhuman. *Arts and Humanities in Higher Education, 13*(1–2), 42–53.

Boulton, G., & Lucas, C. (2011). What are universities for? *Chinese Science Bulletin, 56*(23), 2506–2517.

Brady, N. (2012). From 'moral loss' to 'moral reconstruction'? A critique of ethical perspectives on challenging the neoliberal hegemony in UK universities in the 21st century. *Oxford Review of Education, 38*(3), 343–355.

Brown, W. (2015). *Neoliberalism's stealth revolution*. New York: MIT Press.

Chibber, V. (2013). *Postcolonial theory and the specter of capital*. London: Verso.

Cruickshank, J. (2016). Putting business at the heart of higher education: On neoliberal interventionism and audit culture in UK Universities. *Open Library of Humanities, 2*(1), e3.

de Sousa Santos, B. (2015). *Epistemologies of the south: Justice against Epistemicide*. London: Routledge.

Fichte, J. G. (1805–1806/1926). Deduced scheme for an academy to be established in Berlin. (G. H. Turnbull, Trans.). *The educational theory of J.G. Fichte* (pp. 170–259). London: Hodder and Stoughton.

Franklin, M. (2011). *Orientalist Jones': Sir William Jones, poet, lawyer, and linguist, 1746–1794*. Oxford: OUP.

Fulford, A. (2016). Higher education, collaboration and a new economics. *Journal of Philosophy of Education, 50*(3), 371–383.

Ghosh, K. (2010). Indigenous Incitements. In D. Kapoor & E. Shizha (Eds.), *Indigenous knowledge and learning in Asia/Pacific and Africa* (pp. 35–47). London: Palgrave.

Gibbs, G. (2013). Lectures don't work, but we keep using them. *Times Higher Education Supplement*, 211113.

Grosfoguel, R. (2013). The structure of knowledge in Westernized Universities: Epistemic racism/sexism and the four genocides/epistemicides of the long 16th century. *Human Architecture: Journal of the Sociology of Self-Knowledge, 11*(1), 73–90.

Hall, D. (2001). Just how provincial *Is* western philosophy? 'Truth' in comparative context. *Social Epistemology, 15*, 285–298.

Hauschild, T. (1997). Christians, Jews, and the other in German anthropology. *American Anthropologist, 99*(4), 746–753.

Irwin, R. (2006). *For lust of knowing: The orientalists and their enemies*. London: Penguin.

Israel, J. (2002). *Radical enlightenment: Philosophy and the making of modernity, 1650–1750*. Oxford: OUP.

Kant, I. (1798/1979). *The conflict of the faculties* (M. J. Gregor, Trans.). New York: Abaris Books.

Kant, I. (1803/2003). *On education* (Paul Kegan, Trans.). Mineola: Dover Publications, Inc.

Khoo, S., et al. (2016). Ethical internationalization, neo-liberal restructuring and "beating the bounds" of higher education. In L. Schultz & M. Viczko (Eds.), *Assembling and governing the higher education institution* (pp. 85–111). London: Palgrave.

Kirkwood, A., & Price, L. (2014). Technology-enhanced learning and teaching in higher education: What is 'enhanced' and how do we know? A critical literature review. *Learning, Media and Technology, 39*(1), 6–36.

Kitchen, M. (2015). *Albert Speer: Hitler's architect.* New Haven: Yale University Press.

Kwiek. (2009). The changing attractiveness of European higher education: Current developments, future challenges and major policy issues. In B. M. Kehm et al. (Eds.), *The European higher education area: Perspectives on a moving target* (pp. 107–124). Dordrecht: Springer.

Lepori, B., & Kyvik, S. (2010). The research mission of universities of applied sciences and the future configuration of higher education systems in Europe. *Higher Education Policy, 23*(3), 295–316.

Marcone, J. (2013). Humboldt in the Orinoco and the environmental humanities. *Hispanic Issues On Line, 12,* 75–91.

Marcus, J. (2016). The paradox of new buildings on campus. The Atlantic, 250716.

Marshall, S. (2010). Change, technology and higher education: Are universities capable of organisational change? *Research in Learning Technology, 18*(3), 179–192.

Martín-Díaz, E. (2017). Are universities ready for interculturality? The case of the Intercultural University 'Amawtay Wasi'. *Journal of Latin American Cultural Studies*, Online View, 1–18.

McClintock, A. (1995). *Imperial leather: Race, gender and sexuality in the colonial contest.* New York: Routledge.

McDonald, I. (2013). What are universities for? *Journal of Research Initiatives, 1*(1), 12.

McLaren, P. (2006). *Rage + Hope.* New York: Peter Lang.

Nakata, N. M., et al. (2012). Decolonial goals and pedagogies for indigenous studies. *Decolonization: Indigeneity, Education & Society, 1*(1), 120–140.

Narvaez, D. (2014). *Neurobiology and the development of human morality: Evolution, culture and wisdom.* New York: Norton.

Nybom, T. (2007). A rule-governed Community of Scholars: The Humboldt vision in the history of the European university. In P. Maassen & J. P. Olsen (Eds.), *University dynamics and European integration* (pp. 55–80). Dordrecht: Springer.

Nybom, T. (2012). The disintegration of higher education in Europe, 1970–2010: A post-Humboldtian essay. In S. Rothblatt (Ed.), *Clark Kerr's world of higher education reaches the 21st century: 163 chapters in a special history, higher education dynamics 38* (pp. 163–181). Dordrecht: Springer.

Nylander, E., et al. (2013). Managing by measuring: Academic knowledge production under the ranks. *Confero, 1*(1), 5–18.

Oleseon, A. (2014). Teaching the way they were taught? Revisiting the sources of teaching knowledge and the role of prior experience in shaping faculty teaching practices. *Higher Education, 68*(1), 29–45.

Phipps, A. (2013). Intercultural ethics: Questions of methods in language and intercultural communication. *Language and Intercultural Communication, 13*(1), 10–26.

Pietsch, T. (2015). *Empire of scholars: Universities, networks and the British academic world 1850–1939.* Manchester: MUP.

Rata, E. (2012). The politics of knowledge in education. *British Educational Research Journal, 38*(1), 103–124.

Readings, B. (1996). *The University in Ruins.* Cambridge, MA: Harvard University Press.

Scharfstein, B.-A. (2001). How important is truth to epistemology and knowledge? Some answers from comparative philosophy. *Social Epistemology, 15,* 275–224.

Seuffert, N. (1997). Circumscribing knowledge in Aotearoa/New Zealand: Just epistemology. *Yearbook of New Zealand Jurisprudence, 1,* 97–125.

Shahjahan, R. A., & Morgan, C. (2016). Global competition, coloniality, and the geopolitics of knowledge in higher education. *British Journal of Sociology of Education, 37*(1), 92–109.

Sillitoe, P. (2010). Trust in development: Some implications of knowing in indigenous knowledge. *Journal of the Royal Anthropological Institute (N.S.), 16,* 12–30.

Sutherland, M. (2014). Indigenous and western knowledge: A false dichotomy? In P. Inman & D. L. Robinson (Eds.), *University engagement and environmental sustainability* (pp. 35–47). MUP: Manchester.

Trifonas, P. P., & Peters, M. A. (Eds.). (2005). *Deconstructing Derrida: Tasks for the new humanities*. London: Palgrave Macmillan.

Von Humboldt, W. (1809/1990). Über die innere und äussere Organisation de hoheren wissenschaftlichen Anstalten zu Berlin. In E. Moller (Ed.), *Gelegentliche Gedanken iiber Universititen* (p. 34). Leipzig: Reclam. Translated in Ash (2006).

Von Humboldt, W. (1963). *Humanist without portfolio: An anthology of the writings of Wilhelm von Humboldt* (M. Cowan, Trans.). Detroit: Wayne State University Press.

Warraq, I. (2007). *Defending the west: A critique of Edward Said's orientalism*. New York: Prometheus Books.

Wolf, A. (2015). *The invention of nature: Alexander von Humboldt's new world*. London: John Murray.

Worrall, D. (2015). *Harlequin empire: Race, ethnicity and the drama of the popular enlightenment*. London: Routledge.

Zoontjens, P. J. J. (2010). Protecting 'university' as a designation: Analysis and comparison of the legal position in several countries. *Education Law Journal, 11*(2), 117–131.

The Assessment of Academic Research in the UK: An Ethical Analysis

James C. Conroy and Richard Smith

Introduction

We apologise for what may seem the parochial focus of this paper, focused as it is on the assessment of university research in our own country. However the issues discussed here are of wider importance especially as features of the UK's Research Excellence Framework (REF) are now being taken up in other countries (including Hong Kong and Australia). First, some basic facts about the REF for those who are not familiar with it.

The evaluation and assessment of academic research in the UK has since 1986 taken place by way of a 'research assessment exercise' (RAE: early versions had various names). They now take place every 7 years. The most recent such exercise, completed in 2014, was called the 'Research Excellence Framework'. Each university department (sometimes known as 'cost centre') that wanted to enter the exercise (and of course almost all did) submitted a selection of its work, mostly in the form of publications (these were called 'outputs'). They were also required to provide evidence of the impact of their research on the world outside education, in the form of 'Impact Case Studies'. The number of publications that could be submitted depended on the number of Case Studies. The quality criteria for publications were originality, significance and rigour. Significance meant academic significance, and was not the same as impact. Publications counted for 65% of the final grade awarded and Impact Case Studies counted for 25%. The remaining 10% was based on Environment: this was judged on, for instance, the number of PhDs completed in the

J. C. Conroy (✉)
University of Glasgow, Glasgow, Scotland, UK
e-mail: James.Conroy@Glasgow.ac.uk

R. Smith
School of Education, University of Durham, Durham, UK
e-mail: r.d.smith@durham.ac.uk

© Springer International Publishing AG, part of Springer Nature 2018   25
P. Smeyers, M. Depaepe (eds.), *Educational Research: Ethics, Social Justice, and Funding Dynamics*, Educational Research 10,
https://doi.org/10.1007/978-3-319-73921-2_3

period of the REF, departmental research income, especially from sources such as the UK funding councils, and any significant marks of esteem attaching to particular academics. Further details of the REF will emerge in what follows. It must be said that at the time of writing it is not clear what precise shape the next (2020) REF will take but, from the recommendations of a recent review[1] the overall architecture is likely to see significant continuity with the existing model.

It is worth noting that 'Impact' was a new element in the 2014 REF. Perhaps it was introduced to indicate the importance of university work benefiting the wider community in the kind of terms the wider community would readily understand. Perhaps it was introduced as the result of a compromise in 2010 with the UK Government Treasury, which was pressing for the replacement of these costly assessment exercises with a simpler system based on proxies such as citations. This is often alleged to have been the case, though we can find no hard evidence of it.

The 2014 evaluation was conducted by Panels, consisting of roughly 25 individuals, for each subject or subject area. The authors of this paper sat on Panel 25 (Education).

Protocols and Wider Matters: The Nature of Ethics

It might seem that we should start here with some preliminary remarks, as if to indicate what we mean by 'ethics' before coming on to the more substantial matter of weighing the REF against it. But what is at stake here is partly a sufficiently adequate and rich conception of ethics. It is common, especially in the world of Education, for 'ethics' to be seen as a matter of optional (bolt-on) issues, professional protocols of a largely routine nature, that can be treated in a tick-box fashion. For example: were interviewees anonymised? Was their consent obtained in writing? Was data stored securely? It is a sad comment on academic life that ethics tends to be seen largely as the domain of Ethics Committees, which focus on such necessary but banal questions as these. The Committees would be unlikely to reject a proposed project on, say, a new strategy for evaluating children's performance in literacy tests on the grounds that such an approach to literacy is complicit with a culture of league-tables and testing that is essentially abusive and anti-educational. We could imagine them responding that such large questions were beyond their remit. No doubt they are. Thus we have the irony of Ethics Committees refusing to consider important ethical issues at all.

There is by contrast a long tradition according to which the subject-matter of ethics is very broad. To adopt a well-known way of putting it from Plato (*Republic*

---

[1] The UK government invited Lord Stern (President of the British Academy, to conduct a review now published as 'Building on success and Learning from Experience' July 1916. The findings of the Review were still being considered by the Higher Education Funding Council, which has been consulting with the profession as we write. Url: https://www.gov.uk/government/uploads/system/uploads/attachment_data/file/541338/ind-16-9-ref-stern-review.pdf

352d) it concerns nothing less than how we should live. 'We are not addressing a trivial question' (that is, in the long discussion that constitutes the *Republic*), he has Socrates say, 'but the question of how to live a life' (*hontina tropon chrē zēn*).

For Aristotle ethics was constituted partly by the need to bring flexibility and attention to bear on the details of particular cases that confront us from time to time: in short, to use practical judgement (*phronēsis*). In a famous passage he compares flexibility with a device developed on the island of Lesbos: it is like a builder's comb used today to transfer the pattern of the frame of a door, for instance, to flooring in order to mark what needs to be cut away:

> What is itself indefinite can only be measured by an indefinite standard, like the leaden rule used by Lesbian builders; just as that rule is not rigid but can be bent to the shape of the stone, so a special ordinance is made to fit the circumstances of the case. (Aristotle, *Nicomachean Ethics* 1137b27–32, trans. Ross 1969)

It is thus characteristic of ethics that it does not for the most part consist of laws comparable with the laws of science: as if it was best conceived as the attempt to reach a high level of generality, to be encapsulated in ethical principles and ethical codes. For Aristotle the significant moral or ethical questions concerned not only what we should do and what principles we should follow, but what aspects of character we should think of as admirable and to be cultivated, and what aspects we should repudiate and hope not to find in ourselves, our friends, colleagues or children.

Mary Midgley (1981) offers a helpful perspective on this. Ethics, she writes, is not a label for just 'one kind of serious consideration among many' (p. 106), as though we might discuss separately the ethics of the REF, the politics of the REF, the economics of the REF, and so on. Ethics is, as she puts it, the name for 'the whole country' (p. 117) and not for one part of it only. Ethical thinking involves 'stepping back from all the partial systems and looking at their relation to each other' (p. 130).[2] Some people are disturbed by this, since it seems that the moral philosopher refuses to sit quietly in her own disciplinary box (always a sin in the academe, for all the talk of the importance of interdisciplinary work) but claims the competence and the right to adjudicate across a wide range of specialisms. But if she does this, of course she is not pretending to technical expertise in all of them: only to have something to say about how, in their broadest dimensions, they fit together. In doing this she can of course be challenged: but it is not a criticism to make this point, since it is the nature of philosophy to welcome challenge and debate.

---

[2] Midgley here writes of the 'moral' rather than the 'ethical', but as she herself notes nothing hangs on the distinction in this context. The title of her paper, 'Is "moral" a dirty word?' of course points to another set of reasons why people are uncomfortable with the ethical or moral dimension of life: that it necessarily involves *moralising*, which is rightly to be repudiated as a nasty business with repressive, Victorian connotations, but wrongly imagined as somehow sanitised and neutralised by the substitution of 'ethical' for 'moral'. Some interesting and thought-provoking discussion of the distinction between the two terms can be found in Bernard Williams (1985).

The 'whole country' could be conceived in Plato's terms as a matter of asking what difference the REF makes to how we live: 'we' here meaning university academics, as well as the students that we teach, and the wider community or communities that are affected, for good or ill, by the research we carry out. Do we live more flourishing lives because of the REF, or lives that are diminished? In short, do our lives go better because of it, or worse? In the Aristotelian tradition this broadest of approaches can be thought of as an enquiry into character: what qualities of character are rewarded by the REF, what kinds of people it calls into being and whether, on reflection, these are the kind of people we want to be and to have around us, in universities and elsewhere. The significance of this will emerge in the last three sections of the paper.

The Working of the Panel

Before returning to substantial ethical discussion there are some more preliminary remarks to make. As we noted at the beginning the authors of this paper were both members of the 2014 REF Panel 25 (Education). We have nothing to say about the routine ethics of the workings of the Panel and its protocols – about the kind of aspects that would interest a Research Ethics Committee, as we put it above. This is not because we are bound by any vow of confidentiality. Rather it is because Panel 25, like the other Panels (to the best of our knowledge) went about its business straightforwardly. There was no secrecy about its procedures and protocols or its conclusions, which have been set out in publicly available documents,[3] although confidentiality with regard to the identity of individual researchers whose work had been evaluated was observed – as ethically it should be, on either the thin or the thick conception of ethics – in what was reported back to universities and other interested parties (such as subject associations and research councils). There was no hidden agenda, for example to promote any particular vision of educational research, such as randomised controlled trials at the expense of theoretical work (or vice-versa), or to distinguish an elite group of universities at the expense of the rest, or to reaffirm, in the words of the previous Research Assessment Exercise in 2008, the existence of 'pockets of excellence everywhere'. What membership of the Panel gave the writers of this paper was, from the ethical point of view, simply an extended opportunity to reflect on the REF as an exercise in university research assessment. The ethical interest of the REF, to repeat our point above, lies at a broader level than the detailed workings of the Panel.

---

[3] E.g. Research Excellence Framework 2014: Overview report by Main Panel C and Sub-panels 16 to 26 (January 2015) (http://www.ref.ac.uk/media/ref/content/expanel/member/Main%20 Panel%20C%20overview%20report.pdf).

Objections to the REF

There are arguments against the very existence of the REF, with implications for future funding of research and selectivity. Many of them are familiar (see for instance Sayer 2014). First there is the cost: conservatively put at £47m to universities themselves, in collecting the appropriate evidence and appointing managers and research administrators for this purpose, £12m to the Higher Education Funding Council (HEFCE) in administrative costs, plus the incalculable opportunity costs of time devoted to the REF that could have been spent in the library or the laboratory producing more and better research, or even spent with students in lectures and other kinds of teaching. This is properly to be thought of as an ethical matter and not just a financial one since it concerns universities' obligations and responsibilities and the extent to which they are doing what they exist to do. Secondly, such exercises benefit those who 'play the game', for example by submitting work on the latest fashionable themes, and not necessarily those who do the best research. Thirdly, they militate against slow and patient research that cannot be guaranteed to come to fruition and publication within the time-frame of a research assessment exercise, and against risk-taking, that is working on an area of research which might have spectacular results but equally might come to nothing. The confirmation of the existence of the Higgs boson, first hypothesised by the particle physicist Peter Higgs half a century ago, is often cited as an example. Higgs is now a Nobel Prize laureate but has commented that under the present conditions of university research his career would have been terminated before it properly began. In the field of philosophy Wittgenstein is often mentioned in this context: in his lifetime he published just one book, one academic article and one book review. His major work, the *Philosophical Investigations*, was published 2 years after his death and its importance was at first appreciated in only a small circle of philosophers. On the Platonic view of ethics we might ask ourselves whether we want games-playing, short-term thinking and aversion to risk to be a significant part of the lives we lead in universities; on the Aristotelian one, we might ask whether we might want to reward, favour and promote people who are good at playing games, exploiting trends and making much of the superficial: that is, cynical manipulators of a system rather than respectable academics as they have traditionally been conceived.

   None of these objections is entirely convincing. It would be naïve to expect government to allow universities to revert to a world in which there was no assessment of the research they produced. Alternative forms of assessment, for instance the use of proxies such as citations or the standing of journals, is far more open to 'gaming' in the form of mutual citation agreements, or focusing on the topic of the moment and taking a controversial line about it (to which numerous people will then respond, duly citing you). Allocating quality-related (QR) funding via the research councils (such as the Economic and Social Research Council or ESRC) instead of the REF, an alternative that commends itself to some, would in fact cost roughly five times as much as the REF (Wilsdon 2015) and the opportunity costs of submitting bids to the research councils, with the demoralisation that accompanies failure to secure funding, are already enormous. Peter Higgs, Ludwig Wittgenstein and other 'outliers' do indeed present a problem, but they do so for any form of research assessment and not just for the REF. It is worth noting that it is not the REF itself that would terminate the career of an apparently inactive researcher anyway but the university and its managers, no doubt claiming that the REF makes particular decisions inevitable. We call this the *puer maximus* excuse and return to it below.

There are some sound ethical reasons for supporting the continuing existence of a national research exercise such as the REF. At the national policy level in the UK the REF is significantly instrumental in research being regarded as a major activity in all (or nearly all) universities and departments. The ethical issue here is partly one of equity. The previous Research Assessment Exercise (RAE) in 2008 concluded that there were 'pockets of excellence' everywhere in the UK university sector (and not, for instance, only in an elite group of universities). Research assessment helps to secure the links between research and teaching, if only at the level of rhetoric: we are all in favour of research-led teaching, though there are different interpretations of this phrase. To spell this important point out further, the REF and its predecessors have made it difficult to demarcate 'research-only' (and teaching-only) universities, with the deleterious consequences – construction of hierarchies, demoralisation of the teaching-only sector (and, it must be said, demoralisation of the research-only sector for those research-active staff that enjoy and value teaching) – that would follow from this. These are strong reasons for continuing the REF in something like its present form.

Judgement and Subjectivity

One particularly interesting objection to the REF is that the evaluations made, of publications in particular, came down to the subjective judgements of individual members of the Panels, with the further complaint that they could not in all cases possibly have been competent to evaluate every piece of work that they read. The point is regularly taken as the basis of an argument for the use of proxies such as citations. The idea of judgment is not popular in our time, though more usually this is because its exercise is equated with judgementalism and moralising. Here however the use of judgement is equated with subjectivism and subjective preference, as if a Panel member's verdict was on a level with preferring one kind of cheese or beer over another. But Panel members were recruited on the basis of expertise and experience: they had been referees for journals and journal editors themselves, they had refereed submissions to research councils and so on. Professional judgement, though it can be faulty from time to time, is not the same as subjective preference. Those making this equation would presumably not accept that their marking of student essays or their work as PhD examiners came down to the exercise of personal preference.

Now if all judgement is subjective then the point can be used the other way round: those arguing against the use of judgement are simply registering a subjective preference, and can be safely ignored. This is something of a cheap device but it illustrates the unsatisfactory nature of the identification of judgement with subjective preference. The point can be made too that the use of judgement in this and similar exercises is one way in which the professional expertise of the academic profession is developed and refined, which would not be the case if proxies were used. Moreover there is little to commend the complaint that Panel members must sometimes have been evaluating papers that lay outside of their expertise, given that these were normally passed on to those who were better qualified to judge them; and the complaint of course effectively admits on principle that there is such a thing as relevant expertise in this context.

The Ethics of Language

The nomenclature of the REF is in many ways unfortunate. The word 'research' itself generally points in the direction of empiricism, and the discovery of new facts (however trivial) rather than, say, fresh thinking, the clarification of ideas, the re-evaluation of familiar orthodoxies, the finding of unexamined lines of interest in a classic writer. The word makes it easy to forget that, in the context of Education, unempirical disciplines such as philosophy count as research (see Smeyers and Smith 2014), as can theoretical sociology, or history: an occlusion of which the REF itself was emphatically not guilty but which feeds certain fantasies and empire-building tendencies in university departments and schools of Education. Arguably want many academics consider themselves to be engaged in, is not research but scholarship: that is, the patient study of the thing. It is a mode of advanced attention but of course here too the metricised language of 'Google' as in 'Google Scholar' has (mis) appropriated the conceit of patient attention.

The shibboleth 'excellence' positions all research against some fantasised, almost Platonic ideal, as if the significant things about a highly-rated piece of research might not be that it is interesting, disconcerting, thought-provoking and so on. Perhaps 'excellence' is simply the result of a search for a term so neutral (so empty) that it could provide a common standard against which all might be commensurable. Yet even this tends to make the diversity of research less than visible. Do the latest work on DNA and a radical reinterpretation of Montaigne really sit on the same scale, differing only in having less or more of the same excellence?

A 'framework' can be either a neutral and innocuous skeleton on which things of more substance can be hung, or it can be an all-embracing structure, an endless web from which there is no escape and which we struggle to unweave even during the night: a *Penelopewerk* by which we attempt to postpone the forced marriage to our suitors – business, industry, the market – and keep alive the memory of when things were different and the hope that they might be so again.

Rowan Williams, the former Archbishop of Canterbury, has complained that the REF employs a barbaric language of 'control, closure and somewhat crudely crafted measurement'.[4] 'Outputs' supplies an excellent example. The word was presumably chosen because a performance or a video, for example, could be submitted as well as a book, or a chapter of a book, or a journal article. But 'outputs' are the cousins of widgets. No better word could have been chosen if the desired effect was to make publications appear the outcome of a mechanistic process, eminently suitable to be overseen by university 'research managers' with little understanding of what they are managing.

Impact

We come now to what we regard as one of the ethically most problematic aspects of the REF, yet one whose full implications do not seem fully to be appreciated. To repeat from § above, the 2014 REF gave for the first time a 25% weighting to 'Impact'.[5] Every academic subject department was required to include in its submission some case-studies (roughly one for every ten researchers submitting publications or 'outputs') demonstrating how its research benefits the wider, and specifically non-academic, community. Unless a department submitted sufficient Impact case-studies not be many of its publications could be submitted; conversely, there would be little benefit in having good Impact case-studies without strong publications, since these counted for 65% of a department's submission. There are, first, obvious difficulties in demonstrating such research benefits, especially for a humanities department, of History or English Literature, say, though Pure Mathematics will have the same problem in attempting to show the 'impact' of its work, and of course its economic impact in particular, beyond the world of education. The implicit model seems to be that of working with an industrial partner to invent a light-sabre, or to discover and exploit a new lubricant for artificial hip joints.

A second difficulty is that the idea of impact, despite its relatively minor (25%) standing in the REF, has rapidly colonised the academic imagination. Perhaps academics always secretly longed to be big players in 'the real world'; perhaps economic impact that can be set out on a spread-sheet is the only thing likely to impress the new kinds of managers and administrators that run universities, not least because it funds their salaries and the university's vanity projects, and researchers in search of promotion and favour know who it will pay them to side with. At any rate academics from many disciplines, but from Education especially, are now confusing – whether through deliberate misconstrual, fantasy or honest misunderstanding – the highly specific, and limited, Impact dimension of the REF with the very different

---

[4] Williams is quoted in *Times Higher Education*, 29 Jan. 2015 (http://www.timeshighereducation. co.uk/news/rowan-williams-on-higher-educations-inhuman-and-divisive-jargon/2018188.article).

[5] We have tried to reserve the capitalised 'Impact' for contexts where Impact Case Studies are being discussed, and the uncapitalised 'impact' for the more vague and general idea that university research should hold benefits for the wider, non-academic community. It has not always been possible to be consistent in this convention, partly because of the leakage between the two terms.

criteria for publications. (To emphasise: the criterion of 'significance' did not mean 'Impact' in the sense that the REF used the term.) It is common these days to hear people asserting that 'it's all about impact now', or priding themselves on the usefulness of their research by contrast with people who merely write journal articles or books – which, as we have seen, are merely 'outputs' in any case.

The prioritisation of impactful research thus goes hand in hand with the demotion of what is sometimes called 'blue skies' or 'curiosity-driven' research whose only criterion is academic merit. The very idea of purely academic worth or merit is at stake here: a vague and hardly operationalisable notion, it will be said, compared to the possibility of measuring 'impact' objectively in terms of the invention of light sabres, improved artificial hip joints and their equivalents. Thus the very idea of the university as a place dedicated to academic work, with the complex criteria against which such work is judged and which the work itself constantly challenges and develops, is becoming replaced by a different idea of the university, as a handmaid of industry, commerce and government policy.[6]

A refinement of the obsession with 'impact' involves the growing assumption that academics should prioritise the impact of their research from the outset rather than trying to create it after the work's completion: a remarkable idea which seems to rule out the possibility of open-mindedness on the part of the researcher from the start.[7] This resembles what is sometimes called 'sponsorism': grants from outside the university become the only way to buy time to do research. Academics thus increasingly design their research programmes in the light of what they have reason to think outside bodies – charities, research councils, industry – will fund, rather than, as they once did, identifying an interesting field of enquiry and then looking for sources of funding where appropriate. Otherwise there would be no chance of achieving 'impact' at all.

In this way the REF is widely if wrongly interpreted as in alliance with the other factors driving educational research towards the empiricism and scientism – that is, excessive respect for the image and tropes of science – that render more humane approaches and paradigms ever more marginal. Funding agencies external to the university typically support research that involves extensive collection and analysis of data, rather than research that involves thinking and writing (however is a specific sum of money to be allocated to anything so vague?), with the result that empirical and data-driven projects become prioritised over ones based in the humanities. The pressure to take on high fee-paying overseas students has similar effects.[8]

---

[6]This and the two previous paragraphs are adapted from Richard Smith, Educational research: the importance of the humanities, *Educational Theory* 65. 6, 2015.

[7]Laurie Taylor satirises this: 'Lies, damned lies and impact', *Times Higher Education*, 18 June 2015, p. 60.

[8]Marina Warner (2015) quotes 'a professor who resigned from a Russell Group university': 'The incessant emphasis was on cash … accept anyone for study who could pay, unethical as that was especially at postgraduate level, where foreign applicants with very poor English were being invited to spend large sums on degrees'.

Puer Maximus

We have touched several times on the point that many of the deleterious consequences of the REF come not from the assessment exercise itself, but from the way it is interpreted and its effects manipulated in some universities by the new cadre of research managers. This is such a widespread tendency that it deserves a memorable name, perhaps one with the latinate echo of such fallacies as *post hoc propter hoc,* or *petitio principii.* We offer *puer maximus,* meaning 'a very big boy'. It comes from the regularity with which a child caught in the act of, say, spraying graffiti or pilfering from a shop will allege that 'a big boy came along and made me do it'. A big boy called REF made the university's research managers require academics to explain what will be the impact of their research leave or their conference presentation. The same big boy was responsible for the fact that academics will not now gain promotion unless they can demonstrate, or at least feign, impact. He it was who engineered the demoralisation of those who were not entered for the assessment exercise at all, and he is behind the drive for ever more funded research, irrespective of its academic merit. The REF is a very big boy. The research managers, pro vice-chancellors and 'impact champions' – every department needs one – would never have done these things otherwise.

Nevertheless it can fairly be said that the REF should have seen this coming and done more to safeguard against it. A telling example comes from the way that many academics' careers were 'tarnished by exclusion' from the REF simply because their university could not come up with enough impact case studies to support them. Graeme Rosenberg, who managed the REF on behalf of the Higher Education Funding Council (HEFCE), expected that decisions about the number of staff to be submitted would determine the number of Impact case studies put forward. In fact the process worked the other way round.[9] This may seem a small and rather technical example, but it was more than that for those academics who were excluded and drew the conclusion that the research element of their careers, if not their careers entirely, had no future. It was also, in important respects, the inevitable consequence of introducing a post-hoc metric and attempting to 'back-engineer' the components. Much academic scholarship in the census period was conducted without any regard to its impact so finding a sufficient number of case studies of the 'reqiuisite quality' proved somewhat challenge for many institutions.

Alazony

The demand for impact, or the prioritising of Impact, casts as marginal the researcher who is modest or diffident, who thinks they should have something important to say before they contribute to the mountain, electronic or otherwise, of books and journal

---

[9] *Times Higher Education* 22 Jan. 2015, p. 6.

articles. Self-importance and exaggeration, the 'bigging up' that has now entered the language, become chief among the academic virtues. Aristotle has some illuminating things to say in the *Nicomachean Ethics* about what he calls the vice of alazony (*alazoneia*), which stands at the same extreme on one side of truth-telling as irony does on the other. Irony, Aristotle says, conceals too much while alazony asserts too much. The *alazôn* is the kind of person who exaggerates his qualifications. If he has no ulterior purpose in doing so he is 'feeble rather than bad' (trans. Ross).[10] If he does so because he wants to win fame or honour, we should not censure him excessively: the person who boasts for the same of riches or worldly goods is more disreputable.[11]

The problem with the *alazôn* is not that he makes the wrong choice of ends, nor even that he selects the wrong means for achieving them from time to time. The problem is that he has a settled disposition to behave like this: *alazoneia* is in his character. This is what we dislike in him (*NE* 1127b 16–17).[12]

Aristotle seems here to be thinking indifferently of the person who exaggerates his qualifications (he has them, but not to the extent that he claims) and the person who is lying outright. Translators generally favour the word 'boasting', no doubt because we can boast both about what we have and what we don't have. ('He's always boasting about that new car of his that you saw this morning'. 'He likes to boast that his wife is a doctor – actually she's a nurse'.) Hutchinson captures this neatly: 'the pretentious man [his translation of *alazôn*] claims the things that bring renown when he does not have them, or claims more of them than he has' (1986, p. 102). This is what is objectionable in the demand that every scholar or researcher should demonstrate 'impact'. It is not just that it leads them to exaggerate their impact when they have little, or to lay claim to it when they have none to speak of. It is simply that it turns them into professional boasters: and this, as Aristotle notes (*NE* 1127b9), is wearisome (Ross and Thomson both use this word in their translations).

One of the merits of Aristotle's account of the virtues is that his idea of the mean between excess and deficiency helps us to see what we lose when we fall victim to a vice at either extreme. The *alazôn* lacks the straightforward truthfulness of someone who may say, for instance, that while she thinks that her books and articles have some merit, she doesn't expect them to change the world like the invention of the micro-processor or a cure for ebola. There is something steady, modest and attractively rueful about someone who talks in this way.

At the other extreme from alazony there is the vice of deficiency that Aristotle calls *eirôneia*. Along with most translators, Thomson calls this 'irony'; Ross prefers 'mock-modesty', presumably to avoid the complex connotations of the modern sense of 'irony'. In fact *eirôneia* seems in Aristotle's time to have been moving towards the more modern sense from its older meaning, captured by Ross, which also conveys an intention to deceive (Muecke 1970 pp. 15–16); and of course

---

[10] 'more irresponsible than vicious' (Thomson).

[11] 'is an uglier character' (Ross).

[12] Hutchinson's discussion (1986 pp. 103–4) is illuminating here.

Aristotle had before him the example of Socrates's irony, to which he refers (*NE* 1127b25), as well as Plato's (to which he generally seems obtuse). On Aristotle's account the ironic person misses the truth by excessive understatement ('I'm one of those academics whose work gets read by three people, one of them my mother'). Now his theory of the virtues as the mid-point between extremes means that he should condemn irony as much as alazony. However he observes that the ironic are more attractive (*chariesteroi*) in character (*NE* 1127b22-3): 'Those who make a moderate use of understatement, treating ironically of subjects not too common-place or obvious, make the better impression'. Aristotle finishes his short account of alazony by declaring flatly that the *alazôn* is *cheirôn*, worse – that is, worse than the ironical person.

Conclusion

It will be clear that we believe the REF is a mixed bag from an ethical point of view. We have argued that it is better to have such an exercise than any other way of evaluating research, largely because the REF applies Aristotle's 'Lesbian rule', its Panels being unafraid to make academic judgements, and attempting to do so flexibly and with sensitivity to the kind of work that academic research is. More might be done to prevent the 'gaming' of the system, though complete elimination is probably impossible. More might be done to reduce the barbaric language, as Rowan Williams puts it, of terms such as 'excellence' and 'outputs', and in particular of 'impact'.

Our principal concern is that the introduction of Impact is in danger of changing the character of the people who work in universities: of fundamentally altering the ideal of the academic life and how it is to be lived. The proposal (HEFCE 2016) that Impact should be defined more broadly and more deeply in future iterations of the REF – that is, that there should be even more scope for this particular form of bullshitting (Frankfurt 2005) – makes that concern acute. Professor Lookatme and Dr. Loudmouth have long been familiar figures on campus, of course. Now however they are becoming heroes of popular culture, for example in the sort of people who vaunt their skills in television's *The Apprentice*. Something important departs from the university and leaves it impoverished when they are taken as models of the good scholar.

References

Aristotle. (1969). *The Nicomachean ethics* (D. Ross, Trans.) London: Oxford University Press.
Frankfurt, H. G. (2005). *On bullshit*. Princeton: Princeton University Press.
Higher Education Funding Council for England (HEFCE). (2016). *Consultation on the second Research Excellent Framework*. http://www.hefce.ac.uk/media/HEFCE,2014/Content/Pubs/2016/201636/HEFCE2016_36.pdf

Hutchinson, D. S. (1986). *The virtues of Aristotle*. London: Routledge & Kegan Paul.

Midgley, M. (1981). *Heart and mind: The varieties of moral experience*. Brighton: Harvester Press.

Muecke, D. C. (1970). *Irony and the ironic*. London: Methuen.

Sayer, D. (2014, December 15). Five reasons why the REF is not fit for purpose, *The Guardian*. http://www.theguardian.com/higher-education-network/2014/dec/15/research-excellence-framework-five-reasons-not-fit-for-purpose

Smeyers, P., & Smith, R. (2014). *Understanding education and educational research*. Cambridge: Cambridge University Press.

Warner, M. (2015, March 19). Learning my lesson. *London Review of Books* (pp. 8–14).

Williams, B. (1985). *Ethics and the limits of philosophy*. London: Fontana.

Wilsdon, J. (2015, July 27). In defence of the research excellence framework, *The Guardian*. http://www.theguardian.com/science/political-science/2015/jul/27/in-defence-of-the-ref

Between Research Ethics and Other Interests: Challenges for Historians of Education

Jeroen J. H. Dekker and Inge J. M. Wichgers

Introduction

Much scientific research funded by governments is placed at a distance of possible government interests, especially when governments finance institutions that select research projects and researchers themselves, in particular universities and research funding agencies, among them the Dutch NWO, the Flemish FWO, the British Research Councils, the German DFG, and the French CNRS. Governments also commission research directly, often on request or by pressure of their parliament, and on topics that could easily interfere with the government's interests. When getting such commissions, researchers have to cope with possible tensions between their own research ethics and the interests of the state.[1] Those tensions could manifest itself in various ways, varying from a clash between research ethics and interests of funding agencies to a process of accommodation by researchers with a view to future research commissions. In fact, researchers mostly not only have to cope with interests of funding agencies, but also with interests of other institutions, groups or individuals belonging to the subject of the research.

A case where next to the interests of funding agencies and researchers still other interests are at stake forms the research into historical child abuse, in particular of children placed in homes and foster families, in a number of countries including Ireland, Sweden, Belgium, Norway, Denmark, Canada, and several Australian states (Sköld and Swain 2015a, b). Much of this research was originally triggered by disclosures of incidents of sexual abuse of children within the Catholic Church. Those disclosures, which made public what victims did carry with them as a heavy burden

---

[1] As is also the case when funding comes from private funding agencies connected with a commercial company.

J. J. H. Dekker (✉) · I. J. M. Wichgers
Department of Education, University of Groningen, Groningen, The Netherlands
e-mail: j.j.h.dekker@rug.nl; i.j.m.wichgers@rug.nl

© Springer International Publishing AG, part of Springer Nature 2018
P. Smeyers, M. Depaepe (eds.), *Educational Research: Ethics, Social Justice, and Funding Dynamics*, Educational Research 10,
https://doi.org/10.1007/978-3-319-73921-2_4

for years, led to research into historical child abuse commissioned by several dioceses world-wide. Soon after, governments became conscious of their own responsibility for guaranteeing a safe situation for children in homes and foster families who were placed out-of-home because of legal measures of child protection. Commissions were installed which did research themselves or let do research by research institutes or universities. This history of legal out-of-home placements of children in homes and foster families contains many potentially conflicting interests, among them the interests of the outplaced children and of pressure groups consisting of care leavers, of their parents, of the professionals working in this sector, of the management of child protection institutions, of the inspectorate, the media, last but not least of the state. In this case, the state became both funding agency of the research and responsible and interested subject of that same research into historical abuse. The investigation of this history therefore implicated the challenge for researchers to cope with those different interests, including the interest of their own research ethics.

In the first section, we turn to discussions between researchers on the relationship between research ethics and interests of funding agencies and on the question which ethical dilemmas do the conduct of research encounter in government funded research.? Then we focus on a specific case, namely research into historical child abuse in post Second World War Dutch child care, and to the various interests and ethical challenges involved in such research (section "Investigations into historical child abuse: coping with varying and conflicting interests"). In the concluding section "Conclusion" it will be outlined how interests of various actors within this case, with the state in the dual role of historical actor and research funding agency, could be addressed and coped with.

Interests of Research Ethics and of Funding Agencies

The increase of contractual research, either by private funding or by governments, could result in a shift of power from researchers to funding agencies. In the Netherlands, private funding increased during the past decades, while government funded research through research funding agencies decreased in terms of percentage: in 1990, the Dutch government paid for almost half of research, whereas this was 36% in 2005 (Versleijen 2007, p. 32). Contractual research has strongly increased during the past decades (KNAW (Royal Dutch Academy of Sciences), 2005, p. 44; Köbben and Tromp 1999, pp. 19–20). This shift means a 'major extension of power and control which those who provide the funding exercise over those who carry out the research in the new contractual relationships' (Bridges 1998, pp. 594–595) or, as Köbben and Tromp (1999, p. 20) say: 'he who pays the piper, calls the tune'. The same could occur when governments, instead of funding through research funding agencies, directly commission research on topics that easily could interfere with the government's own interests.

This shift of power to funding agencies, among them the state when directly commissioning research, could affect the main elements of scientific research: the making of the research design, the choice for methods of analysis of data, the evaluation of the research results, and of course what and how to publish results. Resnik (2000, p. 257) distinguishes between objective and unbiased research: 'To be completely objective, a research result (i.e., hypothesis, theory, etc.) would need to be true (or well proven or correct) independent of human interests, concepts, values, and theories'. While objective research remains an unreachable goal, reduction of bias is not (Resnik 2000).

In the following, the power balance between funding agencies and researchers on the research subject, question, design, results and publication will be explored more generally before turning to the specific case of research into historical child abuse.

Problem Selection and Research Question

The first elements of research where researchers have to cope with possible tension between research ethics and interests of funding agencies, including the government, are the selection of the subject and the formulation of the research question. Several authors have found that government funding and research subjects and questions are correlated (Kjaernet 2010; KNAW 2005; Resnik 2000; Rowbottom and Aiston 2011; Useem 1976). Sometimes, this is due to lobby groups (Resnik 2000, pp. 267–268). As early as 1976, Useem showed that a substantial part of social scientists (would) change their topics – and their methods – when federal support leveled off. Resnik (2000, p. 269) even points out that since private funding affects the first step of research plans, the entire research progress and outcomes can be biased. However, not every study shows differences because of variety in funding (Gans and Murray 2011; Thomas 1982). And according to Thomas, the researcher's responsibility is essential in such conditions, for: 'If there is a danger in federal sponsorship, it is not located primarily in federal support of the scientific process, but in the ideological, normative, and epistemological characteristics of researchers and in the fundamental conditions that influence them' (Thomas 1982, p. 361).

That public funding of research is important has to do with closing a 'funding gap' or *selection* perspective, in 1962 articulated by Arrow. He argued that since private incentives to fund research are well below social incentives, without public funding the rate of inventive activity [production of knowledge, Arrow 1962, p. 1] would be suboptimal and its direction would be biased towards more applied, 'close to market' outcomes' (Gans and Murray 2011, p. 2). Public funding could also be related to democratic principles, as 'funding priorities, and by implication problem selections, should reflect human values as well as economic and political circumstances […] in the public's interest'. That means that to 'eliminate these sorts of biases' remains impossible (Resnik 2000, p. 269).

Even more than biased, government funded research could lead to studying non-problems according to researchers (Kjaernet 2010; KNAW 2005; Rowbottom and

Aiston 2011) because of ill-defined research questions and objectives delivered by the funders themselves (KNAW 2005, p. 41) or because 'researchers may be [...] denied the chance to participate in identifying problems (even within a very specific context)'. Sometimes 'prescribing exactly what should and should not be evaluated can prove unnecessarily restrictive, e.g. serve to shield government decisions (and the underlying theories) from criticism' (Rowbottom and Aiston, p. 640). Finally, government funding can lead to not investigating certain subjects and more generally, 'the desire and need to satisfy sponsors may contribute to creating 'blind zones' for research' (Kjaernet 2010, p. 165).

Research Design and Data Analysis

The next stages of conducting research, designing and analyzing, can also be influenced by funding agencies (Dowdy 1994; Kjaernet 2010; Resnik 2007; Rowbottom and Aiston 2011; Useem 1976). Several dilemmas between researchers and funding agencies may exist when funders are able to impact methods in different ways and varying degrees, by rigidly specifying or suggesting a methodological approach (Rowbottom and Aiston 2011) or making tight timescales.

When funders prescribe a design, for example a certain type of data collection, which does not match the research design, the answers to the research questions may possibly not be answered at all. Use of inappropriate methods can also be caused by tight timescales that sponsors require (Rowbottom and Aiston 2011). A rigidly specified approach may prevent scientists from being sufficiently critical, for example from using the severest possible tests or questioning received wisdom, while imposed short time scales can take away input from the best researchers and experts. Genuine scientists should also be open to the possibility that existent methods are not sufficient to the task at hand and should be willing to develop new methods as and when appropriate (Rowbottom and Aiston 2011, p. 642).Tight time scales can also squeeze the analysis stage whereby funding agencies can impact related to the content as well (Rowbottom and Aiston 2011, p. 641), for example 'by insisting on a level of analysis that hides problems on another level, or by supplying the researcher with data that point in a particular direction' (Kjaernet 2010, p. 166).

Research Outcomes and Publication

While various pharmaceutical studies have found effects of funding agencies on conclusions and publication, according to Kjaernet 'there is no reason to believe that social science research is less vulnerable to similar influences' (Kjaernet 2010, p.165). Indeed, many studies have shown that funding can lead to different research outcomes as well as secrecy of results (Bridges 1998; Dowdy 1994; Kjaernet 2010;

KNAW 2005; Köbben and Tromp 1999; Resnik 2007; Rowbottom and Aiston 2011; Useem 1976).

Challenges concerning research outcomes may arise because of pressure to re-write reports, directly from the sponsor or because of the system, for example with respect to the lack of the anonymity of the funders (Rowbottom and Aiston 2011, p. 644). Also, indirect pressure occurs to formulate research findings in a way that communicates with non-scientists, which can be problematic because it may lead to ignoring other important findings (Kjaernet 2010). Most serious is that a change of future funding could be a reason to falsify or even fabricate research results (Kjaernet 2010; Resnik 2007) because of the special relationship between researchers and funders. According to Kjaernet, this relationship 'is akin to a patron–client relation-ship. Finding themselves in a situation of asymmetric dependency, researchers may resort to self-censorship in order not to jeopardize future funding (see Andvig 2008)' (Kjaernet 2010, p. 165).

This self-censorship could lead to changes, subtractions and additions, or to more subtle adjustments (Köbben and Tromp 1999, p. 89), for example ignoring findings that are not interesting to non-scientists. Then, it could 'remove the focus from what is a primary concern of most scientists: How research findings can be made publishable in peer-reviewed journals'. For the 'demands from the project (to be brief, and make it specifically relevant to commercial actors)' could then become in 'conflict with the demands of the profession to make research findings relevant in terms of theory'. (Kjaernet 2010, p. 166). When 'a theory has failed a particular test, this is an important scientific finding' and not reporting this 'or worse, to make a refutation appear to be a confirmation – would be a cardinal Popperian sin' (Rowbottom and Aiston 2011, p. 645).

Publishing research outcomes should be a matter of fact, but that is not always the case. One reason may be that the right to publish research results is not always registered well or explicitly in researchers' contracts (KNAW 2005, p. 41). Also, there might be pressure to cope with interests of the research purchaser to keep research results a secret. So the Dutch General Government Terms and Conditions for Public Service Contracts, in Dutch ARVODI (Algemene Rijksvoorwaarden voor het verstrekken van Opdrachten tot het verrichten van Diensten, used for all con-tracts with the Dutch government), might contribute to such Rapport commissie-Samson. (2012). *Omring door zorg, toch niet veilig. Seksueel misbruik van door de overheid uit huis geplaatste kinderen, 1945 tot heden.* Amsterdam: Boom. pressure as they include demands like secrecy of results, transfer of intellectual property, and even copyright (KNAW 2005, p. 40; General Government Terms and Conditions for Public Service Contracts). Sometimes, also interests of other individuals than researchers are at stake when researchers feel that they have to secure next contracts for themselves and their research assistants or when they would not want to betray relations of trust and respect with colleagues (Bridges 1998, pp. 602–603). Besides, researchers may question whether their work will be oversimplified and whether publicity might embarrass their funding agencies so that a positive change is less likely to happen (Bridges 1998, pp. 602–603). Thus, there are several reasons why secrecy of government funded research is problematic.

This might become an argument in favour of government funding because of the openness of research, for '[…] public-sector researchers can ensure the broad disclosure of research findings that leads to long-term growth' (Gans and Murray 2011, p. 3). 'Disclosure is achieved through the contractual provisions of research funding and, more broadly, because of the norms and incentives for openness found in publish research institutions' [sic] (David 2008, in Gans and Murray 2011, p. 4).

From the perspectives of Kuhn and Popper, to hold information back from the scientific community might impede scientific progress (Rowbottom and Aiston 2011, pp. 645–646). Besides, a democratic government should not deny its citizens access to important information, especially when public money is used to commission research (Bridges 1998, p. 600).

Investigations into Historical Child Abuse: Coping with Varying and Conflicting Interests

The challenges for researchers described above also seem to apply to recent investigations into research into historical child abuse in homes and foster families. Those investigations were funded by governments, which also were among the institutions with specific interests in the outcome of those investigations. Those investigations ask from researchers to cope with varying and potentially conflicting interests. Among them are those from outplaced children, whose protection should be core business of the out-of-home child care system, from care leavers and their pressure groups, from parents, from outplacing institutions among them the juvenile judge and the Guardianship Board, from receiving homes with their management and personnel and from receiving foster families, from the inspectorate, the media, last but not least from the state, next to being the funding agency also responsible for the best interests of out-of-home placed children by guaranteeing them a safe environment. Before turning to the Dutch case, a brief overview will be given of the birth of the international attention for historical abuse of children in out-of-home care.

International Attention for Historical Abuse Focused on Sexual Abuse in Out-of-Home Care

Since the 1990s, historical abuse of children in out-of-home care was put on the agenda in a number of western countries. It started in Australia in the 1995–1997s with the Human Rights and Equal Opportunity Commission investigating the forced removals of Aboriginal Children from their families in the period 1910–1975. From the late 1990s, historical abuse of other groups of children in out-of-home care was investigated in various countries, including the Netherlands (Sköld and Swain 2015b, pp. 1–2). Those investigations focused on two powerful institutions, who eventually also became the funders of those investigations, namely the Roman Catholic Church (Parkinson 2012) and the national state. The reported examples of sexual abuse of children within the Roman Catholic Church worked as a catalyst worldwide. Victim groups in various countries exercised major pressure on the church; they appeared in the media and talked with members of parliament. They were strongly motivated, for they asked for the investigation of a dark side of their own childhood and youth. As a result, in various countries and regions worldwide the Roman Catholic Church installed and financed research commissions. Then, governments became conscious – often under pressure of members of parliament approached by members of pressure groups of victims – of the fact that they also played a role – and an important one – in this history, namely of guaranteeing safety to children placed out-of-home under the responsibility of the state, notwithstanding the fact that the majority of those homes was for decades managed by private agencies, often Roman Catholic or Protestant ones. The occurrence of incidents of sexual abuse in homes and foster families meant that this safety was not guaranteed.

Behind the growing attention for historical abuse of children seem to be at least two phenomena. The first phenomenon was the increasing attention for victims generally in historical research, resulting, among other examples, in research into war victims, including the 1990s Balkan wars (NIOD 2002) and several colonial wars, and into victims of oppressive regimes both from the left and the right wing. The topics on the annual conferences of the dialogues on historical justice and memory network are evidence of this increasing attention for victims in history (http://historicaldialogues.org/).

The second phenomenon is the increasing attention for child maltreatment, a topic firmly put on the agenda in 1962 by the publication of the article "The Battered Child Syndrome" by medical doctor R. Kempe and his colleagues (1962) in the reputed *Journal of the American Medical Association (JAMA)*. In this article in 2008 called a JAMA classic by Carole Jenny, Kempe and his colleagues focused on physical child maltreatment (Dekker 2010a, p. 45; Dekker 2009). But soon the definition of child maltreatment became more embracing and covered also psychological and emotional maltreatment. This resulted in higher prevalence figures (Finkelhor 1979; Finkelhor 1984). From the late 1970s, also serious attention developed for sexual child abuse, starting in the USA. Jenny (2008) quoted a meta-analysis from 1999 reporting that "30% to 40% of women and 13% of men experienced sexual abuse during childhood". She concluded that "understanding of the ways children can be maltreated has expanded greatly" (Dekker 2010a, p. 47). The main impulse for this increasing attention for sexual child abuse came from medical doctors, psychologists, therapists, and from the feminist movement, not from politicians or from the media.

Attention for Historical Child Abuse in the Netherlands

Also in the Netherlands, media and politicians gave almost no attention to this phenomenon of sexual abuse of children until the late 1980s (Vasterman 2004; Vasterman 2005). The reasons why differed over time. It was not as if sexual abuse was not observed before, but it was evaluated differently. In the 1950s, this form of child abuse, although known and observed, mostly was considered a problem of adult staff members who were not able to withstand the seduction of youngsters, not a problem for the abused children themselves. In the 1960s and 1970s, lack of attention for sexual abuse by media and politicians could be related to the seemingly rather indulgent approach to sexual contact between adults and youngsters, also in professional-client relationships within child care homes and foster families, because of the influence of the sexual revolution (Dekker et al. 2012; Timmerman et al. 2012). This indulgent approach changed radically from the early 1990s. Then, child sexual abuse in out-of-home living arrangements became an issue in the media and in society. When it eventually in 2010 came to national inquiries into the abuse of children in public care, little or no attention was given to other types of maltreatment, such as physical abuse or emotional neglect. In 2010 in the Netherlands, after the instalment in 2009 of the commission-Deetman for the investigation of sexual abuse in institutions of the Roman Catholic Church, also the commission-Samson for the investigation of sexual abuse of out-of-home-placed children under the responsibility of the state started its work (Deetman et al. 2011a, b, 2013; Rapport commissie-Samson 2012). The attention for historical child abuse was mainly focused on sexual abuse for several years.

For the clarifying of the dual role of the Dutch state as historical actor and research funding agency and how researchers had to cope with that role, it is important to answer the question why child sexual abuse initially dominated the agenda when it came to a national inquiry into the abuse of children in public care. Two elements are crucial in explaining this: (1) the impact on national politics of incidents within the Roman Catholic Church, and (2) the existence of long-lasting legal and moral values on the impermissible and punishable character of sexual child abuse.

1. In response to publicity generated by victim groups, the Dutch episcopate, together with the society of religious congregations responsible for most Catholic boarding schools, established a commission to investigate claims of sexual abuse in catholic institutions in 2009. The commission was mentioned after its chair Wim Deetman, a Protestant and former minister of education, a member and president of parliament, mayor of the city of The Hague, and until now a member of the Constitutional Council: a man of high repute, trusted by Catholics and by the main political parties. In 2011, his Commission published a report on sexual abuse of boys from the late 1940s until the 1970s. In 2013, a supplementary report followed about physical violence against girls, thus on historical abuse next to sexual abuse. This second investigation was triggered by comments from female care leavers, who complained that the 2011 report only reported on cases

of boys (Deetman 2011a, b, 2013). Triggered by the initiative from the Roman Catholic Church, pressure groups of survivors and care leavers convinced members of the Dutch Parliament about the political and societal necessity of an investigation into the government's role for the sexual abuse of children placed out-of-home under the state's responsibility. The pressure groups made clear that part of the sexual abuse cases reported within Roman Catholic institutions, namely in Catholic residential homes, were not only the responsibility of the Roman Catholic Church but also of the state: those children were placed out-of-home because of legal child protection measures. As a result, members of parliament asked for an investigation into the state's responsibility for those children. The government, anxious to minimize the political risk for example of a Parliamentary Investigation with possible consequences for cabinet members, took the initiative well before Deetman reported. In the summer of 2010, an inquiry commission to study child sexual abuse in residential homes and foster families under the responsibility of the state after the Second World War was installed with as its president Rieke Samson, former attorney-general and public prosecutor. The research for this commission was done by several research groups from Dutch universities, including the University of Groningen (Dane et al. 2012; Dekker et al. 2012; Dekker and Grietens 2015; Grietens 2012; Timmerman et al. 2012). Based on the research reports and on the reports of more than 500 survivors, the Commission Samson wrote her final report (Rapport commisie-Samson 2012).

2. The second reason why child sexual abuse initially dominated the agenda when it came to national inquiries into the abuse of children in public care seems to be the existence of long-lasting legal and moral values on the impermissible and punishable character of sexual child abuse (Wiarda 2011). Sexual abuse of children was a crime in the Netherlands since the introduction in 1806 of the French *Code Pénal* (Dekker 2001). Therefore, it was possible to point at responsible and potentially guilty individuals and institutions when sexual abuse against minors was at stake, this in contrast with other forms of child abuse or violence against children, without a long existing legal umbrella until recently with the implementation of the UN Convention on the Rights of the child (Dekker 2011). As we saw above, also sexual abuse was evaluated differently over time in this period. But underlying moral values about which behaviour was morally permitted and which not did less change for sexual abuse than for other forms of historical child abuse, among them violence against children or emotional abuse: its evaluation over time changed much more radically, together with changing ideas on educational styles and the training of discipline.[2]

Together, those two reasons, the example of investigations by the Roman Catholic Church into sexual child abuse and long-lasting legal and moral values on the

---

[2] This notwithstanding the fact that the law changed from time to time also regarding sexual abuse: with change of definitions and of age minima for minors to have sexual relationships with adults. These changes in the law mirror changes in underlying values, related to the more libertarian sexual culture from the 1960s and 1970s.

impermissible and punishable character of sexual child abuse, seem to explain the initial focus on sexual abuse. Indeed, in the investigations by the Deetman and Samson committees almost no attention was given to other types of historical abuse than sexual abuse. This was the consequence of the formulation of the commissions that asked for research on sexual abuse only.

Coping with Various Interests

Researchers had to cope with interests of a number of institutions and groups during the investigations for the Samson-committee, namely outplaced children whose protection is core business of out-of-home child care, outplacing institutions among them the juvenile judge and the Guardianship Board, receiving homes with their management and personnel, foster families, supervision agencies and inspectorate, last but not least the state with its responsibility for the best interests of those children and for guaranteeing a safe environment.

Outplacement of children did happen within a professionalizing (Dekker 2016a, b) market of supply and demand with various roles and interests for the institutions and groups mentioned. It is clarifying to look over time at the roles, responsibilities and interests of the various parties within this market characterised by some major ups and downs through its post war history by looking at the number of outplaced children, with a sharp decrease in measures in the 1970s after a very high level in the late 1950s, and a steady recovery from the late 1980s. It seems that this historically changing demand for legal out-of-home placements mirrored a changing societal demand and in its ups and downs affected by the society's changing opinions about good and bad parenting and about belief in the effectiveness of legal interventions (Dekker 2016a, b). Increasingly, in the last few decades, societal interests were expressed by professionals, while members of parliament sometimes played the role of representatives of pressure groups (Dekker 2007, 2016a, b; Dekker et al. 2012, pp. 38–39, pp. 78–80).

The delivering of supply, i.e. outplacement of children, was the task of the admitting institutions. Until the 1970s they were in great majority private, mostly catholic or protestant, with a small number of state institutions for criminal children. From the 1990s this transformed into professionalized consortia becoming powerful market players. Both rather small denominational institutions in the past and big consortia from the 1990s did have a great interest of keeping and guaranteeing their market share, for a decrease of children admitted meant decrease of finance and thus of capacity and personnel (Dekker 2007; Dekker et al. 2012, pp. 38–39).

The role and interests of the state in this market were twofold: on the one hand being sensitive for changing societal ideas about out-of-home placements of children, and on the other hand determining the budget. While the societal demand for legal outplacements as mirrored in the number of legal child protection measures was eventually decided by the juvenile judges, advised by the Guardianship Board, the budgets for the supply available were eventually determined by the state. When foster families after the 1970s became the first choice for outplacement this was justified educationally (Dekker and Grietens 2015), but also fitted the government's interest of cutting budgets, necessary in those years (Dekker et al. 2012, pp. 78–80, 417).

The role of children (and of their parents) in the working of this market was very limited. While parents have the constitutional right to choose the school for their children and while most mental health clients have the freedom to stop treatment, this is not the case with legal out-of-home placements of children. The main decisions were made by others, although the problems and behaviour of children and families form the *raison d'être* for this market. When in the 1970s figures of out-of-home placements went down, it was not that parenting styles or child's behaviour suddenly changed, but because its assessment about whether or not to intervene changed. It therefore seems that when looking over time not parent's parenting practices or the child's behaviour directed the ups and downs of out-of-home placements, but that both its supply and demand, although according to the law to be taken "in the best interests of the child", were directed primarily by other agencies mirroring a societal need (Dekker et al. 2012, pp. 78–80). For the rest, although children did not play a major role, they did have their own perspective about how they experienced the out-of-home placement. Some research about the child's perspective is available, before the 1970s consisting of experiences of care leavers recorded through questionnaires and published, and for the more recent period consisting of interviews with children when still staying in homes (Dekker et al. 2012, p. 228). Studying those perspectives was not only in the interest of the children and the researchers, but also explicitly asked by the commissioner of the research, the Samson-committee.

Guaranteeing safety by the state means supervising and inspecting the field. As was generally the case, also for the inspectorate sexual abuse of children during out-of-home placements in the sixties and seventies sexual abuse was not on their agenda, as became clear from an interview with one of the circa five inspectors who were active in the 1970s. Exemplary is that although the serious and critical inspectors of the Heldring-institutions in 1973 wrote critically about the risks of psychiatrist Finkensieper becoming too dominant, they were unable to pick up signals of child abuse by this same psychiatrist, for it was out of the question to think about one of the highest ranked professionals in Dutch Child protection as a child abuser (Njiokiktjien and Lucieer 1973). The same happened when a special commission, the commission Dijkhuis, investigated the institution 2 years later. Eventually, however, Finkensieper's arrest and sentencing in 1992 made clear that both inspectors and members of the committee-Dijkhuis were wrong (Dekker et al. 2012, p. 377; Dekker and Grietens 2015, pp. 112–113). Also the fundamental criticism by the Association of Minors' Interests (Belangenvereniging Minderjarigen) and other alternative pressure groups in the 1970s of the psychiatrist's behaviour did not include accusations of sexual abuse. On May 17, 1974 this association started a campaign against the practices on the Heldring Institutions for the treatment of girls with complaints about misuse of power, knocking girls out with sedatives, and describing the psychiatrist Finkensieper as the embodying person of the new medicalization direction of therapy (Dekker et al. 2012, pp. 411–412).

Also the media before the 1980s only incidentally reported about child abuse. This changed in the late 1980s with attention for among others the Finkensieper-case. The media's publicity was often set in motion by care leavers and victims. By publishing about incidents, they could play a supervising and monitoring role for society. In contrast with the state inspectorate, which was a part of the same ministry that was also responsible for the system they had to supervise, the media could remain outside. Their impact can be influential, for institutions and agencies do never like bad publicity. We also saw this in Sweden and in New South Wales in Australia with TV-broadcastings setting in motion attention for child abuse by the authorities (Sköld and Swain 2015b).

From Research on Sexual Child Abuse to Violence Against Children

During the investigations into child sexual abuse by the Deetman and the Samson committees, it became clear that more went wrong. The publication of the above mentioned second report by Deetman on violence against girls and young women in Roman Catholic Institutions made clear that other forms of violence frequently occurred within Roman Catholic institutions, in particular for girls. During the investigations of the Samson committee, it became clear that most reported incidents of sexual abuse went together with other forms of violence and were part of a broader spectrum of humiliation, misuse of power, and of physical and psychological violence. While not all elements of this spectrum were formally forbidden by the law, they were according to existing educational values after the Second World War educationally and morally not admitted.[3] It became clear that the extraordinary uneven power balance between educators and children in total institutions like residential homes was potentially favourable for stimulating sadistic and immoral behaviour by part of the personnel, also when measured with contemporary norms and values. With Hans Grietens in his report on foster families for the Committee Samson (Grietens 2012) making clear that others forms of maltreatment were represented in foster children's stories too, there is no reason to think that this was basically different for children outplaced in homes.

The question arose what were those other forms of violence. This question, resulting from the Samson investigations, triggered political attention for investigations into other forms of historic abuse of out-of-home children. In the autumn of 2015 a Commission of researchers was set up by the Dutch Minister of Justice with as main task to do a preliminary investigation into violence against children in residential homes and foster families after the Second World War. The results of the

---

[3] Research into history of parenting shows that from the sixteenth century, child rearing advice books warned parents against physically punishing their children (Dekker 2010b).

Preliminary studies, published on May, 17, 2016, showed that violence against children in out-of-home child care seemed to be a serious problem and that investigating violence historically was doable in terms of sources and methods (Rapport en Bijlagen 2016). The government in a letter by the Minister of Justice, G.A. van der Steur and the Health Secretary M.J. van Rijn to the Lower House, decided to a follow up of the investigations (van der Steur and Van Rijn 2016).

Conclusion

When looking at potential tensions between research ethics and other interests when it comes to the formulation of the research subject, question, design, methodology and research methods, and the conclusion and publication of the results, it became clear that increasingly researchers meet tough ethical dilemmas, for example about accommodating results because of the possibility of future funding. They have to cope with a threatening shift of power between them and funding agencies in order to not become situated at the margin or even outside of research ethics. This development occurred both with private agencies and with the state when commissioning research directly and on topics that could interfere with the state's interests. It could be seen both in medical and pharmaceutical sciences and in social sciences. The exception on the rule remained funding which, although eventually paid by the government, is not directed by the government but by universities or research funding agencies that are rather free in their own research policy.

The case of research into Dutch historical child abuse after the Second World War turned out to be an in between case. On the one hand, the government took the initiative for this research and was also the funding agency. Moreover, the government both the departments of Justice and Health and the inspectorate, was subject of the investigations, with strong interests in the outcome of the research. On the other hand, the Samson-committee that commissioned the research was autonomous in asking researchers to develop research projects within the main research question, determined by the government, on sexual abuse of out-of-home placed children. This construction seems to give sufficient counter balance to protect researchers from pressure by interest groups, in this case the state, notwithstanding being paid by this same interest group. It seems to sufficiently prevent the risk of accommodation to the goals of the funding agency. This research situation seems to be rather similar with doing research paid by research funding agencies paid by the state: apart from the research subject and research question, design, methodology and research methods, and the conclusion and publication of the results were and remained the responsibility of the researchers. It is a challenge for researchers in such a situation to remain critical and independent, to maintain their academic ethics, and to resist the temptation to more or less accommodate their research to any interests, among them the interests of funding agencies because of potential new commissions and research grants in the future.

References

Arrow, K. J. (1962). Economic welfare and the allocation of resources for invention. In: Universities-national bureau committee for economic research and the committee on economic growth of the Social Science Research Council, *The rate and direction of inventive activity, economic and social factors* (pp. 609–626). Princeton: University Press.

Bridges, D. (1998). Research for sale: Moral market or moral maze? *British Educational Research Journal, 24*, 593–607.

Commissie Samson. (2012). *Omringd door zorg, toch niet veilig. Seksueel misbruik van door de overheid uit huis geplaatste kinderen, 1945 tot heden. Rapport Commissie-Samson*. Amsterdam: Boom.

Dane, J., Walhout, E. C., & Dekker, J. J. H. (2012). *Overheid en gedwongen jeugdzorg: Een nader onderzoek naar toezicht en inspectie in de periode van de Tweede Wereldoorlog tot midden jaren tachtig*. Den Haag: Commisie-Samson.

Deetman, W., et al. (2011a). *Seksueel misbruik van minderjarigen in de Rooms-Katholieke Kerk. Uitgebreide versie. Deel 1 Het onderzoek*. Amsterdam: Balans.

Deetman, W., et al. (2011b). *Seksueel misbruik van minderjarigen in de Rooms-Katholieke Kerk. Uitgebreide versie. Deel 2 De achtergrondstudies en essays*. Amsterdam: Balans.

Deetman, W., et al. (2013). *Seksueel misbruik van en geweld tegen meisjes in de Rooms-Katholieke Kerk. Een vervolgonderzoek*. Amsterdam: Balans.

Dekker, J. J. H. (2001). *The will to change the child. Re-education homes for children at risk in nineteenth century Western Europe*. Frankfurt am Main: Peter Lang.

Dekker, J. J. H. (2007). Opvoeding onder toezicht. De Nederlandse kinderwetten in de eeuw van het kind. In NN (ed.), *Honderd jaar kinderwetten 1905–2005* (pp. 10–33). Den Haag: Ministerie van Justitie.

Dekker, J. J. H. (2009). Children at risk in history. A story of expansion. *Paedagogica Historica, 45*, 17–36.

Dekker, J. J. H. (2010a). Child maltreatment in the last 50 years: The use of statistics. In P. Smeyers & M. Depaepe (Eds.), *Educational research: The ethics and aesthetics of statistics* (pp. 43–57). Dordrecht: Springer.

Dekker, J. J. H. (2010b). *Educational ambitions in history. Childhood and education in an expanding educational space from the seventeenth to the twentieth century*. Frankfurt am Main/Berlin/Bern/Brussels/New York/Oxford/Vienna: Peter Lang.

Dekker, J. J. H. (2011). The century of the child revisited. In M. Freeman (Ed.), *Children's rights: Progress and perspectives. Essays from the international journal of Children's rights* (pp. 477–495). Leiden/Boston: Martinus Nijhoff Publishers/Koninklijke Brill NV.

Dekker, J. J. H. (2016a). Professionalization. In P. Smeyers & M. Depaepe (Eds.), *Educational research: Discourses of change and changes of discourse*. Dordrecht: Springer. pp. …. (forthcoming).

Dekker, M. (2016b). *Effectiviteit aan de horizon. Een studie rond onderzoek naar resultaat op het gebied van de justitiële kinderbescherming in Nederland tussen 1945 en 2005*. Groningen: Rijksuniversiteit Gorningen. PhD thesis.

Dekker, J. J. H., & Grietens, H. (2015). Sexual abuse of children in foster care and the history of Dutch child protection: Actors in fading spotlights. In J. Sköld & S. Swain (Eds.), *In the midst of apology: Professionals and the legacy of abuse among children in care* (pp. 127–136). Sydney: Palgrave Macmillan.

Dekker, J. J. H., et al. (2012). *Jeugdzorg in Nederland 1945–2010. Resultaten van deelonderzoek 1 van de Commissie Samson. Historische schets van de institutionele ontwikkeling van de jeugdsector vanuit het perspectief van het kind en de aan hem/haar verleende zorg*. Den Haag: Commissie-Samson.

Dowdy, E. (1994). Federal Funding and its effect on criminological research: Emphasizing individualistic explanations for criminal behavior. *The American Sociologist, 25*, 77–89.

Finkelhor, D. (1979). *Sexually victimized children*. New York: Free Press.

Finkelhor, D. (1984). *Child sexual abuse. New theory and research*. New York: Free Press.

Gans, J., & Murray, F. E. (2011). *Funding scientific knowledge: Selection, disclosure and the public-private portfolio*. Cambridge: National Bureau of Economic Research.

General Government Terms and Conditions for Public Service Contracts 2014 (ARVODI). (2014). The Hague: Minister of General Affairs.

Grietens, H. (2012). *Seksueel misbruik van kinderen in pleegzorg. Rapport bij deelonderzoek 4: Aard en omvang van seksueel misbruik in de pleegzorg en de reactie op signalen (periode 1945–2007)*. Den Haag: Commissie-Samson. http://historicaldialogues.org/.

Jenny, C. (2008). Medicine discovers child abuse. *The Journal of the American Medical Association (JAMA), 300*, 2796–2797.

Kempe, C. H., Silverman, F. N., Steele, B. F., Droegemuller, W., & Silver, H. K. (1962). The battered-child syndrome. *The Journal of the American Medical Association (JAMA), 181*, 17–24.

Kjaernet, H. (2010). At arm's length? Applied social science and its sponsors. *Journal of Academic Ethics, 8*, 161–169.

KNAW. (2005). *Wetenschap op Bestelling: Over de Omgang tussen Wetenschappelijk Onderzoekers en hun Opdrachtgevers*. Amsterdam: KNAW.

Köbben, A. J. F., & Tromp, H. (1999). *De Onwelkome Boodschap of hoe de Vrijheid van Wetenschap Bedreigd Wordt*. Alphen aan de Rein: Haasbeek.

NIOD, Institute for War, Holocaust and Genocide Studies. (2002). *Sebrenica-rapport*. http://niod.knaw.nl/nl/srebrenica-rapport

Njiokiktjien, M. A. A. L., & Lucieer, W. J. (1973). *Rapport over de Heldring-stichtingen. KT 178 II, III, IV, V, VI, VII en VIII*. Den Haag: Inspectie Particuliere Inrichtingen/Archives of the OGH-institution Zetten.

Parkinson, P. (2012). What does the Lord require of us? Child sexual abuse in the churches. *Journal of Religion and Abuse, 4*, 3–31.

Rapport en Bijlagen. (2016). *Commissie Vooronderzoek naar Geweld in de Jeugdzorg*. Den Haag: Commissie Vooronderzoek naar Geweld in de Jeugdzorg.

Resnik, D. B. (2000). Financial interests and research bias. *Perspectives on Science, 8*, 255–285.

Resnik, D. B. (2007). *The price of truth: how money affects the norms of science*. Oxford/New York: Oxford University Press.

Rowbottom, D. P., & Aiston, S. J. (2011). The use and misuse of taxpayers' money: Publicly-funded educational research. *British Educational Research Journal, 37*, 631–655.

Sköld, J., & Swain, S. (2015a). *Apologies and the legacy of abuse of children in 'care'. International perspectives*. Basingstoke: Palgrave Macmillan.

Sköld, J., & Swain, S. (2015b). Introduction. In J. Sköld & S. Swain (Eds.), *Apologies and the legacy of abuse of children in 'Care'. International perspectives* (pp. 1–9). Basingstoke: Palgrave Macmillan.

Thomas, J. (1982). Federal funding and policing research the impact of government sponsorship in social science. *Knowledge Creation, Diffusion, Utilization, 3*, 339–369.

Timmerman, M. C., Schreuder, P. R., Harder, A. T., Dane, J., van der Klein, M., & Walhout, E. C. (2012). *Aard en omvang van seksueel misbruik in de residentiële jeugdzorg en reacties op signalen van dit misbruik 1945–2008*. The Hague: Commissie-Samson.

Useem, M. (1976). Government influence on the social science paradigm. *The Sociological Quarterly, 17*, 146–161.

van der Steur, A., & van Rijn, M. J. (2016). *Aanbieding rapport Vooronderzoek naar geweld in de jeugdzorg*. The Hague: Letter dated 17 May to the Lower House, reference 762083.

Vasterman, P. L. M. (2004). Mediahype en de sociale constructie van seksueel misbruik van kinderen. In P. Vasterman (Ed.), *Mediahype* (pp. 133–201). Amsterdam: Aksant.

Vasterman, P. L. M. (2005). Media-hype. Self-reinforcing news waves, journalistic standards and the construction of social problems. *European Journal of Communication, 20*, 508–530.

Versleijen, A. (Ed.). (2007). *Dertig jaar publieke onderzoeksfinanciering in Nederland 1975–2005*. Den Haag: Rathenau Instituut.

Wiarda, J. J. (2011). *Onderzoek naar seksueel misbruik van kinderen die onder verantwoordelijkheid van de overheid zijn geplaatst in instellingen en bij pleegouders. Beschrijving van het relevante juridische kader*. Den Haag: Commissie-Samson.

Research Ethics and a Case of Positionality

Lynda Stone

Several years ago, a research group of university faculty and graduate students met to discuss a study of a middle school classroom in a school of a large number of immigrant families to the United States. The research questions incorporated issues of student identity, school belonging and success, and life outside of school. The study received general support to take place within several months of researcher observation and participation: classroom interactions among the teacher and students and student peers, small survey, focus group and individual conversation especially, and intriguingly, on what students themselves had to say. In the meeting, one of the faculty members raised the question of positionality: to add a statement to the proposal that situated the researcher's background as a former teacher, native-born American, middle class and female. The question was raised by another faculty about the purpose of the statement, that is what, why, and how the researcher's statement was important as ethics for the study. At that point, one of the faculty members piped up: "She will be laughed out of the academy without it!" This closed down the conversation as members of the group indicated their affirmation of the interjection. The group's response did indeed indicate the widespread acceptance of the practice of asserting positionality as a major theoretical and practical standard of ethics.

Introduction

In educational research in the USA and elsewhere ethical practice is a central concern of the work. Various nations have their own standards of ethics amid a general focus on research's aim for furthering knowledge. This chapter takes up current

L. Stone (✉)
The University of North Carolina at Chapel Hill, Chapel Hill, NC, USA
e-mail: lstone@email.unc.edu

© Springer International Publishing AG, part of Springer Nature 2018
P. Smeyers, M. Depaepe (eds.), *Educational Research: Ethics, Social Justice, and Funding Dynamics*, Educational Research 10,
https://doi.org/10.1007/978-3-319-73921-2_5

practices in attending to epistemology and ethics within American quantitative and qualitative traditions and especially within a contemporary emphasis on inquiry for social justice. The principal focus emerges on the practice of positionality. The thesis is that incorporating researcher position as an ethic is a misuse, a misunderstanding of elements of philosophical and social science theorizing based in feminist perspectives. The place to begin is that positionality is basically epistemological.

The hypothetical example that opens the chapter serves as a premise. Following an introductory comment about the methodology, the case incorporates these elements: research ethics in empirical traditions, positionality with its connections to social justice, feminist origins of standpoint and reflexive positionality theories in two sections, and concluding discussion with a final consideration of the opening hypothetical.

The use of "case' in the chapter title is deliberate. This is a case about ethics. Comment on this approach comes from a marvelous philosophical re-start by the late Stephen Toulmin. His point concerned the need for re-affirmation of a tradition within philosophy long taking a back seat as a second, indeed ancient, pillar of modernity. The first pillar was epistemology and the second was ethics. He writes,

> Aristotle saw intimate connections between ethics and rhetoric: for him, every ethical positon was that of a given kind of person in given circumstances, and in a special relation with other specific people, the concrete particularity of a case was 'of the essence.' Ethics was a field not for theoretical analysis, but for practical wisdom, and it was a mistake to treat it as a universal or abstract science. (Toulmin 1990, pp. 75–76)

The case at the close points to the need for an expanded ethics in US educational research today. Overall, it is not surprising that seeking knowledge to combat societal and educational problems takes center stage: education and schooling are enterprises in which improvement for all participants, especially those in most need, is crucial. However, the urgency of this need, especially of social justice for achievement in school of minority males, an important contextual factor. However, there have been two unintended results: One is the masking of ethics and the other is the invisibility of girls and women in contemporary educational research. In the latter regard, It is important that typical researchers today have little or no familiarity with feminist theorizings from a couple of decades ago. The chapter brings these viewpoints to the fore.

Research Ethics

To begin the case, it is important to understand that general ethical practices. are not only desirable but also required in US empirical research. Research is typically organized by methodology, quantitative and qualitative, within disciplines and fields. The Anglo-American model is hierarchical led by the natural sciences followed by the social sciences and applied fields. This hierarchy functions in conceptions of epistemological rigor resulting in funding emphases.

An initial ethical practice is required for all research known as IRB, proposal review by Institutional Review Boards at each institution under federal connections and guidelines. The seriousness of IRB is reflected, in part, in an infamous origin, the Tuskegee Syphilis Study, under the auspices of the U.S. Public Health Service between 1932 and 1972. Therein 600 African American males were unknowingly injected with syphilis and denied treatment when it was available. Revelation of this practice led to *The Belmont Report* in 1978 and legislation enacted by the US Congress. IRB reviews pay special attention to vulnerable populations that include children, students, minorities, and the economically/educationally disadvantage as well as the incarcerated and those with disabilities. As an ethics, thus, it is specifically designed to protect research participants and includes elements of consent and confidentiality. In addition, various academic and professional associations have codes of research conduct that can serve as ethical guides; among them are the international networks around the American Educational Research Association and the American Psychological Association.

There are standard practices that students, researchers, and then mentors follow that are learned through courses, texts, and actual inquiries. Over the past century or so of educational research, specific methodological practices have emerged within quantitative and qualitative traditions. While new knowledge is the 'aim,' this generally means building on past understandings in a process of induction. A key issue across empirical methodologies has been the evolution of theorizing about objectivity for truth claims. One summary statement is found in a late nineties methods textbook in which the author, Donna Mertens, cites a post-positivist position: "Analysts …. place considerable emphasis on science as a method for reducing or eliminating effects of personal values on observations and try to be value-free" (Mertens 1998, p. 21). Specific measures are employed and tests are administered to override subjective bias. Design features might well include standards of survey implementation, population sampling, and the like.

Methods resources take one or both of two tacts regarding ethics; the first is embedded in design as specific tools and the second, considerably less acknowledged, is reference to traditional philosophical positions. Mertens's treatment of ethics incorporates the three principles that are central to IRB: beneficence, respect, and justice (p. 24). Another popular textbook from John Creswell incorporates IRB and emphasis on processes of data collection and reporting. Overall, Creswell states this: "Ethics should be a primary consideration rather than an afterthought and it should be at the forefront of the researcher's agenda" (Creswell 2012, p. 23, citing Hesse-Bieber [and Leavy] 2006). Creswell adds respect for the research site as well as its audience. Moreover, ethical use of specific research tools to which Mertens and Creswell refer in all research is perhaps the most important. This is generally how researchers enact IRB and more. Once again, here is Creswell: "[Research] needs be honestly reported, shared with participants, not previously published, not plagiarized… and duly credited to authors that make a contribution" (Creswell 2012, p. 279). Overall these are matters of right and wrong.

Building on commitment to distinguishing right from wrong in research practice, the second tact is to expose researchers to how western philosophy has traditionally considered ethics. With an extensive background in ethics, Clifford Christians's contribution to *The Sage Handbook of Qualitative Research* (Christians 2011; see Denzin and Lincoln 2011) is very helpful. Christians's starting point is the philosophical project of the Enlightenment with its separation of knowledge and ethics, is and ought, facts and values. Within the dawn of modernity, the center is the promotion, as he puts this, of the autonomous self (see also Stone 2005). Building on ancient ethical values of rationality and virtue, the individual is capable and responsible for this ethics. In Christians's words,

> Consistent with the presumed purity of individual liberty over the moral order, the basic institutions of society.... [and reflecting various European thinkers and states] were designed to ensure 'neutrality of different conceptions of the good. (Christians 2011, p. 62, citing Root 1993)

Much more can be said about traditional western ethics. A modern emphasis on individual autonomy has assumed two paths that researchers might bring to bear on their inquiry. One is Immanuel Kant's logic of ethical duty, in the vernacular to be true to others as one would be true to oneself. The other is from John Stuart Mill and others to instrumentalize a utilitarian calculus for the good of society. While the latter might appeal to social justice, it abstracts from and masks individual actions. Both western views envision society as aggregated individuals. Importantly since these traditions entail processes of self-disclosure, it is thus not surprising that well-intentioned researchers view positionality as an ethical stance.

Positionality and Social Justice

The second element of the chapter's case is positionality, the belief in and practice of inserting an 'ethic' of self-disclosure into the research process. This typically comes in a statement as part of a research design, as in the hypothetical above. Positionality is accepted and affirmed widely across today's educational research methodologies, often taken for granted. Researchers, as implied above, believe that It is especially pertinent for education because of aims for improvement of the lives of children, youth, families, and communities often through schools and schooling.

Positionality has become standard practice across various critical research and scholarly traditions and sub-traditions that do extend beyond education and have been developed within various disciplinary orientations of qualitative research. Many identify themselves with a social justice tradition and thus recognize the central places of identity, critique, and politics in their inquiries. One example of a sub-tradition's initial presentation within positionality is found in a 2004 collection on postcritical ethnography in educational research. Building from a marriage and critique of critical and interpretive ethnographies, here are the editors of the volume:

Positionality involves being explicit about the groups and interests the postcritical ethnographer wishes to serve as well as his or her biography. One's race, gender, class, ideas and commitments are subject to the exploration as part of the ethnography. Indeed position may be so important that it can be seen as an epistemological claim as in… [Patricia Hill] Collins'… standpoint epistemology…. Positionality also involves 'studying up'… [so] that the focus… may well be institutional arrangements and social movements… or more powerful as with whiteness studies. (Noblit et al. 2004, p. 21).

As one of the editors continues about his own research, positionalities, and note the plural, are particular. They do, however, form a unity for him in an investigation, "{carrying] with it its own situatedness, multiplicity, history, and… forms of privilege" (Murrillo 2004, p. 156).

There is some textual evidence of advocacy for positionality in the general teaching of research methods but it is minimal and thus across the academy it remains the purview of specific research courses and mentors. Mertens, cited above, very briefly connects positionality in educational research to an emancipatory paradigm from the mid-to-late nineties with the acknowledgement that all knowledge is contextual (Mertens 1998, p. 185). Juanita Johnson-Bailey, an African-American educational researcher, presents a narrative study in which Collins is also referenced by her. Raising issues of 'researching across cultural boundaries', she concludes this: "There is no righteous ground…. Each story is… a balancing act. The forces to be reconciled change as positions shift" (Johnson-Bailey 2004, p. 138). These shifts are specific to who the researcher and researched are and for her the cultures and margins that are traversed and biases contained (ibid.).

Social justice discourse and aims are increasingly present in social sciences and professions training and methods texts. In the epilogue of the well-regarded *Sage Handbook* referenced above, editors Norman Denzin and Yvonna Lincoln point to this emergence of social justice purposes. They write,

While it is the case that not all qualitative researchers aim for social justice explicitly… it is the case that many now ask themselves what the outcomes of their research will produce in terms of more extended equality and less domination and discrimination. (Denzin and Lincoln 2011, p. 716)

In the same volume, sociologist Kathy Charmaz does address research through a broad definition of social justice:

[Social] justice inquiry… [means] studies that attend to inequities and equality, barriers and access, poverty and privilege… and their implications for suffering…. [It] also includes a critical stance toward social structures and processes that shape individual and collective life. (Charmaz 2011, p. 359)

She continues with suggestions for a wide range of research approaches who take social justice as a "for granted concern" and "who begin with an explicit value stance and an agenda for change" (ibid.). Importantly she embeds an ethic when she states, "[For] those who identify themselves as social justice researchers, "'shoulds and 'oughts' are part of the research process and product" (p. 360).

In education, social justice as an aim is increasingly found in teacher education that might mean greater research emphasis. Examples are critical pedagogy and

culturally-relevant pedagogy, the former with its own roots in the writings of Paulo
Freire. One collection from recent decades is edited by Gloria Ladsen-Billings and
William Tate. This an example from theorists and researchers who have been, for
some, named as 'critical curriculum theorists.' The broad diversity of social justice
approaches is present in the introduction from Ladsen-Billings in ties of social justice to public interest. She summarizes the general issue of justice within research:
"We cannot hide behind notes of neutrality or objectivity when people are suffering
so desperately…. If education research is going to matter, then we have to make it
matter in the lives of real people around real issues" (Ladsen-Billings 2006, p. 10).

From the hypothetical above, positionality claims begin in categories of race,
class, and perhaps gender among brief specifics. Each researcher determines his or
her position and what detail is needed. Given wide use, positionality may have
already achieved a normalization, an acceptance without question. What results is
absent understanding of its epistemological roots—and not as an ethic.

Standpoint Positionalities

The third case element is 'standpoint positionalities,' a catch-all phrase for several
epistemological theories. As indicated above, qualitative social justice researchers
often cite Patricia Hill Collins's writings of a standpoint theory as their source for
their own positionality ethic. Her work is appealing in many ways that emphasize
its narrative form and its politics. Two aspects, however, are misunderstood: a standpoint is precisely an epistemology and it is feminist. This detailed treatment of
Collins's black feminist thought demonstrates its appeal and is meant to render a
corrective understanding of her project. It is followed by additional support for feminist standpoint epistemologies from Sandra Harding and Nancy Hartsock, with a
note about the contribution of Dorothy Smith. In what follows, Collins's capitaliza-
tion of terms is her emphasis and meant to honor this.

Patricia Hill Collins. Collins is currently Distinguished University Professor of
Sociology at the University of Maryland, USA, formerly with a long tenure at the
University of Cincinnati in African American Studies and Gender Studies. Her
undergraduate and graduate academic training was primarily at Brandeis University
with a stop at Harvard. Her project is primarily situated in the now classic, *Black
Feminist Thought* (2009), originally published in 1990 and re-edited subsequently.

Collins's text is a theoretical analysis positing a standpoint position, a privileged
knowledge, based principally on the historical experience of US black women. Its
thesis is a relationship of oppression and activism of individuals and collectives
evidenced textually in literature, music, and other representations most often of
daily life. As asserted in the initial volume preface, its theoretical rigor brings
together insights from "afrocentric philosophy, feminist theory, Marxist social
thought, the sociology of knowledge, critical theory, and postmodernism" (Collins
2009, p. xiii). For present purposes, it is important that the text does not read as
conventional social science inquiry; it is not empirical except in displaying 'reports'

of existential life. While Collins does not employ this terminology, it is more like philosophy as feminist literary criticism.

Black feminist thought is a standpoint theory, an epistemology. First, it is based in unique and predominantly silenced experience. Second, it is a philosophical claim of privilege representing a historical—and contemporary—group. Third, it is feminist, aiming for societal change and empowerment. Fourth, it entails a separation of epistemology and ethics. To begin, Collins's first essay from 1986 and her subsequent text, *Black Feminist Thought* (Collins 1986, 2000, 2009) have to be historically situated both in the evolution of Anglo-American science and social science theory and research and in a similar theoretical trajectory of feminist theory. Now several decades old, this was a period of widespread acceptance of notions of 'social construction of knowledge'; indeed the title of the volume's first part emphasizes this idea. From a base in traditional modern science, Collins introduces her stand toward the objectivity/subjectivity debate from mid-century:

> I found the movement between my training as an 'objective' social scientist and my daily experiences as an African-American woman to be jarring…. I discovered that the both/and stance of Black feminist thought allowed me to be both objective and subjective… to be both a respectable scholar and an acceptable mother. (2009, p. x)

In addition to this basic stand toward epistemology, while Collins brings together insights from a range of theoretical traditions, her unique approach is to place black women's lives and literatures at the center. Specifically, she writes,

> An experiential, material base underlies a Black feminist epistemology, namely collective experiences and accompanying worldviews…. This alternative epistemology uses… standards that are consistent… for substantiated knowledge and… criteria for methodological adequacy. (pp. 274–275)

As a black feminist, Collins writes also about the feminist debates of her day and the movement especially among minority scholars for emphasis on difference rather than sameness in experience and theory (see Kohli and Burbules 2012). Here she is in some detail,

> I have deliberately chosen not to begin with feminist tenets developed from the experiences of White, middle-class, Western women and then insert the ideas of African-American women. While I am quite familiar with a range of… White feminist theorists and certainly value their contributions to our understanding of gender, this is not a book about what Black women think of White feminist ideas… [or about theoretical comparisons of any traditions]. (p. viii)

As indicated above, Collins's writings have strong appeal to social justice researchers perhaps because of the style and content of writing. Her text is lovingly researched, documented, and narrated. Many might desire to emulate it. For example, in a chapter on historical images of black women, she overviews the specific depiction of Black single mothers. Incomplete, stereotyped images of the mammy and the matriarch appeared in social science and in fictionalized accounts beginning in the 1950s. A dominant social science view contrasted to the writings of black women playwrights and novelists such as Lorraine Hansbury and Paule Marshall depicting the lives of strong black women in their families.

Her work raises three issues that concern the use of a black feminist epistemology by researchers seeking an ethic: the uniqueness of speaking as a feminist theorist from self-disclosure for a specific group and an issue of appropriation, a particular ethic stance from Collins that is typically not acknowledged by citation and explication, and the nature and history of standpoint theories themselves. Collins speaks to the first two and very briefly to the third that is turned to in the next section on additional origins of feminist epistemology. Issues one and two are related and take up the issue of whether Collins intended black feminist thought to bean epistemology or and ethic, and what she proposed as a related ethic for her. It seems clear that in the first edition, continuing into the second, her aim was to claim her own voice and through her research advance voices of other Black women (Collins 2000, 2009). Importantly, she writes that as she privileges black women's thought, she does encourage other groups to find their own standpoints but not, significantly, to replicate the knowledge, wisdom, empowerment, and social justice viewpoint that she presents. She offers this invitation: "By placing African-American women's ideas at the center of analysis, I not only privilege these ideas but encourage White feminists, African-American men, and all others to investigate their similarities and differences among their own standpoints" (p. ix). There remains, however, a significant question of when a line of appropriated citation is crossed, a matter of ethics. Indeed, another question is whether standpoints are feminist or must be.

One final significant point from Collins is her own ethics, written about within the standpoint epistemology but distinct. Taken in order in her text are its two components, the ethics of caring and the ethic of personal responsibility. First, she describes the ethics of care initially thus: "[The] ethic suggests that personal expressiveness, emotions, and empathy are central to the knowledge validation process" (pp. 281–282). Here she points to a 'convergence' between this ethic and 'connected knowing' in 'women's ways of knowing" (Collins, p. 283; see Belenky et al. 1987), the important feminist research from the eighties. Significantly too, there must be support for care in "access to social institutions that support an ethic of caring" (Collins, p. 284). Personal responsibility, the second component, means that one is accountable for knowledge claims as they point also to "an individual's character, values, and ethics." She continues,

> Many African-Americans reject prevailing beliefs that probing into an individual's personal viewpoint is outside the boundaries of discussion. Rather all views expressed and actions taken are thought to derive from a central set of core beliefs that cannot be other than personal. (p. 284)

For Collins these ethical components are central to knowledge validation from the specific social location of black women (see p. 289). Pertinently she almost never uses the term 'positionality,' although it does appear in the preface to the second edition of her text from 2009: "Whereas this edition remains centered on U.S. black women, it raises questions concerning African-American women's positionality within a global Black feminism" (p. xiii). New times place her voice within a larger project of social justice. Here is her evolved conclusion: "[The] struggle for justice is larger than any one group, individual, or social movement.... [It] is a collective problem that requires a collective solution" (p. xiv).

Sandra Harding. The turn to Harding's feminist standpoint epistemology helps the case of positionality with additional attention to its roots. It is understandable that Patricia Hill Collins wishes to present her standpoint as original and not derivative of other feminisms and feminist experiences, however, as she acknowledges, other standpoints were extant and indeed encouraged. Harding currently holds professorships at the University of California, Los Angeles, and Michigan State University. Harding's undergraduate training was at Rutgers University, this followed by a dozen years spent in part as an elementary teacher. Her doctorate is from New York University in philosophy. Her professorial career included extensive appointments primarily at the University of Delaware and UCLA. Early writings focused on the nature of science, especially feminist corrections; later writings extended into multicultural and post-colonial approaches to these issues.

Beginning in the mid-seventies, Harding was among few white women and even fewer women of color who were in university departments in philosophy and the natural and social sciences. Many chose to start where they could in response to Enlightenment science and dominant modern epistemology. In writings primarily from the mid-eighties, self-identified feminist philosopher Harding publishes two texts that incorporate and extend standpoint epistemologies. She writes,

> The feminist standpoint epistemologies ground a distinctive feminist science in a theory of gendered activity and social experience.... It is useful to think... [of these theories] as 'successor science' projects: in significant ways, the aim to reconstruct the original goals of modern science. (Harding 1986, pp. 141–142)

With regard to science, the initial point was to argue that it was traditionally—and always—socially situated and representative of "men's distinctive activity and experience" (p. 142). Moreover in science, the feminist project was to be directed by social values and political agendas. The first agenda is largely known as 'liberal,' and sought to place the values and agendas of women alongside those of men.

Whose Science? Whose Knowledge? Thinking from Women's lives (Harding 1991) continues from *The Science Question in Feminism* (1986). In the latter, she offers a series of grounds from and for feminist epistemological claims to science. These are selected and synthesized here in five "grounds,' but not firm foundations (1991, p. 137). First is using women's lives to decrease "partialities and distortions... [from within a gender-stratified society... [in which] women and men are assigned difference... [and unequal] activities" (p. 121) Second of great importance is recognizing women's locations as 'strangers' to the social order. Importantly here Harding cites the work of Collins and what alternative epistemologies can reveal. This 'ground' captures also the observation that within the same culture... [of minorities or majorities] there is in general a greater gap for women than for men... [over] what they say... or how they behave"(p. 125). The additional location of women as oppressed in relation to oppressors is sometimes useful as that of the feminist researcher as "outsider within' a traditional discipline or field (see pp. 131–132).

Third is connecting feminist theorizing to political activism. Harding explains,
The need for struggle emphasizes the fact that a feminist standpoint is not something that
anyone can have simply by claiming it. It is an achievement… [and differs from a perspective… [which] anyone can simple have]. (p. 127)

Importantly in activism, she adds, "some men have been feminists, and some women
have not" (p. 128). Fourth is viewing and valuing the "dailiness of women's lives"
as significant for understanding the lives of both women and men. Credit from
Harding for these insights goes to, among others, sociologist Dorothy Smith and
historian Bettina Aptheker, also both writing in the seventies (Harding, pp. 128,
129; see Smith 1987; Aptheker 1989). Finally fifth is re-conceputalizing historical
and contemporary ideological dualisms that stem from the millenniums-old relationship of nature to culture. Harding understands that men as makers of culture
continue to dominate women's transformations that are still largely invisible
(p. 131).

It is important to see that Harding's work, as that of Collins, has continued to
evolve over her career. Beyond the scope of this case, her continued connections of
science to issues of multicultural and postmodern life remind as in educational
research that issues of dominant theories of epistemology continue. The 'culture
wars,' in which she played a central part, and perhaps especially in educational
research, are not dead.

Nancy Hartsock. Political theorist, the late Nancy Hartsock is largely credited as
the originator of feminist standpoint theory; she died of cancer in 2015. Hartsock's
academic career was spent in the political science department of at the University of
Washington. She earned her doctorate from the University of Chicago in the early
seventies in that field and held several brief professorial appointments before coming to Seattle. In only 2 years following her degree, ground-breaking writing on a
feminist historical materialism began to be published by her. The major work,
Money, Sex, and Power: Toward a Feminist Historical Materialism was published
in 1983. It focused on the sexual division of labor that extended across her academic
lifetime into political attention to global, gendered economic issues. Besides its
origination, the importance of Hartsock's theorizing is its place in a particular tradition within feminisms, that of Marxist-inspired radical formulations. While some
conceptions seem old today, materialist, sociologist researches remain active.

Hartsock's analysis begins with presentation of an ideal type of the social relations of women's and men's activity that is not to be attributed to individuals. Rather
the focus "is on institutionalized… practices and on the specific epistemology…
manifested by the … sexual division of labor" (Hartsock 1983, p. 233). While recognizing the differences in women's lives due to race and sexual preference, nonetheless she asserts that there are commonalities among all women in 'western class
societies.' As a group thus, there are two contributions in common, subsistence and
childrearing. She writes, "Whether or not all women do both, women as a sex are
institutionally responsible for producing both goods and human beings, and all
women are forced to become the kinds of persons who can do both" (p. 234). While
traditionally divided social relations between men and women in the west appear to
have shifted some, the norm and the reality worldwide still exist. One of the most

important contributions from Hartsock concerns the extension of Marxist notions of production to focus on reproduction. She explains, "women's experience in bearing and rearing children involves a unity of mind and body more profound than is possible in the worker's instrumental activity" (p. 237). Here enters 'the body' that assumes feminist significance in later decades.

Part of her treatment also returns in earlier attention to Freud-inspired, psychoanalytic object relations theory. Led by the work of Nancy Chodorow, the point is still that women and men grow up through different experiences in relation of their parents and their separation and individuation from them. This dualism, Hartsock posits plays out in the gendered hierarchy originating from the nature-culture split, the first female-identified and the second male-identified.

Finally Hartsock describes what a standpoint can do: it can move beyond these historical relations. Here she is:

> Just as a proletarian standpoint emerges out of the contradiction between appearance and essence in capitalism... [as historically constituted] by the relation of capitalist and worker, the feminist standpoint emerges... [out of the] differing structures of men's and women's activity in Western cultures. (p. 246)

What brings this standpoint theory forward to today is this conclusion: "it expresses women's experience at a particular time and place, located within a particular set of social relations" (ibid.). Hartsock's aim for this standpoint theorizing is to envision and work toward 'a fully human community,' "structured by a variety of connections rather than separation and opposition" (p. 247).

Dorothy Smith. This third case element ends with one other origin, an honorary mention of the work of sociologist Dorothy Smith. She was born in England, did undergraduate work at the London School of Economics, and emigrating, her doctorate at UC Berkeley. Her academic career centered at two Canadian institutions, the University of British Columbia and the Ontario Institute of Studies in Education, now part of the University of Toronto. She is today in her nineties and retired. Her work too has Marxist roots and as contributing to the early theorizing about standpoint. She is perhaps best known for her intervention in sociology, introducing women's perspective as 'radical critique' of the discipline and into North American social sciences (Smith 1974). One interesting contribution concerns the training of graduate students with which this chapter, this case, began. Here she is: "As graduate students.... we learn to practice the sociological subsumption of the actualities of ourselves and of other people. We find out how to treat the world as instances of a sociological body of knowledge. The procedure operates as a sort of conceptual imperialism" (Smith 1974, p. 8, 1987). As the other feminist standpoint theorists, she is well worth reading.

Reflexive Positionalities

The fourth component of the case of positionality and the second strand of feminist theorizing is found in empirical social science studies, often named as 'feminist ethnography.' This tradition, as standpoint writings, makes knowledge claims but herein are significant differences from standpoints. The theory arises within research in which the basic relationship of researcher and researched is questioned in branches of anthropology and sociology. The reflexivity tradition gains prominence in later decades of the twentieth century; it has complex and multidisciplinary theoretical roots drawing beyond questions of science. It is often identified with postmodernism, a term whose overuse made it virtually irrelevant, while its ties to extended social philosophies such as poststructuralism have been useful. Treatment in this case differs from standpoint theories because the tradition is not primarily identified with key figures, although the work and leadership of Cuban-American anthropologist Ruth Behar is often cited (see the collection, Behar and Gordon 1995). Most important to the case, the tradition has incorporated attention to ethics that will figure both implicitly and explicitly in this brief introduction. A detailed treatment is well beyond the scope of this chapter: educational researchers are encouraged to read across now several decades of writings to gain a broader theoretical overview. Indeed a traditional 'research review' seems contradictory to the tradition. Four exemplars form the basis for analysis in this case: these are from Kim England (1994), Kimberly Huisman (2008), Lorraine Nencel (2014), and Naomi van Stapele (2014).

In addition to reflexivity and positionality, key concepts interwoven throughout these studies include voice, agency, representation, intersubjectivity, and reciprocity—and ethics. Underlying are common feminist themes of differences, fluidities, and multiplicities. Overall in this feminist strand, positionality is embedded in relations of reflexivity and in which ethics often is acknowledged as embedded in epistemological inquiries. In general there appears agreement on values that Nencel related are "grounded in notions of engagement and radical empathy and... [in methodologies that highlight agency and create]... discursive spaces" (Nencel 2014, p. 76).

Reflexivity theory begins with the relationships of the researcher and the researched. In its early formulations, a modern ontology remained but with emerging recognition of problems of differential power relations. Over time feminist researchers desired to undermine the conventional research relationship because of its inherent ethical issues. Kim England offers a set of possible relationships: "reciprocal, asymmetrical or potentially exploitative." She posits that

> most feminists usually favor the role of.... [researcher] supplicant, seeking reciprocal relationships based on empathy and mutual respect... [that] explicitly acknowledge... [her] reliance on the research subject to provide insight... [and] by shifting a lot of power over to the researched. (England 1994, p. 82)

Methods might include what she names as 'real or constructed dialogues' to get to people's own terms, to be open to challenges to the researcher's views, and a "self-critical, sympathetic introspection.... about the consequences of the interactions with those being investigated" (ibid.). Interestingly, in feminist geography, in her own work England complicates the 'ethicality' of identifying place in a study—this beyond conventional confidentiality. What is so crucial to the reflexivity tradition, and to the present case on positionality has been the theoretical centrality of ethics that appears in various terms such as empathy just named. Here is Kimberly Huisman: "the endless... ethical dilemmas that researchers face make it important for them to share their... [own] stories and strategies to address the challenges they... [face]" (Huisman 2008, p. 373). Theory thus emerges within the specifics of research and ethics is not only central to research practice but also to reflexivity discourses.

Two different approaches to discourse are found in the exemplars. The first is 'discourse analysis of a narrative text' that begins from positionality, explains Naomi van Stapele, of both the research participant and the researcher: "The research participant has power in the production of knowledge as she has her own agenda... and decides what to share and how to share, i.e., using words, silence and/or body language.... I am also ascribed subject positions by my research participant because I am positioned... [within relations and discourses]" (van Stapele 2014, p. 75). Both agency and subjectivation are part of the narrative process. For van Stapele, "people are agents of their own positioning.... [and simultaneously shape and are shaped by] discursively demarcated spaces and allotted subject positions" (ibid.). The researcher's discourse analysis seeks to reveal these positionings—part of this process also is to be constantly self-reflective and question the framing of the narrative of the research participant (p. 76).

The second approach to discourse again comes from Nencel who, unlike van Stapele's implicit and self-reflective process, explicitly inserts her positionality into a reflexive text. At one stage of a multi-temporal inquiry, after gathering interview data she made a textual decision as an interpreter, to be an actual protagonist in the study. She writes, "I narrate from my perspective. I tell the stories from within the context I heard them and I do this by using 'I' intermitting this with dialogue" (p. 78). Her general point is that decisions like this occur for the researcher within numerous fieldwork relationships, for the researcher, let alone the researched. Some, one might suggest, positively facilitate the project and others negatively complicate, of course depending on one's point of view. One contribution from her research is evident in specific research context: the historic background and contemporary lives of prostitutes in Peru. While she does not name ethics as central, there is her need to protect participants against harm and to be respectful of their own agency (ibid.).

A final introductory contribution comes from Huisman reporting on dangers within reflexive research, ironically that "can lead to more exploitation than traditional positivist methods" (Huisman 2008, p. 372). Importantly challenges remain even for experienced researchers who 'do structure' through researcher and researched relationships. She names three tensions that "[are] related to my shifting and sometimes contradictory positionalities and the way in which they... [do] not mesh with my own values" (p. 379). These are tensions within the researcher, with the academia, and with the research community. These are entwined as shifting identities and positionalities that at bottom are ethical. This reflexive essay may be especially for to early researchers.

Through the elements thus far presented, the concepts named above are often interwoven through the work of individual researchers. This is important because there is no one 'standpoint', even politically, by which to conduct feminist reflexive research. England adds an interesting aspect to the question of ethics and epistemology: this is the vulnerability that is always present in intersubjective research (England 1994, p. 87); considering this surely is a matter of ethics.

Concluding Discussion

In addition to describing the general system of research ethics in the US, the point of this chapter has been to present a case about positionality, a practice of self-disclosure by educational researchers particularly those with aims of social justice. The major contribution has been a return to roots in feminist epistemologies: standpoint and reflexivity theories as positionalities. This specific focus has left out other aspects of research that constitute a set of pre-concluding comments: a small but significant tradition of feminist research in education itself and a much larger tradition of theoretical and empirical attention to and in intersectionality studies that also has feminist roots.

Prior is an important caveat that there are educational researchers who have attended to ethics. An example is from Sherick Hughes and Julie Pennington in setting out methods for autoethnography. They write, "engaging in autoethnography means welcoming the opportunity to learn about your participation in one or more cultural groups, communities, and contexts while contributing to critical social research" (Hughes and Pennington 2017, p. 1). Such engagement entails "writing against oneself as one… [is] entrenched in the complications of one's positions" (p. 10). They name their ethics stance as 'relational ethics' since "the study of the self is rarely done in a social vacuum… [and must recognize] the connectedness between researcher and researched and the communities in which… [one] lives and works" (Hughes and Pennington 2017, p. 85, citing Ellis 2007). Methods of triangulation and member checking from qualitative research are recommended by them. When these are impossible to use in a self-study, perhaps an ethic of fidelity would apply.

From above, a useful brief summary of contributions by feminist researchers in education is found in Kohli and Burbules's *Feminisms and Educational Research* published in 2012, referenced previously in this chapter. They document the presence of feminist theorizing in education particularly coming to the fore in the nineties (see Stone 1994). Foregrounding the tradition turned to next, they write,

> The intersections of race, class, gender, region, religion, and other identity and subjectivity positions have disrupted… the fiction of a unitary notion of women's experience….
> {Further the] theoretical and political frameworks of feminist materialism and

poststructuralism, as well as postcolonial and critical multicultural theory, have produced some of the most cutting-edge feminist educational research in… [recent] decades. (Kohli and Burbules 2012, p. 88)

They highlight the work of theory and research by feminists in education such as Patti Lather, Deborah Britzman, Leslie Roman, Wanda Pillow, Annette Henry, Cynthia Dillard, and Cris Mayo. Of note, much feminist research in education in very recent decades has been led by minority scholars such as African Americans, Henry and Dillard, and Latinas such as Sofia Villenas. An early, now classic collection is *Working the Ruins: Feminist Poststructural Theory and Methods in Education*, edited by Elizabeth St. Pierre and Pillow (St. Pierre and Pillow 2000). Richard Milner, along with Hughes, are African American researchers in education. The latter's text does briefly mention feminist contributions; the former, in presenting a well-considered theoretical framework of positionality, foregrounds race and culture but does not include gender in his intersections (Milner 2007).

Finally, feminists have also founded a contemporary tradition in intersectionality studies. It might be argued that it has superseded positionality theories: this is beyond the scope of the present case. Similar to the idea of multiple and shifting positions as part to reflexive writings, diversity is emphasized, and most important, intersectionality writings are connected to broader social movements with a leading role by minority scholars and research activists. Collins's later work is part of this tradition but the origin of the term is usually credited to African-American law scholar, Kimberly Crenshaw from 1991. In a recent text written with Sirma Bilge from the University of Montreal. Collins and Bilge name the six core ideas of intersectionality: social inequality, power, relationality, social context, complexity, and social justice (see Collins and Bilge 2016, pp. 25–30). One additional core idea of using intersectionality as an analytic tool is to posit these concepts across contextual domains that are structural, cultural and interpersonal.

It is important to understand that intersectional frameworks are epistemological, paying particular attention to politics, to the interconnections of inquiry and praxis. In the language of Collins and Bilge, the idea is "working at the intersections, especially in the lives of disenfranchised groups. Experiences of these groups are significant because they are especially "to broaden and deepen understandings of human life and behavior" (p. 36). Importantly for this case of educational research, while intersectionality studies are found across the academy, Collins and Bilge especially discuss relevance for professional fields. These range from criminology to public health, to education. In the latter, they name possible applications in "teacher training, curriculum design and research on pedagogy for schools" (p. 39). Three ideas from these authors are pertinent: first, to warn against simplified identity claims, second, to see the complexities of interconnections of race, class, gender and nation within "unjust systems of power… [as 'isms' that get lost in shorthand terms that become meaningless]" (p. 201), and third, to warn against intersectionality's 'success' that might not but must lead to specific activism (see Davis et al. 2015).

The case. These concluding comments are meant to indicate that positionality is part of larger writing and work both in and out of education. The overall point of the case is that research always needs to be more than an individual knowledge claim in inquiry that involves relationships of actual persons. It is always ethical, as the research group participants in the chapter hypothetical intuitively knew: they wanted to be ethical. The problem is that they did not understand, probably know of, the feminist roots of positionality. Both standpoint and reflexive positionalities have legitimacy as knowledge projects, but in social justice research, knowledge typically in educational research is not enough for deep change, to combat the systems of oppression just named.

Both standpoint and reflexive positionalities have value in educational research. A summary of contributions points to a difference in approaches to texts. This moves theory to incorporate experience into representations. As the writings of Collins and Harding demonstrate, standpoints are narrative and analytical and 'stand' on their own. As writings in feminist reflexivity studies demonstrated, reflexive texts are 'positioned' to be returned to explicitly within the actual research process. One initial step for educational researchers set on claiming positionality would be to return to the significance of an individual statement at the conclusion of work and in its write-up.

A concluding suggestion is for a methodological addition to a research project that is explicitly ethical. This call is for conversations, interviews or focus groups perhaps mid-project taking up specifics. This should be part of the initial research design and should be attended to in results and in significance of the study. Mid-project is important as potentially sensitive discussion needs to be built on research experience and trust. One long-range change from these efforts is to extend research discourse with a centrality of ethics; short term changes can come within every project.

For this case, the hypothetical with which this case of positionality began now needs recasting as a microcosm of central tenets. The group was well-intentioned. However, what was missing on the part of all participants, both women and men, was attention, a sensitivity, to issues of gender and power. In the group discussion, none of the participants took account of the feminist roots of the practice of positionality, especially as a knowledge claim and not an ethics. There was no discussion further of the gendered status of research participants; immigrant students were categorized as such but there was no attention to gender influence on their schooling experience, especially at middle school age. The teacher and a researcher were women but their power differential was not mentioned. Finally there was no recognition of the gendered dynamics of the research group itself: it probably seemed unnecessary among these social justice researchers. Therein the majority of the group was male who in addition claimed methodological expertize and who did not question their own 'positions.' Knowledge of positionality theories would have helped but, most important, was a commitment to ethics among themselves.

Acknowledgements This chapter benefited from insights about research from Janice Anderson and Megan Williams, enlightening conversation and crucial sources from Emily Freeman, and special consideration from Paul Smeyers.

References

Aptheker, B. (1989). *Tapestries of life: Women's work, women's consciousness, and the meaning of daily experience*. Amherst: The University of Massachusetts Press.

Behar, R., & Gordon, D. (1995). *Women writing culture*. Berkeley/Los Angeles: University of California Press.

Belenky, M., Clinchy, B., Goldberger, N., & Tarule, J. (1987). *Women's ways of knowing: The development of self, voice, and mind*. New York: Basic Books.

Charmaz, K. (2011). Grounded theory methods in social justice research. In N. Denzin & Y. Lincoln (Eds.), *The Sage handbook of qualitative research* (4th ed., pp. 359–380). Los Angeles: Sage.

Christians, C. (2011). Ethics and politics in qualitative research. In N. Denzin & Y. Lincoln (Eds.), *The Sage handbook of qualitative research* (4th ed., pp. 61–80). Los Angeles: Sage.

Collins, P. H. (1986). Learning from the outsider within: The sociological significance of black feminist thought. *Social Problems, 33*(6), 14–32.

Collins, P. H. (2000, 2009). *Black feminist thought* (1st, 2nd ed.). New York: Routledge.

Collins, P. H., & Bilge, S. (2016). *Intersectionality*. Cambridge/Malden: Polity.

Creswell, J. (2012). *Educational research: Planning, conducting, and evaluating quantitative and qualitative research* (4th ed.). Boston: Pearson.

Davis, D., Brunn-Bevel, R., & Olive, J. (Eds.). (2015). *Intersectionality in educational research*. Sterling: Stylus.

Denzin, N., & Lincoln, Y. (Eds.). (2011). *The Sage handbook of qualitative research* (4th ed.). Los Angeles: Sage.

England, K. (1994). Getting personal: Reflexivity, positionality, and feminist research. *The Professional Geographer, 46*(1), 80–89.

Harding, S. (1986). *The science question in feminism*. Ithaca: Cornell University Press.

Harding, S. (1991). *Whose science? Whose knowledge? Thinking from women's lives*. Ithaca: Cornell University Press.

Hartsock, N. (1983). *Money, sex, and power: Toward a feminist historical materialism*. Boston: Northeastern University Press.

Highes, S., & Pennington, J. (2017). *Autoethnography: Process, product, and possibility for critical social research*. Los Angeles: Sage.

Huisman, K. (2008). "Does the mean you're not going to come visit me anymore?" An inquiry into an ethics of reciprocity and positionality in feminist ethnographic research. *Sociological Inquiry, 78*(3), 372–396.

Johnson-Bailey, J. (2004). Enjoining positionality and power in narrative work: Balancing contentious and modulating forces. In K. de Marris & S. Lapan (Eds.), *Foundations for research: Methods of inquiry in education and the social sciences* (pp. 123–138). Mahwah: Lawrence Erlbaum Associates.

Kohli, W., & Burbules, N. (2012). *Feminisms and educational research*. Lanham: Rowman & Littlefield.

Ladsen-Billings, G. (2006). Introduction. In G. Ladsen-Billings & W. Tate (Eds.), *Education research in the public interest: Social justice, action, and policy* (pp. 1–16). New York: Teachers College Press.

Mertens, D. (1998). *Research methods in education and psychology: Integrating diversity with quantitative and qualitative approaches*. Thousand Oaks, CA: Sage.

Milner, R. (2007). Race, culture, and researcher positionality: Working through dangers, seen unseen, and unforeseen. *Educational Researcher, 36*(7), 388–400.

Murillo, E., Jr. (2004). Mojado crossing along neoliberal borderlines. In G. Noblit, S. Flores, & E. Murillo Jr. (Eds.), *Postcritical ethnography: Reinscribing critique* (pp. 155–179). Cresskill: Hampton Press.

Nencel, L. (2014). Situating reflexivity: Voices, positionalities and representations in feminist ethnographic texts. *Women's Studies International Forum, 43*, 75–83.

Noblit, G., Flores, S., & Murillo, E., Jr. (2004). Postcritical ethnography: An introduction. In G. Noblit, S. Flores, & E. Murillo Jr. (Eds.), *Postcritical ethnography: Reinscribing critique* (pp. 1–52). Cresskill: Hampton Press.

Smith, D. (1974). Women's perspective as a radical critique of sociology. *Sociological Inquiry, 44*(1), 7–13.

Smith, D. (1987). *The everday world as problematic: A feminist sociology*. Boston: Northeastern University Press.

St. Pierre, E., & Pillow, W. (Eds.). (2000). *Working the ruins: Feminist poststructural theory and methods in education*. New York/London: Routledge.

Stone, L. (Ed.). (1994). *The education feminism reader*. New York: Rouledge.

Stone, L. (2005). Philosophy for educational research. In J. Paul (Ed.), *Introduction to the philosophies of research and criticism in education and the social sciences* (pp. 21–42). Upper Saddle River: Pearson.

Toulmin, S. (1990). *Cosmopolis: The hidden agenda of modernity*. New York: The Free Press.

Van Stapele, N. (2014). Intersubjectivity, self-reflexivity and agency: Narrating about 'self' and 'other' in feminist research. *Women's Studies International Forum, 43*, 13–21.

Math and Music: Slow and Not For Profit

Kathleen Coessens, Karen François, and Jean Paul Van Bendegem

Introduction

When Derek de Solla Price published his *Little Science, Big Science* in 1963, little did he realize what the consequences would be. What was meant as a tool to understand the structure of the scientific enterprise, generated not only scientometrics in the hands of Eugene Garfield but also turned into a policy tool in the hands of science foundations world-wide. Science's attempt at 'self-understanding' curiously enough turned into a set of control mechanisms, either generating 'closure'—the scientists' non-involvement in society—or 'economisation', producing patents and other lucrative economic benefits. As descriptions of the 'good scientist' become more and more detailed, see, e.g., the explicit rulings about scientific integrity, educational programmes become themselves equally detailed. 'Ill-fitting' profiles are thus less likely to gain access and hence an internal critique of the scientific enterprise becomes equally unlikely. Counter movements such as 'Slow science' remain marginal, especially in the exact sciences but also affecting the humanities. Nevertheless in the latter a larger 'free space' seems to be available as the cases of mathematical and musical education will show.

The domain of mathematics education questions the scientometrics, closure and (economical) output in terms of attainment outcomes, exclusion of education and math curricula for (economical) profit. Attainment outcomes of 15-year old pupils

K. Coessens (✉)
Vrije Universiteit Brussel (VUB), Brussels, Belgium

Koninklijk Conservatorium Brussel, Brussels, Belgium
e-mail: kathleen.coessens@ehb.be

K. François · J. P. Van Bendegem
Vrije Universiteit Brussel (VUB), Brussels, Belgium
e-mail: Karen.Francois@vub.be; jpvbende@vub.ac.be

© Springer International Publishing AG, part of Springer Nature 2018
P. Smeyers, M. Depaepe (eds.), *Educational Research: Ethics, Social Justice, and Funding Dynamics*, Educational Research 10,
https://doi.org/10.1007/978-3-319-73921-2_6

are internationally measured and compared by Trends in International Mathematics and Science Study (TIMSS) and the Program for International Student Assessment (PISA) international comparative research. These programs as directed by EU and OECD policy determine indirectly national curricula and the exclusion of many pupils as figures on the attainment outcomes show (François and Larvor 2016). Substantial parts of research in the field of mathematics education are explicitly committed to promoting equality and inclusion. Equality, and later on social justice, are central concerns within the research fields of ethnomathematics, critical mathematics education, and gender studies in mathematics education. Intensive research on the parameters of gender, ethnicity, language and socioeconomic level has resulted in comprehensive knowledge about inequalities in mathematics learning and literacy. This research is furthermore characterized by the awareness of the cultural and global contexts of research questions. From this perspective of contextualisation, international comparative research rankings such as TIMSS and PISA are criticised and analysed in terms of ethical and social justice constraints. The ethical challenges of the conduct of these fields in mathematics education research are clear: social justice in mathematics education for all pupils, irrespective of gender, migration background or language background.

The domain of music questions the notions of scientometrics, fast profit and equality from its perspective in paradoxical ways. Music education forces us to revisit the notion of slow science from the inside. An artistic trajectory needs time, takes time and questions time. Music is in se a temporal art; its education and expertise develop slowly by way of experience and exchange. However, music is also threatened by efficiency, by societal speed and productivity. The benefits of music and other arts are difficult to quantify, both on the economic and social level. It follows from this that subsidies and cuts in cultural programs, in music ensembles, are rarely based on solid ground and do not take into account the complexity of the interwovenness of art and society. Moreover, controlling mechanisms of society are normalising the specific pedagogic aspects of the unique master-student relations, leading to new rules for the good musician. Finally, the unravelling of music practice's multiple implicit knowledges has led to the development of an emerging discipline of artistic research that again becomes subject of quantification by way of indicators and categories similar to the scientometrics in other disciplines. While Europe is both cutting in its cultural budget and developing a system of measuring artistic research output, other societies still engage into the experience of music-making as a way to equality—like the Bahia Orchestra project in Brazil or the Venezuelan El Systema program.

In the next section we first present a scientific profile as a teaser to further discuss the representation of a scientific community and its related power laws and ethical consequences.

Table 1 A scientific profile anno 2016s

Query date: 2016-07-11	h-index: 12 (47%)
Papers: 226	g-index: 21 (61%)
Citations: 742	e-index: 14.39
Years: 39	hc-index: 6
Cites/year: 19.03	hI-index: 6.86
Cites/paper: 3.28/0.0/0 (mean/median/mode)	hI,norm: 11
Cites/author: 477.29	hI,annual: 0.28
Cites/author/year: 12.23	hm-index: 11.33
Papers/author: 157.77	AW-index: 7.85
Authors/paper: 1.92/1.0/1 (mean/median/mode)	AWCR: 61.63
	AWCRpA: 38.02
116 paper(s) with 1 author(s)	Hirsch a = 5.15, m = 0.31
47 paper(s) with 2 author(s)	Contemporary ac = 6.83
35 paper(s) with 3 author(s)	
20 paper(s) with 4 author(s)	
8 paper(s) with 5 author(s)	

A Scientific Profile

What is your 'scientific profile'? When confronted with such a question, what seems to be a good answer to it? Is not the most likely answer any form of autobiography, focused on the scientific part of one's life? "Well, I became a biologist because I have always been fond of animals and I wanted to make this world a better place by rescuing species on the verge of extinction", or "… I should say at once that my defence of mathematics will be a defence of myself, and that my apology is bound to be to some extent egotistical. I should not think it worthwhile to apologize for my subject if I regarded myself as one of its failures."[1] If that is the case, why did we end up with the 'scientific profile' in the form of Table 1?

This 'profile' has been obtained through Anne-Wil Harzing's website (http://www.harzing.com), where a program can be downloaded under the ominous but unfortunately well-known title "Publish or Perish". The program roughly imitates *Web of Science* for the humanities. It uses *Google Scholar* as a basis and adds to it a number of filters to eliminate publications that are not considered to be 'scientific'. It is often used in *academia*, especially for the humanities and social sciences, when citation analysis, 'ISI-style', is lacking. Although it is a rather crude instrument, nevertheless one is not really tempted to have it so publicly presented.[2] And is that not an odd thing? But perhaps first the question should be posed how and why we

---

[1] The first answer is made up (although based on frequently heard answers given by starting students in those disciplines, whereas the second answer, strikingly personal, is to be found in Hardy (1967: 65–66).

[2] To avoid readers wasting time to identify the subject of this profile, it is indeed the profile of one of the three authors of this paper, as it happens the senior member.

ended up with tables such as the one presented in Table 1 and why they are actually used in academic and scientific contexts.

Scientific Communities, Power Laws and Their Ethical Consequences

It was the intention of Derek de Solla Price to try to find a way to represent or picture scientific communities. The use of references of one author to another seemed an interesting tool to obtain such graphical representations. It is close to a self-fulfilling prophecy that this work itself gave rise to a new discipline, known under various names but the most prominent being *scientometrics*. Although originally meant as a descriptive tool, gradually it changed into a predictive, hence normative mechanism,[3] whereby new emerging or old disappearing disciplines could be identified. In the hands of funding agencies it helps to make 'wise' investments in scientific research. Nothing in the preceding sentences is new, it is known to us all, especially as members of *academia*, being almost daily confronted with the consequences of these mechanisms. Let us focus on one of these consequences, namely closure.

One of the intriguing aspects of representations of scientific communities as highly connected networks is that boundaries become visible, thus creating an inside and an outside. Being on the inside can be defined in an almost logical-formal way: x is on the inside if there is at least one y, on the inside and different from x, such that x is connected to y. It must be obvious that this definition is circular for how do we know that y is already on the inside? The answer is that it is sufficient to have one or two initial 'identifiers' to get the process going and this is a familiar phenomenon because these are the figures on the inside that have the most connections, i.e., they are the 'leaders' or, to use a mathematical term, the 'attractors' that define the inside and hence the outside.

An obvious consequence of this definition is that the outside is disconnected from the inside for being on the outside means that there is no y on the inside and different from x such that x is connected to y. And that is what closure amounts to: it serves not merely to identify an inside and an outside but it closes the inside, in the very same that a mathematical function is said to be closed. Addition with natural numbers is closed because the sum of two numbers n and m, $n + m$, is itself a natural number.[4]

---

[3] This gradual change from a descriptive approach to a normative one can be found in many cases. A recent nice example is the use of the BMI-index or Quetelet-index. Originally it was nothing more but an interesting mathematical correlation but today it has become an almost purely normative index and not even a stable index at that. In past decennia the "healthy range" has moved from 20–25 to 18–25. No doubt the rise of anorexia is one of the contributing factors.

[4] An intriguing history of mathematics can be told in terms of closure and mathematicians are particularly fond of doing so: natural numbers lead to integers because subtraction is not closed in

There is however a second consequence that is equally important. As the description of a scientific community becomes more and more detailed, it reaches down to the individual level, generating tables as the one at the opening of this paper. Such tables then start to act as a form of 'currency', the academic equivalent of money because first and foremost it introduces comparability. It does not really matter that in most cases this comparability is at best partial because as soon as two parameters are taken into account, decisions have to be made about how to combine these parameters.[5] It suffices to focus on one of the parameters, e.g., the cherished h-index, to introduce linearity and hence full comparability. This in its turn introduces an ideal and here something strange happens. On the one hand, one cannot ignore the famous (or infamous) 'power laws'. Given two variables x and y, a power law takes the form.

$$y = a.x^b,$$

where a and b are constants. A simple example is when x is the side s of a square and y is the surface A of the square, because then $a = 1$ and $b = 2$, as.

$$A = s^2.$$

Apart from squares and other geometrical objects, power laws are to be found almost everywhere as in, e.g., distributions of scientific publications. Take a specific discipline, such that its closure is sufficiently well established and rank the members of the inside according to scientific output and a power law appears. Its meaning is clear: a few publish a lot, a lot publish a few. Or, in geometrical terms, there is an impressive but small head and a rather unimpressive but long tail. This in its turn implies that for an 'ordinary' member on the inside to imitate the head would only amount to the tail shifting towards the head or, in terms of the power law, the constants a and b might change but the 'small-head-large-tail' phenomenon will not thereby disappear. However, on the other hand, there is the fascinating mathematical observation that a power law distribution does not have a well-defined average. In non-mathematical terms one can always publish more and hence the average would change as well and thereby never reached a fixed or stable value. This means that one cannot define an 'average' member on the inside. Or, if the term can be used, there is no such thing as a *prototypical* member of the community. Thus one can only look at the head and do the impossible: make the tail disappear into the head. The phenomenon is well-known: this is the image of the snake eating its tail, that is, the *Ouroboros*. It seems therefore an appropriate name for this impossibility.

---

the natural numbers, which leads to rational numbers because division is not closed in the integers, which leads to ....

[5] Given two parameters x and y, one could consider their sum $x + y$, but then one ignores the possibility of introducing weights a and b, such that $b = 1 - a$ and the sum is replaced by $a.x + b.y$, but then one ignores the importance in powers so that a more general form would be $a.x^n + b.y^m$, but then one has not yet answered the question why we chose to start with an addition.

This mathematically inspired analysis may serve as a (partial) explanation of present-day observed phenomena in *academia*. The number of publications keeps rising, seemingly without any real upper limit, creating along the way a fierce competition as there is no way for everyone to struggle up the tail and make it into the head, producing in its turn violations of scientific integrity, including plagiarism, producing in its turn textbooks on how to be a good scientist. One might be tempted to think that, in terms of the Ouroboros, this process must come to an end at some time but this is the perversity of the whole matter: as more and more scientists join the inside, the tail keeps growing and the poor snake can do nothing but continue to eat and eat. Obviously this raises a host of ethical questions and we will restrict ourselves to two such questions, namely (a) what can be done on the inside, that is, within *academia*, and (b) what can be done towards the outside, and more specifically towards education?

To a certain extent, the answer to the first question is almost trivial: change the community. But that would be an extremely incomplete answer. For even if the community were different, this need not entail that its representation(s) would be different. Is one not entitled to the conclusion that the present-day situation shows an ill-fit between the model and what it is supposed to model? Perhaps one might go as far as to claim that a change in the representation(s) could be sufficient to change the community itself. To get a first idea of such changes, it will be helpful to make the distinction between inside-inside and inside-outside. The former concerns changes within *academia* itself, the latter in the relations between *academia* and the "outside" world but within the practices of the inside. Let us discuss briefly two examples: "slow science" (and similar movements) and "citizen science" (and similar movements).

"Slow science" aims at a reduction of the pace of academic activities, primarily research. Although to a certain extent there is a romantic flavour attached to it—the lone scientist who can be nothing but a misunderstood genius, nevertheless saving mankind by brilliant ideas and innovations, having had plenty of time to develop the ideas for they have to grow and growth has a "natural" rate –, it does question the present-day representation of the scientific world with its emphasis on scientific production, ignoring to a large extent scientific creation. As it is formulated in the manifesto of *The Academy of Slow Science*[6]:

> However, we maintain that this cannot be all. Science needs time to think. Science needs time to read, and time to fail. Science does not always know what it might be at right now. Science develops unsteadily, with jerky moves and unpredictable leaps forward—at the same time, however, it creeps about on a very slow time scale, for which there must be room and to which justice must be done. (The Slow Science Academy, 2010)

One of the key issues surely is that the present mode of functioning induces scientific fraud and similar "wrong" behaviours of scientists. The whole discussion on scientific integrity is therefore more a discussion about the way science is practiced

---

[6]This group was founded in 2010 and based in Berlin. The complete manifesto (though no longer than a single page) is to be found at: http://www.slow-science.org. In Belgium a strong advocate of slow science is Isabelle Stengers, see Stengers (2013).

and represented than about individual ethically high-scoring individuals and, quite inevitably, their "evil" counterparts.[7] What is however less clear is how such changes can be implemented. Creating free-spaces requires a partial isolation from the larger not-so-free space and then the survival question comes up. In concrete, real terms: how are such alternatives funded? Since it is highly unlikely that the inside itself will be sympathetic towards such initiatives,[8] somehow the "outside" must come into play. Citizen science is one such initiative.

The idea of citizen science brings together a set of ideas that have the common feature that the "ordinary" citizen is involved in the scientific process.[9] There is a wide range of such involvements. A minimal type is the participation in scientific research itself by performing small-scale tasks. A typical example is the measurement of pollution in cities by inviting inhabitants to grow plants for a certain period that afterwards can be analysed in the laboratories for toxicity and the like. Because of the direct relation between the living conditions of the participants and the researchers, usually the participants perform these tasks on a voluntary basis and do not expect to be rewarded money-wise. In short, citizen science of this type is less dependent on funds[10] than ordinary science and thereby can afford itself to be slow(er). A maximal type is the determination of research topics by the citizens themselves. Such forms of interaction really challenge present-day scientific practices. Of course, indirectly such determinations already exist through political interaction. Insofar as politicians can be seen as representatives (of the citizens) and they decide what is to be funded and what not, they already steer the scientific process. This is however a world apart from the situation where a local community wants to know whether or not the correlation between the factory next door and a particular illness is a causal connection or not. Or whether the food on their plates is "safe" or not (whatever that may mean). Or whether GMO's are "safe" or not? The most often heard critique of such involvements is that citizens are not the best judges, due to their lack of knowledge, "irrational" (whatever that may mean) attitudes and the like. Usually, the conclusion is drawn from this critique that therefore citizens should not be involved. Rather the conclusion should be a question: why not? Why

---

[7] This observation is sufficient reason, we believe, to doubt the effectiveness of guidebooks on how to be a good scientist. If most instructions are of the form "Thou shall ..." or "Thou shall not ...", then the members of the community are affected and not the structure wherein they are situated.

[8] One of the authors (Jean Paul Van Bendegem) participated in a debate at the University of Antwerp about these very issues. One of the participants was Helga Nowotny who has played a prominent role in the ESF (the *European Science Foundation*) actually described "slow science" as an ugly term, as it suggested that one is slowing down and therefore no longer enthusiast about science. It left one of us completely puzzled what the correlation could be between creativity and speed, an item which will be discussed in the final section on music.

[9] It is not easy to pinpoint the beginnings of citizen science (is a nineteenth-century "gentleman-scientist" more a scientist than a citizen or vice versa?) but for the modern period, i.e., the period that started with the industrialization of science itself, the famous scientific enterprise, the first book on the topic is Irwin (1995).

[10] As one might expect, the phenomenon of crowd-sourcing has also appeared within the framework of citizen science.

are they not the best judges? Why do they lack the required knowledge? These questions lead immediately to the core topic of this paper, namely education.

The tension between science as it is practised today and the attempts to create alternatives is perfectly reflected in the educational process. Roughly sketched, there is on the one hand a demand from the scientific side for new members to keep the scientific community alive and kicking but on the other hand there is a demand from society at large that all members of the community should be sufficiently informed to be able to critically participate in that larger community (which, incidentally, also includes the scientists themselves). Apart from the fact that the particularity of this tension is that both sides cannot be satisfied at the same time as there seems to be an inverse proportional relationship at work. Why that is, can be explained by referring to a feature that connects once again to the power law mentioned. As there is no prototype to use as a guide, the only indicator remaining is the head of the power law. Perhaps phrased too strongly, but future scientists are in principle all Nobel prize winners (and Fields medallists for the mathematicians). Given the ratio of bright versus not-so-bright students one must come to the conclusion that this type of education attends mainly to the happy few. Apart from the fact that it is impossible for everyone to get the highest reward—otherwise the concept of "high" becomes vacuous—it is not clear at all what the conditions are under which such an education can be said to be successful. If no absolute standard can be provided, then one falls back on relative standards: am I doing better than you? It is therefore no wonder at all, seen from this perspective, that we end up with PISA-tests. Analysing such tests shows the tension outlined in this paragraph at its fullest: are we really concerned with mathematical knowledge or rather insights, "meant for all", or are we scouting for the top.[11] Having to choose between sharing with everyone or selecting an elite is surely the top problem on the agenda for anyone concerned with social justice and ethics. The next section focuses on mathematics and mathematics education as a first case study. The last section focuses on music and music education as a second case study.

The Domain of Mathematics

The domain of mathematics and mathematics education questions the notions of scientometrics and equality in terms of Human Rights and the right to education. Let us recall the words of Hans Freudenthal in his inaugural address at the first International Conference on Mathematics Education (ICME1) which was held in Lyon France in 1969.

> Mathematics is more than a technique. Learning mathematics is acquiring an attitude of
> mathematical behaviour. Mathematics was granted a place in education because educators

---

[11] Without going into details, we believe that many STEM-initiatives (Science, Technology, Engineering and Mathematics) show the same tension. It is not really about showing how interesting mathematics is for everyone but rather to find the next generation of brilliant mathematicians.

valued it as a whetstone of wit, as powerful as Latin or even more powerful. [...] Mathematics should not be taught to fit a minority, but to everybody, and they should learn, not only mathematics but also what to do with mathematics. (Freudenthal 1969, p. 4)

From the real beginning of the international interest and collaboration on mathematics education there was a deep and socially sensitive concern with the aim of mathematics for all. Mathematics in the curriculum was key element to the general development of pupils and of society. International collaboration and exchange of information was not based on the outcomes of measurements. Collaboration was perceived in terms of "a great opportunity to exchange experiences and ideas, to meet people from nearby and far away" (Freudenthal 1969, p. 6). Decennia later, international organisations concerned about mathematics education installed the first steps in the direction of metrics. TIMSS was first performed in 1995 as the largest international student assessment study and later on in 2000 the first questionnaire of PISA became a worldwide study by the OECD. It is the same organisation OECD who claims a notion of mathematical literacy for all citizens.

The connection between education and social justice is as old as the foundation of the Universal Declaration of Human Rights in 1948 to which every country is committed. Article 26 indicated that "Everyone has the right to education" and "higher education shall be equally accessible to all on the basis of merit" (UN, 1948, art. 26). The notions of *rights* and *equality* are at the core of the declaration. Moreover the program on education has not only to do with the individual right, it is at the same time directed to a societal achievement of the maintenance of peace.

Education shall be directed to the full development of the human personality and to the strengthening of respect for human rights and fundamental freedoms. It shall promote understanding, tolerance and friendship among all nations, racial or religious groups, and shall further the activities of the United Nations for the maintenance of peace. (UN, 1948, art. 26 §2)

The educational strand of the Universal Declaration of Human Rights was further developed with the World Declaration on Education for All in 1990 by the UNESCO, the United Nations' specialized agency working in the field of education. The core mandate of this world organisation is to bring 'education to all' as expressed in the following statement.

UNESCO believes that education is key to social and economic development. We work for a sustainable world with just societies that value knowledge, promote a culture of peace, celebrate diversity and defend human rights, achieved by providing Education for All (EFA). (UNESCO 1990)

Besides the concepts of *rights* and *equality* from the Universal Declaration of Human Rights, the World Declaration on Education for All includes a project on *social justice*. UNESCO works for "a sustainable world with just societies" where social justice is used as inclusive concept of equality. Both world declarations focus on education in general. One can question the specific role of mathematics and mathematics education within this emancipatory project for the individual and the societal development. This was expressed in the OECD statement on mathematical literacy from 1999.

Mathematical literacy is an individual's capacity to identify and understand the role that mathematics plays in the world, to make well-founded judgments and to use and engage with mathematics in ways that meet the needs of that individual's life as a constructive, concerned and reflective citizen. (OECD 1999)

The general statements on *rights* and *equality* in order to foster *just societies* are now translated in terms of individual capacities of literacy. The description of mathematical literacy includes not only a functional literacy –to analyse and to understand the world– but also a critical literacy as a basic competence to criticise inequalities and social injustice. Based on this overview of the world declarations and the description of mathematical literacy by the OECD one can conclude that there is a clear connection between education and social justice. More specific to mathematics education we can conclude that it has its role in the foundation of global citizenship –as defined by OECD (1999). Regrettably to D'Ambrosio "mathematics educators are generally unfamiliar with these documents". (D'Ambrosio 2008, p. 41).

Nussbaum (2010) focussed our attention again on the emancipatory role of education. Education in general became most often seen as primarily a tool of economic growth and as a gateway to the best economical positions in our industrialized world. Mathematics education became the gate keeper at school curricula and mathematical knowledge is one of the most important admission criteria for higher education (even if the mathematics itself will be no fundamental part of the academic program). Nussbaum (2010) criticises this narrowed function of education and pleads for a new definition of education as the very foundation of citizenship. 'Not for profit' is the main statement of the humanization of education and of society. The dominant model based on economic growth and Gross Domestic Product (GDP) is no sufficient tool to work for a sustainable world with just societies. Instead, the logics of the GDP model has not always made a difference to the quality of people's lives and the model fails to adjust inequalities in society.

Nussbaum (2011) argues for a Capabilities Approach as an alternative of the GDP Approach. The Capabilities Approach links to the Universal Declaration of Human Rights and the World Declaration on Education for All when it comes to the emancipatory project of social justice and equality. It differs from the world declarations in their way of measuring and reporting on capabilities. In their timely reports the notion of capability is used "as a comparative measure rather than as a basis for normative political theory" (Nussbaum 2011, p. 17). It is from this perspective of contextualisation that international comparative research rankings such as TIMSS and PISA are criticised and analysed in terms of ethical and social justice constraints. Coessens et al. (2014) analysed these international comparative test and surveys as the 'olympification' in mathematics education.

The Capabilities Approach differs from the GDP Approach by taking into account the differences of people. The approach is pluralist –instead of universalist– about values, e.g. it holds the idea that the capacity achievements that are central for people can be different in quality and in quantity. Finally Nussbaum (2011) describes the approach as "concerned with entrenched social injustice and inequality, especially capability failures that are the result of discrimination or marginalisation" (Nussbaum 2011, p. 19).

The interesting and new dimension of the approach lies in the interrelation of the individuals capacities and the (societal and political) environment the individual is living in. Nussbaum (2011) describes the capabilities not only as an individual capacity but as an interrelation of these abilities with the political, social, and economical environment. This *ecological* understanding of capabilities provides us a frame of reference to better understand the social justice movement in mathematics education. (Note that Nussbaum herself is not using the term *ecological*. Based on the work of Guattari (1989), we introduced here the notion of ecology to express the generalized interaction between living organisms and their habitat, be it a social, political, cultural, natural, ... habitat).

In the following section we will focus on two research programs that investigated the social justice issue in their project. While mathematics education has an explicit normative dimension as it takes part at the emancipatory project declared by UN/UNESCO/OECD, it is also concerned with best learning and teaching practices –as studied in the different learning theories. A central question is how to reach the emancipatory goals as they are outlined by the world organizations. What is the most successful educational practice to achieve the UNESCO goal "education for all" and how to increase mathematical literacy of all pupils? The answer from the research field of mathematics education came from the two research programs (i) *critical mathematics education* (CME) and (ii) *ethnomathematics*. Both research fields take the social justice issue as a central concern in their program.

Looking back at the origin of the mathematics education research field we can observe a shift from the singular attention on the psychology of the individual to the interdisciplinary attention on the whole learning environment of the learner within the social, political and cultural context (François et al. 2012). Mathematics education as a research field became 'normalized' (in the Kuhnian sense of the word) during the sixties when the (WoS) journal *Educational Studies in Mathematics* was established in 1968. One year later in 1969 we had the foundation of the *International Congress on Mathematical Education* (ICME) in Lyon France. Today the (WoS) journal *Educational Studies in Mathematics* is still a leading journal in the research field and 2016 we will have the 13th ICME conference to be held at Hamburg, Germany.

François et al. (2012) analysed the cultural turn in the research field of mathematics education over the last 50 years. Initially psychology became one of the most important perspectives from which mathematics education was analyzed and investigated. There was a central focus on the cognitive learning theory Piaget and as a real sedimentation of the psychological perspective, the International Group for the *Psychology of Mathematics Education* (PME) was founded at 1976. Since the last two decades there is a growing interest in the sociocultural aspects of math education. The cultural turn became sedimented by the foundation of the Mathematics Education and Society (MES) in 1998. This conference became the central research meeting place for both researchers from the field of CME and from Ethnomathematics. The latest meeting (MES8) was held in Portland, USA and focused from interdisciplinary perspectives on the social, political, cultural and ethical dimensions of mathematics education.

Although both research programs, CME and ethnomathematics, originate from a different geopolitical background, respective the Western and the postcolonial, they are now moving towards a unified community (with their overlapping conferences and publications, e.g. the MES proceedings available at WoS). Ole Skovsmose, perceived as the intellectual father of CME, describes the interconnection in the sense that "CME is represented by many different approaches in mathematics education, and certainly by many approaches that do not use the label of CME" (Alrø et al. 2010, p. 4). He also emphasises that "Much work in ethnomathematics shares the interest and concern of CME. And today several people in Brazil contribute explicitly to the development of CME." (Alrø et al. 2010, p. 4). All these different approaches represent concerns with respect to mathematics education that are in line with the normative layer of the world declarations. They indicate a critical position.

Skovsmose and Borba (2004) gave us a more detailed description of CME and the diversity of concerns CME is dealing with:

> Critical Mathematics Education is concerned with the social and political aspects of the learning of mathematics. It is concerned with providing access to mathematical ideas for everybody independent of colour of skin, gender and class. It is concerned with the use and function of mathematics in practice, being an advanced technological application or an everyday use. It is concerned with the life in the classroom, which should represent a democratic forum, where ideas are presented and negotiated. It is concerned with the development of critical citizenship. (Skovsmose and Borba 2004, p. 207)

We can agree on D'Ambrosio's (2008) regret that "mathematics educators are generally unfamiliar with these [World declarations on Human rights and education] documents" but we have to emphasise that researchers in mathematics education are. The main challenge will be to transmit research findings into teaching practices to realise mathematical literacy for all citizens.

The Domain of Music

The domain of music questions the notions of scientometrics, fast profit and equality from its perspective in paradoxical ways. It seems strange that the previous topics and comments on the changing tendencies concerning quantification, time and societal impact of knowledge and research concern also the domain of music. But it does. The above described shared cultural ideology clearly influences all domains of human behaviour.

In the first place, music education forces us to revisit the notion of slow science. An artistic trajectory needs time, takes time and questions time (remember the quote in the beginning of this text of the manifesto of *The Academy of Slow Science*). Music is in se a temporal art; its education and expertise develop slowly by way of experience and exchange. Looking back to the evolution of the music system at the higher education level in Europe since the twentieth century, the whole organisation in terms of both content and time path have changed drastically. At one side, until the eighties, the educational music system focussed uniquely on the profile of the excellent musician: music education had nothing to do with a more global culture nor with philosophy, sociology or psychology; it was a practice that had to be acquired by hard training and in dialogue with an expert musician, transmitting the tradition. On the other side, the music education system considered time as an ally instead of as a dictate. Indeed, apart from the rather narrow but focussed content, the system offered an educational process that allowed for the development of a personal artistic expertise. A student entered by way of an admission test and then started to study with a great musician. The ultimate aim was to become a good professional musician, which was defined by obtaining a 'first prize' at the Conservatoire. There was no pre-defined number of years to follow: the student could take two, three, four, even 7 years before participating and obtaining a first prize. Participation to the concluding examination was decided by the music teachers and the student and based upon reflections as: Does your level (knowledge, practice) allow you to obtain a first prize? Are you ready? When a student participated, he or she could obtain a first prize, and if not, obtained a second prize—which meant he or she had still to develop further skills. Failure was very different in this kind of program. Brilliant, fast or already high level students went in a couple of years through the program, others took more time.

Nowadays, following the Bologna agreements, the artistic educational system has copied academic curricula (see AEC).[12] The content has opened the narrow perspective with more general courses like philosophy, culture studies or research practice. The structure however has fixed the curriculum in a general program for every student of 3 years of bachelor and 2 years of master. Students can fail now and the result is that when entering the conservatoire, they desire to obtain their bachelor in 3 years and master in 2 years. Of course, you can postpone, but this is strongly discouraged. Time efficiency of the educational program is prioritized over the personal mastery of an expertise and the process of working and practicing for the 'necessary' period with an expert musician—dependent upon personal development. Moreover, the institution too wants to obtain as fast as possible results, as failed courses are not subsidized by the government more than once.[13] Controlling mechanisms of society are normalising specific pedagogic aspects of the unique master-student relations, leading to new rules for educating towards musicianship. This is one example of how music and music education are threatened by efficiency, societal speed and productivity.

---

[12] Since 2010, a research group of the AEC, Association Européenne des Conservatoires, Académies de Musique et Musikhochschulen, "has developed several tools for higher music education institutions in order to assist the institutions with the requirements proposed by the Bologna process. The group has studied issues related to curriculum design and development, and therefore has also dealt with three key elements that have been much talked about in European Higher Education in recent years and that have been given additional impetus by the Bologna Process: Learning Outcomes, Credit Points and Quality Assurance." http://www.aec-music.eu/work--policies/curriculum-design

[13] At least not in Flanders.

Another example of this notion of 'efficiency' is the changing role of the performer over the last 100 years. A music performer, until the beginning of the twentieth century, had a diverse music educational trajectory, often adding composing and improvising skills to his or her performing expertise. The last century, the need for perfection and highest level of performance itself pushed musicians from a more creative to a more Olympic artist—playing faster with technical superiority. This resulted in specialised and heavy educational trajectories for different kinds of musicians: the performer, the composer, the music-theoretician.

In the second place, music education has not escaped other knowledge-oriented societal moves, of which the last one is the institutionalisation of artistic research. Artistic research is the investigation and inquiry into the own artistic practice and should inform, sustain as well as lead to and benefit an excellent and informed artistic output. While artistic research has been for long an implicit process, an integral part of many artistic creations—think of Leonardo da Vinci —, the recent emerging discipline of artistic research aims at unravelling and explicating the music practice's multiple implicit knowledges in institutional formats. This is an interesting move, which can make musicians stronger and more informed both inside the own discipline and in the prevailing society. However, this again is subject to quantification by way of output indicators and categories, similar to the scientometrics in other disciplines. Artists themselves fall in the trap of the system, and not once, but twice. A first defence of the artistic researchers was to counter the requirement for written output—articles in journals, books. Discussions between universities and academies led to the following suggestion of output indicators:

> academies should invent 'analogous' tools for measuring artistic research output. And thus it happens that some people are beginning to dream of an 'art citation index' while others are talking about the need to classify artistic venues in the same way as academic journals are classified according to their 'impact factor'." (Lesage 2013, p. 151)

In different parts of the world artistic research indeed obtained a broader system of measuring research: a classification that took into account the specificity of the discipline. For example, the Australian measurement of research output, called Excellence for Research Australia (ERA), has decided some 10 years ago to take into account both 'traditional research output' (TRO) such as books, articles, conference papers and 'non-traditional research output' (NTRO) as performances, creative work, exhibitions. However, there are still problems with the reviewing system and the transparency of the assessment (Julie Robson 2013, p. 132). In Belgium the Centre for Research & Development Monitoring (ECOOM) developed as an inter-university consortium some 6 years ago to realise a broad system of indicators of research output—with special attention to the humanities.[14] A dialogue with

---

[14] See https://www.ecoom.be/en/introduction: "The Centre for Research & Development Monitoring (Expertisecentrum Onderzoek en Ontwikkelingsmonitoring, ECOOM) is an interuniversity consortium with participation of all Flemish universities (KU Leuven, UGent, VUB, UA and UHasselt). Its mission is to develop a consistent system of R&D and Innovation (RD&I) indicators for the Flemish government. This indicator system has to assist the Flemish government in mapping and monitoring the RD&I efforts in the Flemish region."

artist-researchers soon followed for the new discipline of artistic research. A lot of discussion evolved where difficulties raised because of the singularity of the 'output'-idea as well as of the academic formats proposed. At this moment different types of output are proposed for the arts—artefact, event and design—as well as different types of researcher position—creator, performer and contributor. While the arts received an adapted system for quantifying their research output, they still lost their independency and have entered the quantifying system of output: they fall into the trap of rationalising and predetermining the discontinuities and the multiple possibilities of artistic research. As Lesage (2013) mentions: "we are developing an Artometrics, like the scientometrics" (Lesage 2013, p. 151). The problem is then that artistic research, instead of a tool for coping with and understanding the contingencies, contexts, singularities and creativity of each artistic practice again and again, becomes a paid labour that needs to enter into a system of output or products that can be counted, moreover separated in that context from art itself—part of a 'research catalogue'. This is a tough conclusion, knowing that artistic and aesthetic experience is neither for profit nor for output. Artistic research in practice should be an *ars vitae*, as Anthony Gritten (2015) writes. Such an *ars vitae* requires time, it is a slow science:

> Cultivating an *ars vitae* involves a willingness to wait: a mixture of patience and resistance. It invokes a persistent, soft-edged, and hard to phrase feeling of resisting Ideas of practice and research (…), of resisting the system's desire to rationalise what lies on each side of the boundary. (Gritten 2015, p. 85)

How then can a measuring system cope with the artistic research aim of

> doing justice to the incommensurability of all ways of reflecting on the relationship between practice and research (recall the many definitions of it, of its field, of its methods, and of how to evaluate it)? (Gritten 2015, p. 86)

The benefits of music and other arts are indeed difficult to quantify, both on the economic and social level. The benefits of artistic research in music seem to be only valuable if they can be measured in research output indicators. While artistic research can still obtain recognition this way—by offering artistic output—this cannot be considered as a victory, because, finally, art as a practice loses in this debate. Moreover, we can remark that subsidies and cuts in artistic educational and research systems as well as in cultural programs, in music ensembles, are rarely based on solid ground and do not take into account the complexity of the interwovenness of art and society and as such the importance of art education.

This finally brings us to the third element: citizen art. Like the idea of citizen science, citizen art involves the "ordinary" citizen in the artistic process. While Europe is both cutting in its cultural budget and developing a system of measuring artistic research output, artists still engage into sharing the experience of music-making as a way to equality. We will develop here shortly two examples. The first one is the Kunstorchester Kwaggawerk: an educational experiment in musical performance and teaching that works with an amateur group and was founded to cause interaction with artists and the "non-artistic" public. The second example is offered by diverse Latin-American projects of communicating and teaching classical music to the whole society—especially attracting poor families: the Bahia Orchestra project in Brazil and the Venezuelan El Sistema program.

The Kunstorchester Kwaggawerk Project in Germany was launched by Reto Stadelmann to bring art as an engaging process in society. The project aims at a new form of

> interdisciplinary artistic work that would combine musical, pedagogical, interpersonal and managerial skills to create opportunities and events for the promotion of social activities in order to offer sensuous artistic experience for a broader "non-artistic" public. (Stadelman forthcoming 2017)

Music teaching and music making, skill and personality, were combined in a process of continuous moving and redefining the limits of social difference and to create art. The name "Quagga" comes from an extinct animal from South Africa, a species made up of half a zebra and half a horse. A first characteristic of the project was that everyone was welcome: no restriction in musical knowledge, in age, social class, occupational position.

A second characteristic was the unconventional approach to music teaching. The enjoyment of the activity prevailed upon the knowledge in notes and technique— referring to F. Schiller's " Man only plays when he is in the fullest sense of the word a human being, and he is only fully a human being when he plays." (1967, p. 107).

The group started to rehearse in a rather socially difficult district with an increased level of crime and immigration, a high unemployment rate and a low educational background—the edge of the Humboldt-Gremberg district. The group grow over some months from six to fifty members. Old second hand instruments were bought and an invitation of Cologne to play at different occasions like street parties, demonstrations, art exhibitions, carnival and processions, offered the orchestra an unexpected value. The evenings with Kwaggawerk became big social gatherings. Pedagogically, at least fifty people learned to play a music instrument, and to find confidence in artistic self-expression. Composers wrote music for this specific group and worked following the individual 'strengths' of the musicians.

The Bahia Orchestra project in Brazil or the Venezuelan El Sistema program aim at similar processes of education in a free way. Venezuela's state-supported music education project, El Sistema, offered since 1975 free instruction to nearly 600,000 young people in all corners of the country. El Sistema offers a music program that both can create great musicians and dramatically change the life trajectory of hundreds of thousands of the nation's neediest kids. As El Sistema founder José Antonio Abreu says: "El Sistema breaks the vicious circle [of poverty] because a child with a violin starts to become spiritually rich." Children and parents are involved; the music broadens from Venezuelan to international classical music.[15] A similar pioneer initiative emerged in 2007 and lead to the Brazilian Bahia Orchestra project. This orchestra is part of the long-term educational program NEOJIBA: a governmental program, aiming at multiplication and excellence while promoting social

---

[15] See http://www.theguardian.com/music/2014/nov/11/venezuela-el-sistema-music-scheme-disadvantaged-children-geoffrey-baker-study-uk

development and integration through the orchestral and choral practice. The program provides, at no cost to its musicians and without any social distinction, musical instruments for the orchestral practice, learning materials, musical practice and classes of musical theory by highly qualified professionals.

Conclusion

The examples of mathematics education as well as the three points made on music education show that a certain evolution of thinking about knowledge and research in terms of quantifiable products is a non- negligeable fact that impacts heavily upon the domains of science—mathematics—as well as upon less 'scientific' domains as arts. Whatever the value for funding and measuring knowledge production, scientometrics offers us a reduction of the processes of knowledge and experience. What remains after this reduction is indeed a potentially interesting and objective outcome of specific facts for certain domains, but mainly an overall poor apparatus to (ac)count for human knowledge, its experience, creation, development and communication.

A basic question from the perspectives of life quality, social justice and equality remains indeed the following: what is the output of life, if the process of life itself is not worth living—hereby potentially exchanging the word 'life' by 'knowledge production'? Not only 'what is counted' matters, but also 'how and why this is counted'. It remains a question beyond this approach if scientometrics could be directed to broader aims. This brings us back to the half century old statement on education where ethical issues and justice matter more than just (fast and economical) profit:

> Education shall be directed to the full development of the human personality and to the strengthening of respect for human rights and fundamental freedoms. It shall promote understanding, tolerance and friendship among all nations, racial or religious groups, and shall further the activities of the United Nations for the maintenance of peace. (UN, 1948, art. 26 §2)

Slow science, a poetic approach to knowledge and research and the relation of knowledge to and in society should be cherished in a human society where quality, experience and process are the important factors.

References

Alrø, H., Ravn, O., & Valero, P. (Eds.). (2010). *Critical mathematics education: Past, present, and future. Festschrift for Ole Skovsmose*. Rotterdam: Sense Publishers.

Coessens, K., François, K., Bendegem, V., & Paul, J. (2014). Olympification versus aesthetization: The appeal of mathematics outside the classroom. In P. Smeyers & M. Depaepe (Eds.),

Educational research. Vol. 8. Material culture and its representation (pp. 163–178). Dordrecht: Springer.

D'Ambrosio, U. (2008). Peace, social justice and ethnomathematics. In B. Sriraman (Ed.), *Social justice, International perspectives in mathematics education. Monograph 1 in the Montana mathematics enthusiast. Monograph series in mathematics education.* Charlotte, NC: Information Age Publishing, INC.

De Solla Price, D. (1963). *Little science, big science.* New York: Columbia University Press.

François, K., & Larvor, B. (2016). Cultural and institutional inequalities: The case of mathematics education in Flemish schools. *Journal of Mathematics and Culture, 10*(2), 37–54.

François, K., Coessens, K., & Van Bendegem, J. P. (2012). The interplay of psychology and mathematics education: From the attraction of psychology to the discovery of the social. *Journal of Philosophy of Education, 46*(3), 370–385.

Freudenthal, H. (1969). Inaugural address to the first international congress on mathematical education (ICME1). In *Proceedings of the first international congress on mathematical education (ICME1)* (pp. 3–6). Dordrecht: D. Reidel Publishing Company.

Gritten, A. (2015). Determination and negotiation in Artistic practice as research in music. In M. Doğantan-Dack (Ed.), *Artistic practice as research in music* (pp. 73–92). Ashgate.

Guatterie, F. (1989). *Les trois écologies.* Paris: Éditions Galilée.

Hardy, G. H. (1967). *A mathematician's apology.* Cambridge: Cambridge University Press.

Irwin, A. (1995). *Citizen science. A study of people, expertise and sustainable development.* London: Routledge.

Lesage, D. (2013). PaR in continental Europe: A site of many contests. In R. Nelson (Ed.), *Practice as research in the arts* (pp. 142–151). New York: Palgrave MacMillan.

Nussbaum, M. (2010). *Not for profit. Why democracy needs the humanities.* Princeton: Princeton University Press.

Nussbaum, M. (2011). *Creating capabilities. The human development approach.* Cambridge, MA: The Belknap Press of Harvard University Press.

OECD. (1999/2004). *Learning for tomorrow's world: First results from PISA 2003.* Paris: OECD.

Robson, J. (2013). Artists in Australian academies: Performance in the labyrinth of practice-led research. In R. Nelson (Ed.), *Practice as research in the arts* (pp. 129–141). New York: Palgrave MacMillan.

Schiller, F. (1967). *On the aesthetic education of man in a series of letters* (E. M. Wilkinson & L. A. Willoughby, Ed. & Trans.). Oxford: Clarendon Press.

Skovsmose, O., & Borba, M. (2004). Research methodology and critical mathematics education. In P. Valero & R. Zevenbergen (Eds.), *Researching the socio-political dimensions of mathematics education. Issues of power in theory and methodology* (Mathematics education library, Vol. 35, pp. 207–226). Dordrecht: Springer.

Stadelmann, R. (2017 forthcoming).The Kunstorchester Kwaggawerk project – an original culture education programme. In Kathleen Coessens (Ed.), *Experimental encounters in music and beyond.* Leuven: University of Leuven Press.

Stengers, I. (2013). *Une autre science est possible! Manifeste pour un ralentissement des sciences.* Paris: Les Empêcheurs de penser en rond.

UNESCO. (1990). *World declaration on education for all.* Paris: Secretariat of the International Consultative Forum on Education for All.

Competing Values Within Language Education Research

Jeff Bale

On April 7, 2015, leaders of the Toronto Catholic District School Board[1] announced $30 million in budget cuts. A week later, they announced plans to open a new elementary school by fall 2016 with an emphasis on language education. Specifically, the school would offer immersion programs[2] in four different languages: French, Spanish, German, and Mandarin. In its press release announcing the proposal, the board explained they would follow a "European-style international school model" (TCDSB 2015, n.p.) for using multiple languages to teach academic content. It stated the school would have a "strong academic focus, and may also include an elementary International Baccalaureate program option" (TCDSB 2015, n.p.). Speaking with the media, one board leader justified the choice of languages to be offered in terms of their being the languages of "economic superpowers." He continued, "There's a new, global mindset among some of the new urbane community parents who see language as opening up opportunities for commerce in the future" (Brown 2015, n.p.). In the same report, another district leader "confessed" (Brown 2015, n.p.) that they hoped the school would attract more students—and the funding they bring with them—to the board.

---

[1] In Canada, education is the domain of its ten provinces and three territories, not the federal government. Funding for schools is distributed to both public and Catholic school boards, as well as to separate Anglophone and Francophone boards in most provinces. In Ontario, there are four separate types of government-funded boards: Anglophone public, Anglophone Catholic, Francophone Catholic, and Francophone public (listed in order of total student enrolments).

[2] Immersion programs use the target language almost exclusively to teach the full curriculum, versus learning the language as a subject for 50 or 60 min at a time. Some models stay 100% in the target language across the grades, while others begin to introduce the national/official language back into the curriculum in the upper grades (see Baker 2011).

J. Bale (✉)
Department of Curriculum, Teaching and Learning, Ontario Institute for Studies in Education, University of Toronto, Toronto, ON, CANADA
e-mail: Jeff.bale@utoronto.ca

© Springer International Publishing AG, part of Springer Nature 2018
P. Smeyers, M. Depaepe (eds.), *Educational Research: Ethics, Social Justice, and Funding Dynamics*, Educational Research 10,
https://doi.org/10.1007/978-3-319-73921-2_7

The languages proposed for this new school are noteworthy for several reasons. First, they complement the board's extensive program in International Languages. This program, funded in part by a provincial policy, offers 2.5 h per week of instruction in some 20 languages outside the regular school day.[3] At the elementary level, 22 languages are taught, almost always after school. Typically, only one language is offered at a given school, often the language spoken at home by a plurality of students in that school. At the secondary level, 19 languages are offered on Saturdays, and students may receive up to one credit towards graduation from high school. At this level, language programs are clustered and distributed across the city to facilitate student attendance; adolescents are typically less interested in extra-curricular language education, even with the bribe of a graduation credit.

Second, the languages for this new school complement the board's popular French immersion programs, offered in nine elementary and two secondary schools. This model of language education was pioneered in Canada in response to a number of political developments in the late 1960s, including the naming of English and French as Canada's two official languages. While this model is internationally renowned, less acknowledged is that French immersion has taken on a sorting function in Canadian schools. Anglophone children who are considered high performing, often from a middle- or upper-middle-class background, and destined for university attend French immersion programs at disproportionately high rates. Indeed, even though there is widespread support among immigrant parents for learning both of Canada's official languages, their children are often discouraged from learning French until they have "mastered" English (Mady and Turnbull 2010). Streaming has been a contentious topic in public discourse about schooling in Ontario for several decades (Gidney 1999). Nevertheless, French immersion has provided a different—and politically more tolerable—mechanism for achieving the same end.

Third, the languages proposed for this new school stand in contrast to the languages most spoken in the Scarborough-Agincourt neighbourhood in which the school will be located. (The board owns a school in the neighbourhood that was closed in 2011 due to low enrolments and currently stands empty.) Data from the 2011 census for this part of Toronto indicate that 24% of residents landed in Canada after 2001, and that 75% speak a non-official language at home. The primary origins of immigrants to this neighbourhood since 2001 include China, Sri Lanka, the Philippines, and India, while in 2011 the most frequently spoken non-official languages were Cantonese, Mandarin, Chinese n.o.s.,[4] Tamil, and Tagalog (Statistics Canada 2011). Although there is some overlap between the frequency of Mandarin in this corner of the city and the inclusion of Mandarin in the proposed school, recall that board leaders explained their choice based on Mandarin's perceived global status, not on community needs.

---

[3] See https://www.tcdsb.org/programsservices/schoolprogramsk12/internationallanguages/Pages/default.aspx for more information.

[4] "N.o.s." indicates the respondent listed "Chinese" without further specifying a language or dialect.

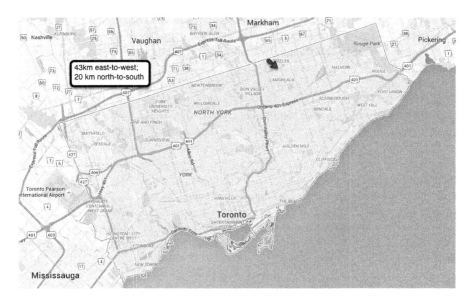

Fig. 1 Location of proposed language immersion school within the city of Toronto

Beyond the languages to be offered, there were other noteworthy aspects of the board's announcement. For example, the reference to a "European-style international school model" (TCDSB 2015, n.p.) stands out because there is no such model recognized in language education research. It is indeed common for international schools to use a prestigious language as the medium of instruction. That choice is either determined by the country associated with the school,[5] or because of the prestige of the language.[6] Although other languages are typically offered in international schools, most often they are taught as subjects, not used as medium of instruction for delivering academic content.[7]

A final detail about this proposal concerns the school's enrolment and transportation policies. While all students in the Catholic board from across the city will be eligible to apply for admission, the board will not provide transportation. Parents are thus responsible to get their elementary-aged children to and from a school located on the northern edge of a city covering over 630km² (see Fig. 1).

These developments at Toronto's Catholic board reveal competing values associated with language education, values implicated in two fundamental questions: to

---

[5] For example the German school in Manila uses German as the medium of instruction for the program it offers to children of German nationals.

[6] For example, English is used as medium of instruction irrespective of where the school is located or what students' language profile is.

[7] For example, the United World College chain of international schools uses English as the medium of instruction, and then teaches the respective national/official language where the school is located to non-native speakers. See Fee et al. 2014 for a discussion of International Baccalaureate schools, some of which use multiple languages as medium of instruction.

what end and on whose behalf do we create opportunities to learn languages? In its proposal, the board has revealed its answers to these questions by: (1) referencing parents with a certain kind of "mindset" about the role languages can play in "opening up opportunities for commerce in the future;" while (2) establishing a contradictory set of attendance and transportation policies that will likely inhibit other kinds of families from taking advantage of the new school; (3) choosing languages based on perceived economic power rather than community interest or need, and creating space within the formal curriculum for those languages to occupy; (4) choosing a model for teaching those languages that has been shown to exacerbate the sorting of Canadian students; (5) excluding most of the languages already offered through their International Languages program, thereby leaving those languages on the margins of the curriculum where they have lived since the 1970s; (6) ignoring altogether any First Nations, Métis, or Inuit languages; (7) using references to prestigious, private school forms to index a particular kind of academic environment; and (8) doing so in the context of budget cuts that led to dozens of staff losing their job.

Taken together, the board has indicated that this new school, and by implication the language-learning opportunities it will create, are designed to attract and meet the needs of Toronto parents with a particular set of economic, social, and indeed linguistic resources. Meanwhile, the vast majority of Scarborough-Agincourt's residents are visible minorities with a migration background, living on a median income of just over $20,000 per year—less than one third of that for the city overall (Statistics Canada 2011). It remains to be seen whether these families will be included in the "new urbane community" the board has imagined and to which it targeted its proposal.

I start with this example from the north end of Toronto to demonstrate how competing values associated with language education reveal themselves in such everyday ways. In this paper, I argue that similar competing values are equally present in *research* about language education, but are sometimes more difficult to recognize. I develop this argument in two parts. The first focuses on the explicit juxtaposition in language education research between viewing language as a *resource* and language as a *right*. The first part of the paper historicizes this distinction by tracing the emergence of resource-oriented discourses to the demise of broad civil rights movements in North America in the late 1970s/early 1980s. The second part of the paper turns to more recent critiques of language rights within language education research. These critiques are rooted in post-structuralist approaches to understanding language that, in general, reject rights as a response to language-based discrimination. Part of the complication in identifying the values within this research is that its authors explicitly frame their inquiry in social-justice terms. The paper does not doubt these authors' commitments, but rather seeks to get beyond claims to social justice to clarify for what purposes and on whose behalf we conduct language education research.

Historicizing the Rights-Versus-Resource Distinction

In his seminal article just over 30 years ago, Richard Ruiz (1984) was among the first applied linguists to name and analyze the competing values associated with language education and language policy. He distinguished among three ideological orientations to language that guide policy-making, namely language as problem, as right, and as resource. By the early 1980s, the language-as-problem orientation had already enjoyed a long run. Not only was this the primary way in which settler-colonial societies such as the United States viewed speakers of minoritized languages, for example construing populations deemed unable or unwilling to learn English as a threat to national unity. But also, the nascent academic field of Language Planning and Policy had founded itself on the premise that language presented manifold problems that scientific investigation and rational planning could resolve (Ricento 2000). Especially in newly de-colonized states in Africa and Asia, a generation of (mostly Western) applied linguists set themselves the task of assisting state functionaries in deciding which language(s) (and which varieties of those languages) should be made official, in which combination and sequence they should be taught in schools, in which societal domains they should be used, and so on.

However, Ruiz was writing at the tail end of a period in which significant social movements had imposed a new orientation on society, namely viewing language as a right. From this perspective, historical structures of discrimination could be dismantled in part by establishing the right for speakers of minoritized languages to use the language(s) of their choice throughout society, including at school. Demands such as these were central to the American Indian, Asian, Chicano, and Puerto Rican civil rights movements that had profoundly shaken US society (see Bale 2012), as well as to the Francophone (especially Québécois) and Indigenous movements that had challenged the legitimacy and even the existence of the Canadian state (Martel and Pâquet 2010). Indeed, with respect to the Canadian example, naming French and English as dual official languages and providing millions of dollars per year in federal funding to support official language education (e.g. the French immersion programs discussed earlier) were two important efforts to rescue the Canadian state in this period (Haque 2012; Hayday 2005; Martel and Pâquet 2010).

Although Ruiz (1984) acknowledged the social-justice gains made possible by a rights orientation, he also raised a number of pitfalls to this approach. I return to this topic in greater detail in a moment; for now, the point is to understand that the objective of Ruiz's paper was to elaborate a third orientation, language-as-resource, that could undo what he framed as the bind of problem-versus-rights. Ruiz defined the resource orientation in several ways. Most obviously, language serves as a resource for identity formation and social cohesion for those who speak and share a given language. In the context of multilingual societies, the resource orientation can also work to reframe societal multilingualism and/or individual plurilingualism as an asset to cultivate, not a deficit to redress. Indeed, Ruiz argued that a resource orientation has the potential to alleviate the social tension between speakers of different languages insofar as each has a linguistic resource to share with the other. It is the

social-justice intentions of this definition of the resource orientation that has made
it so popular in language education research over the last 30 years.

Yet, there was an additional definition of the language-as-resource orientation
that has since become the subject of sharp debate within language education
research. Ruiz (1984) also defined language as a resource for military, political,
diplomatic, and economic objectives. In the United States specifically, almost all
formal language education policies at the federal level have framed language in this
way; indeed, the paltry amount of money made available to fund language (education) research in the US has only ever been tied to explicit geopolitical and economic security objectives (Bale 2014). Following the events of September 11, 2001,
the US government renewed its commitment to language education in the name of
national security. This move touched off another round of academic fretting about
the consequences of understanding language as a resource in this way. At issue was
whether manifold definitions of language-as-resource could operate at once, thus
appeasing dominant policy discourses in Washington, DC while simultaneously
facilitating more scholarly and/or community ambitions for language education. Or,
do some definitions of the resource orientation predominate, in effect limiting both
our imagination and practice of language education (e.g. Bale 2011; García 2005;
McGroarty 2006; Petrovic 2005; Ricento 2005; Ruiz 2010; Wiley 2007).

To make the terms of this debate more concrete, recall the example from Catholic
board in Toronto that opens the paper. In the context of a budget crisis, the board
managed to make room for new forms of language education; this is as laudable as
it is unusual. Their choices for this language education opportunity are clearly
informed by what Ruiz would call a resource orientation, namely construing language as a twofold resource: for its students, in the belief that they will then secure
lucrative jobs in an increasingly globalized economy; and for the board itself, in
hopes of recruiting new students and the provincial funding they bring with them.
This particular approach solidified the position of community languages at the margins of the board's curriculum, where they have long lived, and ignored First
Nations, Métis, and Inuit languages altogether.

As noted above, some language education research has endorsed the resource
orientation precisely because it is conceptually malleable. In principle, it can be
used both to serve dominant discourses (such as economic competitiveness and
revival, as in the Toronto case) and to further community ambitions for language
maintenance. McGroarty (2006) has referred to this malleability as "strategic simultaneity" (p. 1), arguing:

> A logical implication for those who consider themselves pragmatists or political realists is
> that advocates for positive language-in-education policies must constantly articulate the
> value of bilingualism, and be able to do so in varied terms that respond to a protean environ-
> ment of public discussion. (pp. 5–6)

As we see with the case in Toronto, however, this simultaneity rarely presents itself
in practice. Rather, more often than not, the resource orientation to language education functions to relegate minoritized languages—yet again—to the margins of
society. Since McGroarty has introduced a claim to realism: the reality, then, is that

a resource orientation both contradicts and contravenes the social-justice goals of the language education researchers who espouse it.

While I was an active participant in the debate over the resource orientation, I have since come to see the terms on which it was carried out in a different way. In particular, what has made the resource orientation both significant and controversial is not only what Ruiz defined it to be, but also how he counterposed it to a rights-based orientation. By framing the rights orientation in a particular way, Ruiz is thus able to present the resource orientation as an alternative. Here, I offer an extended quote from Ruiz (1984) to give a better sense of his argument:

> What should be our attitude toward the [rights] orientation? To be sure, the importance of the legal argument in U.S. society is not to be denied. It is essential that for short term protections and long term guarantees, we be able to translate the interests of language-minority groups into rights-language…Yet, one cannot deny the problems of this approach. The most important of these could be that terms included in the legal universe of discourse do not incline the general public toward a ready acceptance of the arguments. Terms like "compliance", "enforcement", "entitlements", "requirements", and "protection" create an automatic resistance to whatever one is talking about. Their use creates confrontation. Confrontation, of course, is what the legal process is all about…This atmosphere creates a situation in which different groups and authorities invoke their rights against each other: children vs. schools; parents vs. school boards; majority vs. minority groups; some minority groups vs. others; states rights vs. federal authority; and so on. In the case of language rights, for example, the controversy could be seen as one where the rights of the few are affirmed over those of the many. (pp. 23–24)

This excerpt, as with the entire article itself, contains many hedges, suggesting that Ruiz is thinking out loud as much as he is making a fully developed argument. Yet, it also reveals certain conceptual moves that since have come to be taken for granted within much language education research. The first of these is to discuss rights primarily in terms of formal legal discourse and legal processes. Absent here is any sense of the immediately recent history in the United States that made language rights possible to discuss at all. In addition to the linguistic implications of civil rights legislation from the mid-1960s, the Bilingual Education Act was first passed in 1968, and a series of four Supreme Court decisions between 1974 and 1982 had expanded the definition and scope of formal language rights, up to and including the rights of speakers of non-standard varieties of English at school. None of this "legal process" would have been possible without the breadth and strength of popular social movements, yet there is no sense of the connection between the two in this excerpt (or in the article). In fact, there is little historical evidence that the social movements advocating for their "rights" were much interested in the particular legal form those rights would take. Even in the instances of individual families serving as plaintiffs in cases that reached the Supreme Court, these cases were typically seen as one tactic as part of mass civil rights movements (see San Miguel 2004). In other words, these broad movements set their sights on transforming US society, not necessarily on codifying rights as an end unto themselves.

Another important consequence of conflating rights with formal legal processes within language education research is that it suggests the primary venue for contesting rights is within official channels of government. The history of language education rights, by contrast, suggests that the primary battlegrounds were the front steps of schools, where students, parents, community members, and political activists picketed; the board rooms of local school authorities, where the same collection of people sat-in or submitted petitions signed by hundreds, at times thousands of people demanding bilingual and bicultural curricula; or in church basements, where teachers and community activists set up *huelga* and other forms of liberation schools as alternatives to the regular schools that students at times struck or boycotted (e.g. García 1997; Navarro 1995; Miguel 2001, 2004; Trujillo 1998).

Perhaps it is these experiences from the civil rights movements that Ruiz (1984) is referencing at the end of the above excerpt, with his mention of different groups squaring off against each other as they invoke their rights. Yet, even here there is a conceptual flattening of the contesting parties. In running through the various configurations in which conflicts over language rights can (and do) play out, Ruiz suggests that, like roses, a conflict is a conflict is a conflict. Yet, surely there are vast disparities in the social, material, and ideological resources available to the different parties named in each pairing, disparities that make some of those conflicts qualitatively different from others. To suggest otherwise is to fundamentally misunderstand how power is exerted and resisted in society.

Finally, and most consequentially, Ruiz's critique of a rights-based approach identifies a particular—and peculiar—source of backlash against those same rights. He lists a number of terms specific to US legal discourse and argues that, "their use creates confrontation" (p. 24). While he goes on to acknowledge that policy-making is by nature about confrontation, this particular formulation suggests that it is the *codification of specific rights* that creates discord between majority and minority language groups in society—and not the *existence of language-based discrimination or racism* in the first place.

This conceptual slippage has since become commonplace in language education research addressing the history of language rights in the United States. To offer but one example, Kenji Hakuta was honoured in 2010 for his remarkable career as a scholar of bilingualism and bilingual education by giving a prominent lecture sponsored by the American Educational Research Association. In fact, the lecture series at which he spoke is named for the Supreme Court case that marked the legal end of school segregation in the US. Hakuta (2011) used his own career as a foil to analyze the history of policy-making and research on bilingualism and bilingual education. As his discussion turned to the same period in which Ruiz was writing, namely the early 1980s, Hakuta stated,

> Although the bilingual programs were primarily transitional in intent … this transitional period also supported a zeitgeist of maintenance bilingualism fortified by a spirit of "affirmative ethnicity" … Advocacy for the value of bilingualism created a counterforce from new coalitions such as U.S. English … and other defenders of the melting pot ideal who wanted to support the common language of English and saw bilingual education as needless pampering of immigrants. (p. 163)

(Some of the terms Hakuta uses are specific to the US and require brief explanation. For example, transitional bilingual models, as their name suggests, use the student's home language in decreasing proportions over time to prepare the student to join

English-only classrooms; typically that transition from the home language to English occurs between kindergarten and grade 3 or 4. Maintenance models, by contrast, have as their goal that students become bilingual and biliterate. U.S. English was an organization founded in the early 1980s that aimed to have English declared the official language of the US. While they failed repeatedly at this, their state chapters have been more successful: 31 states have declared English as their official language.)

Different from Ruiz's (1984) discussion, Hakuta (2011) does make mention, albeit oblique, to the social movements that produced what he calls a zeitgeist of affirmative ethnicity. Similar to Ruiz, however, Hakuta locates the cause of the anti-bilingual education backlash *in that advocacy itself* and, again, not in the deep wells of anti-immigrant racism that characterize US society. The implication is the same: demands for maintenance language education, demands animated by "a spirit of 'affirmative ethnicity'" create, rather than resolve, social divisions based on language.

This conceptual slippage is similar to that identified by Fields and Fields (2014) with respect to race and racism in the United States. They name this slippage *race-craft*, that particular brew of ideology, social practices, and structures that functions to transform racism into the social construction of "race" so as to organize social life. To explain the term, they reference an incident in 2009 in New York City in which an off-duty, African-American police officer died. The off-duty officer had encountered a car theft in process and decided to pursue the thief. As on-duty officers joined the pursuit, one of them, a white officer, concluded his off-duty colleague was the thief, and shot him. As Fields and Fields write:

> The instant, inevitable—but, upon examination, bizarre—diagnosis of many people is that black officers in such situations have been "killed because of their skin color." But has their skin color killed them? If so, why does the skin color of white officers not kill them in the same way? … Everyone has skin color, but not everyone's skin color counts as race, let alone as evidence of criminal conduct. The missing step between someone's physical appearance and an invidious outcome is the practice of a double standard: in a word, racism. (p. 27)

Applying the same rhetorical questions to the case at hand, all parents make demands of the school system, but not all parents' demands are seen as controversial, let alone as the *cause* of a concerted political backlash. Indeed, as bizarre as it is to claim in the US that a cop has shot and killed someone "because" the victim is black, it is equally bizarre to argue that bilingual education comes under political attack "because" speakers of minoritized languages have demanded it.

Finally, it seems to me that it is no coincidence that this conceptual slippage emerged at the same historical moment in which the social movements that had won those rights in the first place were in decline. By the late 1970s and early 1980s, the most radical wings of these movements had either been disrupted by state infiltration or had grown demoralized by the failure to achieve more revolutionary change; while more mainstream (and some radical, especially Maoist) wings entered and became stable constituents of the Democratic Party. The election of Ronald Reagan in 1980 only hastened the rate of decline, insofar as his administration worked quickly to turn back as many gains as possible from the civil rights era. This contributed to the widespread sense that a period of fundamental transformation had ended, indeed, had failed (see Smith 2006). To be sure, the world has changed dramatically in the 35 years since. It is telling, though, that within language education research the dominant read on this era has not.

The Current Critique of Rights in Language Education Research

Part of those changes in the last 30 years includes the development of post-structuralism as an intellectual current and its subsequent spread throughout the academy. Post-structuralism has had a profound impact on language (education) research, both in terms of challenging our very understanding of what language is, and in re-conceptualizing the role language plays in society. Interestingly, post-structuralism's impact in many wings of the academy is often referred to as "the linguistic turn," in reference to discourse as the unit of analysis and how it structures disciplinary knowledge. Since language, of course, is the bread-and-butter of applied linguistics, the impact of post-structuralism within our field is more often labeled "the social turn," referencing a shift away from the putatively objective investigation of language as the domain of a single individual (or their mind) and instead understanding language—indeed, discourse—in its social, historical, and value-laden contexts (see, e.g. Block 2003). Nevertheless, despite the considerable theoretical differences between the interpretation of language rights as discussed in the first part of this paper and the critique of language rights from post-structuralist perspectives, the conclusions drawn by both are remarkably similar.

This second part of the paper focuses on examples of recent language education research informed by post-structuralism, namely Makoni and Pennycook (2007), Pupavac (2012), and Wee (2011). Although they get there by different paths, they arrive at the same conclusion: that language rights exacerbate rather than ameliorate social divisions based on language. Moreover, while each of them uses history in different ways, each intends to write useful history (Inoue 2004). While I fundamentally disagree with the conclusions this research draws, I am extremely sympathetic to the questions it poses and to the critical historiography it represents.

In each case, this research begins by raising ontological questions about language itself. Makoni and Pennycook (2007) do this by describing language as an invention in two ways. First is the more widely acknowledged idea that what counts as a "language" is, in fact, the historical product of specific forms of nationalism that attended the advent of capitalism (e.g. Anderson 1991; Hobsbawm 1990; Wright 2004). The division of Latinate, Germanic, Slavic vernaculars into things called Portuguese, French and Romanian, or German, Dutch, and English, or Croatian, Czech, and Russian, are historical artifacts—or social constructions, as per the preferred term of the moment. That division had nothing to do with any objective properties of humans' capacity for language or of those language families themselves. Second is a more novel and controversial argument that many of the languages now considered to be "indigenous" to post-colonial contexts are also invented; that is, they are equally the artifacts of historical processes and conflicts. Colonizers with limited proficiency in the language practices they encountered in turn codified those practices using grammars based on Western languages. Employing an Enlightenment sensibility to categorize and enumerate the world around them, they transformed linguistic practices among those they colonized into discrete, named "languages." In most cases, the peoples being colonized had not recognized these divisions historically, but suddenly found themselves assigned to this or that language as "native speakers."

Wee (2011) opens with a similar move, but extends the argument by defining the nature of language as both hybrid and unavoidable. To be sure, there is no shortage of examples of policies that have attempted to repress the use of a given language, or to enforce the separation of various languages (e.g. the traditional 50–50 approach to bilingual education, in which language x is used exclusively for one part of the day, language y for the other, or permitting only one language to be used in the media, etc.). Moreover, this repression and separation also exists relative to varieties of the same language, for example how the English forms "mines" (for "mine") or "aks" (for "ask") are racialized and stigmatized. Yet even in the most restrictive context, languages—and different varieties of the same language—are always in contact with one another, influencing, shaping, displacing, re-creating each other. In this sense, language can only ever be hybrid and unstable. Language is also unavoidable insofar as it mediates nearly every human interaction. Wee thus distinguishes language from other cultural practices and artifacts, such as religion, diet, and dress. It is on this ontological basis that he argues, "There will always be cases of discrimination simply as a consequence of human interaction and communication, even within what is ostensibly the same variety" (p. 92).

It is, in part, from this ontological perspective that these authors object to language rights. They argue that rights in their liberal democratic form require a stable and fixed object to protect. But if language by nature is unstable and fluid, it cannot be the object of rights in the first place. Moreover, not only do language rights reinforce otherwise invented boundaries between this or that language group, they also ignore the variation in language practice within a language group, and thus fail to resolve the competing interests among speakers of the same language. For Makoni and Pennycook (2007), their objection is even stronger. Insofar as liberal language rights target putatively indigenous languages (which, for them, are colonizers' inventions), those rights continue to inflict "epistemic violence" (p. 16) on the very populations they aim to protect. This violence is carried out through mother-tongue education policies, for example, which allow for instruction in "indigenous" languages in the early grades, when in fact there are considerable differences between the language being taught and the language practices of the children whom these policies were designed to support.

A second objection to rights raised by each of these authors is that language rights reproduce the historical structures and processes that led to language-based discrimination in the first place. Wee (2011) and Pupavac (2012) focus in particular on liberal political theory (e.g. the work of Will Kymlicka and Alan Patten) and how that theory has been taken up with applied linguistics (e.g. the work of Stephen May and Tove Skutnabb-Kangas). They draw our attention to an implicit hierarchy written into language rights in their current forms around the world, which position some minoritized language groups (indigenous and national minorities) as more deserving of formal protections than others (immigrant and refugee groups). As Wee argues, a liberal approach to language rights "merely attempts to replace a set of historical processes that have worked to the advantage of one language historically (the current dominant language) with another set of the same processes that are now intended to work to the advantage of another language (the current minority language)" (p. 68). Makoni and Pennycook cite the work of Selma Sonntag (2003) to make the same point more emphatically, by connecting the reproduction of these historical processes within a given nation-state to the reproduction of imperialism. As Sonntag argues, using a rights-based approach to oppose the English-Only movement in the United States has had little impact on how that country imposes its interests around the globe in the name of liberal democracy.

The relationship between language and international governance regimes are in fact the core of Pupavac's (2012) argument. For her, international language rights have grown into a new kind of restrictive, neoliberal governance. Regulating how and what we speak is based on anti-humanist assumptions that individuals are incapable of negotiating the interactive, generative nature of language on their own. In one of the sharper iterations of her thesis, she writes:

> Contemporary language rights advocacy, like human rights advocacy more broadly, is wary of the *demos* and believes that it is necessary to circumscribe democracy in order to protect minority rights. In short, expert international or regional governance is preferred over popular national government. Language rights advocacy seeks to preserve diverse, plural societies, but its cultural and linguistic identity strategies are at the expense of political speech and experimentalism. Maximising such rights fixes divisions between people. Identity rights governance mummifies cultures in the name of cultural authenticity, and is antithetical to fostering diverse experiments in living and communication between people. (p. 250)

Pupavac (2012) links the rise of liberal language rights advocacy (and the broader human rights advocacy of which it is part) to the demise of emancipatory social movements in the early 1990s. This lowering of political horizons has had two important consequences. First, language rights advocates have romanticized past cultural practices as the object of revitalization policies. She argues, "The collapse of belief in future-oriented politics and political movements has fostered attraction towards *ante*-capitalist solutions" (p. 166) that attempt to resurrect essentialized notions of past linguistic and cultural practice. Second, such advocacy relies on the state, rather than on individual or group agency, to resolve conflict through increased governance. The irony, Pupavac notes, is that language rights advocates in effect have swapped linguistic imperialism for legal imperialism; that is, they provide political and moral cover for Western states and governance regimes (such as the United Nations) to intervene internationally in the name of "human rights."

As I suggested in the introduction to this second part of the paper, I am extremely sympathetic to many aspects of the language education research discussed here. For one, not only has it expanded our understanding of language in society from Western contexts to post-colonial ones. But also, it has challenged and fundamentally changed many of the core assumptions that past language education research had made, even and especially when it was conducted in non-Western contexts. For another, this research takes a critical stance towards historiography so as to make history available to us for contemporary analysis and debate. Finally, each of the authors whose work I have discussed here sets their research and scholarship in service of social justice, in this case, on behalf of those people around the world whose language practices are stigmatized, restricted, or even formally repressed. My argument is that these claims to social justice can make it more difficult to recognize the values that are embedded in this language education research, values that may in fact contradict the social-justice aims these authors have so clearly expressed.

Let us return to the ontological case these authors made, in particular that of Wee (2011). As mentioned above, to make his case about the distinct ontology of language, Wee compares it to other cultural practices, namely religion, diet, and dress. Besides categorizing language as a subset of culture, it is noteworthy that Wee does not consider conflicts over language in relation to those over other categories of difference, such as race, gender, or sexuality. This is a revealing move insofar as these categories are as much a social construction—they are as unavoidable and hybrid— as language is. That is, there is an objective and fluid spectrum of human phenotypes, gender expressions, and sexual orientations. As with language, there are a number of ideological, social, and material processes, situated in specific historical contexts, that have transformed each into social categories of "race," "gender," and "sexual orientation." Whole systems of oppression have been constructed based on those invented categories so as to organize social life to the advantage of some at the expense of others. As with language, these social categories are also at odds with the hybridity and unavoidability of the continua on which they are based. This begs the question whether Wee would be equally critical of formal rights meant to mitigate the oppression based on them, such as affirmative action in hiring or protections from police violence and harassment, abortion rights and equity-in-pay policies, same-sex marriage rights, equal housing or bank lending policies, and so on. Clearly, each of these policies or rights is incomplete, partial, and at best relieves a bit— sometimes even the worst bits—of oppression, rather than ending it. Would Wee consider these policies or rights as merely reifying the invented differences between "races," "genders," and "sexualities," or swapping an old set of discriminatory processes with a new one? This is the logical extension of his argument about language and language rights. However, such a stance would be much more controversial, and rightfully be subject to much greater scrutiny. It is thus extremely revealing that Wee avoids the topic altogether by comparing language to how we might pray, eat, or clothe ourselves.

A second concern relates to the relationship assumed or expressed in this set of language education research between ideology and material reality. Debates over this relationship are nothing new. Yet, it is worth acknowledging that while the language education research discussed here is able to nod towards the material consequences of the conflicts over language they examine, their arguments frame the causes of those conflicts in purely ideological ways. This assumption can be difficult to see, since, as with Makoni and Pennycook (2007), they make explicit statements about the material consequences of the ideas they explore. They write, "while our argument is not one that could be described as materialist in the sense that languages are nothing but the product of real social and economic relations, it may be seen as materialist in that it is a way of conceptualizing language that focuses on the real and situated linguistic forms deployed as part of the communicative resources by speakers to serve their social and political goals" (p. 22). I agree with how they characterize their argument. However, their analysis of invention—"the invention of Africa and African tradition" (p. 5), of the "British colonial project…to turn Indian languages, culture and knowledge into objects of European knowledge" (p. 5), indeed the "inventions of a very specific ideological apparatus" for regulating the colonial world (p. 9)—offers no explanation of what impelled Europe into these spaces in the first place. That is, why did Europe need or want to carry out these inventions at all? Without considering the social and materials processes that fuelled European colonialism, we are left at best with a description of this language invention, but remain in need of an explanation for it.

Finally, each author focuses on individual solutions for getting out of—and for getting over—conflicts based on language. Makoni and Pennycook (2007) are explicit: "Through [language] disinvention we prefer to argue that it is more realistic to think in terms of alternatives than solutions" (p. 30). In each case, those alternatives are based on individual linguistic practice, even when that practice is theorized in a social context. For Wee, the alternative to language rights is also individual language practice, but in conditions that support individuals in participating in "deliberative democracy" (p. 164) over language use in society. Here, Wee applies a theoretical framework from political science to the question of language use, but it is noteworthy that this framework is premised on individuals and their participation in the public sphere, not on collective or group deliberations. Pupavac (2012) arrives at the same conclusion, but from a considerably different direction. Her response to the linguistic governance regimes she analyzes focuses on individual free speech and, from a left-libertarian perspective, limiting the state's encroachment on regulating individual speech. This pattern of individual alternatives to the social problem of language-based discrimination brings a certain irony to "the social turn" applied linguistics is presumed to have made. Individuals and individual language use are still at the heart of the matter. To be clear, the critical historiography this research conducts and the ontological questions it poses are firmly rooted in social analysis. In fact, it is this focus that makes this work so compelling to read. And yet, with conclusions based mostly on individual alternatives, we end up not very away from the methodological individualism that has long characterized applied linguistic research.

Conclusion: Reading Across Language Education Research

In considering both sets of language education research and their critique of language rights, there are considerable similarities in their argumentation and the conclusions they draw. This is striking to me, given the significant differences in theoretical orientation of each. In both cases, rights and how they are codified are seen as the source of ongoing conflict over language, not ideological, material, and structural systems of oppression in the first instance. In both cases, language rights are viewed predominantly, if not exclusively, in terms of the legal forms they take or the governance regimes they comprise. Absent is any sense of the historical processes (which most often include considerable grassroots social struggle) that created these rights at all. In both cases, appeals to realism and pragmatism are made to frame what should be thought of as alternatives, rather than solutions, to social conflict. The effect is to lower our political horizons for what is possible. Instead of imagining, and then working towards changing the social constellation we encounter, we are urged to be realistic and pragmatic and merely react to it. Finally, the question of individual versus collective alternatives is present in both sets, as well, albeit in different ways. In the former case, there is an implicit focus on the individual insofar as the collective, group-based struggles of civil rights movements are either absent from the analysis or criticized. In the latter case, language rights are seen as getting in the way of individual language practice in one way or the other.

There is no question that the language education research discussed here is motivated by social-justice values and aims to serve the interests of speakers of minoritized languages, whether in Western or post-colonial contexts. What is unclear, however, is whether the assumptions informing this research and the conclusions it draws on can deliver. By restricting analysis of rights to formal legal processes and not including popular efforts to campaign for those same rights; by misidentifying the source of hostility to certain forms of language education meant to alleviate language-based discrimination, while framing alternative forms of language education with dominant discourses in the name of pragmatism or realism; and by eschewing collective alternatives to language-based discrimination for individual ones, it seems to me we are leaving ourselves both theoretically and practically hamstrung to respond to everyday experiences of language-based discrimination.

References

Anderson, B. (1991). *Imagined communities: Reflections on the origins and spread of nationalism.* London: Verso Books.

Baker, C. (2011). *Foundations of bilingual education* (5th ed.). Clevedon: Multilingual Matters.

Bale, J. (2011). Tongue-tied: Imperialism and second language education in the United States. *Critical Education, 2*(8), 1–25.

Bale, J. (2012). Linguistic justice at school. In J. Bale & S. Knopp (Eds.), *Education and capitalism: Struggles for learning and liberation* (pp. 77–107). Chicago: Haymarket Books.

Bale, J. (2014). Heritage language education in the "national interest". *Review of Research in Education, 38*, 166–188.

Block, D. (2003). *The social turn in second language acquisition*. Edinburgh: Edinburgh University Press.

Brown, L. (2015, April 28). Multi-language elementary school proposed by Toronto Catholic board. *Toronto Star*. Retrieved from http://www.thestar.com/yourtoronto/education/2015/04/28/multi-language-elementary-school-proposed-by-toronto-catholic-board.html

Fee, M., Liu, N., Duggan, J., Arias, B., & Wiley, T. (2014). *Investigating language policies in IB World Schools: Final report*. Washington, DC: Center for Applied Linguistics.

Fields, K. E., & Fields, B. J. (2014). *Racecraft: The soul of inequality in American life*. London: Verso Books.

García, I. (1997). *Chicanismo: The forging of a militant ethos among Mexican Americans*. Tucson: University of Arizona Press.

García, O. (2005). Positioning heritage languages in the United States. *The Modern Language Journal, 89*, 601–605.

Gidney, R. D. (1999). *From hope to Harris: The reshaping of Ontario's schools*. Toronto: University of Toronto Press.

Hakuta, K. (2011). Education language minority students and affirming their equal rights: Research and practical perspectives. *Educational Researcher, 40*, 163–174.

Haque, E. (2012). *Multiculturalism within a bilingual framework: Language, race, and belonging in*. Canada: University of Toronto Press.

Hayday, M. (2005). *Bilingual today, united tomorrow: Official languages in education and Canadian federalism*. Montreal and Kingston: McGill and Queen's University Press.

Hobsbawm, E. (1990). *Nations and nationalism since 1780: Programme, myth, reality*. Cambridge: Cambridge University Press.

Inoue, M. (2004). Introduction: Temporality and historicity in and through linguistic ideology. *Journal of Linguistic Anthropology, 14*, 1–5.

Mady, C., & Turnbull, M. (2010). Learning French as a second official language: Reserved for Anglophones? *Canadian Journal of Educational Administration and Policy, 99*, 1–23.

Makoni, S., & Pennycook, A. (2007). Disinventing and reconstituting languages. In S. Makoni & A. Pennycook (Eds.), *Disinventing and reconstituting languages* (pp. 1–41). Clevedon: Multilingual Matters.

Martel, M., & Pâquet, M. (2010). *Langue et politique au Canada et au Québec: Une synthèse historique*. Montréal: Éditions du Boreal.

McGroarty, M. (2006). Neoliberal collusion or strategic simultaneity? On multiple rationales for language-in-education policies. *Language Policy, 5*, 3–13.

Navarro, A. (1995). *Mexican American youth organization: Avant-garde of the Chicano Movement in Texas*. Austin: University of Texas Press.

Petrovic, J. E. (2005). The conservative restoration and neoliberal defenses of bilingual education. *Language Policy, 4*, 395–416.

Pupavac, V. (2012). *Language rights: From free speech to linguistic governance*. New York: Palgrave Macmillan.

Ricento, T. (2000). Historical and theoretical perspectives in language policy and planning. *Journal of SocioLinguistics, 4*, 196–213.

Ricento, T. (2005). Problems with the 'language-as-resource' discourse in the promotion of heritage languages in the U.S.a. *Journal of SocioLinguistics, 9*, 348–368.

Ruiz, R. (1984). Orientations in language planning. *NABE Journal, 8*, 15–34.

Ruiz, R. (2010). Reorienting language-as-resource. In J. E. Petrovic (Ed.), *International perspectives on bilingual education: Policy, practice and controversy* (pp. 155–172). Charlotte: Information Age Publishing.

San Miguel, G., Jr. (2001). *Brown, not white: School integration and the Chicano movement in Houston*. College Station: A&M University Press.

San Miguel, G., Jr. (2004). *Contested policy: The rise and fall of federal bilingual education in the United States, 1960–2001*. Denton: University of North Texas.

Smith, S. (2006). *Subterranean fire: A history of working-class radicalism in the United States*. Chicago: Haymarket Books.

Sonntag, S. (2003). *The local politics of global English: Case studies in linguistic globalization*. Lanham: Lexington Books.

Statistics Canada. (2011). *National household survey, Scarborough-Agincourt, Ontario, 2011* [data file]. Retrieved from https://www12.statcan.gc.ca/nhs-enm/2011/dp-pd/prof/index.cfm?Lang=E

Toronto Catholic District School Board. (2015, April 23). *TCDSB considering first ever multi-language Catholic elementary school* [Press release]. Retrieved from https://www.tcdsb.org/news/othernews/2015/pages/proposed-multi-language-school.aspx

Trujillo, A. L. (1998). *Chicano empowerment and bilingual education: Movimiento politics in Crystal City, TX*. New York: Garland Publishing.

Wee, L. (2011). *Language without rights*. Oxford: Oxford University Press.

Wiley, T. G. (2007). The foreign language "crisis" in the U.S.: Are heritage and community languages the remedy? *Critical Inquiry in Language Studies, 4*, 179–205.

Wright, S. (2004). *Language policy and language planning: From nationalism to globalization*. New York: Palgrave Macmillan.

Epistemology, Ethics and Educational Research

David Bridges

> Educational research is fiction – written under oath. The question is: what is the oath?
> (Barry MacDonald)

Barry MacDonald's aphorism, dropped out at a seminar at the University of East Anglia several years ago, has echoed through my own thought ever since, posing questions as to the relationship between ethical principles and epistemological principles in the conduct of research, which is the territory I want to explore in this paper. It is an enquiry into the relationship between the epistemic and ethical requirements which shape research activity which leads me to be sceptical of the invitation to conclude that one might in some way 'trump' the other.

Educational Research As an Epistemic[1] Project

> Educational researchers aim to extend knowledge and understanding in all areas of educational activity and from all perspectives including learners, educators, policymakers and the public. (British Educational Research Association 2011)

---

[1] In this paper I use 'epistemic' to refer to purposes or projects that are concerned with development of knowledge and understanding and 'epistemology' to refer to the theory of knowledge and understanding.

D. Bridges (✉)
University of East Anglia, Norwich, UK

St Edmund's College, Cambridge, UK

Homerton College, Cambridge, UK
e-mail: db347@cam.ac.uk

© Springer International Publishing AG, part of Springer Nature 2018   109
P. Smeyers, M. Depaepe (eds.), *Educational Research: Ethics, Social Justice, and Funding Dynamics*, Educational Research 10,
https://doi.org/10.1007/978-3-319-73921-2_8

There are, importantly, a number of *epistemic* purposes that govern the conduct of educational or any other research. These might include, for example, requirements:

- To unsettle or question established belief
- To conjecture about possible alternatives and develop new ways of seeing things
- To describe or illuminate aspects of experience
- To search for reasons, evidence and/or argument – for warrant – that might support one belief rather than another
- To test beliefs and establish at least provisionally the truth of the matter under investigation

In the context of work honoured as 'research' (this is, I think, an honorific concept) any of these epistemological projects come with a requirement that they are conducted in a manner that is 'systematic and sustained' (Peters and White 1969; Stenhouse 1980), with rigour.

The range of tasks I have illustrated above, clearly reflects some different priorities for research; some different ontologies perhaps and certainly some different methodologies and methods of inquiry. Some attach more significance to reason and evidence; some to imagination and empathetic engagement; some (in philosophy for example) to argumentation, but (nearly) all result in some form of representation of what is, might be or ought to be the case. Hence they affirm in some form what the researcher believes to be the case, what is (provisionally at least) true.[2] This holds even for research that is self-consciously seeking to represent alternative perceptions of educational experience in a non judgemental way. Such research has its own disciplines, its own rigour, aimed at a faithful (a true?) representation of such perspectives.

As I have argued previously (Bridges 1998), even those who seek most vigorously to escape the discourse of truth – like Stronach and MacLure in *Educational Research Undone* 1997) – end up, as inevitably, as they must offering claims as to what is the case, what is true, unless perhaps they stick to the questioning format that they adopt in their opening paragraphs.

Sometimes, of course, we look for qualities in research writing (as in literary and other work) which are not directly stated in the language of truth seeking but are, none the less, dependant on such a notion. We look for *authenticity* in, for example, biographical, historical and ethnographic portrayals; we look for *honesty* in research reports; we look for *integrity* in the relationship between research, participants and research publication. But none of these ethically laden concepts are intelligible without invoking some notion of truthfulness and, hence, truth.

The association I am making here between diverse forms of research and inquiry shaped by a search for the truth of the matter may well be contested, but this is the starting point for the discussion in this paper. Even for MacDonald, the description of research as 'fiction' was as much as anything an exhortation to doubt it, question it, look always for the counter argument and evidence, gather alternative

---

[2] I am inclined to refer to such affirmations as proposition.

perspectives. The 'oath' is perhaps to distrust everything they (including or especially researchers) tell you and indeed what you yourself assume or believe – but
why? If one is to be so rigorous in one's scepticism is it not nevertheless in the
interests of discarding untruths in preference for what, at least provisionally and
pending further sceptical treatment one might regard as true? From Socrates to
Popper philosophers have extolled the benefits to be gained from others' refutation
of their own beliefs, because the discarding of falsehood leaves them with what on
some epistemological criterion is more deserving of belief. Neither Socrates nor
Popper conclude that they cannot believe anything and even Descartes found comprehensive scepticism incoherent.

This is not to say that truth is the only criterion of the merit of a piece of research.
The truth can be banal, predictable and boring: research might seek to excite the
reader with new perceptions and ideas; to bring wider or deeper understanding, to
cultivate a more sensitive or imaginative rendering of experience. Of course it is not
alone in this, and a good novel, drama or painting even may offer more when judged
against these criteria than a piece of research, but whatever research offers it has to
be judged *inter alia* on the basis of its success in providing compelling reasons,
evidence or argument to support what it affirms and its claims to truth.

So, I take the view that educational research is always in some sense focussed on
the development of knowledge and understanding – what is commonly called the
epistemic project. My central question concerns the relationship between this project and a variety of other, broadly ethical and social obligations.

Ethical Obligations As a Constraint on the Epistemic Project of Research?

In particular in a university research environment ethical principles – usually articulated in ethical codes and policed by ethics committees – function to constrain what
researchers might otherwise do in the untrammelled pursuit of truth. They set conditions under which research sites can be entered and what information can be
accessed; they protect vulnerable participants from intrusive inquiry; they protect
confidentiality; and they set limits on what can be published. To this extent – and of
course this does not obstruct all worthwhile inquiry – ethical obligations trump and
constrain epistemological ambitions. In the most difficult cases they simply make
certain areas of inquiry impossible to enter.

There are, however, two important qualifications to this assessment. The first
is a purely pragmatic consideration. It is, I think, the experience of many researchers that by offering the sort of protection to potential sources contained in these
codes you give potential participants greater confidence in sharing their information and perspectives, and so you end up with richer data than you would otherwise have gained.

This response is however a culturally located one associated with a climate of distrust and anxiety about exposure which increasingly pervades western countries. International students studying in the UK, however, frequently have problems returning to their own communities clutching 'consent forms' that tell their communities only that the researcher is not someone to be trusted and is possibly trying to get them to hand over their land (Adugna 2008). Attia describes in similar terms the basis for her relationship with participants in an Egyptian university in which she had previously worked and its inevitable embeddedness in Arab culture:

> For example, "*asham*" is a well-established social concept in Egyptian culture. It may be defined as an expectation and hope that one gets a preferred response, that is, acquiescence to a request .... On the basis of "*asham*", full access was guaranteed and complete assistance was granted. (Attia 2011: 97)

And then:

> The anticipation of assistance that I returned with was based on a history of shared lived experiences which in Arabic may be referred to as "*ishra*". The concept is related to a kind of expected solidarity and mutual assistance stemming from belonging to a "*asheera*", that is, a tribal community, clan, or kinsfolk. (Attia 2011: 98)

In such settings openness is secured not by the reassuring terms of contractual engagement (the consent form) but by culturally embedded relationships of trust. The bureaucratisation of ethics in UK and other universities is both a symptom of and a contributor to the breakdown of relationships of trust between researchers and their communities. The rejection of a bureaucratically shaped ethical code and the requirement for a signature of consent does not, however, mean that it these contexts the researcher is free from moral obligation. Such obligations of care, loyalty and trust are if anything stronger when they are part of the social fabric and not just a short term contract, and they still serve to limit what can be said and what use can be made of what is known.

The second qualification to the suggestion that ethical codes constrain researchers is to be found in some of the clauses that have relatively recently be introduced into the ethical codes of, for example, the British Educational Research Association (BERA) in response to the tendency of sponsors of educational research to demand excessive control over what is published out of the research. The BERA *Ethical Guidelines for Educational Research* (2011) gives strong endorsement to researchers' right and obligation to place their findings in the public domain.

> The right of researchers independently to publish the findings of their research under their own names is considered the norm for sponsored research, and this right should not be lightly waived or unreasonably denied. This right is linked to *the obligation on researchers to ensure that their findings are placed in the public domain* and within reasonable reach of educational practitioners and policy makers, parents, pupils and the wider public.
>
> Researchers must avoid agreeing to any sponsor's conditions that could lead to serious contravention of any aspect of these guidelines or that undermine the integrity of the research by imposing unjustifiable conditions on the methods to be used or the reporting of outcomes. Attempts by sponsors or funding agencies to use any questionable influence should be reported to the Association. (BERA 2011 my italics)

In this way ethical codes can – and should – be used to support rather than to disable the epistemological project.

Can Ethical and Social Goals Substitute for Epistemological Ones in Educational Research?

'Where, previously, ethical considerations were believed to set boundaries on what researchers could do in pursuit of knowledge, now ethical considerations are treated by some as constituting the very rationale for research…. The possibility and, perhaps the desirability of knowledge have come to be downplayed by instrumentalism and postmodernism, [and] a concern for ethics has expanded to fill the space. (Hammersley 1999: 18)

What should drive educational research? To what ends should it be directed? At one end of the spectrum, I suppose, this might be answered by reference to something like the pursuit of truth, however, esoteric, trivial or remote from contemporary concerns. Whether or not it is 'relevant' to contemporary problems, whether or not it contributes to 'evidence based' policy or practice, whether or not it has any 'impact' on anything is neither here nor there.

At the other end of the spectrum are two sets of people both demanding 'relevance' and expecting educational research to contribute to policy and practice, but with rather different political agenda.

One group is framed by the discourse of evidence based policy (see on this Bridges et al. 2009). It has its sights set on improved educational performance; it has an already established political agenda (focussed in the UK on policies like the establishment of educational academies and free schools, frequent testing and a politically defined curriculum); but it is seeking information of an instrumental rather than critical character from the research community about how best to implement its policies as well as, by preference, validation of their success.

The second group, which might find itself uncomfortably aligned with the first, is also concerned with relevance and impact, but has a different political and social agenda focussed on, for example, democratic values, social justice and inclusion. This seems to me to be of particular interest in the context of this seminar.

There are I think at least two lines of argument that link educational research to what, by way of shorthand, I will call the social justice agenda. The first is to urge researchers to work towards the goal of a more just society by giving their critical attention to the aspects of contemporary policy and practice which contribute to injustice and their creative imagination to alternatives. The achievement of greater social justice (etc.) thus provides the substantive agenda for research and its hoped for outcome. In other words, the substance of the research is expected to inform understanding of unjust structures and practices and help to address them.

Note that this model is not so different in principle to 'evidence based policy' though this has been largely inspired by a neo-liberal political agenda rather than an egalitarian one. Those who want educational research to be 'for justice' are, like their neo-liberal counterparts, seeking 'relevance' and 'impact' – in Hammersley's terms, they still judge research in instrumental terms – but they want the impact on education and society to be of a different kind.

Even if we allow that the imperative to be 'for social justice' through educational research is a powerful one, where does this leave the epistemological principles and ambitions which I outlined at the beginning of this paper. Is the advancement of social justice or democracy a sufficient condition for determining the merit of educational research, a sufficient focus for the concerns of the researcher?

Clearly the concern for social justice or any other such principle cannot be detached from a researcher's fundamental commitment to knowledge and understanding. 'All our choices depend on estimates of what is the case' argues Bok (Bok 1978: 19), and she might have added also estimates of what are the most likely consequences of our actions. A judgement that a particular practice, policy or set of relationships is unjust always has two elements: one is an *empirically* based observation (on which researchers have some claims to authority) about the differences in the ways in which people are treated or the circumstances in which they live; the second is a *normatively* based assessment of such differences as being unjustifiable, inappropriate or unfair. On such questions researchers can make no particular claim to authority, though philosophers in particular find the nature of such normative arguments of particular interest. To make an assessment about some injustice, we typically need to know that facts of the case; we need to have some understanding of what Quinton (1973: 4) calls the 'rationally expectable' consequences of acting in one way rather than another, and it might well be useful to know about alternative ways of doing things that would avoid the criticism of the case under scrutiny. Even while advancing the case for educational research for justice, Griffiths acknowledges that 'educational research is about getting knowledge' or perhaps, as she calls it 'better knowledge' (Griffiths 1998, 129). Veck, recounting his own attempts at 'emancipatory' research, explains that he came to the conclusion that:

> In committing to social justice, I was logically bound to the pursuit of truth. If the outcome of my research was to uncover injustice, to pronounce what is wrong, then what I had to say had to reflect the reality of that social injustice with the utmost accuracy. (Veck 2002: 334)

In short, the pursuit of social justice and a more democratic society requires as much as any other social political cause and the sound basis of knowledge and understanding as well as the critical questioning and argumentation that 'research' is properly designed to provide.

Principles of Social Justice As Integral to the Construction and Design of Research

More interesting in some ways, however, is the way a social and political agenda becomes integral to, not just its *focus* or *purposes*, but to the process of research, to *the way in which research is constructed and conducted*, which may itself becomes a contribution to the achievement of a more just and inclusive society.

This is not just a matter of observing certain clauses in an ethical code but a much more substantive project in its own right that carries implications for: the identification of the research questions (whose questions?); the identification of those recognised as 'researchers' (not just those from the academy); the voices that are given expression in the research; control over access and data; who is involved in the interpretation of data; whose authorship or other contributions are recognised; how the research engages with policy and practice; what happens to any research outcomes. Each of these (and other) features of a research project can be designed so as, as far as possible, to re-balance unequal power relations, give voice to those who have previously been excluded; open closed areas of policy and practice to more democratic scrutiny and inform and engage a wider community. These are indeed key areas of attention for that post-colonial researchers, feminist researchers, gay and lesbian researchers and researchers with disabilities, who have sought to change power relations, not only by the published *outcomes* of their research but by the *processes* through which it has been conducted. The slogan that emerged from the disability camp was 'Nothing about us without us!' (Charlton 1998) while in New Zealand, according to Marshall and Martin (2000), a growing body of Maori researchers are operating under the motto 'By Maori; in Maori; for Maori'. This is at least one sense in which educational research can be 'for social justice' (Griffiths 1998).

There is an important sense in which researchers do not have to take sides in educational debates –not even on the side of the marginalised or disadvantaged – in order to promote democracy and a more just society, and this is part of what MacDonald's et concept of 'democratic evaluation' set out to achieve.[3] Of course not all the 'facts' in any educational development will be unambiguous and they may well be contested. Different interest groups may very well have different perceptions of what is the case and why. But how different groups perceive the situation is also a matter of fact that can be investigated empirically – and not necessarily judgementally. For example, MacDonald describes 'democratic' evaluation in the following terms:

> Democratic evaluation is an information service to the whole community about the characteristics of an educational programme. Sponsorship of the evaluation study does not in itself confer a special claim upon this service. The democratic evaluator recognizes value pluralism and seeks to represent a range of interests in his issue formulation. The basic value is an informed citizenry, and the evaluator acts as broker in exchanges of information between groups who want knowledge of each other. (MacDonald 1976)

Interestingly, in terms of the distinction I have drawn between social justice as the substantive focus of research and as a procedural principle governing its conduct MacDonald also suggests that, though there will be a place in the future for different types of evaluation study (including 'autocratic' and 'bureaucratic'), 'there may be

---

[3] MacDonald was at some pains to distinguish evaluation from research, not least because in programme evaluation the 'researcher' does not control the agenda in quite the same way a s research (though many forms of contemporary commissioned research including that of the UK Department for Education and Science render this distinction meaningless. I think, nevertheless, that the issues in both contexts are very similar.

a special case for exploring in practice some of the principles which characterise the democratic model. For those who believe that means are the most important category of ends, it deserves refutation or support' (MacDonald 1976). Democracy is served in 'democratic' evaluation not just by the knowledge and understanding that it places in the public domain, but by the processes by which this is generated.

Belief As an Ethical Obligation

The debate in the literature is sometimes expressed in terms of whether ethical considerations should 'trump' epistemological ones, not just in research but in the wider domain of policy and practice (Chisholm 1956). Hall and Johnson (1998) seem to suggest, for example, that: that when you epistemically ought to gather more evidence and you morally ought to do something else, the moral ought "wins" and you just plain ought to do that other thing (Hall and Johnson 1998: 131). But this seems to me to be an inadequate account.

There is an important sense in which the contrasting views that we are examining is not simply between an epistemic project focussed on achieving knowledge and understanding and an ethical project focussed, let us say, on a just society, but between two sets of ethical obligations, though I will continue to refer to the 'epistemic' project in the interests of clarity.

William Clifford, in his seminal "The Ethics of Belief" – a paper published in 1877 in *Contemporary Review* – pioneered a body of literature (including James 1896a, b; Chisholm 1956; David 2001; Feldman 2000; Heil 1983; Sosa 2000, 2003) that has explored the question of the conditions under which belief is not just subject to epistemological validation but becomes also a matter of ethical obligation. It is not simply that one is entitled to believe that something is the case but one *ought* to believe that something is the case or *ought not* to believe in the absence of sufficient evidence or faced with compelling contradictory evidence: the question 'what ought we to believe?' is intelligible both as an ethical and as an epistemological question. Similarly, a stubborn refusal to face facts, self-serving distortions of an argument, careless use of evidence all carry an element of *moral* censure and not merely consequences for the erroneousness of one's beliefs.

If we take seriously the arguments from the literature on the ethics of belief, the juxtaposition becomes not one between ethical considerations and something quite other, but rather the compatibility between two ethical principles; one of which demands that we seek as far as possible to ground our actions on properly warranted beliefs and offers this as a moral responsibility; the other is expressed in a moral imperative, for example, to act justly and with respect for others. But Feldman (2000) argues that talk of one of these sets of obligations 'trumping' the other 'makes no sense' (p. 692): 'There is no meaningful question about whether epistemic oughts "trump" or are trumped by other oughts' (p. 694). There is on this view no greater 'ought' that can settle the issue (though other ethicists, for example in the Utilitarian tradition, might disagree.)

Secondly, as I have argued, social and ethical causes themselves depend on rigorous, open and honest inquiry. Indeed such inquiry is in an important sense one of the constituents of a more democratic society and not merely a means to the end. In the context of educational research the management of inquiry so as to ensure that, for example, the voices of the weak, the powerless and the marginalised are heard is not just a contribution to the cause of social justice: it also creates the conditions for the success of the epistemic project of inquiry. We *need* to hear the voices of the disenfranchised; we *need* to escape the hegemonic views of the powerful; we *need* the widest possible public debate and an open society if we are even to begin to get to the truth of the matter. To this extent then the social justice agenda supports rather than conflicts with the ambitions of researchers to get to the truth. An unjust society provides neither the open access to evidence that the researcher requires nor the opportunity to make the research freely available for the informing of a democratic citizenry and for critique.

So are there other sources of conflict which might lead us to want ethical, social or political considerations to 'trump' epistemological ones?

I can only make sense of this as a legitimation of dishonesty – if not, in legal terms, of *suggestio falsi,* expressing falsehood, then of *suppressio veri,* concealing the truth or not even wanting to know it.

This becomes significant when research evidence threatens, for example, an important ethical, social or political cause which one seeks to advance. A colleague is a passionate spokesperson in public arena trying to warn about the risks of global warming. But his research into the Antarctic ice suggests that this has survived previous 'warmings' for two or three million years. He knows that this is evidence which could be used by 'global warming deniers' to challenge the urgency of appeals for action. He is faced with two dilemmas: can he really believe what his own evidence seems to suggest? If he does, should he put this evidence in the public domain? In answering both questions in the affirmative (pending further research, of course!) he is driven not just by academic argument but by an ethical imperative that he has to believe what his evidence shows him, even if this runs counter to both his expectations and what he would really rather believe.

In educational settings debates about race, intelligence and educational attainment have been rendered both complex and intense by confusion between what evidence might sometimes indicate and what, for the very best of moral reasons, one would like it to indicate. If research showed that redheads were scored lower marks on intelligence tests than those with other hair, might we consider it better to suppress the finding, for fear that they would then be discriminated against? I might be ideologically opposed to the privatisation of education. Might I prefer not to examine its impact on children from poorer families for fear that the results might actually be rather positive (albeit only part of the picture)? And if I believe sufficiently passionately in some cause, might I not tweak the evidence a little or use it very selectively to support my case.

I might even invent parts of a story so as better to tell the 'greater truth' or what Rolfe (2002) calls 'a lie that helps us to see the truth'? though to express the 'fiction' in these terms is not to reject the epistemic project in favour of some of some social or political cause, but to have an enlarged view of how the epistemic project of knowledge and understanding might be achieved. 'I am well aware' wrote Foucault, 'that I have never written anything but fictions. I do not mean to say however that truth is therefore absent. It seems to me that the possibility exists for fiction to function in truth, for fictional discourse to have effects of truth' (Foucault, 1980: 193. See also this Bridges 2002, 2003.)

This falls short of Plato's 'noble lie' which makes no pretence at truth but knowingly deceives – usually from a position of arrogant superiority – in the cause of some expected wider social benefit.

As with any case of dishonesty, there is a spectrum of moral censure. Preferring not to open certain boxes for fear of what one might find does not in general carry much moral censure though it represents a certain intellectual cowardice in a researcher. Avoiding drawing too much public attention to one's results and managing carefully their presentation is, similarly, against the spirit of research – 'systematic and sustained inquiry *made public*' as Stenhouse defined it (1980 my italics) – but perhaps an acceptable compromise with other moral demands. Deliberately misrepresenting one's findings in the belief that this would advance a particular social cause, even or especially the cause of social justice and democracy, seems to me, however, to be step too far, not least because both principles themselves require (at least in general terms) a climate of openness and honesty. We thus return again to the principle enunciated by Sissela Bok in her excellent discussion of 'Lying'. It is possible to go beyond the notion that epistemology is somehow prior to ethics. The two nourish each other, but neither can claim priority' (Bok 1978:13) – *a fortiori*, one might add when it comes to questions of honesty.

It is perhaps worth considering the particular responsibilities of researchers *qua* researchers in the field of social and political action. As people and as citizens we can of course participate in many forms of social and political action and it may be argued that indeed we should and on the side of justice. This is a duty that can be laid on everyone, though some see it as part of the full set of obligations laid on the researcher:

> Thus I am arguing that the researcher/author has three tasks; the researcher engages the researched in a reflective encounter; the research 'act' – the book, article or presentation – brings to light the inequities of power that may exist; and the researcher actively works for care and change. (Tierney, 1994: 111)

But lawyers, journalists, civic servants and politicians make a distinctive professional contribution to these wider social causes – and so do researchers. In this last case it surely has something to do with providing both rigorous critique, carefully and systematically gathered evidence, faithful analysis and, hence trustworthy reasons and argument. As I have argued, this itself requires a commitment to, for example, giving voice to those who might otherwise be excluded, challenging the hegemonic discourses of the powerful and their control over sources of evidence, putting evidence into the public domain and supporting open discussion. These are both requirements for the conduct of a successful educational inquiry and conditions for an open, just and democratic society.

***

So what is the oath? An oath to question all but especially one's own most cherished beliefs? to be rigorous and inclusive in one's attempts to understand experience? to be open and honest in the presentation of one's evidence and argument? And, who knows, perhaps the 'fictions' thus created might yet contain a glimmer of truth, because these are principles that well serve a traditional epistemic project as well as the cause of a more just society.

References

Adugna, W. G. (2008). *The nature and practice of teacher education via distance learning: The case of Addis Ababa University and the Educational Media Agency.* Thesis submitted in fulfilment of the requirements for the award of the degree of Doctor of Philosophy by the University of East Anglia
Attia, M. (2011). *Teacher cognition and the use of technology in teaching Arabic to speakers of other languages.* A thesis submitted to the University of Manchester for the degree of Doctor of Philosophy.
Bok, S. (1978). *Lying: Moral choice in public and private life.* Brighton: Harvester Press.
Bridges, D. (1998). Educational research: Pursuit of truth or flight into fancy. *British Educational Research Journal, 21*(5), 597–616.
Bridges, D. (2002). Narratives in history, fiction and educational research. In R. Huttinen, L. J. H. Heikinnen, & L. Syyälä (Eds.), *Narrative research: Voices of teachers and philosophers.* Jyväskylän, SoPhi: University of Jyvaskylää.
Bridges, D. (2003). *Fiction written under oath': Essays in philosophy and educational research.* Dordrecht: Springer.
Bridges, D., Smeyers, P., & Smith, R. D. (Eds.). (2009). *Evidence-based edicational policy: What evidence? What basis? Whose policy?* Oxford: Wiley Blackwell.
British Educational Research Association. (2011). *Ethical guidelines for educational research.* London: British Educational Research Association.
Charlton, J. I. (1998). *Nothing about us without us: Disability power and oppression.* Berkley: University of California Press.
Chisholm, R. M. (1956). Epistemic statements and the ethics of belief. *Philosophy and Phenomenological Research, 16,* 447–460.
Clifford, W. K. (1877 [1999]). The ethics of belief. In T. Madigan (Ed.), *The ethics of belief and other essays* (pp. 70–96). Amherst: Prometheus.
David, M. (2001). Truth as the epistemic goal. In M. Steup (Ed.), *Knowledge, truth, and duty* (pp. 151–170). New York: Oxford.
Feldman, R. (2000). The ethics of belief. *Philosophy and Phenemonological Research, XL*(3), 667–699.
Foucault, M. (1980). *Power knowledge: Selected interviews and other writings, 1972–77.* Brighton: Harvester Press.
Griffiths, M. (1998). *Educational research for social justice: Getting off the fence.* Buckingham: Open University Press.
Hall, R. J., & Johnson, C. R. (1998). The epistemic duty to seek more evidence. *American Philosophiical Quarterly, 34*(2), 129–139.
Hammersley, M. (1999). Some reflections on the current state of qualitative research. *Research Intelligence, 70,* 16–18.
Heil, J. (1983). Believing what one ought. *Journal of Philosophy, 80,* 752–765.
James, W. (1896a [1979]). The will to believe. In F. Burkhardt et al. (Eds.), *The will to believe and other essays in popular philosophy* (pp. 291–341). Cambridge, MA: Harvard.

James, W. (1896b). The will to believe reprinted in *The theory of knowledge* (2nd ed., pp. 555–562).

MacDonald, B. (1976). Evaluation and the control of education. In D. Tawney (Ed.), *Curriculum evaluation today: Trends and implications* (pp. 125–136). London: Schools Council and MacMillan Education.

Marshall, J. D., & Martin, B. (2000). The boundaries of belief: Territories of encounter between indigenous people and western philosophies. *Educational Philosophy and Theory, 32*, 1.

Peters, R. S., & White, J. P. (1969). The philosopher's contribution to educational research. *Educational Philosophy and Theory, 1*, 1–15.

Quinton, A. (1973). *Utilitarian ethics*. London: Macmillan.

Rolfe, G. (2002). 'A lie that helps us to see the truth': Research truth and fiction in the caring professions. *Reflective Practice, 3*(1), 89–102.

Sosa, E. (2000). For the love of truth. In A. Fairweather & L. Zagzebski (Eds.), *Virtue epistemology: Essays on epistemic virtue and responsibility*. New York: Oxford.

Sosa, E. (2003). The place of truth in epistemology. In L. Zagzebski & M. DePaul (Eds.), *Intellectual virtue: Perspectives from ethics and epistemology*. New York: Oxford University Press.

Stenhouse, L. (1980). *What counts as research?* Unpublished mimeo, CARE Archive, University of East Anglia.

Stronach, I., & MacLure, M. (1997). *Educational research undone: The post-modern embrace*. Buckingham: Open University Press.

Tierney, W. G. (1994). On method and hope. In A. Gitlin (Ed.), *Power and method: Political activism and educational research*. New York: Routledge.

Veck, W. (2002). *What are the proper ends of educational inquiry: Research for justice, for truth or for both*? Paper presented to the Biennial conference of the International Network of Philosophers of Education, Oslo, 9th August 2002.

Taking the Long View: Longitudinal Surveys and the Construction of Educational Inequality in America

Ethan Hutt

Americans have grown accustomed to thinking about educational inequality in national terms. Since the 1970s, the yearly release of college admissions tests scores (SAT) and the biannual release of the "nation's educational report card" (NAEP) have become the education version of a national holiday. Indeed, the cycle of anticipatory commentary – "Who is to Blame if NAEP Reading and Math Scores Fall?" (Klein 2015) – analysis – "NAEP Scores Extend Dismal Trend in US Education Productivity" (Coulson 2013) – and counter-analysis – "When Bad Things Happen to Good NAEP Data" (Sawchuk 2013) – has all the fireworks, nationalism, and selective history of the Fourth July just without the camaraderie and good cheer.

Beyond providing a perennial occasion for finger-pointing and recriminations, these scores have come to provide the most prominent evidence and potent language for discussing educational inequality in the US – the "Black-White Achievement Gap" (e.g. Gamoran and Long 2007; Ladson-Billings 2006). Addressing this achievement gap has become a primary and explicit goal of federal educational policy, as the full title of the 2001 *No Child Left Behind Act* makes abundantly clear: "An Act to Close the Achievement Gap with Accountability, Flexibility, and Choice, so that No Child is Left Behind."

Though we have grown accustomed to thinking about and describing inequality in national terms – NAEP did not even start collecting representative state level data until 2001, well after the "achievement gap" had become a dominant policy frame – it is not at all obvious why we should do so. It seems natural in some respects, of course, given that despite the tradition of localism, the federal government has long used a variety of resources – money and land – to support education.

E. Hutt (✉)

Department of Teaching and Learning, Policy and Leadership, University of Maryland, College Park, MD, USA
e-mail: Ehutt@umd.edu

© Springer International Publishing AG, part of Springer Nature 2018   121
P. Smeyers, M. Depaepe (eds.), *Educational Research: Ethics, Social Justice, and Funding Dynamics*, Educational Research 10,
https://doi.org/10.1007/978-3-319-73921-2_9

The federal government has consistently used those resources to secure educational opportunity whether via the educational land grants of the Northwest Ordinance in 1787; the construction of public school buildings during the Great Depression; or the funding of vocational education programs in the early 1950s (Kaestle and Smith 1982). More recently, the federal government invested in science and math curriculum after the launching of *Sputnik* and compensatory educational funding became explicit tool for fighting President Johnson's "War on Poverty" and for building his "Great Society" – a society that would transcend the regional legacies of inequality and racism (Phillips 2014; Cohen and Moffitt 2010).

    That education became an issue of national concern does not necessarily mean that we would come to talk about a national system of education. Indeed, there are probably few countries in the world where it makes *less* sense to describe a school system in national terms than in the US. In 1963, the year NAEP was first conceived, there were nearly 32,000 school districts in the US containing more than 100,000 public schools and nearly 18,000 private schools (NCES 1993). Even today, after some considerable consolidation, there are still more than 13,000 school districts and 132,000 public and private schools in the U.S (NCES 2012). These schools are governed by 50 distinct state constitutions; regulated by a patchwork of tens of thousands of federal, state, and local laws and regulations; actualized by more than 3 million school teachers certified via 20,000-plus teacher degree and certificate programs; and the entire calico patchwork is cloaked in the mantra of "local control". Despite the pervasiveness of the phrase, it seems fair to ask: given the lack of centralized control, differing constitutional rights to education, and unequal provisions for schooling, what does it *mean* to talk about the average achievement of the American 9-year-old? Let alone to talk about, as the NAEP reports so often do (NCES 2008), how this achievement compares to the average 9-year-old student of different races or the average American student achievement from four decades ago?

    As a historian, I am less concerned with what we currently mean – or think about – when we talk about a national educational system than I am with tracing the shifts in our thinking about the American education system overtime. One important aspect of this story – the allure and value of quantification – has already begun to be addressed by education scholars in history and philosophy (Smeyers and Depaepe 2010). This article builds on this important earlier contribution by considering a specific kind of quantification – the nationally representative longitudinal dataset. These datasets, which were first imagined during the 1950s when the power of systems analysis was at its peak, have provided the basis for an incredibly generative body of scholarship on the American education system – one that, from its inception, was explicitly aimed at securing greater educational opportunity. As the National Center of Education Statistics NCES explained at the outset, the aim was "to establish a factual basis for verifying and refining federal policy concerned with maximizing individual access to educational and vocational opportunity" (Peng 1977).

    Though collection and dissemination of statistics had been the primary goal of the federal government since the nineteenth century, these longitudinal efforts distinguished themselves from earlier data collection efforts by promising to provide not just a snapshot of the system's exterior but a time-lapse picture of the inner workings of the school system. As I will argue below, this shift represented a relatively new way of thinking about American schools that allowed policymakers to view the American education system as relatively uniform and the goal of policy to optimize its function. The use of data in this way produced, somewhat paradoxically, a higher precision and more distorted view of the American schooling. The detailed picture that could be rendered by scholars using these datasets offered policymakers new and important insights about the pathways of individual students through school while at the same time presenting policymakers with an increasingly abstract and decontextualized view of the American education system as a whole. That is to say, the datasets afforded the opportunity to view the system as uniform and in *national* terms.

This development is significant in no small part because it ran against a growing body of evidence – from these same data – that pointed to the considerable limitations of ignoring contextual and individual differences between schools in favor of universalized comparisons across schools. Yet, in the hands of researchers these datasets – the first of which was heralded as producing "probably the richest archive ever assembled on a single generation of Americans" with 1900 variables covering 22,000 individuals across 12 years – seemed to place a growing arsenal of simple fixes within the grasp of policymakers: curricular differentiation, Algebra by 8th grade, school vouchers, etc. In other words, the upshot of the unprecedented scale and detail of the data collection effort was a more stylized portrait of the American education "system" – one that appeared more amenable to federal intervention but no more likely to secure educational equity for its students.

This article sketches the broad outline of these historical developments and presents them in two parts. The first section provides an examination of the first attempts in the late 1950s to secure longitudinal system data. I argue that these efforts were intimately tied to the ambition to bring systems analysis to bear on questions of school reform – an ambition that created a demand for larger, more precise statistics on school operations – as well as to the Progressive Era view of educational equity as providing appropriately differentiated schooling. Though these early efforts failed to deliver on the promise to identify the precise relationship between identifiable school characteristics and school outcomes, they demonstrated the general viability of these techniques and pointed the way toward this new frontier of research.

In part two, I consider the second generation of longitudinal systems in which the federal government took direct control of these efforts and examine how the failure of prior attempts to produce usable insights were recast as a justification for still more and greater data collection efforts. These efforts required researchers to construct an increasingly stylized view of the education system. Rather than consider how different systems might produce different results for different children, the emphasis was now on how education systems, despite their differences, could be made to produce the same results for all children. I also examine some of the "policy ready" recommendations that have come from the analysis of these datasets and how they reflected and co-constructed the vision of a national school system in which de-contextualized data could be used to provide universal answers to the local problems of schooling.

In considering this history, I hope to make three contributions to literature on the history of educational research and social science more generally. First, in considering the historical origins of longitudinal data, this article seeks to draw attention to what has become a foundational part of the American educational research infrastructure and the influence that this infrastructure has had on education research. Second, I hope this article will contribute to a growing body of scholarship that has examined the ways in which – across fields ranging from meteorological modeling to poverty research (Edwards 2000; O'Connor 2001) – large-scale data collection and the decisions they make possible become profoundly interdependent and thus self-perpetuating. That is, they become a primary means for thinking about and acting on the underlying phenomenon. Thus, in the same way that the decision to view poverty in terms of an "income deficit" led to a demand for longitudinal "microdata" on the income of individuals and households and these data, in turn, defined our understanding of the "nature and causes of poverty," (O'Connor 2001, 182) so too did the federal desire to view the school system in national terms and view its deficiencies as rooted in that system led to datasets that allowed it to see the problems and respond in those terms.

Thirdly, I hope to complicate the history of the federal involvement in American education policy and research. Normally that story is dominated by the failure of federal efforts to spur "basic research" or to produce a R&D infrastructure analogous to those developed in defense and medicine (e.g. Kiesler and Turner 1977; Vinovskis 1996). Though the hope of turning education into a hard science proved disappointingly "elusive" in many respects, these failures should not prevent us from seeing the success of concurrent efforts to construct – at least at the level of datasets and statistics – a national education system. Considering education research from this angle helps to make greater sense of the trajectory of education research in a field disillusioned, but not dissuaded, by the Coleman Report. Though the headline message of the Coleman report was that schools matter quite a bit less than society had hoped, and certainly less than non-school factors like social background, the secondary message was that school *processes* likely mattered more than the overall amount of school resources (Coleman et al. 1966).

While educational scholars, like the public at large, were dispositionally and, perhaps, culturally immune to the first message, the collection of longitudinal data concerning students' movement *through* the system and into the world promised to speak – when translated into a certain statistical dialect – directly to the second. Indeed, it is no coincidence that Coleman himself would use the second federal longitudinal dataset (High School and Beyond) to argue that students who attend Catholic achieve more academically even when accounting for race and socioeconomic background – claims that perfectly reflect the triple move provided by longitudinal data: moving at once "inside" the school, outside of any particular context, while at the same time laying claim to an expansive portion of an individual's life course (Coleman et al. 1982; Hoffer and Coleman 1987).

Part I – The Search for Talent and Equity in the Age of Systems

"Schools are extremely complicated organisms," observed two RAND analysts J.A. Kershaw and R.N. McKean in a little read but widely searching memo in October of 1959 (Kershaw and McKean 1959). The pair knew something about complicated systems. McKean was, with fellow RAND analyst Charles Hirsch, in the process of developing Planning-Programing-Budgeting System (PPBS) and writing the "bible of defense spending" the *Economics of Defense Spending in the Nuclear Age*; Kershaw had already begun to distinguish himself as an analyst of social problems and would soon join the Johnson administration's War on Poverty as head of the Office Research and Planning in the Office of Economic Opportunity.

"The learning process is only dimly understood even by those who have spent their lives studying it," they explained before concluding "If we have anything to contribute, it is not as experts on education, but as interested outsiders who may be able to bring to bear a new methodology on old problems" (Kershaw and McKean 1959, 6).

The old problem was the efficient organization of school systems and the new methodology was RAND's in-house specialty: "systems analysis."

The immediate impetus for considering the amenability of school systems to systems analysis was the concern for how America, locked in an Cold War arms race, could continue to supply "high quality education" given that "with each passing year the flood of school-age children swells" (Kershaw and McKean 1959, 56). To do so inefficiently was not only to be wasteful, they argued, but to risk certain failure. The broader impetus was an effort – pursued by RAND analysts and a growing number of people inside the federal government – to ensure that the quantitative analytical techniques that were seen as instrumental in winning World War II were profitably applied to all sectors of American society from the design of electrical grids to the management of paperwork inside the Social Security Administration (Heyck 2015; Akera 2000). Hunter Heyck has recently argued that these efforts should be understood as indicative of a much broader cultural and intellectual shift in the social sciences in the 1950s – a shift which he calls the "Age of System".

The Age of System, according to Heyck, was characterized by both the re-imagining of the world as a complex, hierarchically structured bureaucratic system and by the redefinition of role of the social scientist as describer and analyst of these systems (Heyck 2015). A key driver of this shift was the "data explosion" that had begun inside the federal government during the Great Depression and accelerated during World War II. The sheer volume of these data pointed both to the increased complexity and interconnectedness of systems in general but also to the difficulty of making the right choice without being overwhelmed by the available system information. In an increasingly complex, fast-changing, and dangerous world, decisionmakers' choices were both more consequential and more difficult than ever to make. The role of the social scientist, then, was to help rationalize the *process of decisionmaking* and to refashion the world as necessary in order to make it possible for such structured, rational choices to be made (Heyck 2015, 128–30). Indeed, Hayek notes, one hallmark of the Age of System was the re-framing of numerous fields around the science of decisionmaking and the exaltation of this science's ability to produce optimal outcomes in the face of uncertainty – think Game Theory – and rational choices even in light of the limited cognition and potential irrationality of individual deciders.

The reverberations of the bold intellectual agenda of the age can be heard resounding throughout Kershaw and McKean's exploration of the possible applications of systems analysis in education. In their view, the ultimate upshot of systems analysis techniques would be the ability to make "formal quantitative comparisons of specific systems with variants of them in which changes and innovations are incorporated…that can help administrators and others *choose* improved educational systems" (Kershaw and McKean 1959, iii, emphasis added) While the idea that individual school system variables could be isolated and manipulated to induce measurable educational changes reflected the unbridled analytic confidence of the day, the sheer size of the analysis required to frame reasonable policy choices did give the analysts pause. "The collection of data would, of course be an enormous job" they conceded (Kershaw and McKean 1959, 35). "For instance, if one used only eight variables and allowed each to have two levels, there would be 256 possible combinations. To speak realistically, we doubt if a very helpful analysis could be made with a sample that comprised less than 500 schools. And, it should be remembered that one would have to visit and examine a good many more school systems [to locate ones with suitable traits] than the number of combinations used in the final analysis" (Kershaw and McKean 1959, 17).

Still, the pair took solace in the fact that the federal government had already funded two massive data collection efforts. The result of these efforts, the RAND men hoped, would provide the necessary raw data inputs for the analyses they envisioned. Their optimism on this account even led them to suggest that subsequent systems analyses be postponed until the data from the second of these studies was available – a delay that "might not ultimately cost anytime to speak of" on account of the amount learned and the possibility that the study "will tell us what we need to know about the relationship between school characteristics and educational output" (Kershaw and McKean 1959, 57).

Though the RAND memo perfectly captures the analysts' abstract ambition to view American schools as a rational system with variables available for selection and manipulated from afar, the concrete experiences of the early data collection efforts revealed how much the reality of schooling diverged from the analysts' vision and how much data infrastructure and statistical airbrushing was required in order to produce a school system available for analysis.

The first of the two federally funded efforts to secure longitudinal data on school operations referenced by the RAND analysts was the Quality Measurement Project in New York State. With money from the Office of Education, the Quality Measurement Project aimed to provide quantitative answers to four deeply pressing and interrelated questions: How much did the quality of school systems (as measured by pupil outcomes on standardized tests) vary within New York state?; Did variation exist even among schools systems with similar system contexts (e.g. urban/rural; socio-economic status of community)?; When accounting for system context, did systems produce similar results for students with similar academic potential (IQ-scores)?; Could any of these variations be accounted for by "factors that are within the control of school administration?" (Goodman 1958, 3–4). The elementary nature of the questions reflected both the immaturity of the field but also the particular educational goals of the moment. The aim was not to secure uniform achievement across school systems and students, but, in the words of the project's lead investigator, "to capitalize maximally the potential of all types of pupils" (Goodman 1958). Given that "a rural district cannot be transmuted into an urban district," the goal was to identify relative deficiencies by category of system and suboptimal outcomes for kinds of students within those systems (Goodman 1958, 34).

If these gaps, and the variables that predicted them, could be identified, the state could take a huge step forward in optimizing its education system and creating the necessary data infrastructure to allow for its continued monitoring and maintenance. In this respect, the goals of the project were unprecedented. Even the most ambitious longitudinal attempts to study school systems – notably the Eight Year Study (Aikin 1942) – had sought to demonstrate the possibilities of deliberately experimenting with the high school curriculum and the results of doing so. This was a far cry from monitoring variation in existing systems with an eye toward exploiting that "natural" variation for the sake of collective system optimization.

The researchers hoped that their role would primarily be as aggregators of available information rather than as creators of new information. But these hopes were quickly dashed. Even in a relatively centralized state like New York, with system was overseen by a Board of Regents and with a uniform test for high school graduation, the researchers found that when it came to documenting student achievement, the system varied in every conceivable way: the standardized tests that were used, the grades that they were used in, and the frequency that they were administered. (Goodman 1958, 10). Even the researchers' hope that they could gen-erate standardized longitudinal data from a direct observation of student records were dashed when the they found "only a small percentage of systems in the sample was found to have readily available longitudinal data on their pupils; and, among those that did have such data, variation in the span of years covered, in the tests used, and in the procedures for reporting was too great to permit use of the records by the Project" (Goodman 1958, 10).

In order to subject the system to study they would have to generate their own standardized data first – a task they gave over to E.F. Lindquist's Iowa Tests of Basic Skills, not because of its wide use in New York or its alignment with local curriculum, but in large part because of "the availability of an electronic scoring service, which had considerable appeal in an enterprise of the size of the Quality Measurement Project" (Goodman 1958, 11) Standardization, in other words, not only had to occur but it had to occur apace.

Once in possession of their new data – covering roughly 70,000 students in grades 4, 7, and 10 – the researchers could finally go ahead with their planned analyses. The results they found were "an arresting fact." According to their data, the *mean achievement levels* varied by as much as four grade levels across the state systems (Goodman 1958, 17).

Faced with such massive differences in system quality, the Quality Measurement team performed what would become for education researchers in subsequent decades the ritual parsing of achievement gap responsibility. The researchers found that even with their limited statistical controls, half the variation could be accounted for by school location and parental occupation level. They also found, to their dismay, that the most obvious and readily observable school level variables – student expenditures and teacher experience – had very weak, and at times *negative*, correlations with student achievement particularly for those at the lowest levels (Goodman 1958, 38). Again foreshadowing decades of coming research on inequality, the scholars, undeterred, concluded "the finding about within-group differences means that variation in process, that is, in what schools in similar settings do with pupils, has a demonstrable effect upon pupil outcomes. This is the essential finding – the finding that supports the hope that substantial improvement of education in a state or in a nation can come from programs of quality assessment." Having just acknowledged that 50% of the variation was beyond school control, they chose to see the systems analysis glass as half-full.

Extracting this hope from the system, however, would require more data. In particular, the Quality Measurement Project noted the need for "the development of longitudinal data on system outcomes and patterns of pupil progress" (Goodman 1958, 66). This data would allow them to peer both inside the system and into the future. Developing and standardizing more variables would provide for a better understanding of the "dynamics of school system effectiveness" – information which, in turn, could be used to "develop better procedures for more precisely classifying systems in terms of institutional potential" and "for classifying pupils in terms of educative potential" (Goodman 1958, 67). The developing data loop would provide the means for maximum efficiency and optimal utilization of education potential given the inherent differences between pupils and school systems (See Gamson 2007); it would also provide the basis for subsequent and on-going management of the school system.

Just about the time the researchers for the Quality Measurement Project were submitting their final report to the Office of Education, John Flanagan of the University of Pittsburgh and the President of the American Institute for Research (AIR), was in negotiations with the Office of Education to take up the call for longitudinal data with one of the most ambitious education research projects ever attempted. During World War II, Flanagan, a Harvard trained psychologist, had served in the Army Air Forces' Aviation Psychology Program (Flanagan 1962). Flanagan spent the war devising instruments and procedures to better predict which aspiring pilots were most likely to complete their aviation training. The work was deemed a critical success – credited with saving hundreds of lives and millions of dollars and ultimately earned Flanagan a Legion of Merit award (Freeman 1996).

When the war ended, Flanagan believed that these same aptitude-based testing techniques could be used to solve the nation's manpower problems by providing better guidance to high school students about their likely career trajectories. Just as a battery of tests could be used to determine who would succeed as a pilot and who was better suited to be the navigator, a much larger battery could be used to identify the unique talent signatures of each individual American student, which career would best suit them and, in turn, how their time in school might best be spent (Flanagan 1962, 5). Echoing the sentiments of the famous Cardinal Principles Report on Secondary Education (1918) and the researchers in the Quality Measurement Project, Flanagan believed that equitable treatment of students involved the individualization and differentiation of their curriculum. Talents, like aptitudes, were innate but they were also multi-dimensional and could be prosperously developed for the benefit of both the individual and the nation. Flanagan believed that embracing this view, as the military had in World War II, represented a fundamental shift in thinking about human development and schooling – drawing an analogy between scientists' rejection of phlogiston theory for modern chemistry to his rejection of Spearman's unitary intelligence for a multi-dimensional view of talent (Flanagan 1962, 21–22; see also: Kett 2012).

What was required, then, to pursue this vision was a massive, longitudinal "census" of American talent. Only a large-scale survey, Flanagan believed, carried out over an extended period of time would allow for the repeated sub-division of the sample by talent measures and the linking of those measures backward to particular features of the school in which they were developed and forward to success (or not) in the multitude of possible career paths. The result of this grand vision; funding from the Office of Education, National Institute of Mental Health, Office of Naval Research and National Science Foundation; assistance from 90 regional coordinators; and guidance from a technical panel of 31 prominent researchers – including luminaries Ralph Tyler, Franklin E. Frazer, Henry Chauncey, and Robert Thorndike – was a brand new two and a half day long academic and psychological test battery consisting of 25 academic and aptitude tests sub-tests, a student interest inventory, student activity inventory, a measure of student "preferences," and two short open-ended essays. The battery was given to a representative sample of 440,000 American high school students in 1353 high schools nationwide. These students, representing roughly 1 out of every 20 high schoolers in the country, would be followed into the working world and surveyed again 1, 5, and 11 years after graduation (Flanagan 1962).

The belief that this avalanche of a *billion* pieces of data – again helpfully generated by E.F. Lindquist's computerized scoring machines at the University of Iowa – would unlock the secrets of the high school system is reflected in the astounding 93% cooperation rate that Flanagan received from the nation's high schools (Flanagan 1962, 51). Town papers throughout the country even proudly announced the selection and participation of local schools in this unprecedented effort (e.g. *Hartford Courant* 1960; Beatty 1960). The reality of the initial data, however, proved somewhat less than the dream.

Flanagan had hoped – much like the researchers in New York – to use his data to create a taxonomy of 17 different kinds of high schools based on location, community demographics, etc. and to identify their unique strengths in developing certain forms of talent (Flanagan et al. 1962). Instead the research mostly offered support for the "small relation to the amount of student learning" of such school factors as "size of school, size of classes, age of building, rural versus urban location, and dropout rate" (Flanagan 1978, 17). He also found strong evidence of the limited influence of schooling on college going, finding instead a strong correlation between family socioeconomic status and achievement of the student: knowing a student's academic ability was only a slightly better predictor of college attendance than knowing a student's socioeconomic status (Flanagan 1978, 18–19).

With respect to improving student guidance, Flanagan was able to demonstrate, in addition to the low college attendance of academically capable poor students, that many students' possessed "unrealistic" career plans – defined as a gap between vocational aspirations and current achievement and latent talent. Flanagan characterized these findings as evidence of his overriding concern in the ineffective guidance programs and talent waste in American high schools. But they did not come close to fulfilling the promise of being able to divine a student's most promising occupation by charting their talent scores (Flanagan 1962). Indeed, Flanagan had fallen well short of the RAND analysts' hopes that his study would "tell us what we need to know about the relationship between school characteristics and educational output" (Kershaw and McKean 1959).

Though Flanagan was fond of likening standardized testing to the physical scientist using X-rays to study the crystalline structure of molecules (e.g. Flanagan 1962, 1), the seeming failure of his immense dataset to reveal the core structure of the school system – to unlock its secrets – has led many modern scholars and historians to ignore Flanagan's effort outright or to dismiss it as "an exercise in overkill" that was crushed by the weight of its own empiricism (Kett 2012, 157). Such dismissals however, fail to recognize how path breaking this work was and how much its results – and the reaction to them – would portend a defining trend of education research over the next four decades.

First, and perhaps most importantly, Flanagan's massive Project Talent demonstrated to the federal government and other researchers that the technical tools – test batteries, survey instruments, and data processing machines – and analytic techniques necessary to conjure a stable, if fuzzy, image of the *American* school system. Flanagan's portrait of the American High School and the American student provides a telling contrast when placed next to the other famous study of the American high school from this period: James B. Conant's best-selling *The American High School Today* (1959). Completed only 2 years prior to the launch of Flanagan's survey, Conant conducted his study by driving around the country visiting American high schools in person in order to understand the unique, subjective characteristics of each school. Indeed Conant doubted whether it was possible "to obtain information which one could generalize the success or failure of the American school in regard to the education of any group of children" and he characterized his evaluations of the schools he visited as "impressions" (Conant 1959; see also, Hampel 1983).

The contrast with Flanagan's survey design and published reports could not be more stark. Flanagan absolutely believed that such broad comparisons and generalizations were possible – a view reflected in his decision to make the data representative of the nation only – not of individual states or districts. He believed in the immutable traits of the schools as systems even if the optimal relationship between input and system characteristics might vary. As Flanagan explained in a brief section of one the Project Talent Reports entitled "Can Schools Really Be Compared?", the answer had been 'no' but only because the proper variables had not been identified or the information available. Producing that information, however, necessarily imposed a level of abstraction on the rendering as academic test batteries reflecting no particular textbook or curriculum had to be created from scratch for the job. Flanagan's study, like the New York study, loudly announced the ambition and intention of researchers to bring the American high school under study and to transform it, if necessary, in the process.

Second, the study also underscored the importance of tying school inputs and characteristics – longitudinally – to particular higher education and labor market outcomes. Though scholars normally associate the "shift to outcomes" with the Coleman Report and the Nixon Administration, Flanagan's explicit concern with these relationships casts these later efforts in slightly different light. What changed was not so much the focus on outcomes as the meaning of providing equity to students. Both the Quality Measurement Project and Project Talent took the reality of differential outcomes as a starting point and sought to optimize schools and, in the case of Flanagan, course offerings to local conditions recognizing that "a rural district cannot be transmuted into an urban district." This reflected more of the Cold War imperative to identify the gifted and talented and utilize the full manpower resources of the nation than the Supreme Court's "all deliberate speed" declaration in *Brown v. Board*.

The issue of shifting equity standards raises the third point about the contemporaneous interpretation of the Project Talent results. Foreshadowing decades of debates in education research, the fine grain-data of Project Talent – the most detailed picture of American education ever produced – became more of a mirror than a microscope – reflecting back the commitments of researchers. Christopher Jencks, for instance, would use the Project Talent data to argue, repeatedly, that it provided the "best currently available evidence" of the complete inability of schools – regardless of their characteristics – to address inequity (Jencks 1972; Jencks and Brown 1975). For him, the data led to the inevitable conclusion that if Americans wanted to address inequality they should do so directly and leave the schools out of it. Others, however, like economist Alice Rivlin who would serve as Johnson's Assistant Secretary of Planning and Evaluation in the HEW, explained away the Project Talent results by arguing that the dataset was large but *not large enough*. What was needed, in her view, was "a longitudinal data system for keeping track of individual students as they move through school" including information about the class they take and the resources they are exposed to (Rivlin 1972, 64). The real value of Project Talent, Rivlin's argued, was that it justified still "more complex and expensive longitudinal studies" (Rivlin 1972, 65). Studies that the National Center for Education Statistics (NCES) would initiate while she was serving in the Johnson administration.

Even with these newly launched longitudinal studies, Rivlin conceded "the problem may be that the real world is not organized to generate information about production functions, no matter how cleverly the statistics are collected. Perhaps the schools are too uniform, with too few important differences that are not correlated with the socioeconomic status of students" (Rivlin 1972, 65). However plausible these concerns, they would hardly prevent educational researchers from endeavoring to try. If schools as they were found were not organized to divulge their inner secrets then they would need to be reimagined; if the schools were too uniform to the gaze of existing statistical controls, then new variables would need to be devised and new statistical ways of seeing would need to be constructed.

Part II – National Longitudinal Survey and beyond

It is impossible to tell the history of American education research in the second part of the twentieth century and not address the Coleman Report. The report, commissioned by the federal government as part of the passage of the Elementary and Secondary Education Act, produced some of the most controversial – and enduring (Gamoran and Long 2007) – findings in education research. The findings called into question the basic American assumption that schools could be an engine of upward mobility by providing evidence that race and socioeconomic status were strong predictors of school success than were in-school factors such as school facilities, teacher qualities, student body characteristics, etc. (Coleman et al. 1966). What is so striking – and strange – about the American response to these findings is how little they caused people to rethink the central role of schools in the pursuit of equality. As Leah Gordon has noted, this was, with few exceptions, no less true when one considers the responses to the Coleman Report emanating from inside the academy regardless of whether they appeared in white or black social scientific outlets (Gordon 2014).

If the report did not drive Americans to rethink their general faith in schooling, it did propel a narrative that the American education system was fundamentally broken. While scholars before had imagined a mismatch between system design and its location and inputs, now scholars, and the wider public, suspected something more fundamental might be amiss. This narrative neatly dovetailed with the new brand of analyses that were being underwritten and undertaken by a newly emboldened federal government. The creation of the National Assessment of Education Progress (NAEP), which debuted in 1969 was intended to provide an "educational thermometer" that its designers explicitly likened to the education version of the GDP. While NAEP could provide a running tally of the nation's "achievement gap" and provide a basis for thinking about the nation's education system as a coherent whole (disaggregation of test scores by state was impossible), passive indicators of this kind could not provide the "solutions" or the kind of actionable information that could serve as the basis for new policies.

One way that education researchers and those in the federal government hoped to fill this gap was through the newly designed National Longitudinal Study of the high school class of 1972 (NLS72). Coupling the empiricism of the old systems analysis and the post-*Brown* language of educational access and opportunity, those working in the National Center for Education Statistics described the purpose of the NLS72 project as "establish[ing] a factual basis for verifying and refining federal policy concerned with maximizing individual access to educational and vocational opportunity, with improvement of the general education system as it impinges upon young people" (Peng 1977, 1). The survey would accomplish this, like Project Talent before it, by repeatedly surveying a nationally representative sample of the high school class of 1972 as they made the transition from high school to higher education and/or the workforce. Implicit in this research design was that the "impinging" factors of the education system were inherent to schools as systems rather than to particular locales as the findings from the data were only generalizable to the nation as a whole rather than to any school, district, or even state level system.

In many respects, this design paralleled the shifts in the larger intellectual outlook within the discipline of economics. During this period there was fundamental reimagining of the ways in which big systems, like "the economy," should be studied. Rather than consider the larger forces at work in macroeconomic systems like national economies, they flipped the analysis around and began to "place macroeconomics on microeconomic foundations" (Rodgers 2011, 47). That is to say, many economists came to believe that they could develop a picture of the strength and structure of the economy as a whole, simply by aggregating a large enough group of individual actions.

Even granting the ascendancy of economics – and microeconomics in particular – as a discipline, this post-Coleman Report design choice was particularly strange given that one of the other major findings of the Coleman report was that 80% of the variation in student achievement existed *within* rather than between schools (Coleman et al. 1966). This finding suggested that there was less to be learned by looking across schools than by looking within them – the kind of particularized analysis undertaken by Conant (and so many qualitative researchers) and also precisely the kind of study explicitly foreclosed by the survey design.

The implications of Coleman's findings did not prevent scholars from utilizing national survey data to try and open up the black box of schooling in order to determine which features of the school organization – beyond resources – might contribute to differential school achievement when controlling, of course, for socioeconomic factors. One key parameter was curriculum, which has been a perennial source of complaint and presumed culprit for the presumed ineffectualness of American education.

Scholars had begun developing structural "school process" models to account for the differential allocation of school resources to students within a school building particularly on account of tracking. Differentiating curricular tracks – college preparatory, commercial, and vocational – had long been a feature of the American high school particularly after the Comprehensive High School movement of the 1950s.

Anecdote and a growing body of largely qualitative evidence suggested, however, that tracking had been reappropriated as a strategy for addressing the challenges posed by school desegregation – middle class white advantage could be preserved in the college preparatory even as African American students were given access to the lower curricular tracks at integrated schools (Gamoran and Berends 1987; Labaree 1992; Reed 2014).

What these qualitative studies had a more difficult time substantiating was whether the differences in achievement by track stemmed from the track placement itself or from differences in prior achievement levels. Venturing an answer to this question was a task well suited to the new crop of national representative longitudinal datasets (Alexander et al. 1978). Not only could they attempt to disentangle prior achievement from track placement, but, in the case of NLS72, it could associate these curricular placements with life outcomes in an unprecedented way.

This line of research appeared to reap large dividends when researchers found that the large gaps in college degree attainment by race disappeared – though they remained for socioeconomic status – when researchers controlled for the "academic resources" of the student including, notably, curricular track (Alexander et al. 1982). The final lines of the article reporting these findings reflect the ascendance of the "can do" attitude of education policy researchers:

> Clearly, differences involving student background, especially SES, still exist and these fully warrant our concern. As a practical matter, though, the more pressing problem seems to be to assure that all youth who desire a college education acquire the sorts of academic resources that will enhance their prospects for doing so. We recognize that this may be no easy task, but the potential payoff is considerable. Improving student qualifications would serve much more to promote high levels of educational attainment than would even a wholly successful assault on the remaining background liabilities uncovered in our analysis (Alexander et al. 1982, 330).

These conclusions place the potential and pitfalls of the longitudinal survey on full display: the ability to provide a comprehensive, longitudinal description of racial and socioeconomic educational inequality; the potential to identify specific past bottlenecks in the system; and the temptation to associate their mitigation with profound changes in an individual's future life-course (i.e. graduating from college or not).

The elided caveat in findings of this sort was that their precise meaning was not as evident as it appeared. Because of a complete lack of standardization in American education curricula, the only way to measure a student's track was by self-report of the student and the school. On account of the need to keep things standardized, these tracks could only be characterized in the broadest possible terms. In the case of the study above, and NLS72 more generally, "college track" and "non-college track" (Alexander et al. 1982, 318). What these designations meant in practice – in terms of the actual experiences of students residing in states from Massachusetts to Mississippi – with respect to actual course-taking, specific curricular content, educational experiences, or academic socialization was anyone's guess.

The response to these concrete but indeterminate findings was a push for more precise and more chronologically expansive longitudinal data. Indeed, one major criticism of the NLS72 design was that it contained only one set of cognitive measures obtained from students when they were seniors. This design did not allow for measures of cognitive growth during high school or for much disentangling of track placement and academic growth (Rock 2012). These deficiencies were addressed in the second longitudinal study – High School and Beyond (HSB) – which followed the high school class of 1980 and obtained measures in both tenth and twelfth grade (and the follow up to HSB, NELS88, went one step further by following students beginning in the eighth grade).

Given the running 1970s controversy over the reality and cause of the declining SAT scores of America's college bound seniors and the enduring concerns about academic rigor, the issue of curricular tracks and the differential course taking patterns they implied, clearly struck a nerve with lawmakers.

The National Commission on Educational Excellence commissioned a study of a representative historical sample of high school American transcripts by Clifford Adelman a researcher in National Institute of Education. A study of actual course-taking patterns – the "time on academic subject matter" – would reveal, the theory went, the trends in academic quality of the American school and the relationship between those trends and higher education outcomes. The result of these efforts would feature prominently in the "Findings" section of the Commission's reform document *par excellence*, the infamous, *A Nation at Risk*: "Secondary school curricula have been homogenized, diluted, and diffused to the point that they no longer have a central purpose"; "The proportion of students taking a general program of study has increased from 12 percent in 1964 to 42 percent in 1979"; "We offer intermediate algebra, but only 31% of our recent high school graduates complete it" (National Commission on Excellence in Education 1983; Adelman 1983).

While the study's inclusion in *A Nation at Risk* highlights the policy relevance of these findings and the growing comfort of policymakers and scholars of speaking generally about the American student, the process by which these findings were produced underscores an important point about the weight of the work and measure of abstraction required to allow us to speak in these terms. It took the National Center of Education Statistics more than *two years* of study to develop a classification system capable of comprehending the variety and idiosyncrasies of the American high school transcripts collected as part of the HSB study (Adelman 1983, 2).

Because of the specific parameters of the study, Adelman and his colleagues had to use a modified version of the NCES scheme which nonetheless involved a nested coding scheme involving grouping course titles under 131 course name categories, 13 general headings, and three curricular tracks (Adelman 1983, Appendix A, B; Ludwig 1982). And though the authors of *A Nation at Risk* discussed the findings in terms of students, the actual unit of analysis in the study was the course title/code not the curriculum or student. This was, as Adelman explained, because "the course is a standard 'house' within which students live for measured periods of time…it is thus a category that allows one to analyze aggregate behavior, and it was aggregate behavior in which we were interested" (Adelman 1983, 6). It was on this basis that he was able to report that American students' course-taking had become "diffuse," less academic, and that the value of a course credit had become "devalued".

In subsequent years Adelman and fellow researchers would press further into this, now standardized, course-taking transcript data in order to better foreground the individual American student as the unit of analysis. As with the more generalized research on the mediating effects of academic resources on race and socioeconomic status, scholars were able to tie macro-life outcomes with even more micro elements of schooling. Notably, researchers found that a student's highest level mathematics course turned out to be a very strong predictor of their likelihood to persist in college. Just as importantly, they found that the specific timing of math achievement was crucial: "early access" to algebra was strongly associated with advanced high school math achievement and "socialization" in math (Smith 1996).

Findings like these, gleaned from the analysis of longitudinal transcript data, lent credence to the massive push in the 1990s to make algebra by eighth grade a new "civil right" – between 1990 and 2007 the percentage of eighth graders enrolled in math courses nearly doubled from 16 to 31% (Loveless 2008, 1). Not only did scholars identify early algebra taking as predictive of later math achievement but, the HSB transcript data revealed one variable in particular – HIGHMATH – was "an extremely powerful construct" (Adelman 1999, 12; see, also Pallas and Alexander 1983) for predicting college level degree attainment.

Of course the origins of any particular policy development are numerous and complex, but the ease and authority with which scholars could move from research findings utilizing representative, longitudinal data to tidy policy prescriptions are well captured by the definitive Department of Education summary of the findings from NLS72 and HSB, appropriately titled "Answers in the Toolbox". In its pages one can almost hear the echoes of John Flanagan's voice and ambition from Project Talent:

> the story told by this voyage is clear…it helps us advise and guide students no matter what paths of attendance they follow through higher education. It tells us that if degree-completion lags for any student or group of students, the situation is fixable. We learn where to take the tool box, and what tools to use…One must acknowledge that SES has a continuing influence in life-course events. But the analysis here (and elsewhere) indicates how much education can mitigate those effects – and in both directions (downward mobility is not a chimera). If SES were an overpowering presence the tool box directions would be futile. Optimism is the preferred stance" (Adelman 1999, 83).

Putting aside the inappropriately causal language for conclusions based on a regression analysis, what is striking about this statement is its imagining of an individual student and the capacity to speak to her amidst the babel of local system dialects. Not only that, but the findings also bear the other hallmark of research involving longitudinal data: a comfort with the elision of time. Though the data the study is based on reflects the experiences of the previous two decades of students, the author has no trouble projecting those same experiences onto future generations of students. The data, having provided secure ownership of the past, provides certain purchase of the future.

It is worth noting that the search for universal tools invited by longitudinal datasets like NLS72 & HBS, was not limited to student level or curricular interventions. They proved just as useful for devising system level interventions as well. Though conservatives had long advocated for the introduction and expansion of school choice programs, these arguments received a big boost in the 1990s with the publication of John Chubb and Terry Moe's *Politics, Markets, and Schools* (Chubb and Moe 1990b). The book, which purported to show the irredeemable flaws of public schools and inherent superiority of choice-based systems, was rooted in their analysis of the HSB data. In providing these conclusions, Chubb and Moe were building on the earlier work of James Coleman and his colleagues who had used the same HSB dataset to claim that Catholic schools, on account of their internal organization, produced superior academic outcomes to public schools even when controlling for student characteristics – controversial findings that sparked considerable debate in the academy (Coleman et al. 1982). In the ultimate illustration of how available data co-create both methods and findings, Coleman's findings along with a quirk in the design of the HSB survey allowed for the application of a brand new statistical analysis – Hierarchical Linear Modeling (HLM) – to be applied in the adjudication of school quality (Bryk and Raudenbush 1988; Raudenbush and Bryk 1986). As with the student level findings, the survey data allowed one to confidently ignore specific context to formulate a national reform and to easily jump from statistical association in the past to future policy solution: a universal choice program would be, the words of Chubb and Moe, a "panacea" for the challenge of providing educational opportunity for all American children – and they had the long-term, nationally representative data to prove it (Chubb and Moe 1990a).

Conclusion

A 1997 *New York Times* editorial cartoon nicely captures the dangers inherent to research fields from too much data. The cartoon depicts a newscaster announcing "According to a report released today…" while sitting next to three board game spinners – one each listing a random behavior, a medical condition, and segment of the human/animal population – under the headline "Today's Random Medical News from the New England Journal of Panic-Inducing Gobbledygook" (Borgman 1997 as cited in Plantin et al. Forthcoming). Though not stated in these terms, the underlying premise is that researchers armed with too much data on too many variables are bound to find and report some – likely spurious – correlation. Indeed in many fields – from epidemiology to meteorology – researchers have found that more data – "big data" – is not always an unqualified good (Plantin et al. forthcoming).

In the case of education and education research our version of this story is clearly complicated. There is no question that some of our most important and enduring findings have been the result of the accumulation and analysis of very large datasets. Given the American education traditions of federalism, inequality, and unbridled optimism, there is something unquestionably valuable and important about our ability to produce cross-cutting, statements that represent the experiences that are nationally representative for our student population. And, given how often our thinking in education policy is driven by visions of "other people's children," there is something important, too, about being able to speak about the "average American student." But, there are also dangers inherent in this style of thinking. Too often there is a temptation set aside our otherwise intimate knowledge of the historical legacies of "local control" and of our immensely idiosyncratic education system and to imagine a coherent, uniform system available for our inspection and intervention. I think these dangers are particularly acute, as I have tried to argue in this chapter, when we are dealing with datasets that give us a window unto the lives of not only a nationally representative of students but unto a substantial portion of their life-course as well.

To be sure these efforts were always undertaken with the best of intentions: during the Cold War the belief was that systems analysis would ensure the maximum development of talent and optimal match between school system and its local context; when notions of equality shifted after *Brown*, researchers shifted from considering the maximum developed in light of local context, to searching for ways to produce equity *in spite of* local context. This meant using data collection – from Project Talent student profiles to NLS72 surveys to HSB student transcripts – to create a national system that, in turn, could be the subject of search and policy intervention; it also meant freezing the future by projecting onto it insights gleaned from the past. Though these developments well-served the needs of education researchers eager to demonstrate their utility in reforming a broken system – analyzing NCES datasets has become more than a cottage industry – the broader outlook is less clear. Though we have reached the point where it has become common to speak about the educational and career trajectory of each child – "No Child Left Behind"; "K-16 pipeline" – the irony of this kind of attention to individual needs is that in doing so we have found the need to efface that student's individual context.

References

Adelman, C. (1983). *Devaluation, diffusion and the college connection: A study of high school transcripts, 1964–1981*. Washington, DC: Department of Education.
Adelman, C. (1999). *Answers in the toolbox*. Washington, DC: Department of Education.
Aikin, W. M. (1942). *The story of the eight-year study*. New York: Harper Brothers.
Akera, A. (2000). Engineers or managers? The systems analysis of electronic data processing in the federal bureaucracy. In T. P. Hughes & A. C. Hughes (Eds.), *Systems experts and computers* (pp. 191–215). Cambridge, MA: MIT Press.
Alexander, K. L., Cook, M., & McDill, E. L. (1978). Curriculum tracking and educational stratification: Some further evidence. *American Sociological Review, 43*(1), 47–66.
Alexander, K. L., Riordan, C., Fennessey, J., & Pallas, A. M. (1982). Social background, academic resources, and college graduation: Recent evidence from the National Longitudinal Survey. *American Journal of Education, 90*(4), 315–333.
Beatty, M. L. (1960, April 3). Fish bowl test may reveal next Einstein. *Chicago Daily Tribune*.

Borgman, J. (1997, April 27). Today's random medical news. *New York Times*, p. E4.

Bryk, A. S., & Raudenbush, S. W. (1988). Toward a more appropriate conceptualization of research on school effects: A three-level hierarchical linear model. *American Journal of Education, 97*(1), 65–108.

Chubb, J. E., & Moe, T. M. (1990a). America's public schools: Choice is a panacea. *The Brookings Review, 8*(3), 4–12.

Chubb, J. E., & Moe, T. E. (1990b). *Politics, markets, and America's schools*. Washington, DC: Brookings Institute Press.

Cohen, D. K., & Moffitt, S. L. (2010). *The ordeal of equality: Did Federal Regulation fix the schools?* London: Harvard University Press.

Coleman, J. S., Campbell, E. W., Hobson, C. J., McPartland, J., Wood, A. M., Weinfeld, F. D., & York, R. L. (1966). *Equality of educational opportunity*. Washington, DC: U.S. Government Printing Office.

Coleman, J. S., Hoffer, T., & Kilgore, S. (1982). *High school achievement: Public, Catholic, and private schools compared*. New York: Basic Books.

Conant, J. B. (1959). *The American high school today: A first report to interested citizens*. New York: McGraw-Hill.

Cooley, W. W., & Lohnes, P. R. (1968). *Multivariate procedures for the behavioral sciences*. New York: Wiley.

Coulson, A. J. (2013). New NAEP scores extend dismal trend in U.S. Education productivity. http://www.cato.org/blog/new-naep-scores-extend-dismal-trend-us-education-productivity

Edwards, P. N. (2000). The world in a machine: Origins and impacts of early computerized global systems models. In T. P. Hughes & A. C. Hughes (Eds.), *Systems experts and computers* (pp. 221–248). Cambridge, MA: MIT Press.

Flanagan, J. C. (1962). *Design for a Study of American youth*. Washington, DC: Office of Education.

Flanagan, J. C. (1978). *Project talent and related efforts to improve secondary education*. Bloomington: Phi Delta Kappa International.

Flanagan, J. C., Dailey, J. T., Shaycroft, M. F., Orr, D. B., & Goldberg, I. (1962). *Studies of the American high school*. Washington, DC: U.S. Office of Education.

Freeman, K. (1996, April 28). John Flanagan, 90, Psychologist who devised pilot aptitude test. *New York Times*. http://www.nytimes.com/1996/04/28/us/john-flanagan-90-psychologist-who-devised-pilot-aptitude-test.html

Gamoran, A., & Berends, M. (1987). The effects of stratification in secondary schools: Synthesis of survey and ethnographic research. *Review of Educational Research, 57*(4), 415–435.

Gamoran, A., & Long, D. A. (2007). Equality of educational opportunity a 40 year retrospective. In R. Teese, S. Lamb, M. Duru-Bellat, & S. Helme (Eds.), *International studies in educational inequality, theory and policy* (pp. 23–47). Dordrecht: Springer.

Gamson, D. (2007). From Progressivism to Federalism: The Pursuit of Equal Educational Opportunity, 1915-1965. In C. Kaestle & A. Lodewick (Eds.), *To education a Nationa: Federal and National Strategies of school reform* (pp. 177–201). Lawrence: University Press of Kansas.

Goodman, S. M. (1958). *The quality measurement project: A research activity conducted by the new York State Education Department*. New York: New York State Department of Education.

Gordon, L. N. (2014). *Opportunity and results: The coleman report and varied uses of 'equality of educational opportunity, 1966–1972*. Paper presented at History of Education Society Conference, Indianapolis, IN.

Hampel, R. L. (1983). The American high school today: James Bryant Conant's reservations and reconsiderations. *Phi Delta Kappan, 64*(9), 607–612.

Hartford Courant. (1960, March 12). Talent tests to begin at weaver high. *The Hartford Courant*. http://search.proquest.com/docview/552553171?accountid=1469

Heyck, H. (2015). *Age of system: Understanding the development of modern social science*. Baltimore: Johns Hopkins Press.

Hoffer, T., & Coleman, J. S. (1987). *Public and private high schools: The impact of communities.* New York: Basic Books.

Jencks, C. (1972). *Inequality: A reassessment of the effect of family and schooling in America.* New York: Basic Books.

Jencks, C., & Brown, M. (1975). Effects of high schools on their students. *Harvard Educational Review, 45*(3), 273–324.

Kaestle, C., & Smith, M. (1982). The Federal Role in elementary and secondary education, 1940–1980. *Harvard Educational Review, 52*(4), 384–408.

Kershaw, J. A., & McKean, R. M. (1959). *Systems analysis and education.* Santa Monica: Rand Corporation.

Kett, J. F. (2012). *Merit: The history of a founding ideal from the American revolution to the twenty-first century.* Ithaca: Cornell University Press.

Kiesler, S., & Turner, C. F. (1977). *Fundamental research and the process of education: Final report to the National Institute of Education.* Washington, DC: National Academies.

Klein, A. (2015, October 22). Who is to blame if NAEP reading and math scores fall? http://blogs. edweek.org/edweek/campaign-k-12/2015/10/who_is_to_blame_if_naep_reading_and_math_scores_fall.html?cmp=SOC-SHR-FB

Labaree, D. F. (1992). *The making of an American high school: The credentials market and the central high School of Philadelphia, 1838–1939.* New Haven: Yale University Press.

Ladson-Billings, G. (2006). From the achievement gap to the education debt: Understanding achievement in US schools. *Educational Researcher, 35*(7), 3–12.

Loveless, T. (2008). *The misplaced math student.* Washington, DC: Brown Center, Brookings Institute.

Ludwig, M. (1982). *A classification of secondary school courses.* Washington, DC: National Center for Education Statistics.

National Commission on Excellence in Education. (1983). *A nation at risk: The imperative for educational reform.* Washington, DC: Department of Education.

National Education Association of the United States. (1918). *Cardinal principles of secondary education: A report of the commission on the reorganization of secondary education, Appointed by the National Education Association.* Bulletin (United States, Bureau of Education), 1918, No. 35. Washington, DC: Government Printing Office.

NCES (National Center for Educational Statics). (2008). *The nation's report card: Long-term trend 2008.* http://nces.ed.gov/pubsearch/pubsinfo.asp?pubid=2009479

NCES (National Center for Educational Statistics). (1993). *120 Years of American education: A statistical portrait.* http://nces.ed.gov/pubs93/93442.pdf

NCES (National Center for Educational Statistics). (2001). *Educational achievement of black-white inequality.* http://nces.ed.gov/pubsearch/pubsinfo.asp?pubid=2001061

NCES (National Center for Educational Statistics). (2012). *Digest of educational statistics.* https://nces.ed.gov/programs/digest/d12/tables/dt12_098.asp

O'Connor, A. (2001). *Poverty Knowledge: Social science, social policy, and the poor in twentieth-century U.S. history.* Princeton: Princeton University Press.

Pallas, A. M., & Alexander, K. L. (1983). Sex differences in quantitative SAT performance: New evidence on the differential coursework hypothesis. *American Educational Research Journal, 20*(2), 165–182.

Peng, S. (1977). *National Longitudinal Study of the high school class of 1972. Review and annotation of study reports.* Washington, DC: National Center for Education Statistics.

Phillips, C. (2014). The new math and midcentury American politics. *Journal of American History, 101*(2), 454–479.

Plantin, J. C., Lagoze, P. N., Edwards, C., Sandvig, C. (Forthcoming). Big data is not about size: When data transform scholarship. http://pne.people.si.umich.edu/PDF/Plantin%20et%20al.%202015%20Big%20Data%20is%20not%20about%20Size%20-%20pre-press%20version.pdf.

Raudenbush, S., & Bryk, A. S. (1986). A Hierarchical Model for Studying School Effects. *Sociology of Education, 59*(1), 1–17.

Reed, D. (2014). *Building the Federal Schoolhouse: Localism and the American education state.* New York: Oxford University Press.

Rivlin, A. M. (1972). *Systematic thinking for social action.* Washington, DC: Brookings Institute.

Rock, D. A. (2012). *Modeling change in large scale longitudinal studies of educational growth: Four decades of contributions to the assessment of growth.* Princeton: Educational Testing Service.

Rodgers, D. T. (2011). *Age of fracture.* Cambridge: Harvard University Press.

Sawchuk, S. (2013, August 7). When bad things happen to good NAEP data. *Education Week.* http://www.edweek.org/ew/articles/2013/07/24/37naep.h32.html

Smeyers, P., & Depaepe, M. (2010). *Educational research the ethics and aesthetics of statistics.* Dordrecht: Springer.

Smith, J. B. (1996). Does an extra year make any difference? The impact of early access to algebra on long-term gains in mathematics attainment. *Educational Evaluation and Policy Analysis, 18*(2), 141–153.

Vinovskis, M. A. (1996). The changing role of the Federal Government in educational research and statistics. *History of Education Quarterly, 36*(2), 110–128.

Validity-Versus-Reliability Tradeoffs and the Ethics of Educational Research

Lynn Fendler

Current educational research projects that rely on testing and measurement are evaluated according to (several types of) validity and (several types of) reliability criteria. In empirical research discourses, the term *reliability* rarely appears except in the company of the term *validity*; one synonym for reliability is "external validity." However, it is not entirely obvious (to me) why validity and reliability are treated as a pair in the research literature. First, reliability and validity are not parallel concepts. *Reliable* describes an instrument; *valid* describes a way of reasoning. Tests can be judged as reliable; but tests cannot be judged as valid. Inferences can be judged as valid or not. Judgments of validity cannot be applied to tests, but only to particular ways of reasoning about testing protocols and the relationship between evidence and results. In those ways, reliability and validity are not epistemologically parallel or comparable concepts.[1]

Moreover, reliability and validity function as competing criteria in research designs; their relationship involves a tradeoff (Matters and Pitman 1994). That is, the stronger the bases for validity, the weaker the bases for reliability (and vice versa). The more a research protocol attends to the particulars of specific cases, the less generalizable the data become. In other words:

> An […] issue related to the reliability of performance-based assessment deals with the trade-off between reliability and validity. As the performance task increases in complexity and authenticity, which serves to increase validity, the lack of standardization serves to decrease reliability. (Paloma and Banta 1999, p. 89)

---

[1] There is some conceptual fuzziness in this paper between educational *research* and educational *testing*. For purposes of this paper, I think the distinction is not very important; much empirical educational research is conducted on the basis of educational test results, and testing instruments constitute the data-collection instruments of much empirical research in education. The validity-reliability tradeoff pertains in empirical educational research whether or not tests are involved.

L. Fendler (✉)
Department of Teacher Education, Michigan State University, East Lansing, MI, USA
e-mail: fendler@msu.edu

© Springer International Publishing AG, part of Springer Nature 2018
P. Smeyers, M. Depaepe (eds.), *Educational Research: Ethics, Social Justice, and Funding Dynamics*, Educational Research 10,
https://doi.org/10.1007/978-3-319-73921-2_10

To some extent, the development in recent decades of increasingly sophisticated statistical instruments can be seen as a series of attempts to ameliorate the problems of the tradeoff between validity and reliability (i.e. between internal and external validity).

This paper does not investigate the issues of tradeoff in the usual terms of "threats to validity" or by differentiating various types of validity and reliability; also, I do not focus on the problems of poorly executed, or unethically implemented research protocols. Rather, I am interested in an investigation of the social justice implications of the validity-reliability tradeoffs in an ideal sense, when the research is done as carefully and competently as possible. There is nothing really new in this argument; rather, my paper attempts to compile perspectives on validity vis-à-vis reliability in a way that shines a spotlight on ethical implications that have been overlooked in the debates about how to conduct good empirical research in education.

Validity and Reliability in the History of Social Science Research

In this section "Validity and reliability in the history of social science research" draw from a range of secondary sources (Baker 2013; Campbell 1959; Kadir 2008; Moss 1992) to trace a brief history of the concept of validity relative to reliability in social science research. A history of the concept of validity provides us with the perspective that validity is not a stable or universally accepted concept; rather validity has been conceptualized variously in different historical contexts and with varying commitments to philosophical stances of realism and pragmatism.

The generally recognized authoritative statement on validity for educational research is the AERA Standards for Educational and Psychological Testing (1985) that specify three categories for validity, namely construct, content, and criterion. The 1985 AERA Standards were based largely on the work of Cronbach (1969, 1971) and Messick (1980), who continued to develop and publish refinements to theories of validity through the 1990s. Although Cronbach and Messick are recognized as giants of validity theory, Moss (1992) provides an analysis that shows how their respective theories of validity do not always agree. Moreover, there have been theories of validity other than those of Cronbach and Messick in the social science research literature (Baker 2013; Kadir 2008; Moss 1992). In general, Messick tended to defend a more objectivist (i.e. philosophical realism) ontology for validity, while Cronbach's stance tended to be more pragmatic. According to Moss (1992):

> For Messick, it seems that adverse social consequences are a source of invalidity only if they are a result of construct invalidity, whereas for Cronbach, adverse social consequences, in and of themselves, call the validity of a test use into question. (Moss 1992, p. 236)

Moss (1992) shows that the meaning of validity vis-à-vis reliability is affected by differences in researchers' stances on realism, positivism, and pragmatism. In psychology, the meaning of validity is also affected by researchers' commitments to idiographic or nomothetic approaches to research (Karson 2007). Idiographic psychological approaches study what makes people unique, and are therefore focused primarily on (internal) validity issues. Nomothetic psychological approaches, in contrast, study what makes people the same; it is in nomothetic approaches to educational research that the issues of the validity-reliability tradeoff are most salient.

In addition to the conceptual variations across schools of thought, the meaning of validity has also been affected by changes over time in the role and importance of statistics in social science research. In general, educational research protocols have moved away from direct observation and replication, and toward the development of models for making inferences: "In the social sciences, statistical tools have changed the nature of research, making inference its major concern and degrading replication, the minimization of measurement error, and other core values to secondary importance" (Gigerenzer and Marewski 2015, p. 423). The increasing importance of inference as a tool of analysis for educational research has greatly elevated the attention paid to reliability as a criterion for evaluating research, and has in turn changed the relationship between validity and reliability in research designs.

In a longer-term historical view, statisticians generally agree on two big shifts in the role of statistics in the history of social science research: the "probabilistic revolution" and the "inference revolution" (Baker 2013; Gigerenzer and Marewski 2015; Moss 1992; Siegfried 2015). The probabilistic revolution (conventionally located in the mid-nineteenth century) refers to a shift away from earlier deterministic and mechanistic assumptions about the world to allow instead for change, chance and mutation (isomorphic with Darwinian evolutionary theories). This nineteenth-century episteme favored statistical models of probability (such as the bell curve) for interpreting data. A century later, the inference revolution (conventionally located in the mid-twentieth century) signaled the new dominance of inference (compared to observation, measurement, and replication) as the highest priority for analysis in social-scientific studies. As Gigerenzer and Marewski (2015) write:

> The qualifier *inference* indicates that among all scientific tools—such as hypothesis formulation, systematic observation, descriptive statistics, minimizing measurement error, and independent replication—the inference from a sample to population grew to be considered the most crucial part of research. (p. 425)

The inference revolution signaled a new relationship between validity and reliability in the social sciences because inference began to take on greater prominence among all the various analytical tools deployed in educational research to establish credibility.

But it is Gigerenzer and Marewski's (2015) next sentence that more dramatically conveys the magnitude of the change ushered in by the inference revolution:

> [The shift to inference] was a stunning new emphasis, given that in most experiments, psychologists virtually never drew a random sample from a population or defined a population in the first place. (p. 425)

If it is true that prior to the inference revolution "psychologists virtually never drew a random sample from a population or defined a population in the first place," then previous educational and psychological research would have been concerned not with reliability, but with measurement accuracy, internal validity, and replicability as the salient criteria on which to evaluate research designs and reports (i.e. an idiographic approach to research). Later however, when inference became the most important factor in the analysis of research data, a new dimension of concepts and classifications was developed on which to formulate those inferences. The social science research literature agrees uniformly that inference-based nomothetic-oriented educational research has become the dominant approach.

One effect of the inference revolution in educational research was to create "populations," a process that eventually reified aspects of human variation, which was captured in language such as "at-risk student." Populational classifications stipulated which aspects of human variation count as "the same" (i.e. one population), and which aspects of variation count as "different" (i.e. different populations). The rising prominence of inference and the tendency to think of research results in terms of populations became mutually reinforcing. Following the inference revolution, the people on whom educational research had been conducted were no longer regarded as individual people but objectified as "members of a population."

In sum, prior to the inference revolution, social scientific research had been concerned primarily with idiographic research criteria of internal validity, observational acuity, measurement accuracy, and replicability; there was little importance attached to extrapolation of findings from one context to another, and so reliability was not a major issue. After the inference revolution, however, the value of direct observation was overshadowed by attempts to use inference to generalize from one context or one population to another on the basis of a relatively small sample size, a movement that underscored the need for standards of reliability (external validity). In this rendition of history, we can see that reliability is a relatively recent addition to the criteria for good research. Reliability became increasingly important in the twentieth century in the wake of the inference revolution, and the tradeoff between validity and reliability has become more dynamic year after year since the mid-twentieth century.

The criterion of reliability is associated primarily with generalization; reliability refers to the degree to which research findings pertain to people in times and places other than those on whom the research was conducted (see also Fendler 2006). It has become a commonplace assumption in the United States that research in all fields and all paradigms ought to be generalizable. Currently in my university, for example, generalizability is a required component in the definition of research. Here is the language from the Institutional Review Board of Michigan State University that defines research as having two necessary components, "systematic investigation" and "designed to contribute to generalizable knowledge."

This definition of research clearly reflects priorities consistent with the inference revolution because it is stipulated that all research presents generalizable knowledge. If an activity does not present generalizable knowledge, that activity is no

Generalizable Knowledge

To be considered "generalizable knowledge," the activity would include the following concepts:

- Knowledge contributes to a theoretical framework of an established body of knowledge
- Results are expected to be generalized to a larger population beyond the site of data collection or population studied
- Results are intended to be replicated in other settings

MSU HRPP Manual Section 4-3, Determination of Human Subject Research

The IRB chair, staff, or member will evaluate whether the activity is a "systematic investigation" and whether it is "designed to develop or contribute to generalizable knowledge."

To be considered a "systematic investigation," the concept of a research study must:

- Attempt to answer research questions (in some research, this would be a hypothesis)
- Is methodologically driven, i.e. it collects data or information in an organized and consistent way
- Data or information is analyzed in some way, be it quantitative or qualitative data analysis
- Conclusions are drawn from the results

To be considered "generalizable knowledge," the activity would include the following concepts:

- Knowledge contributes to a theoretical framework of an established body of knowledge
- Results are expected to be generalized to a larger population beyond the site of data collection or population studied
- Results are intended to be replicated in other settings

Presently, Michigan State University (MSU) masters' theses and Ph.D. dissertations are considered to present generalizable knowledge. (From HRPP website: http://hrpp.msu.edu/definitions-generalizable-knowledge)

longer called research. Because generalizability is a requirement for research, and validity is the primary criterion on which research is evaluated, there is a built-in and inevitable tradeoff between validity and reliability in virtually all scholarly activities that are officially designated as research in education and elsewhere.

It is relatively easy to see how validity and reliability function together as a trade-off in quantitative educational research. However, it is also worth noting that similar and parallel values are built into most qualitative research designs in education.[2] When qualitative research protocols attempt to address credibility and trustworthiness, the aim is quite similar to the efforts to establish validity and reliability in quantitative research. According to the popular textbook on qualitative research by Lincoln and Guba (1985), the four criteria for establishing trustworthiness in qualitative research are:

1. *'Truth value'*[3]: How can one establish confidence in the 'truth' of the findings of a particular inquiry for the subjects (respondents) with which and the context in which the inquiry was carried out?
2. *Applicability*: How can one determine the extent to which the findings of a particular inquiry have applicability in other contexts or with other subjects (respondents)?
3. *Consistency*: How can one determine whether the findings of a particular inquiry would be repeated if the inquiry were replicated with the same (or similar) subjects (respondents) in the same (or similar) context?
4. *Neutrality*: How can one establish the degree to which the findings of an inquiry are determined by the subjects (respondents) and conditions of the inquiry and not by the biases, motivations, interests, or perspectives of the inquirer? (Lincoln and Guba 1985, p. 290)

In this widely cited passage, we can see parallels between the epistemological values in quantitative and qualitative research criteria: "truth value" and neutrality correspond with validity; applicability and consistency correspond with reliability. In this way, the ethical issues in the tradeoff between validity and reliability pertain to both quantitative and qualitative projects in educational research. Even idiographic social science research may aim for generalization when insights from individual cases are meant to contribute to more general knowledge about people and phenomena related to education.

Ethical and Social Justice Issues

This part of the chapter describes four ethical and social justice issues associated with the validity-reliability tradeoff in educational research: bootstrapping, stereotyping, dehumanization, and determinism.

---

[2] Thanks to Jeff Bale for pointing this out.

[3] I don't know why scare quotes appear around the term "truth value" but not around the other terms on the list.

Bootstrapping: Ethical Issues of Construct Validation

I wouldn't have seen it if I hadn't believed it. (Marshall McLuhan)

Construct validation is the means by which research protocols are operationalized, and is therefore foundational for all research that calls itself empirical (see, e.g. Cherryholmes 1988; Cronbach and Meehl 1955; Fiske 2002; Mackenzie 2003). Cizek (2007) wrote: "All validity is construct validity" (slide 9). Constructs are – by definition – not empirical, and yet construct validity is the foundation of empirical research in the social sciences.

"Bootstrapping" refers to the conservative and reproductive features of closed-system research designs. Constructs are located within a famously designated "nomothetic network" (Messick 1998), which means that constructs are validated by making reference to existing constructs – not by making reference to observed data. Westen and Rosenthal (2003) describe construct validation as theory-dependent in this way:

> Construct validation is a bootstrapping operation: Initial (often vague and intuitive) theories about a construct lead to creation of a measure designed to have content validity vis-à-vis the construct as understood at that point in time. (Westen and Rosenthal 2003, p. 609)

The bootstrapping feature of construct validation builds reproduction into the system because new constructs are considered valid if and only if they align with existing constructs. The bootstrapping nature of construct validation is an ethical issue in educational research when existing hierarchical stratifications of populations tend to get reproduced. Bootstrapping occurs as a function of the tradeoff between validity and reliability because the goal of construct validation is to capture both categorical specificity and generalizability at the same time. As a matter of contrast, replicability (unlike construct validation) is a criterion for evaluating research that does not necessarily rely on bootstrapping.

Constructs are culturally and historically specific; they are products of intuition and discourse. Statisticians and psychometricians repeatedly remind us that constructs do not exist; they are "the product of informed scientific imagination" (Crocker and Algina 1986, p. 230). The bootstrapping nature of construct validation sometimes implies that features of outdated social views continue to get built into research instruments and to influence judgments of validation because the constructs of new research must be validated by aligning them with the constructs of previous research.

The conservative effect of bootstrapping is an ethical issue to the extent that harmful constructs are tacitly reproduced and reinforced in research projects that purport to build upon previous research findings. Perhaps one of the most egregious examples of the harmful effects of bootstrapping is IQ testing. The development of the Stanford version of IQ tests entailed a series of revisions to the testing instrument, each of which was "normed" relative to previous tests (Terman 1916). This means that test items were repeatedly revised until new tests reproduced the same distribution that had been established by previous versions of the instrument (see also Fendler and Muzaffar 2008). The Stanford version of the IQ test was designed in the context of the eugenics movement, explicitly to sort people on the basis of race. Therefore, we know that construct validity in IQ tests is rooted in the heinous assumption of White racial superiority. The construct continues to be reproduced in the validity-reliability loop of construct validation of IQ and other standardized testing instruments. This reproduction can be seen in current educational research on the so-called "achievement gap."

Stereotyping: Reification in Sampling and Representation

Reduction of confusing variables is the primary desideratum in all experiments. (Gould 1981, p. 367)

The validity-reliability tradeoff contributes to the (re)production of stereotypes by working to specify demographic specificity and generalizability at the same time. Validity alone would not contribute to stereotyping because there would be no attempt to generalize claims; reliability alone (if there could be such a thing) would not contribute to stereotyping because there would be no attribution of general tendencies to individuals. Schwartz and Arena (2013) raise the point that the validity-reliability tradeoff has had the effect of reification: "the methodological demand of reliability coincides with a tendency of people to take an essentialist perspective that reifies assessments into stable traits or essences of a person" (Schwartz and Arena, p. 117). Reification works to interpellate identities according to the classifications that have been invented to define and specify populations. The concepts and practices of sampling in social science research work only when a researcher believes that (1) there is an identifiable population, and (2) a given sample can represent that population.

Statistical tests that attend to both validity and reliability provide descriptions of aggregates, not descriptions of individuals; however, the combination of validity together with reliability has had the discursive effect of specifying individual characteristics in populational terms (i.e. reification). Eubanks' (2012) articulation helps to pinpoint the difference between inference and probability in the reification of constructs. He wrote:

To me, the only sensible sorts of questions that can be checked for validity are ones like this: "The probability of X happening is bounded by Y." This involves a minimum amount of theoretical construction in order to talk about probabilities, but avoids the reification fallacy of statements like 'Tatiana has good writing ability.' (Eubanks 2012, online)

This caveat offered by a statistician calls attention to the difference between a research framework based on probability and a research framework based on inference. The nuance expressed in Eubanks' cautionary statement is less fashionable in a research context that focuses almost exclusively on inference, as does the current research climate.

Similar arguments about reification fallacies have been made in the U.S. popular press since at least 1922. For example, journalist Walter Lippman, in response to Lewis Terman's (1910s) statistical work at Stanford on IQ tests wrote:

> [The IQ test] tends to show that the gross result is reached in the mass by statistically impartial methods, however wrong the judgment about any particular child may be. But the fairness in giving the tests and the reliability of the tests themselves must not be confused. The tests may be quite fair applied in the mass, and yet be poor tests of individual intelligence. (Lippman 1922, p. 276)

The issues of validity-reliability tradeoff have been controversial in debates about educational research ethics for at least a century, and yet the emphasis on inference has continued to grow, and the reification effects have contributed to the perpetuation of stereotypes.

Inferences in social science research are derived from data taken from "samples." Sampling techniques are evaluated as a component of an overall judgment of validity. To begin with, all sampling requires that we first create a population, a set of descriptors that circumscribes one group of people and separates that group from all other groups. In order to create populations, it becomes necessary to control variables, and to control variables means to control variation. As Eubanks (2012) writes:

> Unlike electrons, humans are intrinsically variable. So in order to squeeze out all the variability in human performance, we have to imagine idealizing them, and that automatically sacrifices reality for a convenient theory (like economists assuming that humans are perfectly rational). (Eubanks 2012)

Controlling variation is an inevitable product of the validity-reliability tradeoff, and the control of variation tends to produce stereotypes in research findings through the invention of populations and reification fallacies. When it is assumed that we can "sample a population," the populational attributes (i.e. stereotypes) get applied not only to aggregates, but also to individuals who are seen as "representative" of stereotypes.

Steele and Aronson's (1995) famous study that has become known as the "stereotype threat" serves as one example of the ethical problems of stereotyping, even within the domain of educational research itself. In their controlled-experiment study, standardized tests were administered to different groups of students. Just before students began the test, the treatment groups were told that the test results were going to be used in a study about demographic differences. The control groups were told that the test results were going to be used in a study about mental processing. In the treatment groups, when the focus was on race and gender, the test scores for African American and Latino students were significantly lower than in the control cases. In Steele and Aronson's study, the test scores of high-achieving African American students were lowered in conditions when it was merely suggested that negative racial stereotypes could affect the test they were about to take.

Another way to think about the relation between stereotypes and behavior is what Hacking (1995) calls the "looping effect" of human kinds. Hacking introduces his concept of looping in the context of a book about causal reasoning. By looping, Hacking means that as categories get constructed from averages, causal connections are made to help "explain" the categories. In discourse, these categories and causes about human kinds become part of knowledge, of which we humans are both subjects and objects. Hacking provides examples from psychiatry and pediatrics to illustrate that the relation between classification and the attribution of cause is a chicken-and-egg loop:

> Which comes first, the classification or the causal connections between kinds? [T]o acquire and use a name for any kind is, among other things, to be willing to make generalizations and form expectations about things of that kind. The kind and the knowledge grow together. [In the case of pediatric X-rays and child abuse] cause, classification, and intervention were of a piece. (Hacking 1995, p. 361)

Similarly, in the case of Steele and Aronson's stereotype threat, the test scores of the African American students can be seen as a reiteration of stereotypes in a kind of self-fulfilling prophecy with disastrous effects.

Dehumanization in Operationalization

Much empirical research in education is based on psychological studies, which have for decades included experiments on lab rats. Edward Thorndike's (1898) doctoral dissertation, *Animal Intelligence* included the line: "this hitherto unsuspected law of animal mind may prevail in human mind to an extent hitherto unknown" (Thorndike 1898, p. 105). Thorndike was evidently entertaining the belief that experiments on animals could yield insight into human learning. In 1899 Thorndike was appointed to the faculty of Psychology at Teachers College where he applied findings and research designs from his lab-rat experiments to the study of human teaching and learning.

There is some disagreement in the psychology literature about whether Thorndike ought to be considered a behaviorist. In any case, it is generally agreed that Thorndike's approach to the study of learning at least paved the way for the strictly behaviorist theories of B.F. Skinner and Ivan Pavlov. Behaviorist research operationalizes constructs such as learning in terms of the behavior that is exhibited under conditions of reward and punishment. Researchers don't care what the rat is thinking when it pushes a lever for food; they care only about the frequency and conditions of that repetition. Despite the claims by psychologists that behaviorism became outmoded in the mid-twentieth century, educational research still subscribes to behaviorism in most studies of motivation, including all studies that involve so-called incentives and disincentives like evaluation marks and test scores. To the extent that behaviorism is based on assumptions derived from experiments with lab rats, it is not difficult to recognize how operationalization contributes to dehumanization in educational research.[4]

---

[4] I have never understood how research methods or findings could be extrapolated from animals to humans. I just don't get how it could have occurred to researchers (such as Thorndike) to imagine that findings from experiments on lab rats could be applied to teaching and learning for the people

The ethical issue of dehumanization in operationalization can be illustrated with Biesta's (2010) specification of subjectification as one of the purposes of education[5]:

> The subjectification function might perhaps best be understood as the opposite of the socialization function. It is precisely not about the insertion of 'newcomers' into existing orders, but about ways of being that hint at independence from such orders, ways of being in which the individual is not simply a "specimen" of a more encompassing order. (Biesta 2010, p. 20)

In this specification, we can understand subjectification as that which makes us uniquely human. Idiographic research, which is concerned with internal validity, may serve discursively to illustrate subjectification. However, in the context of a validity-reliability tradeoff, the demands of nomothetic validation render subjectification a confounding variable. In that way operationalization contributes to dehumanization.

Prediction and Determinism

Modern social-science research has been characterized by its twin agenda of scientific neutrality and social improvement since its inception in the late nineteenth century (see, e.g. Heilbron et al. 1998). If research agendas were scientifically neutral, then researchers would not work so hard to make predictive claims. The purpose of prediction is to provide warrants for social policy, and specifically for establishing social management policies that will avoid and/or correct mistakes of the past. Educational research agendas that provide predictions are based on a historiographical assumption that shares Santayana's belief that "Those who cannot remember the past are condemned to repeat it."

In his Foucault-style genealogy, Castel (1991) traces shifts in discourses of medicine and public health from dangerousness to risk from the mid-nineteenth through later twentieth century in France and in the United States. Castel's genealogy covers the period identified by statisticians as the time of shift from probability to inference. Castel's analysis of the shift from dangerousness to risk is commensurate with the shift from probabilistic to inferential models for calculations of data, and in that way, Castel's analysis provides insight into the way the validity-reliability tradeoff in research has come to determine what has become (im)possible for us to think.

Castel defines "dangerousness" as an immediately present threat, and distinguishes it from "risk" which is a calculated and probabilistic estimation of a future threat. The shift from dangerousness to risk can be seen in the implementation of eugenics programs in the early twentieth century:

---

in Teachers College. But we humans can be taught, and apparently we have learned to behave like rats when we are treated as such.

[5] The other purposes specified by Biesta (2010) are qualification and socialization. Biesta uses the term *subjectification* very differently from the way Foucault uses it.

Eugenics also starts to reason in terms of risks rather than dangers; the goal of an intervention made in the name of preservation of the race is much less to treat a particular individual than to prevent the threat he or she carries from being transmitted to descendants. Accordingly, the prophylactic measure of sterilization can be applied in a much more widespread and resolute preventive manner than confinement, since it can suppress future risks, on the basis of a much broader range of indication than those of mental illness strictly defined. (Castel 1991, p. 285)

Castel's analysis traces shifts in the roles of public health administrators relative to doctors and practitioners. When research is shaped by calculations of risk (rather than dangerousness), then the administrator becomes more important than the doctor because risk is calculated on the basis of abstract statistical relationships (the knowledge base of administrators), and not face-to-face meetings with patients (the knowledge base of doctors). We can see parallel trends in the history of educational research and the increasing importance of administrators' knowledge relative to teachers' knowledge for shaping educational policies and practices.

When research modalities shifted from probability to inference, further implications arose. In a research climate dominated by inferential models, educational administrators tend to establish policies that are based on the predictions of inference-driven research. These administrative policies have come to replace the findings and diagnoses created by professionals (i.e. teachers). In that way, the prophecies engendered by probability models have been replaced by inferences that function to determine what is possible for any given child. As Castel wrote:

Instead of segregating and eliminating undesirable elements from the social body, or reintegrating them more or less forcibly through corrective or therapeutic interventions, the emerging tendency is to assign different social destinies to individuals in line with their varying capacity to live up to the requirements of competitiveness and profitability. (Castel 1991, p. 294)

The trends in medicine and public health documented by Castel can also be seen in education when results of testing and measurement are used to determine children's futures. Educational test results in the twenty-first century are products of research that balances specific information about individual children (internal validity) with generalizable descriptions of populational trends (reliability). In that way the validity-reliability tradeoff functions administratively to determine children's futures using social constructs that were validated with reference to the same nomothetic network as the constructs that underpinned the eugenics movement.

Recent Trends in Validity-Reliability Studies

All tests are wrong all the time. It's only a matter of degree. (Eubanks 2012)

Educational research in the twenty-first century is facing changes in technological affordances, political demands, and economic fashions. In these changing contexts, there are emerging trends in social science research that have the potential to displace the validity-reliability tradeoff as a central concern for the evaluation of educational research. Four of those trends are: the introduction of translational sciences, a shift from significance to replicability, a move from inference to Big Data, and the increasing importance of consequential validity.

Introduction of "Translational Sciences"

The gap between laboratory research and clinical application has become particularly salient in biomedical fields. Laboratory research on pharmaceutical interventions, for example, does not always translate well into clinical applications. In an effort to manage the gap between research and clinical practice, a field called "translational sciences" has been invented to concentrate on bridging laboratory findings with findings in clinical settings. The U.S. National Institutes of Health now sponsors a National Center for Advancing Translational Sciences (NIH 2007), and it is now possible to get a Ph.D. in Translational Sciences in some U.S. universities. From these trends we can see that there is increasing attention to the gap between research and practice.

Translational sciences have been developed for biomedical research, and the concepts of translational sciences do not apply precisely to the field of education because educational research is (for the most part) not laboratory based. However, the recent flourishing of this new field of translational sciences does signal more attention to the problems that arise from inferential models of research whenever attempts are made to apply research in practice. The introduction and rapid growth of translational sciences signal a departure from some of the issues of the validity-reliability tradeoff insofar as it is no longer assumed that inferences from controlled studies will "translate" directly into clinical settings.

From Significance to Replicability

There is evidence that some recent social science research trends have begun to de-emphasize "statistical significance" as a major criterion for determining the quality and importance of research findings. For example, p-values are becoming more suspect as indicators of good or important research findings; some scientific journals have even banned p-values as criteria for evaluating research (Nuzzo 2014). The move away from inference and significance has turned instead to the importance of replicability of research findings as a criterion of quality.

Nuzzo (2014) describes the misuse and overemphasis on statistical significance as "p-hacking," the analytical process of trying multiple approaches until p-values reach the magical "significance" number of 0.05. Nuzzo wrote:

> Such practices [as p-hacking] have the effect of turning discoveries from exploratory studies — which should be treated with scepticism — into what look like sound confirmations but vanish on replication. (Nuzzo 2014, online)

With increasing rejection of p-values as the "holy grail" of good research, there seems to be an indication that social science researchers are becoming more aware and critical of the degree to which inference has taken over other kinds of judgments about research quality. In place of an overemphasis on p-values, researchers and statisticians are beginning to advocate a return of replicability as a more important criterion for evaluating research.

From Inference to Big Data

The term Big Data refers to data sets that are so massive that they cannot be managed using conventional analytical processing tools. For example, biomedical research has begun to use social-media data mining to make predictions about such things as disease outbreaks. These research practices reduce the need for inference in data analysis because there is more actual data than just a sample size. With less emphasis on inference, reliability becomes less of an issue. For example, the Center for Disease Control (U.S.) had previously been dependent on reliability functions for developing models to predict the outbreak of diseases. However, the CDC now monitors social-media and Google-search trends to find indications of disease outbreaks. When the CDC can receive data analytics that show a sudden spike in Google searches for "TheraFlu," the inference about disease patterns is not based on a statistical model that has sacrificed specificity for reliability.

Educational assessment designers, Schwartz and Arena (2013) advocate that educational assessments in the digital age would be improved if we moved away from an emphasis on inference-heavy models and moved instead to the analysis of Big Data (data mining): "If we let go of inferential statistics and dreams of proof, we can embrace a new set of *data-mining tools* for handling behavioral data" (Schwartz and Arena 2013, p. 117; emphasis in original).

From Internal Validity to Consequential Validity

The second decade of the twenty-first century has brought attention to yet another category of validity, namely consequential validity. Shepard (2013) elaborates on consequential validity by distinguishing two competing purposes of assessment: accountability and learning. She wrote:

> Accountability tests cover too broad a range of content (a year's worth at a minimum) and too broad a range of proficiency levels to be useful to diagnose the learning needs of specific students.... To be truly instructionally relevant for individual students and to serve formative purposes, very different assessments are needed.... Reliability is not as great a concern when the purpose of assessment is to support learning. (Shepard 2013, p. 7)

Consequential validity addresses the impacts of assessments on educational performance, including both accountability and learning. The emergence of consequential validity as an issue is associated with the increase in the use of performance assessments (portfolios, etc.) instead of multiple-choice tests. Because so much educational research uses assessments as data, consequential validity has implications for the ethics of educational research. Philosopher of validity Moss (1992) wrote:

> Beyond considering the social consequences of assessment-based interpretations and actions, … we need to consider the social consequences of the methods by which we warrant those interpretations and actions. We need to expand our conception of validity to include questions about why particular methods of inquiry are privileged and what the effects of that privileging are on the community. (Moss 1992, pp. 253–254)

Consequential validity is an assessment of the impact of research instruments on the very educational processes those instruments purport to measure.

Whose Interests Have Been Served by Research?

In general, I have found that statisticians tend to be more tentative and nuanced in their claims of findings than are social scientists who appropriate statistical methodologies as protocols for designing and reporting on educational research. Remarking on the differences between statisticians and social scientists, Gigerenzer and Marewski write:

> Practicing statisticians rely on a 'statistical toolbox' and on their expertise to select a proper tool; social scientists, in contrast, tend to rely on a single tool. (Gigerenzer and Marewski 2015, p. 422)

Gigerenzer and Marewski (2015) go even further to suggest that the inference revolution took hold because "significance levels" (e.g. p-values) provided journal editors with a convenient and seemingly objective basis on which to decide which research articles to publish:

> Indeed, the inference revolution was not led by the leading scientists. It was spearheaded by humble nonstatisticians who composed statistical textbooks for education, psychology, and other fields and by the editors of journals who found in 'significance' a simple, 'objective' criterion for deciding whether or not to accept a manuscript. (Gigerenzer and Marewski 2015, p. 429)

According to Gigerenzer and Marewski, the tendency for social scientists to emphasize inference has grown to the point of absurdity. In efforts to evaluate research objectively and impartially, the research community has come to the point of sacrificing common sense and professional judgment in the determination of what counts as good research.

When we ask whose interests are served by research, it becomes easy to see that the research that is most useful for policy makers may not be the same kind of research that is most useful for teachers. Policy makers want generalizable knowledge; teachers want context-specific knowledge. Fenstermacher (1994) defined "practical knowledge" as knowledge confined to a particular time and place, and distinguished that from "formal knowledge," which can be generalized across contexts. Cochran-Smith and Lytle (1999) draw on that distinction to explain how teacher research is practical knowledge that does not aim for generalizability. Moreover, they add, generalizable knowledge is rarely useful for teachers because it does not pertain to the specific context of teaching in which teachers work. In this way, generalizability raises the ethical question of who benefits from research. Research that aims for generalizable knowledge may serve university researchers insofar as it advances their publishing careers and garners grant funding. Generalizable knowledge may also help policy makers who are seeking warrants for advancing particular reform agendas. However, research that aims for generalizable knowledge does not serve teachers or students.

Another example of serving disparate interests is the issue of purpose in research. For example, it is reasonable to ask whether educational research is designed to measure qualifications that are most valued by universities and/or the qualities that are most valued by societies and/or the qualities that are most valued by individuals and/or the qualities that are most valued by institutional establishments. Berkeley law school researchers Shultz and Zedeck (2008) asked exactly that question about standard law school admission tests (e.g. LSAT). They conducted an extensive study of the relationship between test scores and desirable qualifications for lawyers, and found that the LSAT did predict grade-point average in law school; however, LSAT scores did not predict (or were negatively correlated!) with the characteristics of effective lawyers (Shultz and Zedeck 2008). This is an example of research serving the interests of institutional administrations, and failing to serve the interests of the general public who need qualified and effective lawyers. (For similar arguments about other fields, see also Bloomberg 2005; Jenkins 1946).

The inference revolution in research and the derivatives market in the stock exchange are both examples of contemporary trends that have removed our work from the plane of bodily and material interactions far away onto the plane of abstract inferences. When that happens, experts are put at an advantage, and ordinary people have a more difficult time getting access to the complicated and esoteric tools that have become necessary for the production of research knowledge and/or the production of wealth.

Current practices in financial sectors in most parts of the world are homologous with current practices in statistical modeling because both have resulted in the creation of a particular kind of expert elite whose models of stock trading or educational policy are not available to the general public, or even to other kinds of experts. Stock-market trading used to be dominated by direct investments so that when a business profited, stockholders would also profit. However, since the twentieth century, stock-market transactions have been dominated instead by derivative trading. Derivative trading is based on complex statistical models of prediction and contingency. In derivative trading, it is not the case that investors will profit when a corporation does well; in fact, there is no necessary relationship between a corporation's performance and stock market profits. Rather, it has become possible to invest abstractly in the stock market by betting on the outcome of a complicated algorithm. "Shorting" a stock means to bet against a stock price (to bet the stock price would decrease) or to bet that the price of a certain stock would change X points in Y days, or change relative to a competing stock.

These trends in futures/options/derivative trading in the stock market are homologous with the inference revolution in research in which knowledge production relies on increasingly esoteric and specialized manipulations of data relative to claims. Both trends support the creation of an administrative elite who establish research/investing models that benefit those who have designed the models, and exclude other points of view and other epistemologies. Voices and perspectives that do not speak the language of high-brow inferential models are generally dismissed from serious "data-driven" conversations about educational research. When the validity-reliability tradeoff dominates the standards and criteria by which research is evaluated, then perspectives from other research paradigms are rendered irrelevant. This univocal trend works against diversity and democratic access to participation in debates about what education might mean, and how educational policy or teaching decisions might be made.

Finally, validation is the opposite of critique. When research focuses primarily on the validity-reliability tradeoff as the criterion for inclusion in educational decision-making, critique is foreclosed. The current relationship between validity and reliability in research makes it virtually impossible to raise dissenting opinions and to include the perspectives of anyone other than a small and homogeneous group of privileged research traditions for which nomothetic validity is a euphemism for maintaining a closed loop of inference.

References

American Educational Research Association, American Psychological Association, & National Council on Measurement in Education. (1985). *Standards for educational and psychological testing*. Washington, DC: American Psychological Association.

Baker, E. L. (2013). The chimera of validity. *Teachers College Record, 115*(9), 1–26. http://www.tcrecord.org. ID Number: 17106. Date Accessed: 4/23/2015 3:06:16 PM.

Biesta, G. (2010). *Good education in an age of measurement: Ethics, politics, democracy*. Boulder: Paradigm Publishers.

Campbell, D. T. (1959). Convergent and discriminant validation by the multitrait-multimethod matrix. *Psychological Bulletin, 56*, 81–105.

Castel, R. (1991). From dangerousness to risk. In G. Burchell, C. Gordon, & P. Miller (Eds.), *The Foucault effect: Studies in governmentality* (pp. 281–298). Chicago: University of Chicago Press.

Cherryholmes, C. H. (1988). *Power and criticism: Poststructural investigations in education*. New York: Teachers College Press.

Cizek, G. J. (2007, August). *Introduction to modern validity theory and practice.* Invited *presentation to the National Assessment Governing Board*, McLean, VA. Available: https://www.nagb.gov/content/nagb/assets/documents/naep/cizek-introduction-validity.pdf

Cochran-Smith, M., & Lytle, S. L. (1999). The teacher research movement: A decade later. *Educational Researcher, 28*, 15–25. https://doi.org/10.3102/0013189X028007015.

Crocker, L., & Algina, J. (1986). Introduction to classical and modern test theory. Orlando: Harcourt Brace.

Cronbach, L. J. (1969). Validation of educational measures. In P. H. H. DuBois (Ed.), *Proceedings of the invitational conference on testing problems* (pp. 35–52). Princeton: Educational Testing Service.

Cronbach, L. J. (1971). Test validation. In R. L. Thorndike (Ed.), *Educational measurement* (2nd ed., pp. 443–507). Washington, DC: American Council on Education.

Cronbach, L. J., & Meehl, P. E. (1955). Construct validity in psychological tests. *Psychological Bulletin, 52*(4), 281–302. https://doi.org/10.1037/h0040957. PMID 13245896.

Eubanks, D. (2012, June 8). *Bad reliability, part two.* http://highered.blogspot.com/2012/06/bad-reliability-part-two.html

Fendler, L. (2006). Why generalisability is not generalisable. *Journal of the Philosophy of Education, 40*(4), 437–449.

Fendler, L., & Muzaffar, I. (2008). The history of the bell curve: Sorting and the idea of normal. *Educational Theory, 58*(1), 63–82.

Fenstermacher, G. (1994). The knower and the known: The nature of knowledge in research on teaching. In L. Darling-Hammond (Ed.), *Review of research in education* (Vol. 20, pp. 3–56). Washington, DC: American Educational Research Association.

Fiske, D. W. (2002). Validity for what? In H. I. Braun, N. Jackson, & D. Wiley (Eds.), *The role of constructs in psychological and educational measurement* (pp. 169–178). Hillsdale: Lawrence Erlbaum.

Gigerenzer, G., & Marewski, J. N. (2015, February). Surrogate science: The idol of a universal method for scientific inference. *Journal of Management, 41*(2), 421–440. https://doi.org/10.1177/0149206314547522.

Gould, S. J. (1981). *The mismeasure of man.* New York: W.W. Norton.

Hacking, I. (1995). The looping effects of human kinds. In D. Sperber, D. Premack, & A. J. Premack (Eds.), *Causal cognition: A multidisciplinary debate* (pp. 351–394). Oxford: Clarendon Press.

Heilbron, J., Magnusson, L., & Wittrock, B. (Eds.). (1998). *The rise of the social sciences and the formation of modernity: Conceptual change in context, 1750–1850.* Boston: Kluwer Academic Publishers.

Jenkins, J. G. (1946). Validity for what? *Journal of Consulting Psychology, 10*, 93–98.

Kadir, K. A. (2008). *Framing a validity argument for test use and impact: The Malaysian public service experience* (esp. chapter 2 on history of validity p. 29). Dissertation.

Karson, M. (2007). Nomothetic versus idiographic. In N. J. Salkind & K. Rasmussen (Eds.), *Encyclopedia of Measurement and statistics.* New York: Sage. https://doi.org/10.4135/9781412952644.

Lincoln, Y. S., & Guba, E. G. (1985). *Naturalistic inquiry.* Newbury Park: Sage.

Lippman, W. (1922, November 8). The reliability of intelligence tests. *The New Republic* (pp. 275–277).

MacKenzie, S. B. (2003). The dangers of poor construct conceptualization. *Journal of the Academy of Marketing Science, 31*(3), 323–326.

Matters, G., & Pitman, J. A. (1994). The validity–reliability trade-off. *20th annual conference of the International Association for Educational Assessment (IAEA).* Wellington.

Messick, S. (1980). Test validity and the ethics of assessment. *American Psychologist, 35*(11), 1012–1027.

Messick, S. (1998). Test validity: A matter of consequence. *Social Indicators Research, 45*(1–3), 35–44.

Moss, P. A. (1992). Shifting conceptions of validity in educational measurement: Implications for performance assessment. *Review of Educational Research, 62*(3), 229. Retrieved from http://

ezproxy.msu.edu.proxy1.cl.msu.edu/login?url=http://search.proquest.com.proxy1.cl.msu.edu/docview/1290947129?accountid=12598.

NIH [National Institutes of Health]. (2007, October 15). *National center for advancing translational sciences*. Available: https://ncats.nih.gov/. Accessed 31 Oct 2015.

Nuzzo, R. (2014, February 13). Scientific method: Statistical errors. *Nature, 506*, 150–152. https://doi.org/10.1038/506150a.http://www.nature.com/news/scientific-method-statistical-errors-1.14700

Paloma, C. A., & Banta, T. W. (1999). *Assessment essentials: Planning, implementing, improving*. New York: Jossey-Bass.

Reliability vs. validity. (2005, September 26). *Bloomberg business*. Online version available: http://www.bloomberg.com/bw/stories/2005-09-28/reliability-vs-dot-validity

Schwartz, D. L., & Arena, D. (2013). *Measuring what matters most: Choice-based assessments for the digital age*. Cambridge, MA: MIT Press.

Shepard, L. A. (2013). Validity for what purpose? *Teachers College Record, 115*(9), 1–12. http://www.tcrecord.org ID Number: 17116, Date Accessed: 10/14/2015 8:12:55 AM.

Shultz, M. M., & Zedeck, S. (2008). *Identification, development, and validation of predictors for successful lawyering*. Berkeley Law School Research Grant Report. https://www.law.berkeley.edu/files/LSACREPORTfinal-12.pdf

Siegfried, T. (2015, July 2). Science is heroic, with a tragic (statistical) flaw. *Science News* Online. https://www.sciencenews.org/blog/context/science-heroic-tragic-statistical-flaw

Steele, C. M., & Aronson, J. (1995). Stereotype threat and the intellectual test performance of African-Americans. *Journal of Personality and Social Psychology, 69*(5), 797–811.

Terman, L. M. (1916). *The measurement of intelligence: An explanation of and a complete guide for the use of the Stanford revision and extension of the Binet-Simon intelligence scale*. Boston: Houghton Mifflin.

Thorndike, E. L. (1898). Animal intelligence: An experimental study of the associative processes in animals. *The Psychological Review: Monograph Supplements, 2*(4), i–109. https://doi.org/10.1037/h0092987.

Westen, D., & Rosenthal, R. (2003). Quantifying construct validity: Two simple measures. *Journal of Personality and Social Psychology, 84*(3), 608–618. https://doi.org/10.1037/0022-3514.84.3.608. Accessed 23 Oct 2015 4:30:19 PM EDT.

Schwab's Challenge and the Unfulfilled Promise of Action Research

Chris Higgins

Introduction

Action research began as an ambitious epistemological and social intervention. As the concept has become reified, packaged for methodology textbooks and professional development workshops, it has degenerated into a cure that may be worse than the disease. The point is not the trivial one that action research, like any practice, sometimes shows up in cheap or corrupt forms. The very idea that action research already exists as a live option is mystifying, distracting us from the deep challenge that action research ultimately represents. Though Joseph Schwab is sometimes credited as a forerunner of action research, it is likely that he would see the new talk of 'the teacher as researcher' as indicative of the very epitomization of which he warned. Dewey's new conception of knowledge, action, and communication—and the vision of the teacher as learner it entails—requires nothing short of a radical rethinking of teaching and inquiry, schooling and teacher education. In what follows, I make the case that the promise of action research remains unfulfilled and recall us to the force of Schwab's challenge.

A Double Negation

Only in formal logic does the negation of a negation get you back where you started. Actual concepts, embedded in cultures and histories, do not work this way: double reversals lead to strange new places. Action research is a case in point. To see why,

C. Higgins (✉)
Department of Education Policy, Organization & Leadership, University of Illinois at
Urbana-Champaign, Champaign, IL, USA
e-mail: crh4@illinois.edu

© Springer International Publishing AG, part of Springer Nature 2018   163
P. Smeyers, M. Depaepe (eds.), *Educational Research: Ethics, Social Justice,
and Funding Dynamics*, Educational Research 10,
https://doi.org/10.1007/978-3-319-73921-2_11

we must defamiliarize the modern notions of research and methods. A useful guide here is Bruce Wilshire (1990) who offers a redescription of modern disciplinarity as kind of extended purification ritual. As Wilshire shows, the disciplines represent not only a division of epistemological labor, but also a process of abstraction away from the messy particularity of the lifeworld. We know a serious discipline by its narrowness, and we know a sophomore by his silly habit of trying to connect his coursework with lived life.

Consider the radical *askesis* undergone by philosophy. As those three little letters, Ph.D., remind us, philosophy was once synonymous with the serious search for understanding in any form, from dialogue in the *agora* to rolling balls down inclined planes. With the rise of experimental science, philosophy has repeatedly hived off each part of itself seen as newly set on an empirical foundation. Its deepest self-laceration may have been its ceding of questions of human development to empirical psychology and the new social sciences of education.[1] From Plato to at least Rousseau, philosophers still turned to the scene of education not as an applied afterthought but precisely in order to understand the psychological, the ethical, and the political. By the time we get to the twentieth century, philosophy has become the study of abstract and fully formed human beings, if not simply of words and concepts themselves. This helps us to appreciate the irony that the word "philosophy" is encoded in the name for our highest degree. The idea was that you have not fully matured as a knower unless you have come to understand the place of your specialized discipline within the full ambit of human knowing. The mature knower seeks not only knowledge but understanding, even wisdom. Now philosophy is just another mode of specialized research and the letters 'Ph.D.' signify command in this or any other specialized field. William James (1987) was alert to this irony when, in 1903, he warned of the tightening grasp of the 'Ph.D. Octopus'. For James (1987, 1111), far from being a proper prerequisite, the demand to 'exhibit a heavy technical apparatus of learning' could warp the aspiring scholar and derail him from fulfulfilling his potential as a thinker and teacher.

With the rise of the research university, we find not only hyper-specialization, but a dichotimization of knowing and doing and an overshadowing of practical intelligence by propositional knowledge. Dewey (1916, 9) saw this as 'one of the weightiest problems with which the philosophy of education has to cope.' The expansion of formal education leads us to overestimate the importance of what one consciously knows because one is 'aware of having learned it by a specific job of learning.' We create 'sharps in learning' who take pride precisely in the marks of a failed educational engagement: when learning remains 'abstract and bookish', 'remote and dead' and fails to rise to the level of 'ordinary vital experience' in which knowledge is forged with a 'depth of meaning' and is 'transmuted into character' (Dewey 1916, 8).

What makes the problem of scholasticism weighty for Dewey (1916, 269–70) is that the separation of knowing from doing grows out of, and further reinforces, a classing of people as knowers or doers, 'a division of human beings into those

---

[1] On the divorce of philosophy and psychology see Lear (1998, 7 and passim).

capable of a life of reason and hence having their own ends, and those capable only of desire and work, and needing to have their ends provided by others.' In the sphere of education, this means a distinction between teachers and educational researchers. While it is certainly possible to make the transition from the former to the latter, the gap between the two pursuits persists. This is where the purification rituals described by Wilshire come in handy: to become a priest of the modern research university, to make the ontological leap from a doer to a knower requires sacred rites indeed. That many current educational researchers are former teachers does nothing to elevate the intellectual status of teaching. The hierarchy remains intact, forming one part of the famous lack of a career path in teaching in which the only way to move up is to move out, into administration or research. Indeed, far from elevating the practice of teaching, the close proximity of educational research to practice has tended to lower the status of educational research, contributing to what Labaree (2004) calls 'The Trouble with Ed Schools.'[2]

Thus, we find hierarchies within hierarchies. Within the academy, educational research has a lowered status because of its proximity to practice. Within education, we find teachers as the serfs of the vast empire that is educational practice-policy-research. Teachers have always experienced relatively low levels of autonomy. The heteronomy of teachers has several sources including Lortie's (1975) famous 13,000 h 'apprenticeship of observation' (leading all who have been students to think they understand teaching), the fact that teaching is a feminized profession in a sexist society, and the understandable desire for all to have their hands on what we imagine as our great lever of social change (see, for example, Perkinson 1991, and Labaree 2008). Already in 1932, Willard Waller could speak of the authority of teachers in 'unremitting danger' undermined by students, parents, school board, and even one another (Waller 1932, 10–11). And this was before the rise of social science, technicism (the tendency to view practice not as the exercise of situated, practical wisdom but as the application of research about the most efficient means to given ends), and the audit culture. The rhetoric of accountability and standards has driven a new era of hyper-reform, rooting out what little autonomy teachers still possessed. Concepts such as 'evidence-based practice' and 'value-added measures' have given the hyper-reformers new tools for bullying and blaming teachers. Neither Michelle Rhee nor Scott Walker invented teacher blaming, which David Berliner calls our other national pastime, citing vivid examples from the 1920s. Nonetheless, despite this long, depressing history of 'semi-professionalization' (Etzioni 1969), the bullying and scapegoating of teachers has improbably gotten even worse.

It is helpful to situate the rise of action research—from Dewey and Lewin, through Schwab and Corey, to Stenhouse, Elliott, Carr, and Kemmis—within this context, as an intervention targeting both epistemological dualisms and social

---

[2] The problem is not merely one of perception. Far too many doctorates are granted in education, many to practitioners seeking only professional advancement but with no real proclivity toward scholarship. On this, see McClintock (2004, paragraphs 26–7). Here and in the paragraph that follows what I say applies especially to the U.S., though parallels surely exist in other national contexts.

divides.[3] The goal was not merely to add one more tool to the methodological tool-box, nor simply to encourage teachers to try their hand at an unreconstructed social science, but to think our way past the knowing/doing dichotomy and interrupt our professional version of Dewey's classed society in which some know and set aims while others (teachers) do as they are told. In this way, the ambition and the promise of the program of action research is clear, but how well have we lived up to that promise? Have we healed the rift between action and reflection, or merely soldered a deactivated cognition on to a decognitivized action? Now teachers can be research-ers too. Does this negation of a negation signify a return or merely a double alienation?

Action Research as Methodolatry and Clip Art

Action research aims to rethink both the nature of inquiry and who participates in it. In traditional, nomothetic, social-scientific educational research—with its founding trope of the data-collecting, distantiated knower wielding methods to fend off bias and randomness—teachers show up only as subjects (though, in a case of language as wish-fulfillment, we call them 'participants'). For a long time, this was the only game in town. As mentioned previously, there were researchers who had once been teachers, but one role had to be abandoned for the other to be taken up. What does it mean to promote teachers as researchers? There are at least three basic models.

In the first model, the dominant conception of inquiry remains the same. Teachers are encouraged to think of their classrooms in social scientific terms, to run small-scale experiments, collect data, and so on. Thus, while we start to see some teachers thinking of themselves as researchers some of the time, the gap between teaching and research remains. This conception is plagued with problems. It perpetuates the idea that knowing and doing are separate, which leaves teachers *qua* teachers in a position of perceived social inferiority, and saddles teachers with a kind of double consciousness (the part of me that is like the mere doer and the part of me that is like the knower).

This conception of the teacher as researcher is liable to suffer from the method-olatry pervasive in educational research. Methods are simply tried and true proce-dures for heading off common pitfalls of inquiry. The most we can say is that when adapted to a specific case and employed insightfully they help us avoid some sources of misunderstanding. To be circumspect enough to avoid the other sources of mis-understanding, let alone to be able to pose fertile questions, to notice what matters, to argue cogently, to frame insightfully, this requires a robust and well-rounded education. Even a thorough training in methods would be radically insufficient to produce someone capable of breaking new ground on questions of importance. Educational research is plagued by 'methodolatry,' the tendency to fetishize

---

[3] See, for example, Lewin (1946), Corey (1953), Schwab (1969), Stenhouse (1975), Elliott (2006), and Carr and Kemmis (1986).

methods, as if they themselves contained the powers of the scholar's educated imagination, the expansive network of tacit knowledge that enables one to select, modify, and intelligently make use of methods not to mention to engage in all of the aspects of inquiry that go beyond methods as such.

About the first model there is bad news and really bad news.[4] The bad news is that it is likely to create only would-be social scientists, wielding reified, brittle understandings of methods and procedures. This either will or will not help such teacher-researchers achieve a kind of parity with university-based researchers, and either way, the news is not good. If we do find parity, then this means that the standards for social science in education are extremely low, that our doctoral programs in education themselves tend to treat research as a recipe, the ingredients of which (research question, literature review, theoretical framework, method, limitations, findings) are thin and hypostasized (for more on this, see Higgins 2007). If we find a lack of parity, then this conception has done nothing to lift the condescension built-in to the traditional model. Those teachers who research their classrooms become something like educational research's junior varsity.

The really bad news about this model is that it is likely not only to fail to enable teachers to see their classroom in powerful new ways, as if through the eyes of Freud or Weber, Geertz or Ehrenreich, but it may well also blind their teacherly eyes.[5] As van Manen (1991) argues, pedagogy is about perception, a special mode of tact rooted in the teacher's relationship with the student. Teaching is, for Manen, an existential stance, a special form of intentionality: the teacher orients himself to the student as becomer, opens himself to the experience of the student. If van Manen is right, a teacher who steps out of this relational stance to become a scientific observer, framing his students as participants in an action research study, will, paradoxically, notice less. Imagine a carpenter looking at a cabinet. She is seeing more than we would, seeing details of materials, design, and geometry hidden to us. Now imagine that this carpenter is hired by a sociologist and asked to determine the average number of cabinets per household. Whether or not this helps the sociologist see more about, say, décor and class, what seems clear is that the carpenter is seeing less about cabinets. Action research may all too easily amount to one of the worst-of-both-worlds compromises identified by Dewey (1916, 257): rather than rethink a dichotomy, we forge 'an inorganic composite' and produce something 'perhaps worse than if either ideal were adhered to in its purity.' Under the thrall of action research, we may find a teacher who, while never fully apprenticing herself to one or another craft of scholarship or research, has nonetheless alienated herself from the relationships to her students and work that afford singular access to sources of practical wisdom.

The second model, like the first, affirms that traditional social science is capable of generating knowledge about education, but adds that such knowledge is not in a form suitable for guiding practice. The second model therefore calls for a division of labor, holding that while there may be a place for basic educational research,

---

[4] For a colorful use of the trope of bad, worse, and really bad news, see Egan (2008, Chap. 2).

[5] I refer to Max Weber, Emile Durkheim, Clifford Geertz, and Barbara Ehrenreich.

action research is needed to generate the kind of grounded, situated knowledge that can influence practice. This model suffers from at least two major flaws. First, it is simply false that ideas far removed from the terms and texture of practice cannot be useful to improving practice. We can easily imagine a teacher who, say, finds his own participatory action research on homogenous and heterogenous grouping uninstructive while it is Ehrenreich's *Nickel and Dimed* (2011) that gives him a whole new way to come at his social studies class or deal with class tensions in his school. Indeed the catalyst for a given teacher in a given term may have no topical connection at all. As Kafka (1977, 15–16) once asked, "If the book we're reading doesn't wake us up with a blow on the head, what are we reading it for?' For Kafka (1977, 16), what we need from books is 'an axe for the frozen sea inside of us.' While someone somewhere right now is leading a professional development exercise, projecting a power-point slide picturing the action-reflection cycle, a teacher somewhere else has just found his axe in the form of Neil's *Summerhill*, or maybe it was Neil Young's lead riff in 'Cowgirl in the Sand', jolting him from a cynicism that had without his knowing it infected his entire practice. In short, the notion that the only ideas that can influence practice are those derived from and couched in the terms of classrooms is patently false. The second flaw is that its distinction between and general and situated knowing is likely to collapse back into the pure/applied distinction and reinforce the dichotomies and hierarchies of which Dewey warned.

There are, then, irremediable flaws in both models. In the first model, teachers try their hand at traditional social science. In the second, teachers supplement basic research with their own brand of situated inquiry. This suggests that what is needed is a third model in which teachers take the lead in inquiry, and inquiry itself is rethought along the lines of participatory action research. So it seems that all we need is Dewey's ideas about the inseparability of knowing and doing and we are ready to launch a new paradigm of participatory action research. Not so fast, says Schwab, who reminds us of the doing that is necessary for this knowing, who forces us to ask whether we truly have the stomach to reconceive teaching, schools, and teacher education from the ground up so as support the teacher as intellectual, as someone richly and rigorously reflective.

Schwab sounds this caution in the very title of the essay on which I would like to focus, speaking of 'the "impossible" role of the teacher in progressive education'. Schwab (1959, 139) begins the essay by noting that education is plagued by 'epitomes'. Ideas to think with become ideas to think about until they finally degenerate into inert, 'isolated terms,' 'rendered with a specious simplicity.' Such epitomes abound in education—achievement, accountability, differentiation, grit, metacognition—their speciousness hidden behind protective coatings of obviousness and self-importance. And in educational research, as we have already noted, we have a special way of dignifying and thus disguising our epitomes: we call them methods.

That 'action research' has tended to degenerate into another of our epitomes, to become another victim of our methodolatry, seems as undeniable as it is ironic. Schwab did not live long enough to see the rise of Powerpoint, a technology beautifully designed to ease and accelerate the process of epitomization (for more on the message that is the medium of powerpoint, see Tufte 2006). Action research has become as easy as selecting an image from the ocean of professional development clip-art. One typical image shows the sequence "Plan-Act-Observe-Reflect" spiraling around a central upward arrow marked "continual progress"[6]. Such diagrams are designed not to provoke epistemological reflection about the relation of knowledge and action but simply to evoke the basic meme of modernity. Scientists (or scientists and engineers in tandem if you prefer) poke nature, observe how she flinches, reflect a bit, and plan a new intervention. The result: 'continual progress.' What might at first blush appear like a return to *phronesis* turns out to be something more artificial, encouraging the teacher to view her classroom as a series of (uncontrolled) experiments.

Any idea can degenerate into slogans and clip art, it will be replied. It is easy to attack a thing by its abuses. Action research, the skeptic will remind me, was meant not as one more method in the toolbox of the traditional social scientist but as a rethinking of the nature of inquiry. True enough, but what also comes all too easily to us is the assumption that, having named something, it exists. Talk of action research as a live option in the current landscape amounts to a kind of mystification, distracting us from the structural changes necessary to realize the transformation of teaching and inquiry it entails. If Schwab's choice of the word 'impossible' seems too pessimistic, we can take comfort in the fact that he puts it in scare quotes. On the other hand, no one ever said it would be easy.

Schwab's Challenge

Action research, as I have tried to show, was an important intervention that has largely fossilized into a banner or method. Educational research, however, does not need one more method; nor do teachers need one more hat to wear. What is needed, Schwab suggests, is nothing more nor less than to make good on the promise of genuine education. 'The effective "learning situation"', Schwab (1959, 147) writes, 'is not the one which leads by the quickest, most comfortable route to mastered habit and attitude, used precept and applied knowledge, but the one which is provocative of reflection, experiment, and re-vision.' At the heart of progressive education (and indeed, in another way, in traditions of liberal learning), Schwab reminds us, is the idea that the scene of learning itself must feature inquiry. If inquiry is to be interwoven with practice, and not a task for a special caste of researchers, this must become part of primary and secondary schooling. Given that even in so-called "higher education" we are witnessing a regression to the FedEx model of education, content plus delivery, this may seem a tall order. For Schwab, though, the 'impossibility' centers around a simple but profound corollary of this basic premise: that teachers themselves must be learners and indeed intellectuals.

As Schwab (1959, 158–9) explains,

---

[6] See https://valenciacollege.edu/faculty/development/tla/actionResearch/ARP_softchalk/mobile_pages/index.html

The teacher must be a learner—even unto the fourth level of Dewey's intellectual space. It is not enough for the teacher to master certain ways of acting as a teacher. This is only a capable apprentice. It is not enough to be master of flexible ways of acting. This is only to be a competent 'hand' who can function well when told what to do but who cannot himself administer. It is not even enough to possess organized knowledge of ways and means. This is to interpret a policy and tend to its efficient execution but not to be able to improve a policy or change it as problems change. Only as the teacher uses the classroom as the occasion and the means to reflect upon education as a whole (ends as well as means), as the laboratory in which to translate reflections into actions and thus to test reflections, actions, and outcomes against many criteria, is he a good 'progressive' teacher.

Schwab imagines teachers as intellectuals but certainly not as denizens of an ivory tower. It is neither erudition nor method per se that Schwab is after but intellectually mobility. Schwab pictures the intellectual life as one of dynamic movement between various levels of what he calls 'Pragmatic Intellectual Space.' Based on his reading of Dewey, Schwab (1959, 155) identifies six levels of reflective practice: 'mastery of problematic situations,' 'sensitive mastery of variable problematic situations,' reflection on patterns of actions and consequences, 'reflection on ends and means,' 'reflection on the conduct of discovery,' 'invention of means and ends of discovery.' Each practice, Schwab suggests, opens upon fundamental questions about what is true, what is worthwhile, and how we can come to know what is true and worthwhile.

But Schwab does not stop there. He stresses not only the movement among levels of reflection radiating from a particular mode of practice but 'polyprincipality,' or the ability to converse across practical domains where one will be confronted with 'unfamiliar vocabularies' and 'alien considerations'(Schwab 1969, 598). The traditional intellectual seeks breadth of vision in the general, abstracting away from the concrete situations and commitments of practice. Schwab's progressive teacher-intellectual also seeks breadth of vision, but through polyprincipality not abstraction. Schwab's teacher cultivates the ability to think dialectically, comparing rival traditions of action-reflection concerning the means and ends of human growth.[7]

And this suggests, in turn, a progressive mode of teacher education. Teachers, Schwab (1969, 620) suggests, need to be initiated into 'the arts of deliberation.' In this way, teacher education,

Ought to exhibit the material… as matter for reflection rather than as matter for docile mastery. It ought to exhibit proposed ends and methods of instruction in some of their difficult, tangled, and doubtful connection with the imperfect and incomplete researches on society, the learning process, human personality, and similar topics, from which they stem. (Schwab 1959, 148)

The battle cry for alternative certification and the attack on university-based teacher education is that pre-service teachers don't need 'theory,' that learning what Dewey or Freire thought about education is irrelevant to pedagogical practice. And, of course, if by learning, we mean transmission, and if by theory we mean a

---

[7] Much of what I say here echoes my exploration of the teacher as intellectual in Higgins (2011, Chap. 8). On education as a dialectical conversation about the ends and means of human growth, see pp. 254–71. For implications for teacher education, see pp. 271–78.

second-hand account of their conclusions, we can agree. Good riddance. What follows from this, though, is not learning on the job after a six-week boot camp, but that learning is about transformation not transmission, and that theory is a practice not a body of information. Thinking with and about Dewey and Freire can be transformative. University-based teacher education at its best, is an invitation to engage in serious reading and discussion of primary texts and fieldwork, to apprentice oneself to thinkers and traditions of thought, to learn how to think with some depth and precision.

It is not only that changes in learning imply changes in teaching and teacher education, but schooling itself will have to change if teachers are to be dynamic, organic intellectuals:

> The schools, in turn, ought to be so organized that at least some of their capable and energetic teachers find in the classroom and in each other the opportunity to reflect on ends and methods and try alternatives which experience and reflection suggest. (Schwab 1959, 148)

Former UK Minister of Education, Michael Gove, in his effort to replace university-based teacher education, called for the establishment of 'teaching schools,' on analogy to 'teaching hospitals'. As a plan to replace academic pre-service teacher education with learning on the job, this will not do. That said, Gove's rhetoric raises a crucial question. What would it mean to build schools from the ground up, as places of learning for the teacher? Here it will suffice to mention four core principles.

First, the culture of teaching must be supportive rather than punitive. Teachers cannot adopt an attitude of inquiry toward their practice in an environment in which their performance is measured by high-stakes rigid assessments, let alone in a climate in which "value-added" scores become public shame lists. Second, one can obviously not explore alternatives when pedagogy is tightly scripted according to "what works" recipes. The third and fourth principles are complementary. Teachers spend most of their time in a state that is simultaneously crowded (with students and interactions) and isolated (deprived of opportunities to participate in genuine communities of practice). To flourish as reflective intellectuals, teachers need both some sort of studio space, a space of retreat, and opportunities to discuss and collaborate with their colleagues. If this sounds radical, consider that for all of the spurious international comparisons and false borrowing that surrounds talk of success in Finland and China, it seems that one thing that Finland has done well is to create a professional culture around teaching. Finnish teachers spend somewhere on the order of 4 h a day in the classroom, using the rest of their time, like professionals, to reflect, collaborate, design, and prepare (Anderson 2011).

Finally, educational research must change to accommodate these other changes. Schwab (1959, 144) speaks of a pragmatic rhetoric, a mode of indirect communication that eschews proving for 'moving men to reconstruct and test by practice.' Educational writing is potentially miseducative insofar as it takes itself to be offering solutions to known problems (the first level of pragmatic intellectual space). Instead, Schwab calls on us to write in a way that creates challenging experiences for teacher intellectuals, giving teachers solutions to problems that they didn't even know they had, or guidance on problems they are about to have, or other provocations to think more dynamically about educational means and ends. He challenges us to invite teachers to raise practical educational deliberation to the level of criticism and art, the modes by which we open ourselves to think about the concepts we have come to think with and attune ourselves to what matters and why it does.

Schwab is well aware of the difficulty of the challenge he has set for us. Action research was once just another name for this challenge. The irony is that it has become a concept that reinforces both on the level of form and content, the old dualisms and the anti-intellectual conception of teaching. If we care about genuine intellectual life and the teacher as a leading participant in that life, then we ought to adopt as our platform that we are both for and against action research. That just might unstick us a bit to explore pragmatic intellectual space.

References

Anderson, J. (2011, December 12). From Finland, an intriguing school-reform model. *The New York Times*. http://www.nytimes.com/2011/12/13/education/from-finland-an-intriguing-school-reform-model.html?src=me&ref=general&_r=0

Carr, W., & Kemmis, S. (1986). *Becoming critical: Education, knowledge and action research.* London: Falmer Press.

Corey, S. M. (1953). *Action research to improve school practices.* New York: Teachers College Press.

Dewey, J. (1916). *Democracy and education: An introduction to the philosophy of education.* New York: The Macmillan company.

Egan, K. (2008). *The future of education: Reimagining our schools from the ground up.* New Haven: Yale University Press.

Ehrenreich, B. (2011). *Nickel and Dimed: On (not) getting by in America.* New York: Picador. Original edition, 2001.

Elliott, J. (2006). *Reflecting where the action is.* London: Routledge.

Etzioni, A. (Ed.). (1969). *The semi-professions and their organization: Teachers, nurses, social workers.* New York: Free Press.

Higgins, C. (2007). Interlude: Reflections on a line from Dewey. In L. Bresler (Ed.), *International handbook of research in arts education* (pp. 389–394). Dordrecht: Springer.

Higgins, C. (2011). *The good life of teaching: An ethics of professional practice.* Oxford: Wiley.

James, W. (1987). The Ph. D. Octopus. In B. Kuklick (Ed.), *William James: Writings, 1902–1910.* New York: Library of America. Original edition, 1903.

Kafka, F. (1977). Letter to Oskar Pollak (27 January, 1904). In *Letters to friends, family, and editors* (Richard & C. Winston, Trans.), 15–16. New York: Schocken.

Labaree, D. F. (2004). *The trouble with Ed schools.* New Haven: Yale University Press.

Labaree, D. F. (2008). The winning ways of a losing strategy: Educationalizing social problems in the United States. *Educational Theory, 58*(4), 447–460.

Lear, J. (1998). *Open minded: Working out the logic of the soul.* Cambridge, MA: Harvard University Press.

Lewin, K. (1946). Action research and minority problems. *Journal of Social Issues, 2,* 34–46.

Lortie, D. (1975). *Schoolteacher: A sociological study.* Chicago: University of Chicago Press.

McClintock, R. (2004). *Homeless in the house of intellect: Formative justice and education as an academic study.* New York: Laboratory for Liberal Learning.

Perkinson, H. J. (1991). *The imperfect panacea: American faith in education, 1865–1990.* New York: McGrawHill.

Schwab, J. J. (1959). The "impossible" role of the teacher in progressive education. *The School Review, 67*(2), 139–159.

Schwab, J. J. (1969). The practical: A language for curriculum. *School Review, 78,* 1–24.

Stenhouse, L. (1975). *An introduction to curriculum research and development.* London: Heinemann.

Tufte, E. (2006). *The cognitive style of Powerpoint: Pitching out corrupts within.* Cheshire: Graphics Press.

van Manen, M. (1991). *The tact of teaching: The meaning of pedagogical thoughtfulness.* Albany: State University of New York Press.

Waller, W. (1932). *The sociology of teaching.* London: Wiley.

Wilshire, B. (1990). *The moral collapse of the university: Professionalism, purity, alienation.* Albany: State University of New York Press.

On the Commodification of Educational Research

David Bridges

Contracting for Research

This chapter is framed by a recognition that all or most academic research in universities (I shall limit myself to this setting) requires some sort of funding and it further supposes that exactly how it is funded and on what terms and conditions might have some impact on the nature of the research itself. One can usefully observe some different models of these relationships between funder and researchers. Becher (1985) distinguishes five strategies which those paying for research use to control to a greater or lesser degree the research which is done. These include (I have slightly elaborated on Becher's account):

(i) proprietorship: funders create dedicated research establishments in-house – maximising their control over every aspect of the research and their rights over the utilisation (or suppression) of the research;
(ii) purchase: bought-in researchers commissioned by government agencies or private sector organisations under project contracts (which universities are increasingly anxious to win) – i.e. the sort of research relationship I am mainly concerned with here;

This chapter draws on some of the sources referenced in a chapter in the author's *Philosophy in educational research: Epistemology, ethics, politics and quality* published by Springer in 2017, which also expands on the argument set out here in section "Research in the discourses of the knowledge economy" in particular.

D. Bridges (✉)
University of East Anglia, Norwich, UK

St Edmund's College, Cambridge, UK

Homerton College, Cambridge, UK
e-mail: db347@cam.ac.uk

© Springer International Publishing AG, part of Springer Nature 2018   175
P. Smeyers, M. Depaepe (eds.), *Educational Research: Ethics, Social Justice, and Funding Dynamics*, Educational Research 10,
https://doi.org/10.1007/978-3-319-73921-2_12

(iii) prescription: the concentration and steering of, usually government, research resources through the designation of particular centres of excellence, which, once established may enjoy a significant measure of independence;

(iv) persuasion and sponsorship: the identification and designation of a preferred theme and the encouragement of academics to put forward proposals for research relating to this theme (for example the EU Horizon 2020 programme)

 (v) pluralism: responsiveness to researcher demand – selection by perceived merit of proposals (cf. the UK Economic and Social Research Council open bidding process). (Becher 1985: 183)

Beyond these in terms of almost non-existent control mechanism he might have added:

(vi) patronage: David's 'stage theory' interpretation of the development of modern science refers to 'a transitional stage in which aristocrats bestowed patronage on savants as another form of conspicuous consumption' (Mirowski and Sent 2002: 50; David 1991) Today research conducted by individuals on their own agenda under publicly funded posts in universities is in a sense a form of public patronage. Under this form of funding the individual researcher enjoys maximum freedom for 'curiosity led' research (though with only very limited resources), though universities may claim at least a share of ownership of the research if it should prove profitable. (Not an anxiety that keeps many philosophers awake at night). In a sense, however, the story of patronage has come full circle in a modern and highly sophisticated from that Lynn Fendler calls 'philanthrocapitalism', also referred to as venture philanthropy, creative capitalism, assertive philanthropy and impact investing, as developed by the Gates Foundation, George Soros, the Clinton Foundation, etc., and which she describes as 'the fastest growing source of funding for educational (and healthcare) research in the USA' (Fendler 2016: 1) – a phenomenon which is readily recognisable too in the UK.

Of these funding patterns it is the second – the 'purchase' or buying in of researchers under contract – that brings us closest to the idea of research as a commodity that can be bought and sold or otherwise disposed of as the purchaser wishes. Some years ago a senior education adviser in Norfolk commissioned an evaluation by the Centre for Applied Research in Education at the University of East Anglia of the local implementation of a new government scheme. He did not enjoy reading the subsequent highly critical report and proposed that it should go straight into the bin. When the lead researcher protested the advisor reportedly declared: 'I buy research like I buy a bag of coal and when I have bought it I expect to be able to do what the hell I like with it'. This, at least is my recollection of a response that I found disturbing at the time and one that has clearly resonated in my mind over a good many years. The terms of *education* research contracts with the UK Department for Education echo the same construct of research as commodity: they are couched in the same language that might be used for the purchase of a suite of computers or of school furniture:

> The Contractor warrants that any goods supplied by the Contractor forming part of the services will be of satisfactory quality and fit for their purpose and will be free from defects in design, material and workmanship. (Department for Education 2014: par 7.2.10)

Surely, research, or at least educational research, is *not* like a bag of coal or any other material commodity in some significant way; nor does a local government officer have the right to throw it in the bin, does (s)he? But why? This paper attempts to explore some important dimensions of this question.

Research in the Discourses of the Knowledge Economy

> In economies that rely increasingly on the generation and application of knowledge, greater productivity is achieved through the development and diffusion of technological innovations, most of which are the products of basic and applied research undertaken in universities. Progress in the agriculture, health, and environment sectors, in particular, is heavily dependent on the application of such innovations. (World Bank 2002: 76)

Clearly research can and does have commercial value and, when this is aggregated in measures such as GDP, economic value, providing its users with competitive advantage by helping them to produce innovative products, to improve on established products or reduce costs. Having access, and especially exclusive access, to such knowledge can make all the difference between commercial success and failure at the level of an individual company and, by extension again, of a national economy. The capacity to generate such knowledge, not least in universities; to own and control it (hence '*intellectual property*'); and to apply and utilise it ('*knowledge transfer*') has become a key responsibility of universities and, in the UK Research Excellence Framework and others that have followed its path, a measure of their research excellence. This capacity for research based innovation has also become a central element of the sort of '*knowledge economy*' that governments across the world in settings as diverse as the USA and Ethiopia aspire to create.[1] So commercial value and, at the macro level, economic value can be attached to research products, which can be owned, bought and sold like any other commodity. This '*commodification*' of research is a feature of a world in which, as Burton-Jones describes it,, 'Knowledge is fast becoming the most important form of global capital' – hence '*knowledge capitalism*' (Burton-Jones 1999: vi) and subsets that

---

[1] Peters and Besley observe 'an emerging consensus that development on the Third World crucially depends on developing a knowledge economy in which tertiary education has a double role to play: in the creation of knowledge and its translation for local conditions and also in the development of knowledge as human, social and intellectual capital. The form of development education advocated by the bank [i.e. The World Bank] for the third world does not differ greatly from knowledge development strategies adopted by the developed world' (Peters and Besley 2006: 25).

include, for example 'bio-capitalism' (Rose 2007[2]; Peters and Venkatesan 2013) . Universities themselves adopt this discourse: 'When it comes to biotechnology', boasts the motto of the University of California System, 'UC means business', and its income from industry sponsored contract research gives credibility to its claim. Thus a powerful discourse is developed around the idea of knowledge as a commodity with commercial and economic value attached.

> This development is often described as the economization, or economic instrumentalization, of human activities and institutions, or even entire social subsystems. In this wider and more appropriate sense, academic commodification means that all kinds of scientific activities and their results are predominantly interpreted and assessed on the basis of economic criteria. (Radder 2010: 4)

Of course, as soon as one begins to value research on the basis of its potential to create wealth a particular hierarchy develops. Research in the fields of, for example, bio-scienve, material science or communications technology have enormous potential for wealth creation (though the costs attached may also be enormous and the outcomes far from predictable). By contrast, no-one would suppose that a fortune was to be made out of a nuanced reinterpretation of the Arthurian legend, a feminist reading of Plato's Republic or an ethnographic study of Glaswegian bar culture. So, one of the consequences of this observation of a hierarchy of value in terms of the economic or commercial value of different kinds of research is differential investment and the prioritisation of different areas of research, not just by the private sector but also by government. Across the world STEM subjects (Science, Technology, Engineering and Maths) are being given priority over the humanities and social sciences in government funding not only for research but also for teaching. (Ethiopia, for example, is among those countries that have adopted the 70/30 principle in its support for STEM subjects compared with others in higher education).

But where does Education sit in all this as a field of research in higher education? I suggest that it suffers a double penalty. First, its research 'products' very rarely carry the sort of commercial value that might be attached to a new pharmaceutical product or a component for mobile phones. On this basis it joins the social sciences and humanities as a relatively low priority for research funding. But, secondly, and in spite of this, *it suffers by association with the discourse of commodification* which I have briefly described and which is applied without proper examination of the appropriateness of this discourse in the field of Education. Most of the published discussions of the commodification of research (e.g. in the collection of papers edited by Hans Radder 2010), focus on the commodification of scientific research for *commercial* purposes, but I am rather more concerned in the sphere of education with the consequences for *public understanding* of the treatment of research as a commodity, It is to the grounds for this unease that I shall now turn.

---

[2] 'A new economic space has been delineated – the bioeconomy – and a new form of capital – bio-capital' (Rose 2007: 6).

Challenging the Association Between Funding, Ownership and Control

I think we have to start by considering what are the fruits or, in the terms of the UK Research Excellence Framework (www.REF.ac.uk), the 'outputs' of educational research.[3] At one level these are reports, published articles and books; at another level, increasingly rewarded by the UK Research Excellence Framework, these are demonstrable 'impacts' on educational policy and practice; between the two there is an available body of enhanced knowledge and understanding of some aspect of educational theory, practice and/or policy that points perhaps to problems in any of these areas and/or possible responses.

It is this knowledge and understanding on which I want to focus. Let us suppose that what research offers is something that helps anyone who has access to it to have a better understanding of education. Such 'better' understanding may as readily be a better understanding of the complexity of educational practice or a more critical questioning of what is currently assumed to be the case as a clearer direction towards 'what works' (on some criterion of what might count as working) or not.

Now, my starting point is to assume that this sort of knowledge and understanding is something that any member of the public has an interest in (in the sense that they stand to benefit from it) and that any member of the public has the right to access. If education is itself a public good, then surely understanding education and what may and may not contribute to its quality ought to be out there in the public domain? To follow Fuller's distinction (Fuller 2010: 279) such knowledge is not just 'for the public good' ('the technology that is provided exclusively to the rulers') but 'as a public good' (a resource to inform democratic deliberation). As MacDonald and Norris describe very vividly:

> We are not just in the business of helping some people to make educational choices within their present responsibilities and opportunities. We are also in the business of helping *all people* to choose between alternative societies. (MacDonald and Norris 1982: 10 my italics)

What might lead us to qualify this opinion? My senior education adviser is not alone in thinking (imbued with the discourse of commodification) that one important qualification relates to the matter of who has funded or paid for the research and the rights over the control of the research that flow from this relationship. But this seems to me to be a less than compelling argument – for several reasons.

First, government officers at national or local level might remember that this is not their own money they are using, but rather that of the general public, of tax payers at least. The officers are merely their agents, and if the argument is that access to

---

[3] I shall not in this paper make a distinction between educational research and evaluation (as, for example, in programme evaluation, though I recognise that for some purposes this distinction could be distinction. Programme evaluation may, for example, have a particularly high level of political sensitivity and perhaps public interest compared with more fundamental and theoretical educational inquiry.

and control over research belongs to those who pay for it, then local and national tax payers are the ones that can claim that entitlement.

Secondly, in a liberal democracy (and indeed other forms of government) ministry and other officials employed by the state are or should be accountable for their actions. Research and evaluation focussed on local or national government educational initiatives, or indeed any part of what is happening in the public education system are all things for which they may reasonably be called to account, and research into educational policy and practice and its public availability is a key contributor to that accountability.

Thirdly (and I grant that this is a researcher's perspective) research into education or anything else is or should be conducted in a systematic and disciplined way with care and thoroughness and respect for legitimate ethical principles, but always under an imperative to see and to speak truth. This is what research is and does. These principles and purposes become distorted if the seeking and speaking of truth becomes subordinate to other considerations like protecting the minister's reputation or shielding junior officers from ministerial wrath[4] – a phenomenon that Elzinga calls 'epistemic drift'. (Elzinga 1985).

> Epistemic drift may .. be interpreted as a shift from a traditional reputational control system associated with disciplinary science to one that is disengaged from disciplinary science and, thus, more open to external regulation by governmental and managerial policy impositions. The norms of the new system have a strong relevance component, transmitted from the bureaucracies to which the hybrid research community is linked. The bureaucracy thereby influences not only the problem selection but the standards of performance of research, standards of significance and territorial definition of the field or speciality in question. (Elzinga 1985: 209)

Worse – when the imperatives placed on university researchers to bring in income become associated with an expedient desire not to offend funders, then, as Stronach et al. (1997) observed in an editorial in the *British Educational Research Journal* the result is 'a shift in preoccupation away from "research" as knowledge production, to research as an entrepreneurial activity, a question of finding money rather than answers ...' (Stronach et al. 1997: 403).[5]

---

[4] Kushner and MacDonald speak from hard experience when they write: '... civil servant managers who commission evaluations are vulnerable to unfavourable judgements of the policies they are implementing or of the ways in which they have chosen to prosecute them ... They do not want, and will strenuously oppose, policy evaluation of a kind that could embarrass their superiors by raising questions about the validity of the programme rationale.' (Kushner and MacDonald 1987: 152)

[5] Elzinga suggests that research is more susceptible to external determination at different stages in their evolution and epistemic drift: 'during the phase in which a paradigm is being established and articulated the development of a discipline is strongly bound to the function of internal norms and regulatives – these determine the choice of problems and objectives within a research programme. This is taken to be incompatible – as a rule – with strong external regulation or determination' (Elzinga 1985: 208). This might be a fair characterisation of educational research, at least in the Anglo-American sphere of influence as the 'disciplines' of education dominated the landscape in the 60s and 70s. Arguably, as these disciplines have lost their authority in favour of what Donmoyer called 'paradigm proliferation (Donmoyer 1996), and as educational research has become balkanised and hybridised, it has become more sensitive to external rather than internal regulatory systems.

So, there are moral, political and epistemic reasons for challenging the assumption that the purchase of research by government departments carries with it an entitlement to do with it 'what the hell they like'.

But there are other considerations that may leave one uneasy about the idea that one can regard the fruits of educational research in this way.

Ethics and Ontology in the Commodification of Research: Educational Research As a Public Good

I want to return to my consideration in the opening of the last section of education as a public good and, hence, educational research as an important contributor to that public good. And here I use the notion of public good not in the economic sense of something from which the public at large can draw economic benefit, but in the moral sense as something that can contribute to people's capacity to lead a good life, for example in the way that Amartya Sen talks about people's 'capabilities' (Sen 1999). It seems to me that something that can be described in these terms should be made available as freely as possible and that practices that circumscribe this freedom should be opposed. We are not talking here about issues of national security, on which there might be a case for some protection of research findings or even commercial competitiveness, but of education, something central to becoming fully human.

In writing in these terms I approach the thought that there is something in the very nature of education and the research which informs it which suggests that it is inappropriate to treat it as a commodity if the commodification of research is understood, in Brown's terms, as:

> the social process whereby a person or thing becomes understood as a 'mere thing,' as entirely separate from the people and that give it meaning. Commodities are seen as commensurable with each other through the medium of money. When academic research becomes a commodity, it loses any explicit association with either particular scientific communities or society as a whole, and it becomes reduced to a possession of individual agents that can be exchanged on the market. (Brown 2010: 1–2)

Still less is it appropriate to treat it as a commodity over which some people – in government or in commerce – can have proprietorial rights that include the right to withhold knowledge and understanding about it from the public domain. The corollary is that there is something not quite right about a university putting such rights, such knowledge and understanding up for sale and in so doing consenting to such proprietorial claims. Some things, perhaps, are not, or should not be, up for sale in this way, but be freely available to all. This is the uplifting spirit in which Diderot railed against those who sought to keep new discoveries to themselves:

> Nothing is more contrary to the progress of knowledge than mystery. … If it happens that an invention favourable to the progress of the arts and sciences comes to my knowledge, I burn to divulge it; that is my mania. … Had I but one secret for all my stock in trade, it seems to me that if the general good should require the publication of it, I should prefer to

die honestly on a street corner, my back against a post, than let my fellow men suffer. … We exist within such an existence so ignorant, so short, and so sad, that the vicar sparing his money and the philosopher sparing his discoveries, both steal from the poor. Besides, I think that discoveries are safe and valuable, only when they have come into common knowledge, *and I hurry to bring them in*.[6] (Diderot 1755, cited in Hilaire-Perez 2002: 142–143 my italics)

… and Diderot's indignation was a response to those who sought to keep secret only the technique of painting in wax!

The accusations against those who exercise proprietorial rights over knowledge and seek to keep it to themselves, or those who sell out to those who seek such proprietorship, do not stop there. Sandel writes of 'the degrading effect of market valuation and exchange on certain goods and practices' (Sandel 1998: 94). For Brown:

The commodification of academic research violates the distinctive ideals, habits of mind and institutional purposes traditionally associated with science. Commodification corrupts science…, because exchanging scientific knowledge for money threatens the moral integrity, social purpose, and/or epistemic quality of science. Just as prostitution denigrates sex and bribery denigrates government, commercialised research denigrates science. (Brown 2010:263)

Half a century ago Theodore Roszak had already labelled universities easy readiness to sell whatever services that customers desired as a form of prostitution. In a stinging critique of 'the service university' (for which read in contemporary terms the 'entrepreneurial' or 'enterprise' university) he wrote:

"Service", by becoming a blanket willingness to do whatever society will pay for, has led the university to surrender the indispensable characteristic of wisdom: moral discrimination. So it is that the multi-versity progressively comes to resemble nothing so much as the highly refined, all-purpose brothel Jean Genet describes in his play *The Balcony*. (Roszak 1969:12)

For some ethicists and philosophers, the objection to the commodification of certain things is almost ontological in character. They are simply not that sort of thing and what they contribute to human being is incommensurable with notions of financial gain (Brown 2010): it is a kind of category mistake to regard them as commodities. To do so is not just a conceptual error: it is one that, as Sandel suggests, *corrupts* the object that is thus changed (Sandel 1998 and see also Brown 2010). The examples that Sandel gives include the commercialisation of prison services, the sale of babies, surrogate motherhood (for payment), the sale of human organs, the sale of

---

[6] Meeton points to the paradoxical feature of 'intellectual property' that, 'the more freely the scientist gives his intellectual property away, the more securely it becomes his property…. Only when he has published his ideas and findings has the scientist made his scientific contribution and only when he has thus made it part of the public domain of science can he truly lay claim to it as his (Merton 1979:47.). In spite of his enthusiasm for putting his knowledge in the public domain, Diderot was nevertheless a staunch defender of copyright and had a long running dispute with Condorcet who rejected *privilèges de librairie*.in favour of what today we might recognise as the 'public good' nature of knowledge. (Van den Belt 2010:195; Diderot 1763; Condorcet 1776). For Diderot, however, the reward to which the author of new knowledge was entitled was recognition and honour, so it was important that his or her name could be firmly attached to the work.

sexual services, 'the marketing of "Ivy League" sperm' (a new perspective for me on the financial returns of a higher education!), Some popular objections to the privatisation of public health provision or public education and the selling off of national heritage sites are of a similar character, i.e. these are the sort of things that belong in public hands to be employed for public benefit under public scrutiny, not things hived off for private profit. Similarly, 'The substantive findings of science constitute *a common heritage*; they do not enter into the exclusive possession of the discoverer or his heirs. This means that the rights of intellectual property are extremely curtailed' (Van den Belt 2010: 191, my italics). The argument in Van den Belt (and Condorcet) is against the exclusive ownership of 'intellectual property' (a term that Van den Belt prefers to avoid) by the discoverer, the scientist, or the researcher but rather to regard such knowledge as 'a non-excludable and non-rival public good'. In the context of this paper I am more concerned about the claims to proprietorial rights of those paying for the research. But if the research cannot be owned exclusively by the researcher, then the researcher cannot legitimately pass over exclusive ownership to anyone else, nor can they claim exclusive ownership on other grounds, because, unlike a piece of furniture or a plot of land (to use Van den Belt's examples) an idea is not the sort of thing that can be possessed in this way.

The law of patenting and copyright is interesting in the context of this discussion. First, it recognises some (but not all) products of science cannot be patented or copyrighted. For example 'mathematical formulae, newly discovered laws of nature and newly discovered substances that occur naturally in the world traditionally have been considered to be unpatentable' (Elias 1999: 70). DNA sequencing has been an area of dispute, though the Nuffield Council on Bioethics recommends that since DNA sequencing is essentially simply information about a natural phenomenon it should not be patented (Nuffield Council for Bioethics 2002). But also, 'ideas' cannot be copyrighted, only their 'particular expressions' (Elias 1999:107). Unlike most other things you might 'own', copyright and patents are not given in perpetuity. For different kinds of patent the duration is between 14 and 20 years and copyright expires after 50 years in most cases. All this tends to reinforce the idea that, for example, critique of educational programmes, insights into how children learn. Philosophical reflection on the nature of education – all belong in the public sphere, even if there are some restrictions on specific forms of their expression, *because of the sort of thing they are*. Let us examine this, as it were, ontological consideration in more detail.

Ethics and Ontology in the Commodification of Research: Research as a Gift – Or a Conversation?

Should we, as some have argued, regard the outcomes of scientific research as part of 'a gift economy', which Brown compares with the potlatch of certain indigenous cultures: 'a public economy in which the highest honours go to those who give away the most goods' (Brown 2010: 265 and see Bollier 2002, Hyde 1979, Ziman 2002). In a book under the enticing title *The gift: Imagination and the erotic life of property*, Lewis Hyde writes about the commodification not of research but of art, with which there are interesting parallels. For one thing he sees art as something which does not start *ab nihilo* with the artist but rather as something that, as it were a gift to the artist as well as one passed onto others. 'Along with true creation comes the uncanny sense that "I" the artist did not make the work' (Hyde 1979: xii) – a view that resonates with DH Lawrence's 'Not I, not I but the wind that blows through me' (ibid). Research, similarly, does not start at the point at which the researcher begins to work on the project, the commission, perhaps. It depends critically on what precedes it, what is already in the public domain.

> The public domain consists of a great, invaluable bounty of knowledge, art and culture. Its value lies in the paradoxical fact that it is openly accessible to all. It is priceless, indeed, because the shared heritage that constitutes the public domain is indispensable to creativity. Without the ability to draw on shared knowledge and art – to quote past creativity, to modify it as one wishes, to express it in new ways to new audiences – future innovation is doomed. (Bollier 2002: 119)

But in the kind of gift economy or gift culture described by anthropologists, the receiving of gifts is not the end of the relationship. The classical and enduring work on this topic was Marcel Mauss's *Essai sor le don* published in France in 1924. He observed among other things that gift economies were characterised by three sets of obligations: the obligation to give, the obligation to accept and the obligation to reciprocate. Hyde develops this notion of reciprocity by reference to an early settler;s account of encounters with the indigenous population in Massachusets. For this community the key requirement was that 'Whatever we have been given is supposed to be given away again, not kept. Or if it is kept, something of similar value should move on in is stead... The only essential is this: *the gift must always move*' (Hyde 1979: 4 – original italics). The notion of an 'Indian gift', as the settlers called it, stood in contrast with perhaps the 'white man's gift' which these proto-capitalists clung to as their own possession.

This fluid and ephemeral notion of possession resonates too with the account I have given of research as a conversation (Bridges 2014, 2017). In this I cited Oakeshott's view of our intellectual inheritance

> As civilised human beings, we are the inheritors, neither of an inquiry about ourselves and the world, nor of an accumulating body of information, but of a conversation, begun in the primeval forests and extended and made more articulate in the course of centuries. It is a conversation which goes on in public and within each of ourselves. (Oakeshott 1962: 199)

And I added:

> In such conversational conditions, then, each participant arrives with a unique perspective, which is uniquely changed through the conversational encounter. But of course the conversation does not end there; it continues, perhaps with the same participants, perhaps elsewhere and with a different group, and ... it goes on even when we no longer take part, taking forward, perhaps, some traces of our own participation, though their source will almost certainly be lost among the myriad of voices which have shaped any one person's understanding at any one time. (Bridges 2014: 208 and see also Burke 1957: 210–11)

There are two sides to this sort of picture of research, both of which render the idea of drawing proprietorial fences round it, let alone possessing it, seriously problematic. First, as Caffentzis points out,

> There is the history, the antecedents:' Intellectual products are never far from the commons they are produced from,… The 'auteur function' in Foucault's evocative phrase, is no longer played in Foucault's evocative phrase, is no longer played by the isolated, self-sufficient, individual thinker operating like an artisan in control of his/her means of production. The contemporary 'auteur function' is increasingly recognising the communal and social nature of knowledge production. (Caffentzis 2008: 8; Foucault 1977)

So any research report owes much to what preceded it and to the wider community of scholarship, the enduring conversation and not just to what was carried out 'under contract'. 'The material production of knowledge now depends on a vast worldwide network of information, material and knowers' (Caffentzis 2008: 9).

But just as any particular set of knowledge and understanding stands in and depends on a conversation that goes back into the past. The conversation does not stop there. The ideas live on and get absorbed into a similarly wide tapestry of knowledge and understanding, contributing perhaps to new creativity. So who owns that?

Some research contracts try to address at least the first of these problems by distinguishing between 'background knowledge' (individual or social), that the researcher brings with him or her to the contracted piece of work, and 'foreground knowledge' that is developed through the commissioned work itself. The European Community project on European Educational Research Quality Indicators Project was one such. Contributors (of whom I was one) had to report on their contributions in just such terms and the Final Report (available at www.eerqi.eu) lists what the project refers to as 'exploitable foreground'. I don't think I was alone in finding this task impossible without colluding in a number of half-fictions and arbitrary decisions. Knowledge just does not divide up that way. Perhaps there is a particular difficulty for those engaged in philosophical work, but others, required for example to develop new software, developed programmes that built upon and were substantially constructed from pre-existing resources, even if there was a relatively discrete and tangible product.

So What Are We to Do?

I have set out a number of objections or at least risks attached to the commodification of educational research under a relationship between funder and researcher that gives the funder 'ownership' of the research and the right to do with it what he or she wants. These have included considerations of a political character about a wider public's right and need to know both to inform their own decisions and to hold their political masters and mistresses to account; considerations to do with 'epistemic drift' and the erosion of the credibility of the research itself; and considerations of an ontological character which seem to render the conceptualisation of research as a commodity both inappropriate and corrupting.

So does this mean that as universities we should not enter into such contractual relationships? This is almost certainly an unrealistic conclusion, not least given that, according to a survey by the Higher Education Funding Council for England of *Higher education – business and community interaction* 'income from contract research, where academics or paid to do a specific study, nudged up to £1.2 billion' in 2012–3 (HEFCE 2014: par 7). We might recall Mac the Knife's observation in the *Ballade of good living* from Brechr's *Threepenny Opera*:

> I've heard them praising single-minded spirits
> Whose empty stomachs show they live for knowledge
> In rat-infested shacks awash with ullage.
> I'm all for culture, but there are some limits. (Brecht 1928 Act 2 sc.4)

All university research has to be paid for by someone: only the modern day equivalent of the 'gentleman scholars' with a private income – perhaps academic retirees – can afford to disregard such base considerations entirely.

One response perhaps is to acknowledge that one has to live with ambiguity in what is sometimes described as a dual economy. For Hyde the duality combines a market and a gift economy:

> To state the modern case with more precision, … works of art exist simultaneously in two "economies," a market economy and a gift economy. Only one of these is essential, however: a work of art can survive without the market, but where there is no gift there is no art. (Hyde 1979: xi)

On Mirowski and Sent's (2002) account 'Stanford' economists also locate research in 'two economies', which have some resemblance to those described in the anthropological literature. The first is:

> 'a highly idealised invisible college of scholars who operate only according to their own whims and inclinations, whose stature rest purely upon disciplinary reputation and intellectual credibility, and whose evaluations of the quality of research are so tacit and maintained in such multilateral conformity by the relevant reference group that the actual process of producing warranted knowledge can largely be left out of the picture….[The second] is the everyday corporate reality of proprietary information and market-driven research where the coin of the realm is not scientific fame but cold hard cash and success is denominated in tangiblr products and patents. (Mirowski and Sent 2002: 50–51 and see David 1998)

Both, they add, need to co-exist.

But what happens if the second economy dwarfs the first? It is perhaps the collision between these two 'economies' that underlies the issues I have been discussing in this paper.

To return to Becher's earlier set of distinctions – the question is on what terms should such funding be offered and received. For example, as Geiger (1985) argued at the level of government policy for scientific research, research funding in the form of research *sponsorship* on terms that allow large measures of independence (as provided in the UK by the research councils as well as a number of charitable organisations) probably runs fewer risks of offending against the 'scientific ethos' than other funding mechanisms that involve the *purchasing* of research.[7]

---

[7] Geiger argues, on the basis of case studies of government intervention in basic science, that as a

However, one may find oneself under a research contract of a more or less restrictive kind. What then? 'At times', suggests House (1980) 'evaluators may have to resort to their consciences rather than to their contracts.' Norris and Pettigrew (1994) offer a range of more subversive strategies for resistance to unreasonable contractual terms or their unreasonable application:

> (i) exploiting discrepancies between the contract and proposal (ii) appending to the contract statements about freedom to publish (iii) preparing the ground for the reception of bad news (iv) threatening to expose any attempt at censorship or suppression – especially to powerful people or bodies (v) getting reports leaked (vi) ensuring that short-term evaluative research is part of longer term and more general research programmes. (p. 12)

Any of these strategies would require fairly tough minded institutional support as well as tough minded and high risk researchers (Norris and Pettigrew qualify). A Times Higher Education Supplement leader on the reported repression of research scientists' work on BSE ('mad cow disease' on popular parlance) pointed out, however, that the conditions of independence among researchers lie not just in their individual courage and defiance, but in the support they receive from their institutions and in particular the heads of those institutions' (Times Higher Education Supplement 2000: 16). And yet, as the Leader goes on to point out, many academics have no more confidence in the commitment of their contemporary managers to support their academic independence (especially at the price of lucrative research contracts) than they have in government or other patrons.

But the support needs to run further. Universities undermine each other's stands on these principles if they do not stand together. To this end it is important that research associations operate with a code of conduct that affirms strongly researchers obligations not just to those who fund their research (to whom they owe legitimate duties in terms of the rigour and care with which the research is conducted) but also to a wider public. The ethical code of the British Educational Research Association was reviewed in 2011 in the light of member's increasing concerns with the terms on which government departments were issuing research contracts. The review (which, I should acknowledge, I chaired) explicitly 'refines and strengthens the Association's position on the rights of researchers in commissioned research contexts.' (BERA 2011: Preamble) This is most clearly displayed in two paragraphs in the section of the guidelines on the publication of research (pars 40 and 41):

> 40. The right of researchers independently to publish the findings of their research under their own names is considered the norm for sponsored research, and this right should not be lightly waived or unreasonably denied. This right is linked to the obligation on researchers to ensure that their findings are placed in the public domain and within reasonable reach of educational practitioners and policy makers, parents, pupils and the wider public.
>
>   41. Researchers must avoid agreeing to any sponsor's conditions that could lead to serious contravention of any aspect of these guidelines or that undermine the integrity of the research by imposing unjustifiable conditions on the methods to be used or the reporting of

---

matter of science policy, governments gain most from investment in science when this is channelled to universities not on the basis of bureaucratic planning from outside the research community but on the basis of scientific merit assessed by, for example, research councils (Geiger 1985 and see Becher's fifth category in the opening section of this paper).

outcomes. Attempts by sponsors or funding agencies to use any questionable influence should be reported to the Association. (BERA 2011)

… pious sentiments perhaps: I am not aware of any reported cases so far (apart from those that informed the review) and do any but the most powerful and prestigious universities really have the bargaining power to dictate the terms of their own research contracts?

Research journals, too, can contribute to the protection of the independence of research from funders' control. Radder describes how:

Since 2001 a number of prominent biomedical journals require that their authors make public any ties to external funding bodies and even demand them to sign a statement saying that, if such ties exist, the sponsors have not influenced the methods or contents of their research'. (Radder 2010: 14)

Though the processes that lead towards the commodification of research are global and powerful, there are forms of resistance available to us. There are small acts of defiance, such as those proposed by Norris and Pettigrew (above), but, perhaps more encouragingly a shift in the global climate in favour of open access research and publication and what Michael Peters describes as:

the development of knowledge cultures based on non-proprietary modes of knowledge pro- duction and exchange ….[and of] social processes and policies that foster openness as an overriding value as evidenced in the growth of open source, open access and open education and their convergences that characterise global knowledge communities that transcend bor- ders of the nation state. (Peters 2013: 72–3)

(but will they be able to transcend the competing sovereignties of trans-national global capitalism?). Nor are the political implications of such open systems of knowledge production and dissemination lost on commentators. Peters, again:

openness seems also to suggest political transparency and the norms of open inquiry, indeed democracy itself as both the basis for the logic of inquiry and the dissemination of its results. (Peters 2013: 73).

How can a government that claims the high ground of democratic principles defend its imposition of terms for the conduct of research that require anything other than such openness?

Perhaps, like Roszak, we should take inspiration and direction from the *philosophes*:

For the *philosophe*, intellectuality began at the point where one undertook to make knowl- edge work. The intellectual was one who intervened in society for the defence of civilised values: free speech, free thought, free inquiry for the sake of reform. He was one who sought to clarify reality so that his fellow citizens could apply reason to the solution of their problems… It meant performing the service of criticising, clarifying, dissenting, resisting, deriding, exposing: in brief, educating in the fullest sense of the word as a member of 'the party of humanity'. (Roszak 1969: 32)

Not, I think, an account of our 'service' as intellectuals and researchers that sounds much like a commodity. *'Ecrasez l'infame!'*

References

Becher, T. (1985). Research policies and their impact on research. In B. Wittrock & A. Elzinga (Eds.), *The university research system: The public policies of the home of scientists*. Stockholm: Almqvist and Wiksell.

BERA (British Educational Research Association). (2011). *Ethical guidelines for educational research*. London: BERA. https://www.bera.ac.uk/wp-content/uploads/2014/02/BERA-Ethical-Guidelines-2011.pdf?noredirect=1. Accessed 15 April 2016.

Bollier, D. (2002). *Silent theft: The private plunder of our common wealth*. New York: Routledge.

Brecht, B. (1928). *The Threepenny Opera* (J. Willet & R. Manheim, Trans.). (1994). New York: Arcade Pub.

Bridges, D. (2014). Conversation in the construction and representation of research. In P. Smeyers & M. Depaepe (Eds.), *Educational research: Material culture and its representation*. Dordrecht: Springer.

Bridges, D. (2017, forthcoming) Philosophy in educational research: Epistemology, ethics, politics and quality. Dordrecht: Springer.

Brown, M. B. (2010). Coercion, corruption and politics in the commodification of academic science. In H. Radder (Ed.), *The commodification of academic research: Science and the modern university* (pp. 259–276). Pittsburgh: University of Pittsburgh Press.

Burke, K. (1957). *The philosophy of literary form*. New York: Vintage.

Burton-Jones, A. (1999). *Knowledge capitalism: Business, work and learning in the new economy*. Oxford: Oxford University Press.

Caffentzis, G. (2008). *A critique of commodified education and knowledge (from Africa to Maine)*: Russek scholar lecture to the University of Southern Maine, February 12th 2008. Downloaded 18th September 2016 from www.http://commoner.org.uk/wp content/uploads/2008/04/caffentzis_critiqueeducation.pdf

David, P. A. (1991) *Reputation and agency in the historical emergence of the institutions of open science* (Stanford CEPR Publication No 261).

David, P. R. (1998). Communication. Norms and collective cognitive performance of invisible colleges. In P. Navaretti, K. Dasgupta, G. Maler, & D. Siniscaleo (Eds.), *Creation and transfer of knowledge*. Berlin: Springer.

de Condorcet, M. (1776). Fragments concerning freedom of the press. *Daedalus, 131*(2. (2002)), 57–59.

Department for Education. (2014). *Research contract terms and conditions (Updated 10 November 2014)*. London: Department for Education.

Diderot, D. (1755). L'Histoire et le secret de la peinture en cire. In R. Lewinter, & Y. Beleval (Eds.). (1969), *Diderot: Œuvres completes* (pp. 809–810, 15 vols.). Paris.

Diderot, D. (1763). Letter on the book trade. *Daedalus, 131*(2. (2002)), 48–56.

Donmoyer, R. (1996). Educational research in an era of paradigm proliferation: what's a journal editor to do? *Educational Researcher, 25*(2), 19–25.

Elias, S. (1999). *Patent, copyright and trademark* (3rd ed.). Berkley: Nolo.com.

Elzinga, A. (1985). Research, bureaucracy and the drift of epistemic criteria. In B. Wittrock & A. Elzinga (Eds.), *The university research system: The public policies of the home of scientists*. Stockholm: Almqvist and Wiksell.

Fendler, L. (2016, November). *The Gates Foundation MET research project as a case of philanthrocapitalism*. Paper presented to a research seminar on Research Funding Dynamics, Vrije Universiteit, Brussel.

Foucault, M. (1977). What is an author? In *Language, counter memory and practice* (D. Bouchard & S. Simon, Trans.). Ithaca: Cornell University Press.

Fuller, S. (2010). Capitalism and knowledge: The university between commodification and entrepreneurship. In H. Radder (Ed.), *The commodification of academic research: Science in the modern university*. Pittsburgh: University of Pittsburgh Press.

Geiger, R. L. (1985). The home of scientists: A perspective on university research. In B. Wittrock & A. Elzinga (Eds.), *The university research system: The public policies of the home of scientists*. Stockholm: Almqvist and Wiksell.

Higher Education Funding Council for England. (2014). *Higher education – business and community interaction survey*. Bristol: HEIFCE.

Hilaire-Perez, L. (2002). Diderot's views on artists' and inventors' rights: Invention, imitation and reputation. *British Journal for the History of Science, 35*(2), 129–150.

House, E. (1980). *Evaluating with validity*. Beverley Hills: Sage.

Hyde, L. (1979). *The gift: Imagination and the erotic life of poetry*. New York: Random House.

Kushner, S., & MacDonald, B. (1987). The limitations of programme evaluation. In R. Murphy & H. Torrance (Eds.), *Evaluating education: Issues and methods*. London: Harper & Row.

MacDonald, B., & Norris, N. (1982). *Looking up for a change: Political horizons in policy evaluation*. Mimeo, Norwich: CARE Archive, University of East Anglia, but published in *Case Study Methods ER881*, Deakin: Deakin University.

Merton, R. K. (1979). *The sociology of science: An episodic memoir*. Carbondale: University Press.

Mirowski, P., & Sent, E.-M. (Eds.). (2002). *Science bought and sold: Essays in the economics of science*. Chicago: University of Chicago Press.

Norris, N., & Pettigrew, M. (1994). *Evaluation and the profession of research: ESRC end of award report*. Norwich: Centre for Applied Research in Education/University of East Anglia.

Nuffield Council on Bioethics. (2002). *The ethics of patenting DNA: A discussion paper*. London: Nuffield Council on Bioethics.

Oakeshott, M. (1962). The voice of poetry in the conversation of mankind. In M. Oakeshott (Ed.), *Rationalism in politics and other essays* (pp. 197–248). London: Methuen.

Peters, M. A. (2013). *Education, science and knowledge capitalism*. New York: Peter Lang.

Peters, M. A., & Besley, A. C. (2006). *Building knowledge cultures: Education and development in the age of knowledge capitalism*. Lanham: Rowman and Littlefield.

Peters, M. A., & Venkatesan, P. (2013). Biocapitalism and the politics of life. In M. A. Peters (Ed.), *Education, science and knowledge capitalism*. New York: Peter Lang.

Radder, H. (2010). *The commodification of academic research: Science in the modern university*. Pittsburgh: University of Pittsburgh Press.

Rose, N. (2007). *The politics of life itself: Biomedicine, power and subjectivity in the twenty-first century*. Princeton: Princeton University Press.

Roszak, T. (1969). On academic delinquency. In T. Roszak (Ed.), *The dissenting academy* (pp. 11–44). Harmondsworth: Penguin.

Sandel, M. J. (1998). *What money can't buy: The moral limits of markets*. The Tanner Lectures on human values. http://www.tannerlectures.utah.edu/. Accessed 24 May 2016.

Sen, A. (1999). *Development as freedom*. Oxford: Oxford University Press.

Stronach, I., Hustler, D., & Edwards, A. (1997). Editorial. *British Educational Research Journal, 23*(4), 403–404.

Times Higher Education. (2000). *Opinion: Only openness and integrity will reassure the public*. November 3rd 2000:16. London: Times Higher Education.

Van den Belt, H. (2010). Robert Merton, intellectual property and open science: A sociological history for our times. In H. Radder (Ed.), *The commodification of academic research: Science in the modern university*. Pittsburgh: University of Pittsburgh Press.

World Bank, The. (2002). *Constructing knowledge societies: New challenges for tertiary education*. Washington: The World Bank.

Ziman, J. (2002). The microeconomics of academic science. In P. Minowski & E.-M. Sent (Eds.), *Science bought and sold: Essays in the economics of science*. Chicago: University of Chicago Press.

The Funding of Higher Education: Lessons from Europe's Past

Robert A. Davis

Introduction: Runes and Ruins

In some respects, deliberation of the question of university funding in 2016 may seem remote from the concerns of philosophers and theoreticians absorbed in adjudicating the many cultural, academic and technological influences actively moulding the future of Higher Education today. Yet 2016 is the 20th anniversary of the late Bill Readings' widely acclaimed and prophetic *The University in Ruins* (1996) – a book which for many philosophers and critics crystallised, at the dawn of the digital age, the new technico-bureaucratic globalising forces then allegedly gaining control of universities and perniciously subjecting their time-honoured rationale and hallowed purposes to the inimical market logic of late capitalism. Since Readings, a generation of academic and journalistic commentators has extended this critique and mainstreamed it into the thinking of – to say the least – the arts, humanities and social sciences. There it has been enlarged to encompass the Lyotardian unmasking of 'performativity' as the secret driver of a higher education policy process that is seen as inescapably captive to the hostile 'neoliberal' arithmetic calculus of input-output ratios by which university effectiveness and efficiency are now, it seems, to be permanently measured. It is fair to say that these views probably now represent a broadly 'Leftist-Progressivist' intellectual consensus in European and North American academia and a rallying-point for protest against, and resistance to, further encroachments of the market on university integrity.

The issue of funding is never far from these controversies. The international economic collapse of 2008 served to dramatise for many observers the extent to which the fortunes and functions of universities across the world were implicated in volatile global capital flows and in the risk-taking of the buccaneering, often

R. A. Davis (✉)
University of Glasgow, Glasgow, Scotland, UK
e-mail: Robert.Davis@Glasgow.ac.uk

© Springer International Publishing AG, part of Springer Nature 2018
P. Smeyers, M. Depaepe (eds.), *Educational Research: Ethics, Social Justice, and Funding Dynamics*, Educational Research 10,
https://doi.org/10.1007/978-3-319-73921-2_13

191

morality-free hyper-skilled STEM-graduate fund-managers educated (ironically) by those same elite institutions. It also produced a very obvious immediate effect in the sudden and drastic deterioration of the public finances of the nation states sustaining many of the world's leading universities, resulting in a steep contraction of resource and unprecedented pressures on staffing and capacity across the whole sector. Still recovering from these traumatic events, universities now find themselves toiling in their aftermath, where governments struggle often vainly to restore national balance-sheets against a backdrop of polarised ideological conflict over the causes of, and remedies for, the recent international economic debacle. Universities remain an obvious locus, meanwhile, for further expenditure reductions and real-locations of their costs between state, institutional and individual stakeholders. Hence we can see in the concept of 'funding' – with which, according to the popular folklore of university history, academics were supposedly too 'elevated' in the past to concern themselves – an essential element of the 'grammar' through which the philosophy of contemporary higher education and the idea of the university are to be articulated and interpreted.

It is key to the argument of this essay that any sense of 'funding' as a concept traditionally distant from the interests of academics or the institutional values they champion is historically misplaced. Any impression that there was once an arcadian 'pre-performative' age of educational innocence when academics did not need to concern themselves with the funding of their activities and institutions is an entirely false one. If the current fiscal regime and accompanying controversy to which university activity is prey seems without precedent, then this is largely an illusion, even if we acknowledge that there may well be of course undeniably unique features to our current realities and problems. Rather, it may be wiser to see the challenges around twenty-first century university funding as another phase in a long succession of supervening orders of resource and accountability that have been profoundly interwoven with the development of universities and the various endeavours of study and research for which they have been responsible since their origins. Understanding and historicising these factors, by locating them in wider discussions of sovereignty, autonomy, interdependence and governance – and the economics of education – may not only assist us in appraising our present financial circumstances more responsibly, but might also help in deepening our appreciation of a question that is most certainly rarely absent from the attention of professional academics: the place of the modern university in democratic society (Graham 2013).

Funding the Medieval University

Unduly simplified accounts of the origins of the ancient universities often gesture wistfully to an era of Church patronage in which the activities of the *scholae monasticae* evolved organically from the largesse of the great European Cathedral schools and monastic foundations within which the question of funding and resourcing was for the most part incidental, or at least taken care of by means inscrutable to otherwise abstracted teachers and learners. While it is true in the famous words of Hastings Rashdall (1895) that the earliest universities appear to have emerged spontaneously as 'a scholastic Guild, whether of Masters or Students... without any express authorisation of King, Pope, Prince or Prelate', this perceived independence disguises the extent to which the earliest institutions were caught up in the evolution around 1200 of an urban-mercantile Mediterranean society in which the making and spending of money was vital, and within which learning itself routinely carried an expensive price-tag.

Miri Ruben (2012) explains that while the key foundations of this society – the Church, the nascent civil-commercial bureaucracy and the legal profession – each supported and gained from the coming of the universities, the funding packages by which they resourced it were commonly chaotic and improvised. Alongside a basic principle of selective due-exemption, which encouraged early universities to invest in land and agriculture as longterm sources of income-generation, a combination of 'patronage, family support, and paid work' (9) sustained most student matriculations and teaching provision, with the perverse effects of generally high levels of dropout and the almost total absence of the aristocracy from the first seats of learning – their families mistrustful of the cosmopolitan culture of the universities and preferring to maintain for their offspring the surveillance standards of the older practices of domestic clerical tuition. This habit, incidentally, persisted well into modern times in many royal households. In Great Britain, the first heir apparent to attend university was Edward Prince of Wales in the 1860s, though he did not graduate. Princely enrolments in universities did not become the norm until the twentieth century.

Whether Bologna or Paris claims the mantle of Europe's first university, it seems clear that it was well into the thirteenth century before these foundations and a handful of others like them evolved an at least partially self-sustaining system of funding, based still upon these older improvisations, but becoming more organized in legal and fiscal formulae as the importance and influence of the universities and their curriculum of study grew. Despite wide regional variations in the histories of these universities, resulting in a spectrum of legal governance ranging from the student-led Dominican Chapter-structure of Oxford to the professorial and Master-led faculty system of the French and Germans, fiscally speaking, the ancient universities had by 1300 settled upon the financial model of the fully-fledged medieval corporation. This status was intended to secure the forms of longterm financial viability through which university leaders believed their legal and academic autonomy might be preserved in the face of often volatile surrounding civic and ecclesiastical interests.

In practice, as Alexander Gieysztor (1992) has shown, this entailed marshaling several cumbersome income streams, from episcopal benefices, gifts in kind and occasional royal or noble endowment. Its centerpiece was the *collectae*: the sums (and occasionally fines) levied on students ostensibly to pay for non-academic services and personnel and in most universities commonly paid directly to the masters. By c1450, the *collectae* included, controversially in some jurisdictions, fees for matriculation, examination and graduation – exacerbating the problem of non-completion and prompting levels of student dissent that gave rise in universities from Oxford to Cracow to legal statutes limiting tuition costs for students and tying them expressly to the individual ability to pay. Gieysztor points out that in the sophisticated internal dynamics of the Orléans *studium* of 1444, for which we possess some of the first detailed university accounts, a complex diversification of funding and expenditure is evident, portraying a university reliant upon charitable donation from wealthy merchant supporters, sponsored academic posts, student fees and occasional active fund-raising drives, alongside almsgiving and bequests to support more expensive projects such as new buildings and libraries. Orléans is also one of the first universities to record in detail its *spending* on goods and services in its local commune, as if to highlight its contribution to the regional economy on which it had grown heavily dependent.

Towards the end of the Middle Ages, this complex and periodically unstable mechanism of basic resourcing was affected by two major innovations. The first was the rise in the Southern and Eastern European universities of royal patronage as a large-scale source of funding for universities, reflective of the growing prestige and centralizing impulses of the late medieval monarchies eager to showcase universities as expressions of their legitimacy, sanctity and benevolence. The second was the increasing involvement of host towns and cities in the support and resourcing of universities, with foundations such as those in Louvain, Leipzig and Prague entering into formal legal contracts with their civic authorities, which included the transparent inspection of accounts. We are accustomed from university lore to seeing these early town-gown transactions in largely conflictual terms, but at the levels of finance and funding they were far more businesslike than this suggests, echoing the original 'urban moment' in which the first universities had appeared and extrapolating this into the range of specialized professional and other services that university men could provide for the burgeoning towns and cities of the later medieval period. As Laurence Brockliss (2000) concludes, 'The university from the beginning, then, needed the city. Equally the city from the beginning could see the benefits of the university' (153). This relationship was not by any means in all cases harmonious, but neither was it only procedural and calculating. Many towns came to cherish the universities for which they provided material support, strengthening the academic reputation of the region, drawing in wealthy and high-status visitors, enriching commercial activity and integrating the work of Church and State in the healthy maintenance of the civil order. The bustling quasi-independent late medieval town-network of the Hanseatic League perhaps perfected this holistic mercantile-intellectual understanding of university funding most fully, because it came to prize the universities themselves as vital nodes in the profitable circulation of good, services, people and ideas.

Lest we idealise these late medieval arrangements in some of the quite misleading and regressive ways in which several educational movements of the past century and more have done (perhaps most conspicuously in the nostalgia of the Oxford and Arts and Crafts Movements of the later nineteenth century), it is salutary to recall their limitations and to recognise the ambivalence of their legacies for modern conceptions of university funding. Ararat Osipian (2004, 2008) has recently drawn attention to what he terms the 'corruption paradigm' frequently in evidence in the narrative of the medieval university. Just as widespread, systemic *civic* corruption in the modern era is seen as an early indicator of the 'failed state', Osipian argues that the evidence of endemic academic, financial and personal moral corruption in the medieval university system – of a scale previous analyses have failed to recognise – points to grave structural deficiencies in the operation and governance of the whole academic culture of the medieval European university.

According to Osipian and his collaborators, these defects are visible wherever we scrutinize the day-to-day functioning of the university community of the medieval period: in bribes and backhanders for matriculation, assessment and qualification; in payment for office; in usufruct and simony; in chronic misuse of position and money for personal advantage; in common embezzlement and disposal of property; in the levying of exorbitant interest rates for both municipal and master-student loans; in the promotion of gambling and gaming; in selfish profiteering from benefits awarded for the furtherance of the mission and study of the university. The inventory is a detailed and painful one, corroborated in the various waves of reform – religious and academic – which swept the universities from more or less the time of their inception until the Reformation and which repeatedly foregrounded their alleged misappropriation of the revenues allocated to them. Even if we demur at the suggestion that the documented catalogue of abuses normalised corruption as part of the fabric of university instruction, perpetuating it for future generations, the sobering charge sheet ought to alert us to the venality ingrained in the system and to the fundamental instability of a funding model vulnerable to malfeasance at so many points in the academic and institutional cycle. Aside from ridding us then of any illusions of an originary past free from the spectre of mammon compromising the disinterested pursuit of truth, this knowledge also enables us to see that if, in the words of James Conroy's public lectures, money is a form of 'circulating energy' in almost all educational enterprises, it is forever shadowed by a moral entropy which can fatally distort the work and the ambitions of learning, teaching and research.

The Early Modern University

The two vectors of change identifiable in the narrative of the late medieval university – the extension of royal involvement and the deepening compact of town and gown – constitute two of the most important developments in the fortunes of early modern European higher education. The spread of humanism and the flourishing of Renaissance ideas of the Christian polity incentivized these shifts, as universities assumed still greater responsibility for the education of civic elites and, in the same period, became centres for the reproduction of new concepts of enhanced monarchical authority. These activities of course extended the range and scale of university activity and university teaching, but it seems clear from the fragmentary late fifteenth century records that we possess that income routinely struggled to match expenditure, leading to often frantic scrambles on the part of university leaders to generate fresh revenues or strengthen existing ones. These needs understandably opened universities to greater dependence on the towns and cities in which they were located, whether this was enshrined in formal charters or merely the result of incremental integration of the university estates into the commercial and political life of host communities.

As Hilde de Ridder-Symoens (1996) observes, 'from the fifteenth century onwards the municipal and territorial authorities increasingly tended to subsidize the university directly out of city or state funds, but in exchange, naturally, for greater control and authority' (184). She points to new special subsidies such as the *gabelle* in Rouen, the carriage tax in Venice and the full tax-exemptions in Louvain binding local universities more completely into the fiscal structures of their sponsoring cities. By 1536, when the University of Copenhagen reopened as a Lutheran foundation, its dependence on the city was complete, with income streams stemming from confiscated Church properties, a proportion of parish tithes, a new 'study tax' on wealthy dioceses and 27 scholarships for poor students supplied by the chapters of the reformed Copenhagen Cathedral. In this context, as Anderson and Lynch (2003) point out, the controversial emergence in 1582 of the University of Edinburgh seems almost inevitable: a College daringly established and governed not by the Church, but by the Town Council, and ratified not by Papal Bull or Seal of the Presbytery but by Royal Charter. While this innovation of course reflects some of the complex dynamics of Reformation Scotland, it also highlights what we might term the growing 'urbanisation' and nascent 'secularisation' of university learning as the expense and political will required to create a new, major university moved increasingly beyond the capabilities and resources of the Churches alone, whether Catholic or Protestant. Within 30 years, by virtue of its municipal governance and Council funding arrangements, Edinburgh University had possibly the most socially diverse student intake of any university in Europe, its financial affairs overseen and audited closely by the city authorities.

Altered patterns of expenditure also sharpened the university hunger for additional income streams. A well-attested manifestation of the transition from medieval to early modern universities in Europe was the rise of the professoriate, with the additional costs associated with the coming of this new class of vocationally committed Master, intended to be more or less full-time in the service of the establishment and its students. With the withering of clerical prebends as the financial entailments of chairs, especially in Protestant countries, and the growth in the overall number of chairs across the sector, new forms of salaried professorial appointment materialized often subsidized by wealthy individual patronage. This development also signaled, at last, serious direct aristocratic participation in university education in Europe, with the sons of the landed nobility – from families often themselves newly enriched by the expropriation of former Church properties – encouraged to enroll in universities, even if only a minority of them subsequently graduated with a degree. Successful support for chairs helped confirm the humanist credentials of patrons, ostentatiously declared the piety of their almsgiving, and soon extended to the much more lavish endowment of whole colleges by plutocrats such as Thomas Linacre, Henry Savile and Johan Skyte. It is from the mid-sixteenth century onwards that we begin to see strong dynastic and intergenerational associations with specific Colleges and subjects, a development that was to have lasting and far-reaching implications for the wealth later accrued at some highly prestigious institutions across the Continent, including Oxford, Cambridge and Naples (Perkin 2007).

The intensification of royal interest in the fortunes of universities was certainly critical to these complex processes of change. Royal identification with the new learning, in the institutions that were its crucible, became an international badge of the Renaissance Prince, just as the monarch's philanthropy at the heart of the university also sent important political signals to swaggering mercantile towns and cities about status and sovereignty. The creation of Royal or Regius Chairs – professorial appointments paid for by the Crown – epitomized this process and the jockeying for power it signified. Regius Professors became a pillar of the royal presence in universities, demonstrating the monarchical stake in theology, classical learning and the new (and expensive) laboratory sciences (Bann 2013). As the Renaissance matured and spread, the royal imprint similarly expanded, no doubt incentivized by the public, and often rival, educational works of the great noble houses. Henry VIII founded Trinity College, Cambridge, in 1546, after apparently contemplating a raid on the university's property parallel to his assault on the monasteries. Instead, the court party persuaded him of the potential of establishing in his own name, at the heart of a medieval Catholic foundation, a refurbished Protestant theological College that would produce clergy and public servants loyal to the Tudor Reformation settlement. At the same time, Henry's self-projection as a patron of Renaissance humanist learning would be legitimated on an international platform from the resultant publicity of the association.

These practices became the pattern for the next century, culminating, as Sten Lindroth (1976) has argued, in the royal investment in Uppsala University between 1620 and 1632 by King Gustav II Adolph. Gustav's beneficence was on a quite unequalled scale, effectively resourcing from a complicated pipeline of income streams every significant university activity in teaching, collecting, study and writing. It included massive cash subsidies for staffing; transfer to the real estate of the university of over 300 working farms; 14 thousand dollars per annum of local Church tithes; multiple shares in commercial-industrial enterprises and an early provision for the support of professorial sabbaticals. Every staff stipend and every student fee was paid by the Crown. Until mired in the destructive consequences and near national bankruptcy of the 30 years War, Gustav's investments made Uppsala possibly the richest and most dynamic university in Europe and in the period of Swedish recovery after 1648 bequeathed to it a reputation for academic excellence that it succeeded in maintaining for at least two centuries.

None of this should suggest that early modern universities were merely passive beneficiaries of royal, aristocratic or civic generosity, surrendering their freedom to those furnishing their funding. The sophisticated interplay of forces and strategies at work in creating and sustaining corporate relationships includes complex forms of negotiation, bargaining, trade-off, suggestive of the highly transactional guild cultures of the trading elites whose enterprise and wealth production generated the fabric and material of university learning and whose lay and clerical children provided its men of letters, both as students and as teachers. The evidence for this lattice structure of decision-making, revenue-raising and governance, within which universities for the most part skillfully preserved their autonomy while contributing in critically important respects to the life of civil-commercial society and its wider spiritual-ecclesial interests, has led some historians such as Vera Keller (2015) to emphasize universities as powerful institutional actors in the embryonic emergence of an authentic Habermasian 'public sphere' in early modern European society: a shared secular zone of intercultural and organizational communication where money is quite literally a currency or medium of exchange in the use, movement and circulation of which the nascent public sphere is steadily materialized in forms no stakeholder group, least of all the Churches, might dominate.

Thus the university and the determination of its proper funding succeed in disclosing to this society serious moral and legal dilemmas in the incremental resolution of which the rules, boundaries and differentiated domains of influence and legitimacy across the commonwealth begin to be established and moderated. In their very recent case study of the early University of Utrecht, from 1636–1676, Henk van Rinsum and Willem Koops (2016) appear to confirm these insights and perceptions, by showing how in its interactions with its host town, Utrecht University became a laboratory of debate and deliberation on the proper parameters and jurisdictions of the fledgling public sphere and its constituent agents. At the heart of this dialogue was the relationship of knowledge to money – and the consideration of the forms of curricular and philosophical knowledge that the Calvinist ecclesial authorities would sanction, but also for which the increasingly independent and even libertine-anticlerical town magistrates would agree to pay. Rinsum and Koop do not understate the tensions in involved in this, including the infamous altercation around the university's appointment of René Descartes and the disturbances occasioned by the theologically incendiary preaching of some of the university's first, radical students. But in their analysis of the subtle distributions of power and advocacy in the Utrecht setting, they succeed in portraying a quite worldly, flexible, even pragmatic university regime. It works cleverly and proactively with the mayoral authorities to highlight the practical material gains to the town from protecting and nurturing its new university community. It also collaborates with the magistrate class in leveraging power and authority away from the Calvinist Church towards an increasingly autonomous public sphere, within which the control of money and resources is the principal expression of an expanding quasi-secular civil-academic independence. '[T]own magistrates defended the university as an important element in the development of a public space,' Rinsim and Koops conclude, '… stressing the *liberteijt* – the liberty of the academy in opposition to the ecclesiastical authorities and their theocratic aspirations' (17). Hence it may not be too far-fetched to see 'money' and its uses as part of the 'university fuel' of the early European Enlightenment.

Advances of the kind seemingly witnessed in Utrecht did not, however, by any means always signal steady progress for the idea of the university or the security of its longterm funding models. On the contrary, the discussions in Utrecht about whether even to have a university took place against the backdrop of the final years of the 30 years War, with an exhausted European intelligentsia, disfigured by the pan-Continental catastrophe of the Wars of Religion, coming to terms with a century of civil strife, regicide, economic collapse and massive political and cultural trauma. The European universities, it was widely perceived, had done little to avert this disaster and in its aftermath were therefore often appraised in less than edifying terms. It was clear to many sections of academic opinion that nothing had protected the universities from the poison of confessional intolerance and bias, exposing features such as their sectarian intakes, their continuing subservience in key jurisdictions to unyielding religious authorities and their widespread dependence on systems of patronage that left them vulnerable to manipulation and fraud by self-replicating political elites (Davis 2015).

In Utrecht and other European towns a quite viable – and allegedly cheaper – alternative to the university had arisen in the form of the late Renaissance Humanist concept that Jonathan Israel (2002) has called the 'non-confessional universal library' (120). Typified by the collection of the French *erudit* Gabriel Naudé (1600–53), the phenomenon of the universal library grew out of both the dispersal of older medieval monastic *scriptora* and the wreckage of some of the university libraries ruined in the Wars of Religion. The universal library originated in the tumults of the 1630s, reaching its heyday around 1680 and going on to pose for some seven further decades a significant threat to the viability of universities as centres for early Enlightenment instruction. Universal libraries were often superior in content to university libraries and by their nature attracted a broader base of readers and scholars around which salon-style disciples and novices readily gathered and from out of which rudimentary forms of pedagogy also soon arose. 'The community of scholarship around the early universal library collections,' states their latest historian, Evy Varsamopoulou (2013), 'and the independence of those researchers from institutional and economic constraints fostered a spirit of community amongst peers and independence of judgement' (65). Added to this, universal libraries in cities such as Padua, Leiden and Gottingen took heed of the weaknesses in the many areas of the broken seventeenth century European university system and introduced into their activities an informal curriculum of study more modern and flexible than that offered by the ancient universities, including disciplines such as Geography, Modern Languages, the natural sciences and Accountancy. From Oxford to Glasgow to Heidelberg to Uppsala, in the period from 1690 to 1730, medieval universities experienced significant falls in matriculations and records of the period show librarians and bursars lamenting the decline in library stocks and the quality of bibliographic administration. The cost base of universities had grown exponentially in the decades since the 30 years War and the award of degrees lost much of its esteem when so many registered students showed no serious desire to graduate. Universal libraries and the learned societies that began to gather around them were on the other hand reasonably priced, popular and generally non-exclusive and their approach to learning and teaching seemingly better suited to the new age of ideas, empire and discovery.

Varsamopoulou has gone so far as to term this period the first great crisis of the European university, where a genuinely financially viable alternative to university study presented itself to European letters, with a stripped-down infrastructure and a streamlined fitness of academic-professional purpose available to a much broader student base than the universities has ever assayed. That the traditional system of higher education from Scotland to Poland and Uppsala to Salamanca survived this protracted threat is attributable to the rise within it of a new generation of men (such as Adam Smith (1723–90), Glasgow University's reforming librarian and pedagogue) who understood the appeal of early Enlightenment associational culture and who strove to integrate some of its key attractions into the experience of university education, including the active encouragement of new subjects and the provision of novel styles of learning such as the seminar and the tutorial. These reforms of course entailed a monumental overhaul of university funding and investment for which few of the customary resource instruments seemed remotely suited. In the northern European countries recovering from the 30 years War and its many regional variants and parallels, the opportunity to found, refound or radically redesign models of collegiate and university education entailed fresh thinking about the funding base for these revised and enlarged endeavours.

Led by campaigners such as Christian Thomasius at Halle, William Wishart at Edinburgh and – quite extraordinarily – Elector George of Hanover (King George II of Great Britain) at Göttingen, a new combined concept of university funding arose based upon a distributed cost analysis of the services universities could provide and which supposedly eclipsed those available from even the best of the universal libraries. It is important to stress that older forms of resourcing were not abandoned in this reconceptualization. Indeed, they remained vital to the total package. Nor was the model uniform across Europe. But the universities that emerged strongest from the tumults and the threats of the early Enlightenment had come to a profound realization expressed in what came to be termed the 'tripartite model' of university finance: the marshaling of large-scale endowments, the levying of substantial annual fees upon undergraduate students matriculated in large numbers, and, above all, the irrevocable financial guarantee of the state (Appold 2008). It seems clear that the early architects of this new settlement regarded the local or nation-state underwriter of the university as an important but equal participant in the renewed provision of longterm resource. Subsequent history was to demonstrate, however, the naiveté of this position, since the contractual partnership with the state as it was evolving in the middle of the eighteenth century was destined to alter forever not only the funding of higher education, but its core purposes.

Money and Modernity

Paul Gerbod's (2004) simple statement that that 'From the nineteenth century onwards, the financial needs of the universities tended to be covered more and more exclusively by the state' (111) of course captures the central truth of the relationship between modernity, money and university learning. It represents possibly the brightest nugget of historical insight to have come down to our contemporary perception of the challenges facing universities today. With a small handful of exceptions – including perhaps the new Pontifical Universities funded directly by the Roman Curia and also the unusual phenomenon of Oxford and Cambridge in England – in the early 1800s the idea of the European university became increasingly inseparable from the educational goals and unmatched capacities of the burgeoning administrative-bureaucratic state and its seemingly boundless sources of industrial and commercial surplus.

There were several pivotal reasons for this. In the first instance, the Westphalian state model after 1648 began to tie the expression and understanding of national identity to a set of indices for the reproduction and transmission of which universities were held to be uniquely placed. Continuing and fortifying their traditional role in the instruction and formation of key cadres of public and ecclesiastical servants, the evolving university curriculum became one of the chief means of narrating the national story: its language, literature and arts; its history in victory and defeat; its deposits of religious insight and devotion; its founders and great minds; and, latterly, its achievements in industry, architecture, the sciences and imperial-colonial exploration and conquest. Such 'training' functions for which the state appeared increasingly willing to pay in this period ought not to be seen either instrumentally or paternalistically. Across Europe, a broad humanist education, extended and enriched by the additional subject expertise (especially in Science) for which the universal libraries and their offshoots had provided particular academic credibility was regarded as more and more vital to the maintenance of an effective and loyal bureaucracy administering the operations of governments responsible for increasingly specialized areas of national life. Funding the universities for these purposes was then not merely a crude, reductive means of controlling them, it legitimated them as an manifestation of state power and national community (Leerssen 2006).

Beyond this cultural imaginary of ethno-civic identity formation and technocratic leadership, the practical reform of the university in order to address the revenue losses and other hazards posed by alternative forms of Enlightened education, such as the universal libraries, the provincial associations and salon networks – and eventually the lure for the affluent classes of the tutor-led or chaperoned Grand Tour – required levels of infrastructure investment that few of the customary university income streams could yield. Some of the largest contributions made to universities from central state coffers in the decades from 1780–1900 were provided to support the massive expansion of the university estate in the form of new libraries, purpose-built buildings and accommodation for expanded teaching and study precisely in order to neutralize the perceived threats to the existence and prestige of the universities (Gerbod 2004: 107–11). The name most strongly associated with such developments was of course Wilhelm Humboldt, whose refurbished Berlin University, entirely underwritten by a new style of fiscal contract with the Prussian State, came to typify the supposed 'reinvention' of the modern university as a nexus of learning, reformed curricula and assessment, and above all research-intensive enquiry across a spectrum of disciplines. The Humboldt legend has been challenged in the last 15 years by thinkers such as Mitchell Ash (2006, 2008) and Oleg Morozov (2010). It has been in large part defended by Marek Kwiek (2008). What seems clear is that whatever his exact role in the Berlin renewal, Humboldt stands in a lineage of growing, centrally-funded and administered investment which antedates his interventions and which continued gathering momentum long after he left office. It may indeed be chiefly in these essentially monetary respects that we can continue to speak of the 'Humboldtian University' bestowing certain specific credentials on a subsequent European university system to which contemporary higher education remains undeniably the troubled and ambivalent heir.

Measures taken to rebrand European universities as beacons of national excellence were most expensively implemented in two broad areas: research and recruitment. It was quite obvious from 1810 onwards that the scale of investment required to bootstrap research centres, whether in Egyptology or Engineering, could reasonably come from no source other than central government and its increasingly differentiated tax base. This funding regime certainly remained open to private benefactors and commercial-industrial sponsorship. In the early 1770s, the journeyman James Watt had entered into what was effectively a public-private partnership with Glasgow University, renting laboratory space in order to work on the design of the separate condenser steam engine, in the eventually lucrative fruits of which the university purchased shares. This particular agreement built on a strong indigenous culture of state subsidy for university learning in Scotland, reaching back to the terms of the 1707 Act of Union, which made annual government subventions to the nation's five ancient universities a legal requirement. In Scotland and elsewhere, the kind of linkages exemplified by Watt persisted into the early decades of the nineteenth century as the Industrial Revolution helped forge a new class of super-rich technology entrepreneurs increasingly eager to collaborate with universities and to endow research initiatives focused on agreed commercial priorities. But the sheer scale of plant and machinery required for establishing and maintaining state-of-the-art scientific research institutes, alongside the expense of supporting the paleographic and travel costs of research undertakings drawn from the humanities, steadily enmeshed the central government offices for Education across Europe in the detailed economics of the university. It is therefore unsurprising that by the 1840s, in most regional jurisdictions, central governments had in one guise or another become the pivotal sources of supply for almost all of the leading European universities, swiftly dwarfing all others (Neave 2012).

Such developments were of serious political as well as economic import in the countries where they occurred. From the middle of the nineteenth century, the funding of universities from national treasuries in polities such as Britain, France, the Netherlands and the German Confederation led to increased clamor for state monitoring and accountability, particularly in those societies that were coming to regard universities as an important fixture in the provision of mass education and where the public purse was filled increasingly from an expanding tax base of the general citizenry. The danger here was obvious: as groups barred by station or confession or even qualification were called upon increasingly to resource a high-status area of educational activity to which they and their children had no access, the support of public opinion for state-funded universities was placed in serious jeopardy, with consequent peril to the whole academic edifice.

Wherever we look in Europe, however, in the middle and later decades of the nineteenth century, we see fierce university resistance to the idea of state scrutiny of their activities or spending patterns (Rothblatt 1997). It is at this juncture that there is a pan-European reclamation of the so-called 'ethos' or heritage of the medieval university, eloquently elaborated by figures such as John Henry Newman and commonly commemorated in self-servingly heroic narratives by many others as a long struggle to main critical independence from the powers of Church and Court in support of the disinterested pursuit of truth and public service. Many of the so-called new or 'free' universities born in the nineteenth century make just as much play with these claims of right as their ancient peers, demanding respect for their autonomy and calling upon their influential alumni to defend it. We might reasonably conclude that by some important measures these campaigns were successful. Despite the exponential growth of state funding or subsidy, in a wide variety of forms, few if any of the major European seats of learning forfeited their freedom or relinquished responsibility for their own financial accounting. Significant legal statute in several countries did subject university authorities to enhanced levels of fiscal transparency, but this was largely no different from the growing body of law governing the increasingly diverse business combinations appearing throughout industrial society. Few special statutes were instated for overseeing the financial and other affairs of universities *per se* and governments proved for the most part reluctant to pass or enforce them where they were contemplated (Willis 1984).

In one critical area state authorities did incline to exercise their powers to enforce change as the nineteenth century advanced: access and participation. There were wide divergences of view and policy on this topic, but they were marked by common and compelling themes. The growth in the student population was vital to realisation of the state and university objectives that constituted the new, shared rationale for higher education. The contractual understanding that brought universities fresh capital embraced large-scale expansion of intake, most especially among those sections of the middle class educated population achieving new levels of political and economic advantage and situated usually in the vanguard of gradualist franchise reform. These are the sections of society who provide the myriad student characters for classic nineteenth century novels and plays in Britain, France, Germany and Russia: the 'perpetual students' embarked on decade-long degrees and in those specific literary-cultural settings more routinely preoccupied with forbidden extra-curricular reading, sexual dalliance and political agitation.

What are we to make of this first expansion of provision – culturally, politically and economically – in even its piecemeal and imperfect implementation? The initial observation to be made is the obvious one that the pattern of growth reflected other deep-seated and paradoxical trends in the burgeoning of the industrial polity. The culture of 'enrolment management' in the universities mirrored parallel types of emergent human capital and investment theory, which from around 1850 onwards, reframed the centralized state as an enabler and arbitrator of market efficiencies that would, when properly attuned, help ensure the competitive advantage of commercial-imperial nation states through the supply of suitably qualified and leading-edge labour. The clarification in even rudimentary form of cost-comparison mechanisms, enabled by the reprofiling of student contributions as 'tuition fees', placed a notional price on advanced education that could then be aligned or harmonized with other processes of cost-benefit-output analysis across the commercial-industrial complex. Hence students could discern with supposedly greater transparency than ever the true cost of their learning, publicly benchmarked against alternative forms of occupational credentialisation – and within which they could be readily configured as 'customers' as well as matriculating undergraduates. These were the movements in university politics Nietzsche was subsequently to denounce in his fierce polemic 'We Scholars': the subordination of knowledge to the cash nexus and the resultant creation of a new and dangerous kind of graduating technocracy in thrall to the worst aspects of market calculation, personal acquisitiveness and state servitude.

While it may be too early in this financialising narrative to pinpoint at this juncture the direct emergence of the 'entrepreneurial university' – currently the object of much critical scrutiny – it is certainly feasible to discern in the cadences of higher educational policy discourse and institutional practice in the period the gradual appearance of a new conception of corporate knowledge ownership. This was by the economic slump of the 1890s (which inflicted serious damage on the leading universities precisely because of their multiple compacts with state and market) expressed in a variety of new university initiatives, which ranged from patents to corporate partnerships and which were inseparable from the new legislative and fiscal arrangements emanating from an increasingly interventionist state. Increased intakes were then matched paradoxically by an inescapably homogenizing construction of the student, channeled along certain academic-professional facultized pathways towards domains of study conducive to the priorities of mushrooming state and imperial bureaucracies and/or the needs of private enterprise for competitive intellectual specialization.

The late nineteenth-century extension of participation was therefore by no stretch of the imagination a democratic or emancipatory conception of access, nor was it even a cross-class meritocracy of the best and most able. Admission to university remained throughout these decades the privilege of certain self-replicating elites, whose gatekeepers made only the most cautious adjustment to entry and intakes. Nevertheless, the base of these elites was undoubtedly growing dramatically in the period in question and their pressure for greater mobility incentivized governments to look favourably on their financial support for higher education in the form of widespread fee exemptions, direct grants, scholarships and accommodation. As Keith Vernon (2001) and Gavin Moodie (2016) have shown, this was by the years immediately before the First World War an immense undertaking, furnishing a whole new managerial class with meaningful opportunities to attend university for a price in most cases well below its actual costs. For the vast majority of those who completed a successful schooling, of course, university remained permanently out of reach, despite these policies. The new forms of subsidy in consequence remained vulnerable to George Elder Davie's (1961) later potent criticism that, far from extending general educational entitlement, they merely succeeded in harvesting a tiny minority of the most talented minds and initiating them into that same introspective fraternity, which, in various semblances, had controlled the leading

European universities from time immemorial. Whether we accept Davie's famous critique or not, the terms in which it was leveled reflect a whole new moral and political perspective on the meaning of the university in modern society and its relationship to democratic principle and pluralism. This in effect marks a new turn in the conversation on the university and one where history has to all intents and purposes *become* the modernity (and postmodernity) with which higher education now currently grapples.

History Lessons?

This essay began from the quite traditionalist heuristic assumption that there might be something to be 'learned' from a fresh consideration of Europe's university funding experience – particularly those aspects of it, from a perhaps neglected past, that appear to have receded from general academic and social memory. It is be hoped that most of these lessons – if indeed there are any – are discursively embedded in the examination of the issues themselves in their particular historical conjunctures, requiring little in the way of distillation to make them available for inspection or for illuminating comparison with the issues of the present day. Nevertheless, there may be some elements of the critical recount of the 'deep past' that in concluding this exercise merit sharper foregrounding, because their salience for current circumstances is peculiarly – even unexpectedly – resonant.

The first of these in the insistence throughout this analysis that money has *always* been a critically important feature of the university landscape, not only in the form of resource but as a potent signifier in articulating, defending and critiquing the purposes of universities – a form of academic energy, to paraphrase Conroy, materialising concerns and dilemmas that might otherwise remain concealed in the esoteric order of university knowledge-production, curation and expertise.

The second is the challenge to a simplistic, Whiggish view of university progress, which characterises higher education as moving from privilege to entitlement, from private indulgence to public good, from possession by the elites to ownership by the masses. The narrative of university funding is a much more confusing and recursive plotline than these binaries imply, marked by trade-offs, the striking of colossal social bargains and the annexation of university history itself by rival parties seeking domination and control of the idea of higher education.

Somewhat more benignly, the appreciation of university funding in all its complexity across the ages discloses moments of genuine synergy and creativity. This is perhaps most conspicuous in the parsing of the state throughout this assessment as *more* than central government: the understanding of the state, instead, as an interconnected network of actors some of whom, the late medieval guild towns especially, may represent a usable memory of how universities can engage with subsidiary territories and regions, refashioning the social contract from the base upwards and restoring an authentic collaboration with local peoples and communities. If this aspiration seems itself somewhat idealistic, then it is surely a final, paramount lesson from the history of university funding regimes that the preservation and actualisation of ideals of some sort is absolutely vital to reimagining the concept of the university for the generations who will come after us.

References

Anderson, R., & Lynch, M. (2003). *The University of Edinburgh: An illustrated history*. Edinburgh: Edinburgh University Press.
Appold, K. G. (2008). Academic life and teaching in post-reformation Lutheranism. In R. Kolb (Ed.), *Lutheran ecclesiastical culture, 1550–1675* (pp. 65–116). Brill: Leiden.
Ash, M. (2006). Bachelor of what, master of whom? The Humboldt myth and historical transformations of higher education in German-speaking Europe and the US. *European Journal of Education, 41*(2), 245–267.
Ash, M. (2008). From 'Humboldt' to 'Bologna': History as discourse in higher education reform debates in German-speaking Europe. In B. Jessop et al. (Eds.), *Education and the knowledge-based economy in Europe* (pp. 41–63). Sense: Rotterdam.
Bann, J. (2013). Legal terminology in the eighteenth-century Scottish university. *Scottish Cultural Review of Language and Literature, 19*. n.pag.
Brockliss, L. (2000). Gown and town: The university and the city in Europe, 1200–1800. *Minerva, 38*, 147–170.
Davie, G. E. (1961). *The democratic intellect: Scotland and her universities in the nineteenth century*. Edinburgh: Edinburgh University Press.
Davis, R. A. (2015). Archiving the source: Pasts and futures of the humanities. *Educational Theory, 65*(6), 617–634.
De Ridder-Symoens, H. (1996). Management and resources. In H. De Ridder-Symoens (Ed.), *A history of the University in Europe Vol 2: Universities in early modern Europe (1500–1800)* (pp. 155–208). Cambridge: Cambridge University Press.
Gerbod, P. (2004). Resources and management. In W. Rüegg (Ed.), *A history of the University in Europe Vol 3: Universities in the nineteenth and early twentieth centuries (1800–1945)* (pp. 111–122). Cambridge: Cambridge University Press.
Gieysztor, A. (1992). Management and resources. In H. De Ridder-Symoens (Ed.), *A history of the University in Europe Vol 1: Universities in the Middle Ages* (pp. 108–144). Cambridge: Cambridge University Press.
Graham, G. (2013). The university: A critical comparison of three ideal types. In R. Sugden et al. (Eds.), *Leadership and cooperation in academia* (pp. 1–17). Cheltenham: Edward Elgar.
Israel, J. (2002). *Radical enlightenment: Philosophy and the making of modernity, 1650–1750*. Oxford: Oxford University Press.
Keller, V. (2015). *Knowledge and the public interest, 1575–1725*. Cambridge: Cambridge University Press.
Kwiek, M. (2008). Revisiting the classical German idea of the university. *Polish Journal of Philosophy, 2*(1), 55–78.
Leerssen, J. (2006). Nationalism and the cultivation of culture. *Nations and Nationalism, 12*(4), 559–578.
Lindroth, S. (1976). *A history of Uppsala University 1477–1977*. Stockholm: Almqvist & Wiksell.
Moodie, G. (2016). *Universities, disruptive technologies, and continuity in higher education*. London: Palgrave.
Morozov, O. (2010). *Wilhelm Von Humboldt and Berlin University: A new look at the origin of the Humboldt myth*. Moscow: National Research University.
Neave, G. (2012). *The evaluative state, institutional autonomy and re-engineering higher education in Western Europe*. London: Palgrave.

Osipian, A. L. (2004). *Corruption as a legacy of the medieval university.* Annual conference of the Association for the Study of Higher Education (ASHE), Kansas City.

Osipian, A. L. (2008). Corruption and coercion: University autonomy versus state control. *European Education, 40*(3), 27–48.

Perkin, H. (2007). History of universities. In *International handbook of higher education* (pp. 159–205). Dordrecht: Springer.

Rashdall, H. (1895). *The Universities of Europe in the Middle Ages* (Vol. 1, pp. 17–18). Oxford: Clarendon Press.

Readings, B. (1996). *The University in Ruins.* Cambridge: Harvard University Press.

Rothblatt, S. (1997). The writing of university history at the end of another century. *Oxford Review of Education, 23*(2), 151–167.

Rubin, M. (2012). The European medieval universities, from the past and today. *International Higher Education, 67*, 9–11.

Van Rinsum, H., & Koops, W. (2016). University of Utrecht 1636–1676: Res ecclesia, res publica and … res pecunia. *History of Education, 45*(1), 1–17.

Varsamopoulou, E. (2013). The fate of the humanities, the fate of the university. *The European Legacy, 18*(1), 59–73.

Vernon, K. (2001). Calling the tune: British universities and the state, 1880–1914. *History of Education, 30*(3), 251–271.

Willis, R. (1984). *The Universities of Europe, 1100–1914.* Cranbury: Associated University Presses.

The Furnace of Instrumental Reason

Richard Smith

> *We only have to look around us, at the blunt use of metrics such as journal impact factors, h-indices and grant income targets to be reminded of the pitfalls. Some of the most precious qualities of academic culture resist simple quantification, and individual indicators can struggle to do justice to the richness and plurality of our research. Too often, poorly designed evaluation criteria are "dominating minds, distorting behaviour and determining careers." (Lawrence, P.A. (2007) The mismeasurement of science, Current Biology 17. 15, pp. 583–585.) At their worst, metrics can contribute to what Rowan Williams, the former Archbishop of Canterbury, calls a "new barbarity" in our universities.*
>
> Wilsdon et al. (2015, Foreword, p. 3)

Introduction

I take for granted in this paper that the broad answer to our questions concerning the relation between funding and research is that it is, increasingly, the funding and the search for it – for 'grant capture' as the phrase has it – that drive both the kind of research that is done in universities and the way it is done. Many examples could be given, and I touched on several in a previous paper for this seminar, 'Mud and hair: an essay on the conditions of educational research' (Smith 2014a, b) and in the paper that Jim Conroy and I gave in Leuven last year on 'The ethics of the research excellence framework'. In the first paper I noted the speed with which 'sponsorism'

R. Smith (✉)
School of Education, University of Durham, Durham, UK
e-mail: r.d.smith@durham.ac.uk

© Springer International Publishing AG, part of Springer Nature 2018
P. Smeyers, M. Depaepe (eds.), *Educational Research: Ethics, Social Justice, and Funding Dynamics*, Educational Research 10,
https://doi.org/10.1007/978-3-319-73921-2_14

has established itself in academic culture in the UK. I quoted MacFarland (2012) for a definition: 'sponsorism is when someone's research is designed to fit the agenda of funding bodies', and I suggested that the older idea, that an interesting – even theoretically interesting – research question might precede not simply the quest for funding but the very consideration of whether funding would be helpful in any particular case, had come to seem naïve, or even laughably old-fashioned. Certainly colleagues in my own university now take it for granted that, despite what the advertised criteria say – these in any case tend to ambiguity – unless they establish themselves as successful 'grant-capturers' they will have no chance of passing probation or achieving promotion. In a remarkable conflation of these two career hurdles some UK universities are now moving from a three-year to a five-year probationary period, by the end of which the lecturer will either meet the criteria for promotion to Senior Lecturer or be required to leave. There is uncertainty over whether meeting the criteria for promotion will automatically lead to actual promotion. What seems clear is that the increased height of the hurdle will be reflected in ever greater expectations of 'grant capture'.

In the second paper, 'The ethics of the research excellence framework' (now published as Conroy and Smith 2017), Jim Conroy and I drew attention to the criterion of 'Impact' in the regular (once every 7 years) evaluation of academic research in the UK. Every department of the university, from Material Physics to Theology, must submit case-studies showing how its research benefits the wider, ie non-academic, community. For the Material Physicist this might mean working with industry to develop more effective lubricants for artificial hip-joints (a real and of course wholly admirable example). The collaboration can be written up in ways that emphasise both the contribution of the hip-joint manufacturer (which counts as grant-capture for the university) and the wider (that is, more than academic) value of the research to the community. The patients are happier and in less pain; the hip-joints are more effective and last longer, so the benefits can be readily expressed in economic terms too. This is an excellent example of Impact, properly capitalised in REF terms. Theology may seem at a disadvantage here, but it can join in the game by contributing to a multi-faith festival that it organises with the City Council. There will be economic benefits from sales of samosas and chapatis, and even more so from the calculated Social Return from the festival: the enhanced social cohesion that means less racially-motivated crime and thus less demand on the Police, hospital services, magistrates and prison professionals. There will be less anxiety or depression and so there will be fewer days off work, to the further benefit of the local economy. I return to 'Social Return' below.

At least the REF rewards, in theory, good academic work rather than the indifferent 'capture' of funding. Impact case studies carry implications for the number of academics whose publications can be submitted for assessment – roughly ten for every case study – and it is here that the essentially academic criteria apply. Publications are judged on academic originality, rigour and significance: the latter meaning significance to the academic community and in no way to be equated with impact, capitalised or otherwise. A top-rated, 4* publication currently brings in (in

Education) £8337 in each year of the seven-year cycle, ie over £58k in total.[1] This money, unlike so much funding from other sources, does not then leave the university to be shared with industrial or commercial partners, since its academic component is an achievement of the university alone. It does not arrive already ear-marked for redistribution in the way that many if not most external grants do, for instance to pay the salary of a research assistant. The interesting question then is this: why, given the significant income achieved by good publications (and publications accounted for 65% of a department's submission to the last REF in 2014) – do universities set such store by capturing all and every kind of external funding, especially funding that does not carry the academic prestige of REF funding, funding much of which is destined to leave the university almost as soon as it reaches it, and funding the search for which seems bound to distract academics from writing the books and journal articles which constitute their traditional work and which in any case bring a substantial flow of income to the university? Before attempting to answer this question I quote a similar cry of exasperation from Stefan Collini's luminous book, *What are Universities For?* (2012), and then turn to a case-study of the new insanity.

> To meeting of Faculty Board where we are told that the university wants us to 'generate' more 'research income'. Successfully control my temper and express judicious-sounding reservation. But really! High-quality research in my field depends, overwhelmingly, on having time free from other distractions … Regular sabbatical leave is the key, understood not as a period in which you 'complete' a 'project' but as a space in which you start to ruminate about an unobvious question and find out whether you might, one day, have something interesting to say about it. The origin and purpose of grants and other kinds of 'outside income' is to pay for expenses incurred in carrying out such a piece of research, so being told to *pursue* 'outside funding' amounts to the instruction: 'You must find extra ways to incur expenses'. More material for the growing field of tail/dog wag-relation studies. (p. 151).

I return to the significant matter of 'rumination' in the final section below.

Raising the Bar

Here is an example of the requirement for 'grant capture' that vividly illustrates Collini's point. In the summer of 2015 the UK's Newcastle University introduced a new performance management programme called 'Raising the Bar'. All active researchers were given 'minimum expectations for research performance'. This was in response to concerns that the University was slipping down the rankings of Russell Group universities (a self-selecting group of the larger, older and more research-intensive universities that lobbies for its own interests rather than those of the Higher Education sector more widely) and that it was not well positioned to

---

[1] These are the figures for my own university at least.

meet the challenge of the next REF.[2] The 'minimum expectations' entailed individual targets for external research funding, set according to academic subject and individual seniority. Thus a lecturer in the humanities might be expected to secure £3k each year, while a professor or senior lecturer in the same discipline might have a target of £12k; a professor or senior lecturer in a science- or social science-based discipline might have a target of £45k per year. At the same time researchers were expected to produce highly rated publications for the next REF: at least four 3* publications (or 'outputs' as they are of course called) in the case of lecturers and significantly more highly rated publications in the case of promoted staff. 3* is awarded to publications that display 'Quality that is internationally excellent in terms of originality, significance and rigour but which falls short of the highest standards of excellence', in the terminology of the REF.

At Warwick University in the previous year associate professors, readers and professors in the university's medical school were told in late 2014 that research-active staff who had not brought in an average of £90,000 per year as principal investigators (or £150,000 as co-investigators) over the past 4 years were at risk of redundancy. Those opposed to the redundancies were quick to complain that academics were being put in a similar position to 'market traders in the City, who are judged solely on the amount of money they raise' (Jump 2014). They noted that financial targets such as these carry the temptation for academics desperate not to lose their jobs to 'massage data' (which of course has indeed been prevalent in the financial industries). In an echo of Collini's critical remarks above Dennis Leech, president of Warwick's branch of the UCU, pointed out that the financial targets amounted to an encouragement, if not a directive, to academics to 'carry out the most expensive research they could' Jump, ibid. he suggested that this was unacceptable behaviour on the part of an institution funded largely by public taxes. These are just two examples of the performance management strategies now being adopted by at least one in six UK universities (*Times Higher Education* 7 Dec 2015) and of the criticisms made of them.

If we draw these criticisms together it is difficult not to conclude that performance management such as this does not make sense even in its own dismal terms. Academics are driven to chase paltry sums of money – as little as £3k per year in the case of a humanities lecturer at Newcastle – when even the financial return, let along the academic prestige, from publishing a very good (of better than 'international excellence', but let this oddity pass) journal article or book can be twice as much as this. In any case the funding opportunities for, say, a historian or a philosopher are quite limited compared to those for a Material Physicist or a specialist in sustainable technology. The success rate for applications to the various UK funding councils is seldom much more than 35%; in 2015–16 for the Economic and Social Research Council it was 12%. The opportunity cost – the amount of time wasted in chasing

---

[2] It is worth noting that neither at the time when 'Raising the Bar' was proposed, nor at the time of my writing this paper, was there any clear indication of what the requirements of the next REF will be, nor exactly when it will be, nor whether even the title will be the same. All agree however that whatever it is, it will happen.

funding from these sources – is obvious: time that could have been spent in doing research (not to mention teaching, of course). The low success rates for the Funding Councils in turn are partly responsible for the pressure to acquire funding from any and every source; but much the same opportunity costs apply everywhere, and success in 'grant capture' does not carry the same prestige in all cases (the LEGO Foundation is often cited, no doubt unfairly).

In trying to make sense of this phenomenon the comparison with an episode of Chinese history is irresistible. During Mao Zedong's 'Great Leap Forward' in 1958 every local commune was required to set up small backyard furnaces to produce steel from scrap metal, to fulfil Mao's ambition to match the steel production of the USA and the other western powers. Farmers, doctors, teachers and others were forced to turn to this task from their regular work. Farm workers left their fields in search of such stray bits of metal – rusted iron bolts or broken metal tools – as they could find, and agriculture suffered. In their desperation to meet the production targets set for them peasants sometimes threw their pots and pans, their only means of cooking, into the furnaces. The environment was despoiled as whole forests were cut down to fuel the furnaces. Jung Chang records how during this time she went out to gather what the peasants called 'feather fuel', the scrub and twigs that were in fact virtually useless, burning up in no time at all, but were the only approximation to fuel that could be found.

> Once I voiced my regret about the lack of proper trees. The women with me said it had not always been like this. Before the Great Leap Forward, they told me, the hills had been covered with pine, eucalyptus and cypress. They had all been felled to feed the 'backyard furnaces' to produce steel ... I was shocked to come face-to-face, for the first time, with the disastrous consequences of the Great Leap, which I had known only as a 'glorious success'. (Jung Chang 1993, p. 555)

Despite these efforts the furnaces did not produce steel anyway, only low-grade and largely useless pig iron. Metallurgists could have told Mao that this would happen, but he persisted with the scheme in the face of such evidence as people dared to bring to him since it was rooted in the revolutionary zeal of the people rather than the expertise of 'intellectuals' ('experts', we might say, in resonance with today) and scientists.

The comparison between Raising the Bar and the backyard furnaces is of course less than perfect. It does however highlight the absurdity of scratting around for insignificant sums of money down the back of the academic sofa (the equivalent of the backyard furnaces) to the neglect of more important academic goals (the equivalent of advanced methods of steel production). Furthermore the destruction of the natural environment to feed the furnaces parallels only too well the effect on what Wilsdon, in the quotation that prefixes this paper, calls 'the most precious qualities of academic culture' and 'the richness and plurality of our research'. It sidelines cooperation and mutual support in favour of increasingly desperate competition; it puts what can be measured in terms of money 'captured' before consideration of what we value; in the field of education especially it threatens to marginalise all other forms of research, particularly those that, in Collini's words above, call us to 'ruminate about an unobvious question and find out whether [we] have something interesting to say about it' – and this despite the fact that, in the UK, the REF explicitly welcomes and rewards research of this kind.[3] Most of all, however, the comparison with the bizarre and tragic backyard furnaces helps us to see the full ludicrousness of what is thus satirised.

Newcastle University's 'Raising the Bar' performance management programme was withdrawn in the summer of 2016 after trade union 'action short of a strike' that involved refusal to mark essays and examination scripts, a sanction that would have prevented students from graduating and entering the world of work. The University and Colleges Union and Newcastle University's management issued a joint agreement (Newcastle UCU 2016) recognising that, among other things,

- performing well in key metric exercises such as the REF is important even if some of the rules are problematic
- it is problematic to focus exclusively on quantitative targets
- it is necessary to continue to improve the research performance of the University
- we need to establish a non-coercive culture and approach

It is hard not to wonder, though, if the use of bullet-points is not itself a symbolic concession to management.

Instrumental Reason

Since 'grant capture' is deeply irrational, in deflecting academics from their proper and in all senses more profitable work, it is tempting to wonder if it is a symptom of a more pervasive underlying condition. In an interesting blog on the Raising the Bar affair Liz Morrish (2015) writes that it is a symptom of the audit culture and its 'rituals of verification' (Power 1997) that demand constant and obsessive monitoring, reporting and surveillance. Since, as she points out, the REF scores of individuals are confidential to the REF Panel that awarded them, they are not available to the university's management – its monitors and auditors – who accordingly look for something which they *can* measure. This seems right, though I would put it slightly differently: audit and verification are means of holding people to account, and from holding people to account it is a small step to the urge to discipline, to apportion blame and exact penalties. One does not have to be a Foucauldian to make this diagnosis. Those conducting regimes of performance management need to show that they can 'make hard decisions' if they are to rise to the next tier of management, where they will be able to exercise their powers not merely on individuals but on whole Departments and Schools.

---

[3] E.g. 'Although modest in volume, the quality of philosophical outputs was generally very high. World-leading conceptual work addressed and illuminated complex educational issues and contributed to the refinement of theoretical understanding' (Overview report by REF Main Panel C and Sub-panels 16 to 26, HEFCE 2015, p. 108).

Although talk of symptoms is apposite here, perhaps it is more revealing to think in terms of symbols. In any case there are connections between the two terms in the context of the discussion here: a symptom becomes a symbol when it kicks free of the condition that originally underlay it, and takes on a life of its own. Thus the backyard furnaces were a symptom of the way Mao's judgement was impaired by his desire to catch up with the west in steel production, and by his urge to inspire and benefit from the revolutionary fervour of the people. The furnaces then became a symbol to the rest of the world of that fervour and of China's technological progress. As a symbol their failure was intolerable, with the result that the backyard furnaces movement continued despite clear evidence that it was a disaster. Similarly, in the Newcastle case, while grant capture started as a symptom of the culture of audit and heavy-handed performance management it became emblematic of the University's attempt to rise in the Russell Group of universities and display its REF-ready muscles to its competitors. It thus symbolised the essentially instrumental nature of the modern university, whose success is measured by the extent to which it meets the ends of climbing in the various league-tables and improving its scores in exercises of research assessment. What we might call the intrinsic value of the university, or the value of the university when it is true to its intrinsic ends and purposes, has disappeared entirely.

The instrumental thinking that now characterises the universities of the UK can be illustrated in numerous ways. Above all, the charging of undergraduate fees of £9k per year, to be repaid when the graduate's annual salary reaches a certain threshold, naturally causes university students to think that the principal function of university education is to enable them to earn sufficient money, in graduate-level careers, to repay the debts they have incurred. The whole business is thus circular – the outcome of university study is income – though presumably the sterility of this is satisfying to a particular kind of mind. Universities are finding other ways too of concentrating the student mind according to the tenets of instrumental thinking. Some appoint 'academic advisors' from the ranks of lecturers: their job is to conduct a 'skills audit' of their incoming first-year students and suggest ways in which they can improve their CVs during their time at university in the interests of securing good employment when they leave. If they show no evidence of 'leadership skills', for example, perhaps they could found a new university club or society. Other universities are moving to include modules on Entrepreneurship in every degree programme. In one university (not my own) it was only at a late stage that the thought occurred to the proposers of this scheme that it would require the services of a vast number of lecturers competent to teach such modules, of which they could identify only two, from the Business School. There was also the wider problem that very few academics, having spent all or most of their career in universities, had the knowledge of the world of graduate employment that these innovations seem to require. In particular there was no reason to suppose that they had more idea than anyone else in just what fields the jobs of the future would be found.

Should the enthusiasm of academics for this new Idea of the University falter, measures will be taken to re-inspire them. A new Excellence Framework, this time the TEF or Teaching Excellence Framework, proposes ways of rewarding good quality university teaching. A major criterion of this will be the proportion of a department's ex-students who are in good graduate-level jobs 6 months after graduation. To be clear: if the proportion of your ex-students is not up to scratch, this shows that you did not teach them well, and appropriate sanctions will apply. Collini (2016) notes in his analysis of the Green Paper that proposes the TEF that the phrase 'value for money' occurs four times in the one-page foreword to the Paper, 'and it is repeated over and over again in the body of the document (the NUS [National Union of Students] counted 27 appearances, topped only by 35 for 'what employers want')'. Collini reasonably identifies this as an expression of 'consumerist logic', but it is of course before anything else an expression of instrumental reason. The purpose of university is to give its customers value for money and meet the demands of employers. The TEF Green Paper, *Fulfilling Our Potential: Teaching Excellence, Social Mobility and Student Choice* (2015), was published by the Department for Business, Innovation and Skills (BIS), which was at that time responsible for universities, in the clearest possible indication of the instrumental direction of Government policy on higher education. (It is now the responsibility of the Minister of State for Universities and Science, an individual who appears to be located in both the Department for and the Department for Business, Energy & Industrial Strategy, the latter being the successor to BIS. The significance, if any, of these latest semantic shifts currently eludes me.)

Education is naturally not the only field of activity on which the cold hand of instrumental reason has settled. My favourite examples, which I have cited elsewhere (2014), come first from the resignation of the President of the Royal British Legion (which 'provides help and welfare to the serving and ex-Service community and their families') after he was found to have described the annual events to commemorate those killed in war, such as the ceremony at the Cenotaph in London's Whitehall, as a 'tremendous networking opportunity' in which he could help defence companies (that is, arms manufacturers) lobby ministers and senior members in the armed services (*The Guardian* 15 Oct 2013). Secondly, the then mayor of London, Boris Johnson, welcomed the London Olympics as a 'gigantic schmooze-athon', the opportunity to show the world the 'wealth of … amazing investment opportunities' in Britain. The website of the government's department of Business, Industry and skills (BIS) where this appeared without apparent embarrassment or shame quoted other politicians from the Coalition government, such as the Business Secretary, Vince Cable, to the same effect (though they did not use the term 'schmooze-athon'). Thus sport, which might have appeared something of intrinsic value, joins the list of human goods that are now instrumentalised for the benefit of the economy. In a coda to this it is worth mentioning that Great Britain's impressive achievements in the 2016 Rio Olympics now appear largely the result of careful investment in those disciplines, such as cycling, where large numbers of medals stood to be gained because of the plethora of events.

Some of the most remarkable examples of the instrumentalisation of things once regarded as good in themselves come from museums and similar venues. In an editorial to a special issue, *The health and well-being potential of museums and art galleries*, of the journal *Arts & Health*, the editors write that 'In recent years, many museums, including art galleries, have broadened their services to include those directed towards improving health and well-being' (Chatterjee and Camic 2015). Beneficiaries include 'older adults, people with dementia and mental health service users'. They continue:

> Evidence shows that engaging with museums provides: positive social experiences, leading to reduced social isolation; opportunities for learning and acquiring news [sic] skills; calming experiences, leading to decreased anxiety; increased positive emotions, such as optimism, hope and enjoyment; increased self-esteem and sense of identity; increased inspiration and opportunities for meaning making; positive distraction from clinical environments, including hospitals and care homes; and increased communication among families, caregivers and health professional [*sic*].

The editors admit that 'robust studies regarding the efficacy of museum encounters are limited', but they continue: 'Notwithstanding this shortfall, when analysed and valued in a multi-dimensional, multi-attribute and multi-value socio-economic environment, cultural heritage is widely accepted as an important facet of society in providing cultural references for populations and local communities' and also, of course, and inevitably, 'as an economic asset that provides jobs through tourism'. So the lack of good evidence for these implausible claims can apparently be discounted if they are 'analysed and valued in a multi-dimensional, multi-attribute and multi-value socio-economic environment' (ibid.). The language here does not yield its meaning readily. Certainly the 'socio-economic environment here is not 'multi-value': it is an instrumental monoculture (Smith 2014b), the worthwhileness of museums and art galleries lying in health benefits, broadly understood, whose worth in turn will be articulated in fewer claims on expensive medical and welfare facilities. The length of the editorial, just under a page and a half, is exceeded by the list of references, as if to compensate for the paucity of 'robust studies regarding the efficacy of museum encounters', that is, for lack of evidence.

The novelist Jonathan Coe nicely parodies claims such as these in his recent novel, *Number 11* (Coe 2015: the title reflects the way that power in the UK has moved from 10 Downing Street, the residence of the Prime Minister, to 11 Downing Street, the residence of the Chancellor of the Exchequer). Here is an 'academic expert' talking on television about a site in London where construction workers have found twenty-five skeletons in what seems to have been a burial ground for victims of the Black Death. The interviewer asks:

> 'So, Professor Harvey … you think that this discovery may not just be of historical value, but worth something in monetary terms as well?'
> 'Yes', said Laura. 'Of course I'm not talking about the market value of the remains if people were to try and sell them. I'm saying that discoveries like this add to the sense of mystery which attaches to parts of London, and that sense of mystery is one of the things that attracts people here'.
> 'Tourists, you mean'.
> 'Yes'.
> 'And you're part of a movement, I believe, which is tasked with the job of assigning value to phenomena such as this?'
> 'That's right. As members of the Institute for Quality Valuation, we attempt to quantify things that have traditionally been thought of as unquantifiable. Feelings, in other words. A sense of awe, a sense of wonder…' (pp. 258–9).

Laura has written a book, *Monetizing Wonder*. Elsewhere in the novel a character is charged with placing a monetary value on the Loch Ness Monster – that is, on the myths and legends that surround this almost certainly non-existent creature.

Intrinsic Value

This paper so far may seem only to confirm John Dewey's well-known warning about 'the vice of externally imposed ends' in education (Dewey 1916), or to recommend Michael Oakeshott's equally celebrated idea of education as a 'place apart' from the immediate, local world of the 'present and the particular', seen as a site of corruption, servitude and, in the terms of this paper, the narrowness of instrumental reason (Oakeshott 1971). For Oakeshott the assumption of instrumentalism is foremost among the perils that education is to release students from: education does not exist to tell them in so many words that instrumental reason is the only grown-up way of thinking. But this interpretation is too close to the view that education which cannot be thought of as having intrinsic value is really not education at all. On the contrary, education has all kinds of extrinsic purposes, including qualification for a job or career; it may be thought of as rendering a nation-state more civilised and cohesive, as standing to increase its GDP, and so on. I intend little more here by resurrecting the question of its intrinsic value than to argue, or perhaps merely to suggest, that it cannot be reduced exhaustively to those extrinsic aims and purposes, and to return to the old, and now widely abandoned, question of how the claim that there is an intrinsic dimension to the value of education might be justified. There is moreover an important rhetorical or political side to this. When we are asked what are the purposes of education, how can we expect people to respond other than with bewilderment (if not cynicism) if we appear to shrug our shoulders and merely insist that education has no external goods or purposes but it good in and for itself alone?

The form of the difficulty here is one that we should be familiar with, for it appears in the first Book of Plato's *Republic*, at the beginning, and not by accident, of what is generally thought of as western philosophy. As Socrates encounter the difficult in the *Republic* it concerns the nature of *dikaiosunē*, often translated as 'justice' but which bears the wider sense of 'doing what is right'. The question is how we are to understand the value of *dikaiosunē* in itself, apart from its consequences such as good reputation and honour: for if we value it for the sake of these things then we are not valuing doing right in itself. In the first pages of the *Republic* a rich, immigrant business man (with more than a touch of the *mafioso* about him) called Cephalus, who has sent for Socrates to provide some philosophical entertainment, is alarmed to find that his own suggestion, that doing right brings its proper reward in the satisfactions of not having to lie and being able to pay off one's debts, is disputed by Socrates (partly on the grounds that it is not right to return the axe you have borrowed from your neighbour if he has gone mad in the meantime). Cephalus suddenly remembers he has to go and attend to the business of a religious sacrifice, and leaves his son, Polemarchus, to take his place in the discussion. The other interlocutors seem to grasp that some special kind of answer, beyond listing the contingent rewards that doing right may bring, is required. Thrasymachus, in his characteristically forthright way, demands that Socrates supply a definition of *dikaiosunē*: one that is 'clear and precise' (336d).[4] When this demand is not met he withdraws from the discussion. Glaucon offers a barely more sophisticated version of the same demand: 'I want to be told what exactly each of them [doing right and doing wrong: *dikaiosunē* and its opposite] is and what effects it has as such [*auto kath'auto*] on the mind of its possessor, leaving aside any question of rewards or consequences' (358b).

There are at least three interesting things to note here. The first is that both Thrasymachus and Glaucon both think it reasonable to demand a 'precise' or 'exact' answer. Such an answer would presumably have to be quantified and unconditional, as if doing right consisted in absolute adherence to a number of moral principles, or as if, in the museums example above, so many hours spent in a museum or art gallery – and spent in a particular and specifiable way – could be shown not merely to correlate with but unequivocally to cause decreased anxiety, precisely measured by lower blood pressure or a slower heart beat. An answer like this, of course, is (precisely, as we say) the kind of instrumental justification of doing right that both Thrasymachus and Glaucon are asking Socrates not to offer, and it is difficult to imagine a 'precise' and 'exact' answer that does not take this form. The second thing to note is that it will also be a brisk or quick answer: 'causes a reduction in blood pressure to 120 over 80' (with appropriate caveats) is the end of the matter, leaving little room for further thought or discussion. This is as far as could be imagined from Collini's vision of research (above) as finding 'a space in which you start to ruminate about an unobvious question and find out whether you might, one day, have something interesting to say about it'. We should register, and enjoy, the temporal implications of 'start', 'ruminate', 'might' and 'one day'.

The third thing to note is the epistemological dimension of what is at stake here. We are enquiring about what counts as a sound reason for valuing justice, or a museum, or education – or, to put it differently, what justifies us in saying that we *know* that these things are valuable and worthwhile. The demand for precision and exactness of course takes us in a scientific or mathematical direction, to measuring the blood-pressure of museum-goers or to examining large data-sets and concluding that the education system of Singapore is better than the one in England. In short, it is the nature of evidence that is at issue here, and our deep tendency to be held captive, as Wittgenstein put it (1972 § 115), by the picture of science which convinces us that 'scientific' evidence trumps all other kinds.

Here, by contrast, is the journalist and cultural critic Stuart Maconie paying testimony to the educational value of art history, a subject shortly to be cut from the English curriculum as an A-level subject, that is, one that is taken mainly by senior pupils in secondary schools:

---

[4]All translations are from Lee (1974).

> My other A-level … was art history, and almost every moment of it, every darkened afternoon with Keith Spruce, 'Bri' Lewis and Dorothy Taylor chatting informally but authoritatively at the slide machine, looking at Fra Filippo Lippi or Degas or Kandinsky or Mondrian, has stayed with me. Those long, absorbing hours taught me that the creation, appreciation and love of art is not just the mark of any civilised society, it is the clearest mirror you can hold up to that society, telling you more of its time than a thousand academic histories or earnest documentaries. (Maconie 2016)

Many examples of such testimony could be quoted: of how people have found their education expanded their mind, taught them to think 'outside the box', broadened their horizons, revealed to them a world of wider meanings than they could ever have imagined, showed them not simply how to achieve their ambitions and desires but how they might revise their desires and set their ambitions differently. Why should we not say that such testimonies are the best evidence we have for the intrinsic value of education, in a way that the brisk listing and quantifying of its goods ('Graduates earn on average £100k more than non-graduates over a lifetime') could not possibly do? In his later work Wittgenstein, freeing himself at last from the scientific picture that had held him captive, came to recommend the idea of 'imponderable evidence' (1972 p. 228): that is, evidence that cannot be precisely calculated, weighed and measured, but which is good evidence nonetheless. He wrote (ibid.): 'Imponderable evidence includes subtleties of glance, of gesture, of tone … I may recognize a genuine loving look, distinguish it from a pretended one…'. If subtleties of glance or tone can tell us when someone is lying and when they are telling the truth, our faculties should be reliable enough for us to be able in general, if never with the degree of certainty we expect from the mathematician and the engineer, to recognise sound testimony and distinguish it from false.

It is no accident, I wrote above, that the question of intrinsic value stands, in the *Republic,* at the beginning of western philosophy, for Socrates (or Plato: the usual caveats apply concerning how far we can separate the two) knows that we have here no ordinary question, as if it was like asking whether we should take a taxi or catch the bus, but what we would now call a ruminative question, to use Collini's word, or a philosophical one. Part of the great power of Socrates' insight, though, is that this is not the quick way to a solution – as if having identified the problem as a philosophical one we would then know what methods or techniques we would need to employ – but only the beginning of a deeper and more interesting problem. All Socrates knows for sure, or we might say feels in his bones, is what is the wrong way to talk about the intrinsic value of *dikaiosunē*, which is to appeal to its contingent rewards and consequences. (And as we have seen he has some success in convincing Thrasymachus and Glaucon of this.) In the same way he knows that Theaetetus, in the dialogue that bears his name, must be disabused of the idea that it is possible to think about the nature of knowledge as if it was like geometry, a task consisting of clear, sequential steps following from basic axioms; just as he knows that Euthyphro, in his dialogue, will never be able to think sensitively about morality while he identifies moral thinking with having unshakeable convictions about what is and is not the will of the gods.

Thus in trying to answer the question 'what is knowledge?' Theaetetus has to make the move from addressing that question directly, as if it might be solved by taking up this answer or that – he accepts every one of Socrates' proposed answers in turn until Socrates himself exposes their limitations – and to think about the kind of thinking that investigating the nature of knowledge requires. He needs, we might say too easily, to think philosophically: too easily, because while Plato (rather than Socrates here) has shown the power of such thinking he has also succeeded in problematizing it: for example by making no great distinction between the 'philosophical arguments' of the *Republic* and the speculative or mythical elements in the last Book (such as the myth of Er); by putting into Socrates' mouth specious arguments and word-play (e.g. 376a–c: dogs have a 'truly philosophic nature'); by arguing for the superiority of speech over writing in the *Phaedrus* while producing an extensive body of texts. Nor should we forget here the questionable analogy between *dikaiosunē* in the soul of the individual and in the city-state, on which most of the *Republic* rests.

Socrates, we might say, slows us down in our attempts to answer certain sorts of question not only by insisting that we need to learn a new way of thinking about the question and its epistemological presuppositions, a way that we might characterise as philosophical or ruminative: he slows us down further by reminding us frequently that this philosophical or ruminative thinking is no straightforward matter, but slips between our fingers just as we think we have grasped it, or has the disconcerting tendency from time to time to turn into the faulty or clumsy thinking for which we imagined it was the cure. There is in this sense no quick answer, of course, and philosophers might do more to keep this point in view in the various forums and occasions when they are called on for the kind of brisk answer that the world regards as the standard sort of response. 'This is not a question that can be answered quickly' is not a bad start, especially if it can be pursued a little further. This paper has ruminated about the kind of longer answer that might be developed. Shorter and catchier answers, in the spirit of instrumental thinkers of our time and all times, simply feed the furnace whose product is dross.

References

Chang, J. (1993). *Wild Swans*. London: Flamingo.
Chatterjee, H., & Camic, P. (2015). The health and well-being potential of museums and art galleries. *Arts & Health: An International Journal for Research, Policy and Practice, 7*(3), 183–186.
Coe, J. (2015). *Number 11*. London: Viking/Penguin.
Collini, S. (2012). *What are universities for?* London: Penguin.
Collini, S. (2016, January 21). Who are the spongers now? *London review of books*.
Conroy, J., & Smith, R. (2017). The ethics of research excellence. *Journal of Philosophy of Education, 51*(4), 693–708.
Department for Business, Innovation and Skills. (2015). *Fulfilling our potential: Teaching excellence, social mobility and student choice*. London: Department for Business, Innovation and Skills.
Dewey, J. (1916). *Democracy and education*. New York: Macmillan.

222   R. Smith

Higher Education Funding Council for England (HEFCE). (2015). *Research excellence framework 2014: Overview report by Main Panel C and Sub-panels 16–26*. http://www.ref.ac.uk/media/ref/content/expanel/member/Main%20Panel%20C%20overview%20report.pdf. Accessed 27 Oct 2016.

Jump, P. (2014). Warwick academics 'treated like City traders' with financial targets. *Times Higher Education* 11 Dec. https://www.timeshighereducation.com/news/warwick-academics-treated-like-city-traders-with-financial-targets/2017468.article

Lee, D. (Trans.). (1974). *Plato: The Republic*. London: Penguin.

Macfarland, B. (2012, October 4). I'm an academic and I want to be proud of it. *Times Higher Education*.

Maconie, S. (2016, October 17). Cornelia Parker, Stuart Maconie and more on the axing of A-level art history. *The Guardian*.

Morrish, L. (2015). *Raising the bar: The metric tide that sinks all boats*. https://academicir-regularities.wordpress.com/2015/11/26/raising-the-bar-the-metric-tide-that-sinks-all-boats/. Accessed 27 Oct 2016.

Newcastle UCU (Universities and Colleges Union). (2016). *Raising the bar withdrawn*. Posted 17 June. http://newcastle.web.ucu.org.uk/raising-the-bar-withdrawn/. Accessed 27 Oct 2016.

Oakeshott, M. (1971). Education: The engagement and its frustration. *Journal of Philosophy of Education, 5*(1), 43–76.

Power, M. (1997). *The audit society: Rituals of verification*. Oxford: Oxford University Press.

Smith, R. (2014a). Mud and hair: An essay on the conditions of educational research. In P. Smeyers & M. Depaepe (Eds.), *Educational research: Material culture and its representation* (pp. 133–144). Dordrecht: Springer.

Smith, R. (2014b). An epistemic monoculture and the university of reasons. In D. Lewin, A. Guilherme, & M. White (Eds.), *New perspectives in the philosophy of education: Ethics, politics and religion*. London: Bloomsbury.

Wilsdon, J., et al. (2015). *The metric tide: Report of the independent review of the role of metrics in research assessment and management*. https://doi.org/10.13140/RG.2.1.4929.1363. Accessed 27 Oct 2016.

Wittgenstein, L. (1972). *Philosophical investigations* (G. E. M. Anscombe, Trans.). Oxford: Basil Backwell.

Ovide Decroly (1871–1932): The Prototype of a Modern Scientist, Also in the Context of Funding?

Marc Depaepe, Frank Simon, and Angelo Van Gorp

If any Belgian educator belongs to the canon of the New Education, it is, as generally accepted, Ovide Decroly. Particularly in southern Europe and in many Latin American countries, the ideas and work of this French-speaking Brussels doctor have been inspirational for a movement that projected itself – albeit in different modes – as "child-oriented" (Depaepe & Van Gorp 2003). At the ECER conference of 2016, in Dublin, we reported on our wish to, alongside our efforts to reconstruct his work from the perspective of the inner history of science, also write a biography (putting emphasis on the social and personal contexts of his work) (Depaepe et al. 2016). The point of departure for this is the so-called "laundry list", an agenda carefully compiled in retrospect. An analysis of this factual data based on previous archival research – Where exactly was he? What did a typical day look like for him? At what conferences did he speak? etc. – has already yielded two items which caught our attention in light of the topics addressed by this Research Community [on the philosophy and history of the discipline of education] (e.g. Depaepe and Van Gorp 2003; Depaepe et al. 2013). On the one hand there is the idea that for his time, this figure embodied a very "modern" approach to scientific practice (predominantly aimed at producing scientific articles for high quality medical and psychological journals, largely itself a product of team-based research) (Depaepe et al. 2011). This aspect not only raises the question as to precisely who contributed what

M. Depaepe (✉)
K.U. Leuven, Kortrijk, Belgium
e-mail: Marc.Depaepe@kuleuven.be

F. Simon
Ghent University, Ghent, Belgium
e-mail: Frank.Simon@Ugent.be

A. Van Gorp
History of Education, University of Koblenz-Landau, Mainz, Germany
e-mail: VanGorp@uni-landau.de

© Springer International Publishing AG, part of Springer Nature 2018   223
P. Smeyers, M. Depaepe (eds.), *Educational Research: Ethics, Social Justice, and Funding Dynamics*, Educational Research 10,
https://doi.org/10.1007/978-3-319-73921-2_15

competences (and which possible hierarchical compositions were associated with this at the levels of society and gender [such as "master-servant" and "male-female" relationships, whether complementary or not]), but also from an ethical perspective it problematizes the values pattern – be it epistemic or otherwise (Paul 2014; see also the special issue of *BMGN – Low Countries Historical Review*, 131, 4, 2016) – applied by scientists.

These two elements were recently designated as decisive factors influencing the features and characteristics of the scholarly personae of a specific era. On the other hand – and in connection with this – Decroly's approach to securing funding for his research was, at the very least, innovative. Well, at first sight, at any rate. He was able to call on the sizeable financial resources of his wife, Agnes Guisset, for the initial amounts, but how precisely did his degree and medical practice contribute to funding his research? To what extent was he willing to accept payment for providing advice to various people and bodies? What about the lectures he gave? How were the numerous positions he held "remunerated"? Are there any traces of contracts pertaining to the books he published, his educational games, or his famous box,[1] and how did he make money with them? What public funding did he call on (for example the Commission for Relief, National Fund, university endowments), and what about private funding (gifts for his *Institut d'enfants anormaux*, Solvay[2])? What amounts were specifically allocated to his research and/or private educational initiatives? In this regard, to what extent could he count on support from his "clients"?

In this paper we will attempt, based on biographical research, to provide the initial elements of an answer to each of these questions.[3] Quite obviously it is not

[1] The Decroly box, with different locks, was a practical intelligence test. It was inspired by the boxes used in animal psychology, on chimpanzees in particular. Decroly used a set of four boxes that were increasingly more difficult to open (Thieffry 2002, pp. 80, 216).

[2] Cf. Solvay sponsored several scientific enterprises at the *Université Libre de Bruxelles,* see Bertrams et al. (2013). According to the archives (see following note), Decroly seems to have been part of the *Institut de Sociologie* (1904 ff.) and its *Groupe d'études psychologiques* and *Groupe d'études de Sociologie de l'enfant* (Centre des études decrolyennes [= CentreD], Lettres, I, documents bio-bibliographiques, cv OD [= Ovide Decroly]).

[3] Data on Decroly's research funding are not so easy to find. During our wanderings through the records we have from the beginning always been alert to detect financing. The *Centre des études decrolyennes*, located on the site of the Decroly school in Uccle, where the Decroly records are kept, contains most of the information. Furthermore we consulted the archives of the institutions that employed Decroly, such as the *Université Libre de Bruxelles*, the *Institut des Hautes Etudes* (also at ULB, Brussels) and the City of Brussels. Through the exchange of letters with friendly colleagues we traced a few costs and fees for lectures and conferences (cf. the archives of Henri Piéron (*Université Paris Descartes*), Edouard Claparède (*Archives Institut JJ Rousseau,* Geneva) and Cornelia Philippi-Siewertsz van Reesema (National Museum of Education, Dordrecht; The Hague Municipal Archives). Specifically for Decroly's study tour with Raymond Buyse to the United States in 1922 we consulted the file kept in the archives of the Belgian American Educational Foundation (Brussels). About this Foundation see Huistra and Wils (2016), Fit to travel. The Exchange Programme of the Belgian American Educational Foundation: An Institutional Perspective on Scientific Persona Formation (1920–1940). *BMGN – Low Countries Historical Review*, 131, 4, pp. 112–134.

our objective to downplay Decroly's contribution to psycho-educational research, but rather to come to a better understanding of the context in which his work came about.[4] After all, we have to acknowledge that most of what is recently published about Decroly continues to perpetuate the trend that mythologises and idealises the "great educationalist" (E.g. Wagnon 2013; Blichmann 2014).

* * *

Of immense importance to Ovide's financial future was his marriage in 1898 to (Marie) Agnès Guisset, the daughter of a textiles baron from Renaix. Following the wedding, he was keen to get started with his neurology career, which is what brought him to Brussels. The city held a powerful attraction for him. It was his desire to study mental illness that often brought him to a *clinique neurologique* there. It was Dr. Jean Demoor, recently appointed as the chief medical officer for special education in Brussels, who encouraged him to take an interest in "mentally disabled" children. As a result, a special school was founded in the city. Decroly was more interested in working with children than adults, and children with congenital disorders in particular. Doctors Demoor and Hendrickx had toyed with the idea of creating a special environment for the 'disabled' children of the bourgeoisie. While this was the sort of work that Decroly was looking for, he didn't have the money to make it happen. In 1901 he and his wife decided to add a laboratory to their home, which would bring them into immediate contact with "disabled" children. And so the *Institut des Anormaux* was born in Brussels, an *institut d'enseignement spécial*, conceived from the outset as a psychological laboratory and one of the first of its kind in Belgium.

We see, from the handwritten biography put together by Agnès Guisset after her husband's death, in 1932, that equipping the laboratory was something of an administrative headache. "La question financière fut un problème", she confided on paper; the doctors, whom Decroly had managed to drag to the lab with him, were probably very dedicated, but this wasn't enough. "Mon père, très compréhensif, et comme nous n'avions pas d'enfants nous permit d'entreprendre ce projet cher au coeur de mon mari en nous accordant une aide financière", she relates in the same account.[5]

The Decrolys had grand plans, that was certain. In 1907 the Institute of Special Education acquired a wing for "normal" children. Agnès Guisset writes that this was partly achieved by press-ganging a few doctor friends (which indubitably included Jean Demoor, future vice-chancellor of the ULB) and the money for which came from an inheritance left by her father, after his untimely death. From the very beginning the idea was in place for research to also be conducted in the school and that it should eventually develop into a major centre for innovation (for that matter it had already rapidly attracted the attention of the relevant authorities at home and abroad).

This school was also founded in Brussels, at 60 rue de l'Ermitage, and in 1910 the original institute moved from the rue de la Vanne to Vossegat in Ukkel. The Decrolys oversaw the entire project and drafted in specialist personnel, mostly

---

[4] For the importance of such an approach, see, e.g. Halleux et al. (2015).

[5] CentreD, Lettres I.

"schoolmistresses", including J. Degand (headmistress of the school for normal children) and E. Monchamp (head of the mathematics department). In 1914 J. Degand was briefly replaced by J. Deschamps, who quite quickly became ill and was later replaced by Decroly, himself. In 1924, A. Hamaïde, who had served as a schoolmistress between 1910 and 1916, was appointed headmistress. By this time project's crowning was the school's transfer in 1927 to the Drève des gendarmes (adjoining the Avenue Montana, on the outskirts of the Bois de la Cambre), where the Decrolys had bought a new villa.[6]

In 1930, after consulting the parents, the school was extended to accommodate the three highest years of secondary education, thereby opening up the possibility of a university training for its graduates. This was modelled on an inspiring example set by the *Ecole des Roches* in Verneuil. The Decrolys drew their pupils from the moneyed environs of Brussels, a milieu in which they themselves now belonged as people of consequence and standing. It thus comes as no surprise that a few of their former pupils did very well for themselves at the university (in Brussels). It also likely explains why parents so blithely went along with the proposals for change. More than 80% stated their express support for the expansion (100 out of 123 to be precise).

It is safe to assume that the Decroly school was more or less self-sufficient as a result of the tuition fees received from the parents. But this is not to say that the school's history is only one strewn with roses, certainly not in the period following Ovide's death. The Decrolys themselves reported that 1932–34 was a difficult two-year period. We have published papers on several subjects to mark the school's centenary (Van Gorp et al. 2008). It seems that money was always an issue. There was never enough to embody the progressive ideas of Decroly's followers, not even architecturally (Herman et al. 2011). Hence the frequent notes in the archive on the so-called "minerval", or tuition fees, and the likely need to raise them. One case in question was in 1930, after the referendum on the school's expansion. At that time the tuition fees should have been 350 francs, but in addition the school, and the Decrolys, could survive comfortably due to frequent donations. The relative value of the fees can be found by measuring them against a teacher's salary at the time. In 1934, an inner conflict between Agnès Guisset, a few teachers and Hamaïde ended with the discharge of the last one. She cashed 30.000 francs severance pay,[7] 500 francs less than the in Belgium maximum fixed annual salary of an unmarried school principal (scale 1935).[8]

In order to determine the relative value of the amounts in Belgian franc below, it seems that the evolution of teachers' salaries and their purchasing power, which we calculated in the context of a study into the societal position of teachers in Belgium, is one of the best standards (see figure 1, cited in De Vroede and Blomme 1993,

---

[6] CentreD, Ecole nouvelle 1914.

[7] CentreD, Procès-verbaux ASBL Ecole Decroly, 1922–1962; Van Gorp et al. (2008, pp. 165–168). About Hamaïde see Wagnon (2015).

[8] The starting salary totaled 16,000 fr., an unmarried primary education teacher started at 13,000 fr. (De Vroede and Blomme 1993, pp. 191–246).

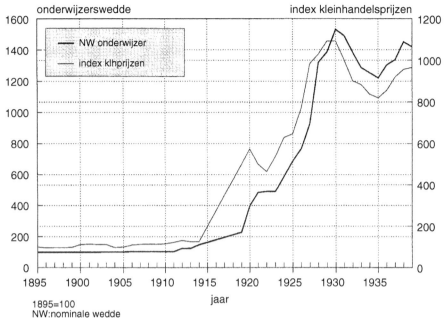

onderwijzerswedde   index kleinhandelsprijzen

1895=100
NW:nominale wedde

Grafiek 1:Onderwijzerswedde, 1895-1939 (vergeleken met index kleinhandelsprijzen)

Fig. 1 Male teacher salary for Belgian primary education in relation to index

p. 219). The big increase of the nominal value of the [Belgian] franc after 1914 was a result of its devaluation at the time. As far as the specialized literature within the historiography goes, this devaluation forms the starting point of a comparison with the contemporary situation. Peter Scholliers calculated that the real gross hourly wage (i.e. the gross wage divided by the index figure) of adult, male workers in the construction sector increased from 0.5 franc in 1914, to 635 franc in 2014 (Scholliers 2015, p. 10) (which means that the incomes in a 100 years span should roughly be multiplied by 1200, to get an idea of what this income would mean today). Self-evidently, during the life of Decroly, the wage curve did not climb that high. According to Scholliers, the average real wages increased with 62% (Scholliers 2015, p. 7) in every sector between 1896 and 1937. On the basis of his calculations for the same target population, the evolution during the interwar years of gross hourly wages in the construction sector can be estimated roughly with a grow factor of 10 (from 1914 to 1928), of 12 (from 1914 to 1929), and again of 10 (from 1914 to 1935) (Fig. 1).

It is against this financial and economic backdrop that the amounts (in Belgian franc) below need to be interpreted.

It is quite clear that the school's expansion was going to cost a lot of money. There were two projects in the offing, one for 165,000 and one for 112,000 francs. Many of the parents offered to put the money forward of their own accord. Following the school's relocation, an amount of 307,450 francs had already been collected from the parents in 1927. It was to be repaid between 1940 and 1945. But the parents had also invested in the school before its relocation, for more classrooms and other facilities. That particular round had yielded 275,000 francs. In 1930, at the time of the referendum, there was the prospect of a new loan, due for repayment between 1945 and 1948. The enrolment fees yielded 130,900 francs and another 30,800 francs in donations, also from the parents.[9]

Of course, the funding of Decroly's school is one thing, but that of his research was quite another. However, where the latter is concerned, the archives provide little of any substance to go on. As a successful researcher, Ovide was in the habit of scooping up prizes left and right, such as the Prix Dieudonné from the *Société Royale des sciences médicales et naturelles de Bruxelles*, already as early as 1900, and he was also regularly receiving royalty cheques, such as those from Swiss publisher's Delachaux & Niestlé in 1905 (being 3000 Belgian and 300 Swiss francs[10] respectively for various editions of *L'initiation à l'activité intellectuelle et motrice par les jeux éducatifs*), and he would also find it relatively easy to get hold of the latest academic work through his editorial contributions for magazines. For the *Sociéte de Médecine mentale de Belgique*, for example, he was librarian, secretary and editor of the *Bulletin*, through which he had access to all of the organisation's subscriptions. As was the norm in those days, he would swap magazines and journals with the colleagues in his network. His friend Claparède, who would come and stay with him from time to time, and vice versa, is a fine example of this (Ruchat 2015).

His membership in academic networks in the city and nationwide meant that he was able to attend foreign congresses on behalf of some of these societies (possibly with expenses paid). In 1906, for example, he travelled to Giessen with Tobie Jonckheere, teacher and later professor of education and teaching at the ULB, for a holiday course on "troubles de l'esprit chez l'enfant", about which he wrote a report for the Belgian *Societé protectrice de l'Enfance anormale*, which had commissioned him.[11]

And yet it goes without saying that the earnings from these side-lines would never have been enough to support him. For that matter, his list of international congresses and educational sojourns abroad was so impressive (Van Gorp et al. 2004; Depaepe 1990), that these earnings would never have been enough to cover them, which makes the issue of Ovide's basic income all the more interesting.

On 1 February 1903 Decroly received, "à titre d'essai", an appointment as "médecin adjoint" for the "special classes" of the school group *Bruxelles Sud-Est*, which illustrates not only his good relations with the local authorities, but the key role played by Brussels in the pedagogic innovation movement in the early

---

[9] CentreD, Procès-verbaux ASBL Ecole Decroly, 1922–1962.

[10] In contrast to guilders or dollars, we have not been able to find conversion tables for the value of Swiss franc in the past.

[11] *Bulletin de la Ligue de l'enseignement*, XLIV, 2, 1908, p. 49.

twentieth century (Depaepe 1993). For his services he received a stipend of 1000 francs a year.[12] In April 1904 this provisional appointment was extended to the whole of the city's special education and he was given the title of "médecin-inspecteur". Nonetheless, Agnès Guisset afterwards stated that he had been counting on more cooperation from the city, especially for the setup of a small laboratory and for carrying out scientific research in the classroom (through tests, for example).[13]

It is hardly surprising then, from this perspective, that the school doctor from Brussels was asked to share his insights with future researchers by way of several different courses and lessons and to expound on the subject for the men and women of the pedagogical practice. In the 1908–1909 academic year Ovide gave at the distinguished *Institut des Hautes Etudes*, one of the most renowned research institutes at the university of Brussels, a "cycle de conférences sur les nouvelles directions de l'enseignement populaire", and a course on "les anormaux au point de vue scientifique". In 1911–1912, possibly as a result of the first and only international congress on paedology, which took place under his chairmanship in the summer of 1911 in Brussels (Ioteyko 1912; Depaepe 1987), he taught, in association with the *Société Belge de Pédotechnie*, a three-year "cours de Pédotechnie" at the very same *Institut des Hautes Etudes*.[14] The first year's subject was: "la culture de l'enfant au point de vue physiologique". In 1912, Decroly also taught a course for teachers (and would-be teachers) in special education, organised by the province of Brabant. This initiative was to be repeated in 1914, just before the German invasion. The province of Brabant held another free course on education for disabled children from 15 January to 15 July. The course was delivered on Thursday afternoons and over part of the Easter holidays. Admitted to the course were male and female teachers, lower secondary school teachers with at least 2 years' practical experience and kindergarten teachers with 2 years' experience of Teachers' (Training) College. Decroly taught the course with a teaching staff of a few friends from the Brussels paedological (and paedotechnic) milieu. That Decroly had become unavoidable in that environment was also evidenced by his joining the ranks of teachers at the Buls-Tempels Higher Institute of Education in 1913, an institution for the education and additional training of teachers.[15]

---

[12] According to the then statutory scales an assistant teacher started at 1400 francs. De Vroede and Blomme (1993, p. 199).

[13] Archives of the City of Brussels, Instruction Publique [= AVB, I.P.], Pers. 1169/19; Comité secret du 25 avril 1904, *Bulletin communal de Bruxelles*, 1904, I/9, p. 661; Conseil communal du 12 avril 1897, *Bulletin communal de Bruxelles*, 1897, I/4, p. 370; CentreD Lettres I (Decroly's biography by Agnès Guisset, pp. 12–13, manuscript).

[14] Since 1908/1909 Decroly was associated with the Institut des Hautes Etudes. Initially, he only gave a few lectures, but from the establishment of the Cours de Pédotechnie (1911/1912) he also taught a course (the course was made possible through a collaboration with the *Société Belge de Pédotechnie*, hence Decroly's involvement). See Despy-Meyer and Goffin (1976).

[15] CentreD, Lettres I, documents bio-bibliographiques, cv Decroly; Despy-Meyer and Goffin (1976, pp. 57, 71, 76).

Decroly was also a force of nature in the field of university education, where the actual foundation of pedagogical institutes had yet to get off the ground. The afore-mentioned "cours de pédotechnie" was already part of the *Université Nouvelle*[16] before the Great War with Decroly a permanent lecturer there. According to Despy-Meyer,[17] whose work is based on the archives of the *Université Nouvelle*, this was an incorporation of the third year of a course organised by the *Société belge de Pédotechnie*. The subject of the 1913–1914 academic year was "l'évolution envisa-gée au point de vue sociologique". Additional "cours supérieurs" were planned for the year to come. But the war would soon cast its bleak shadow here, just as it did in the broader context of paradigmatic shifts in paedology and paedotechnics (Depaepe 1985; Depaepe 1993). The *Université nouvelle* was abandoned after the war and the *Institut des Hautes Etudes* went on as an independent institute, though affiliated with the ULB. Decroly gave both single lectures and full courses there, namely for section VI (1919/1920–1921/1922, the section on "des sciences philosophiques: philosophie, éthique, pédagogie") and section VIII (1922/1923–1926/1927, the newly set up "ergologie" section; the course was taught in the build-ings of the *Université du Travail* in Charleroi and the *Institut d'Hygiène* in Mons).

Owing to the chief medical officer's unavailability as a result of the draft, Decroly was given the wartime post of co-director of the *Institut des Estropiés de la Province de Brabant*, a temporary post which he was forced to vacate after the armistice.[18] However, this hardly got in the way of his professional career. The appointments and commissions came raining down, so to speak. In the Decroly archives there are indications that he not only held the "mandat de médecin-spécialiste de la Fédération libre des Sociétés mutualistes de Bruxelles et ses faubourgs pour le Service médical et pharmaceutique" in 1917, but at the same time also taught courses on "orthoph-onie" at the city of Brussels Teacher's (Taining) College.[19] Whether, and how much, he was paid for this is not entirely clear. It also appears that he wasn't entirely fas-tidious when it came to filling out his expenses… And yet from time to time a letter of thanks would arrive out of the blue, which he could have converted to hard cur-rency. In September 1918, at the end of the works for the "Commission spéciale chargée d'étudier l'avant-projet d'allocation de bourses d'études spéciales en argent aux élèves des écoles communales particulièrement doués", a delightful example of the meritocratically inclined thinking Brussels policy makes, the local authority of Saint-Gilles thanked Decroly profusely for his work on career guidance and awarded

---

[16]About the *Université Nouvelle*, see Van Rooy (1976) and Despy-Meyer (1994). This "New University" was established in 1894 from the dissatisfaction with the conservatism, both in policy and in intellectual life, at the *Université Libre de Bruxelles* (ULB).

[17]CentreD, Lettres I, documents bio-bibliographiques, cv OD; Despy-Meyer and Goffin (1976, pp. xcvii, xcviii, cii, 103, 108, 114, 120 and 126).

[18]CentreD, Lettres I, documents bio-bibliographiques, cv OD.

[19]CentreD, file "Pensée", letter 18 Nov. 1917; CentreD, file "Pensée", V. Devogel to OD, 1917.

him an attendance fee of 1000 francs. For the same advice, 10 years later, he would receive a more modest sum of 30 francs.[20]

When the process of finding an academic footing for the educational sciences finally got going in Belgium after the war, thanks to the (first) School of Education (at the ULB) (Depaepe 2001), it was only to be expected that Decroly would be involved in one way or another. In 1919, the opening year, he was involved as "chargé du cours" for the "Psychologie de l'enfant et de l'adolescence" section. What he received in the way of a salary for this, is unknown. But what we do know is that in 1920 he made 300 francs for his lessons at the *Institut des Hautes Etudes*, and that in 1923 another 135 francs were added by way of a "modeste indemnité" for his work at the institute. In 1926, he received a compensation of 400 francs.[21]

In the meantime, Ovide worked several jobs and combined his teaching with other medical work, where the core of his professional expertise still resided (Depaepe et al. 2011). Already in 1915, he received as medical school inspector of Brussels, 1900 francs from the city.[22] In 1920 he became, moreover, responsible for medical inspections at state and privately run institutions for delinquent youth and by the Ministerial Decree of 17 March he was appointed the inspecting physician for the young boys' institutions of the *Office de la protection de l'Enfance*. In the same year he added another course on "assistance aux enfants anormaux (y compris les troubles de la parole)" as part of the training for social workers, which had started that year on a Monday as a "cours de service social de Bruxelles".[23] Three years later he also taught general psychology and pedagogy for 'normal' and mentally disabled children at the city of Brussels' Teachers' (Training) Colleges of Emile André and Charles Buls (for boys and girls respectively). This involved lessons of two-and-a-half hours, twice a week. On 22 October 1923 the council decided to set his remuneration at two instalments of 1375 francs each. In this job he actually succeeded Demoor, who had retired.[24] In the following year Decroly was promoted to director of courses for special education teachers in the province of Brabant, where, as we have seen, he once worked as a teacher. And in 1926 his position at the ULB, until then in child psychology, came to include the subject "statistique appliquée à l'éducation".[25]

Moreover, it is from that point on that Decroly's activities seem to hit their true stride. A council resolution of 30 April appointed him as chief medical officer for special education in the city of Brussels, with effect from 1 May 1926.[26] Alongside this promotion he starts giving occasional lectures in psychology at the *Institut*

---

[20] CentreD, Correspondances étrangères I, town council St-Gilles to OD, 23 Sept. 1918; CentreD, file "Psychogénèse", Letter 21 Nov. 1928.

[21] Academic file ULB, 1 P 65: Decroly, Ovide; Despy-Meyer and Goffin (1976), p. 92; CentreD, file "Enfant-Développement-", treasurer *Ecole des Hautes Etudes* to OD, 23 Dec 1926.

[22] AVB, IPII, 616.

[23] Archives Institut des Hautes Etudes, ULB, 1919–1920.

[24] AVB, I.P Pers. 1169/19.

[25] CentreD, Lettres I, documents bio-bibliographiques, cv OD.

[26] AVB, I.P Pers. 1169/19.

normal provincial d'enseignement professionnel in November.[27] But his career reached its zenith in December 1928, when he was awarded the title of "extra-ordinary professor", the highest level achievable at university (albeit part-time). Precisely how much that position earned him, we do not know. But the prestige (in that the great pedagogical reformer finally became a professor), must not be underestimated.[28]

The city of Brussels provides us with more specific details for his salary in this period. In 1929 this amounts to 15,000 francs for his work as a physician and 4125 francs for his teaching activities. In 1930 the second figure rose to 4200 francs and in 1931 the two figures rose respectively, to 16,200 and 4275 francs.[29] This was a considerable income, especially if we add the university salary, which can hardly have been less than the pay at Teachers' (Training) College. To this we can add occasional earnings from the sale of books, talks for scientific societies and so on. We cannot know for sure if this was enough to cover Decroly's foreign travel, but there are plenty of indications to suggest that it was.

For example, in August 1923 in Podebrad (in the present day Czech Republic) he received 200 Swiss francs for his lecture on "les types d'enfants et l'instinct comba- tif" at the "cours de vacances international de la Ligue internationale des femmes pour la paix et la liberté". This likely covered more than the costs of a summer trip on which Mrs. Decroly was also in attendance, for she was entirely wrapped up in her husband's work and continued to support him financially.[30] A few weeks earlier, through A. Ferrière acting as intermediary, she had lent Elisabeth Huguenin 1000 francs to assist the publication of a book on the *Odenwaldschule*.[31]

Decroly regularly received sums for other commissions abroad, however, they were more symbolic (and therefore modest) in nature, and hardly sufficient to cover the full cost of his numerous educational trips. That said, we should remember that savings were also made in those days, because the members of the newly crystallis- ing international networks often stayed in each other's homes. This was certainly the case in Easter of 1927, when Ovide stayed in the home of his Dutch friend (and admirer) C. Philippi-Siewertsz Van Reesema and, in return for his contribution to commemorate 25 years of the Child Studies Foundation, received the sum of 100 guilders.[32] For taking part in the Fourth International Conference of the New

---

[27] Centre D, file "intelligence", Province du Brabant, Conseil de perfectionnement de l'enseignement technique to OD, 12 Nov. 1926.

[28] Academic file ULB 1P 65: Decroly, Ovide; Letter in CentreD, file "Psychogénèse".

[29] AVB, I.P Pers. 1169/19.

[30] CentreD, Correspondants étrangers II, Andrée Jouve, secretary *Section française de la Ligue Internationale des Femmes pour la Paix et la Liberté* to OD, Paris; CentreD, Correspondants étrangers II, flyer of the Summer course.

[31] CentreD, Correspondants étrangers III, Ferrière to OD, Genève; Huguenin, 1923. Elisabeth Huguenin (1885–1970), former teacher at the *Odenwaldschule* (Heppenheim); in 1923 she taught at the *Ecole des Roches* in Normandy.

[32] National Museum of Education, Dordrecht, Archive C. Philippi-Siewertsz van Reesema, minutes of the meeting "Afdeeling Onderwijs", 17 Febr. 1927. (According to the search engine of the International Institute for Social History-http://www.iisg.nl/hpw/calculate2-nl.php retrieved on 12/19/2016-, today 100 guilders should amount to approximately 767,78 Euro).

Financial Cushion:

- **Substantial fortune Agnes Guisset: ???**
- ***Instituts des anormaux*, medical practice, Decroly School (extension annual fee, 350 Belgian Francs)**
- **Copyright on publications: ???**
- **Annual salary as extra-ordinary professor at the *ULB*: ???**
- **Annual salary doctor of the city of Brussels (15,000 Belgian Francs), salary as theacher at the Brussels normal schools (4125 Belgian Francs)**
- **Annual attendance fee *Comité de Séléction...* Saint-Gilles (30 Belgian Francs)**
- **Free lecture at Bloemendaal (the Netherlands) (50 Dutch Guilders)**

Fig. 2 Estimation of income of Ovide Decroly, 1928–1929

Education Fellowship in Locarno, in August 1927, Decroly, who was one of the main speakers, received a reimbursement for the return leg of his trip plus 3 days in a first class hotel, or the cash equivalent of 42 Swiss francs.[33] And for his presentation at The Hague, in October 1928, he received a fee of 50 guilders.[34] According to the search engine of the International Institute for Social History (http://www.iisg.nl/hpw/calculate2-nl.php retrieved on 12/19/2016), this should amount to approximately 381,13 Euro).

In sum, it is difficult to put together the pieces of Decroly's total income. There are many aspects that (for now?) remain unknown. Our efforts to estimate to Decroly's total income around 1928/1929 – virtually the highlight of his career – unavoidably result in an incomplete, yet informative estimation of his (yearly) salary. He received namely 19,125 francs from the city (as doctor and as teacher, see Fig. 2). If we apply to these figures an appropriate coefficient derived from the data of Scholliers (of which one can estimate a grow factor 120 for the period 1928–2014 – as the grow factor was 1200 between 1914 and 2014 and already 10 between 1914 and 1928), we can say that his Brussels' city salary as physician and teacher was around 2,295,000 Belgian francs a year (one euro being c. 40 francs at the inception of euro's in 2001), which means, in our terms, a year salary of 57,375 euro and a salary of 4,781,25 euro each month. However, this conversion is an a-historical standard for comparison. This is demonstrated by the very fact that today's gross incomes (with taxes of more than 50% in Belgium) cannot be compared with the fiscal policy of the time. Again, teachers' wages provide a much better point for comparison. In 1928, the basic wage of a married male teacher varied, according to the type of school, between 13,600 to 27,200 franc (De Vroede and Blomme 1993, p. 212). As a result, it can be concluded that Decroly, with the wage he received

---

[33] CentreD, Correspondants étrangers II, Clare Soper, secretary New Education Fellowship to OD, London 6 July 1927.

[34] CentreD, file "Mensonge", A. De Vletter, headmaster Kennemer grammar school, Overveen, 11 Oct. 1928.

from the city of Brussels, found himself somewhere in the middle. Yet, to this should be added the salary he received from the ULB, probably per presentation, as well as occasional revenues from lectures and publications.

In his archive, we found proof that his publications indeed generated incomes. On 10 September 1924 he had a meeting with publisher Fernand Nathan in Ukkel about his forthcoming publications. Though we know nothing of the ensuing financial arrangements, there was plenty in the pipeline, if Decroly's health (he suffered pain in the legs) would allow it.[35] A similar lack of clarity applies in his contracts with Felix Alcan, for the books he published with Raymond Buyse. For *La pratique des tests* a contract was signed on 8 July 1925 stipulating that the text was to be delivered in the third quarter of 1925 and that 3000 copies of the book would be printed. The authors would share 10% of the sales, a half each.[36]

Decroly's (numerous) publications with Buyse, who played the part of the young assistant to the "master" from Brussels, but who stemmed from a different ideological background, i.e. Catholic, were the result of a shared educational trip to the United States in 1922, to study the condition of (applied) psychology in general, and more particularly the use of tests in education and in the social sphere.[37] It lent significant momentum to the professional and academic aspects of their careers. It was undoubtedly a factor in Buyse's appointment as a lecturer at the (Catholic) University of Leuven, for the opening of the School for Education in 1923. And it is not implausible that it played a direct (or indirect) role in Decroly's promotion in 1927.

Decroly's investment, in taking unpaid leave for this trip, leave granted him by the Ministry of Justice from the schools he inspected, and by the university, had clearly paid off. It is not clear whether he had to forego his salary from the city, still his basic income at the time, during his period of absence. In any case, for that four-month trip, which had undoubtedly cost a great deal of money, Decroly and Buyse benefited from an ample grant from the Commission for Relief of Belgium – Educational Foundation, which had been set up to rebuild academic research in Belgium.[38] In the end, the commission decided to award a budget of 5000 dollars for the trip, including a monthly fee of 500 dollars for Decroly and 250 dollars for Buyse (according to the website "measuring worth", 5.000 dollar today amounts to about 70.700 dollar in purchasing power (https://www.measuringworth.com/ppowerus/ retrieved on 12/19/2016). It seems too, that for a congress in Barcelona immediately prior to this, Decroly had received a partial reimbursement of his expenses from the same organisation. He had obviously ventured the demand for an additional 2500 dollars as a bargaining ploy, when it turned out that the US was also interested in sending the Belgian partnership to the El Dorado of the intelligence testing movement.

---

[35] CentreD, Correspondants étrangers I, F. Nathan to OD, Paris, 12 Sept. 1924.

[36] CentreD, Correspondants étrangers I, contract.

[37] See Depaepe et al. (2013). This travel diary has been published with a critical introduction by Depaepe and D'hulst (2011).

[38] Archive Belgian American Educational Foundation Inc., C.R.B. Educational Foundation, Inc., Minutes of Meeting, 1919–1922.

However, making money was not Decroly's sole objective. In 1925, he was invited to Colombia by his friend Augustín Nieta Caballero (1889–1975) to give a series of lectures about the "New Education Movement" (Herrera 1999, 74, pp. 110–112; Saenz Obregon et al. 1997, pp. 320–331). Decroly took an unpaid leave for 4 months (for his job for the city of Brussels), starting on July 1st 1925.[39] He took a vacation for 2 months; during the other 2 months visited relevant places (amongst others, the Brothers of the Christian Schools and the *Gimnasio Moderno* of Nieto Caballero). Apparently, he received an additional payment for his lectures at and advices for the *Gimnasio*. Initially, he refused the money, but later accepted. After his return to Belgium, however, he donated his payment to the *Foyer des Orphelins*, one of the key institutions in his network (Negrin Fajardo 1992, pp. 149–150). A similar involvement in society is to be found in his work for the *Société Belge de pédotechnie*. The so-called "paedotechnical consultations" for children which Decroly performed on Sunday morning were free of charge for parents.[40] As the society had almost no money, we can assume that the doctor was not paid for these consultations – which again seems to fit with "altruism" rather than with "egoism", whatever these words in the history of science do mean...

* * *

In conclusion: Was Decroly, from a financial point of view, a "modern" scientist? The answer needs to be put in a nuanced light. He certainly was in terms of networking and the conference and publication culture that went along with it. However, money was not the only factor in knowledge and scientific production – certainly not in a context that was not marked by competition in applications for funding. Supposedly, Decroly and his entourage aimed for a break even as far as the school was concerned (e.g., staff and learning materials). However, for his research, he needed a staff and the financial means. To what extent did he use his personal accounts to pay for this? In other words, what were his family's expenses? Again, we cannot entirely answer this question. Surely, the technology in his laboratory could not compete with today's often astronomical budgets, but still, Decroly's (self-made) box needed to be developed, the photo and film cameras needed to be paid for, as well as the tests, the measuring equipment, etc.

If, indeed, Decroly can rightly be considered as a "modern scientist", a modern "moi", a "scientific persona", whose cultural identity bridges the gap between personal background and the social institutions for which he worked and lived (Daston and Sibum 2003; Paul 2014), this is mainly the result of his incentives for the construction of a new scientific model of experimental and clinical research. However, despite the rhetoric of reform and possibly also philanthropy, even these initiatives for a "new" model needed to be paid for. This is exactly where the troubles lie in the history of science. Until today, the material conditions in which the attractive rhetoric of modern scientific practices came into being, remain virgin territory. With this somewhat fragmentary and partly thematic-chronological contribution we have sought to make a modest start, pending a more detailed biography.

---

[39] AVB, I.P Pers. 1169/19.

[40] CentreD, file Pensée.

References

Bertrams, K., Coupain, N., & Homburg, E. (2013). *Solvay: History of a multinational family firm.* Cambridge/New York: Cambridge University Press.

Blichmann, A. (2014). *Ovide Decroly und sein Weg vom Arzt zum Pädagogen.* Paderborn: Schöningh.

Daston, L., & Sibum, H. O. (2003). Introduction: Scientific personae and their histories. *Science in Context, XVI,* 1–8.

De Vroede, M., & Blomme, J. (1993). Inkomen en levensstandaard. In M. Depaepe, M. De Vroede, & F. Simon (Eds.), *Geen trede meer om op te staan. De maatschappelijke positie van onderwijzers en onderwijzeressen tijdens de voorbije eeuw* (pp. 191–246). Kapellen: Pelckmans.

Depaepe, M. (1985). Science, technology and paedology. The concept of science at the "Faculté Internationale de Pédologie" in Brussels (1912–1914). *Scientia Paedagogica Experimentalis, XXII*(1), 14–29.

Depaepe, M. (1987). Le premier (et dernier) congrès international de pédologie à Bruxelles en 1911. *Le Binet Simon. Bulletin de la Société Alfred Binet et Théodore Simon, LXXXVII*(3), 28–54. (nr. 612).

Depaepe, M. (1990). Soziale Abnormität und moralische Debilität bei Kindern. Ein Diskussionsthema auf internationalen wissenschaftlichen Zusammenkünften am Anfang dieses Jahrhundert. *Paedagogica Historica, XXVI*(2), 185–209.

Depaepe, M. (1993). *Zum Wohl des Kindes? Pädologie, pädagogische Psychologie und experimentelle Pädagogik in Europa und den USA, 1890–1940.* Leuven/Weinheim: Leuven University Press/Deutscher Studien Verlag.

Depaepe, M. (2001). La pédagogie. In R. Halleux (Ed.), *Histoire des sciences en Belgique 1815–2000* (Vol. I, pp. 329–342). Bruxelles/Tournai: Dexia/La Renaissance du livre.

Depaepe, M., & D'hulst, L. (2011). *Un pèlerinage psycho-pédagogique aux Etats-Unis. Carnet de voyage de Raymond Buyse, 1922. Introduction et édition annotée/An Educational Pilgrimage to the United States. Travel Diary of Raymond Buyse, 1922. Introduction, edition, and comments.* Leuven: Leuven University Press.

Depaepe, M., & Van Gorp, A. (2003). Constructing the Eden of our earthly existence. Empiricism and the history of educational research in Belgium before the second world war. In P. Smeyers & M. Depaepe (Eds.), *Beyond empiricism. On criteria for educational research* (pp. 53–64). Leuven: Leuven University Press.

Depaepe, M., Simon, F., & Van Gorp, A. (2011). L'expertise médicale et psycho-pédagogique d'Ovide Decroly en action. Utiliser le "fardeau" qu'engendre inadaptation sociale au profit de la société. In A. François, V. Massin, & D. Niget (Eds.), *Violences juvéniles sous expertise(s) XIXe-XXIe siècles. Expertise and Juvenile Violence 19th–21st century* (pp. 39–54). Louvain-la-neuve: UCL Presses Universitaires de Louvain.

Depaepe, M., D'hulst, L., & Simon, F. (2013). Crossing the Atlantic to gain knowledge in the field of psycho-pedagogy: The 1922 mission of Ovide Decroly and Raymond Buyse to the USA and the travel diary of the latter. In P. Smeyers, M. Depaepe, & E. Keiner (Eds.), *Educational research: The importance and effects of institutional spaces* (pp. 47–60). Dordrecht: Springer.

Depaepe, M., Simon, F., & Van Gorp, A. (2016, August). *Writing a biography based on a "laundry list": Ovide Decroly (1871–1932).* Some methodological questions and theoretical considerations. (Presentation at ECER, Network 17, Dublin).

Despy-Meyer, A. (1994). Un laboratoire d'idées: l'Université Nouvelle de Bruxelles (1894–1919). In G. Kurgan-Van Hentenryk (Ed.), *Laboratoires et réseaux de diffusion des idées en Belgique: XIXe-XXe siècles* (pp. 51–54). Bruxelles: Editions de l'Université de Bruxelles.

Despy-Meyer, A., & Goffin, P. (1976). *Liber Memorialis de l'Institut des Hautes Etudes de Belgique.* Bruxelles: Institut des Hautes Etudes de Belgique.

Halleux, R., et al. (2015). *Tant qu'il y aura des chercheurs. Science et politique en Belgique de 1772 à 2015.* Liège: Lucpire.

Herman, F., Van Gorp, A., Simon, F., & Depaepe, M. (2011). The organic growth of the Decroly school in Brussels: From villa to school, from living room to classroom. In S. Braster, I. Grosvenor, & M. Del Pozo Andrés (Eds.), *The Black Box of Schooling. A cultural history of the classroom* (pp. 241–259., 305–308). Brussels/Bern/Berlin: Peter Lang.

Herrera, M. C. (1999). *Modernización y escuela nueva en Colombia: 1914–1951*. Santafé de Bogota: Universidad Pédagogica Nacional/Plaza & Janés.

Huguenin, E. (1923). *Paul Geheeb et la Libre Communauté scolaire de l'Odenwald: Une expérience moderne de l'éducation*. Genève: Bureau international des Ecoles nouvelles.

Huistra, P. A., & Wils, K. (2016). The exchange program of the Belgian American educational foundation 1920–1940 – An institutional perspective on persona formation (1920–1940). *Bijdragen en Mededelingen Betreffende de Geschiedenis der Nederlanden, 131*(4), 112–134.

Ioteyko, J. (Ed.). (1912). *Premier congrès international de pédologie tenu à Bruxelles, du 12 au 18 Août* (Vol. 2). Bruxelles: Misch & Thron.

Negrín Fajardo, O. (1992). El Gimnasio Moderno de Bogotá, pionero de la escuela nueva Iberoamérica. *Historia de la Educación, XI*, 143–175.

Paul, H. (2014). What is a scholarly persona? Ten theses on virtues, skills, and desires. *History and Theory, LIII*, 348–371.

Ruchat, M. (2015). *Edouard Claparède. A quoi sert l'éducation?* Lausanne: Editions Antipodes.

Saenz Obregon, J., Saldarriaga, O., & Ospina, A. (1997). *Mirar la infancia: Pedagogía, moral y modernidad en Colombia* (Vol. 2). Santafé de Bogota/Antioquia: Colciencia, Ediciones For Nacional Para Colombia/Ediciones Uniandes/Editorial Universidad de Antioquia.

Scholliers, P. (2015). Honderd jaar koopkracht in België (1914–2014). *Brood en Rozen, XX*(3), 5–22.

Thieffry, V. (Ed.). (2002). *La mesure de l'homme, instruments et tests du musée d'Histoire naturelle de Lille*. Paris: Somogy.

Van Gorp, A., Simon, F., & Depaepe, M. (2004). Backing the actor as agent in discipline formation: An example of the "Secondary Disciplinarisation" of the educational sciences, based on the networks of Ovide Decroly (1901–1931). *Paedagogica Historica, XL*(5–6), 591–616.

Van Gorp, A., Simon, F., & Depaepe, M. (2008). Persistenz einer Nischenschule. Hundert Jahre Decroly-Schule in Brüssel, Belgien. In M. Göhlich, C. Hopf, & D. Tröhler (Eds.), *Persistenz und Verschwinden. Persistence and disappearance. Pädagogische Organisationen im historischen Kontext. Educational organizations in their historical contexts* (pp. 159–173). Wiesbaden: VS.

Van Rooy, W. (1976). L'Agitation étudiante et la fondation de l'Université Nouvelle en 1894. *Revue belge d'histoire contemporaine, VII*(1–2), 197–241.

Wagnon, S. (2013). *Ovide Decroly, un pédagogue de l'Education nouvelle, 1871–1932*. Bruxelles, etc.: Peter Lang.

Wagnon, S. (2015). Amélie Hamaïde (1888–1970) l'illustre inconnue de la pédagogie Decroly. *Cahiers Bruxellois – Brusselse Cahiers, XLVII*(1), 132–149.

The Gates Foundation MET Research Project As a Case of Philanthrocapitalism

Lynn Fendler

In 2009 the Bill & Melinda Gates Foundation launched the Measures of Effective Teaching [MET] research project. The goal of the MET project was to develop instruments and protocols for evaluating teaching and distinguishing teachers who are effective from those who are not. The MET project was a massive three-year, $45 million undertaking. It studied six school districts and 3000 teachers in the United States, collected digital video of 13,000 classroom lessons, administered surveys to students, and tracked student scores on two separate tests in efforts to stipulate the parameters of effective teaching. Reports from the MET project publicized research results about how effective teaching might be defined and measured. MET project analyses and conclusions were published in scholarly academic venues, policy briefs, and popular media from 2010 through 2013 when the project closed. The $45 million MET Project was directed and funded entirely by the Bill & Melinda Gates Foundation.

The Gates' MET project is just one instance of philanthrocapitalism, currently the fastest growing source of funding for educational (and healthcare) research in the United States. Philanthrocapitalism – also called venture philanthropy, creative capitalism, assertive philanthropy, and impact investing – pertains not only to the Gates Foundation, but also to the Eli Broad Foundation, the Clinton Foundation, the Walton Foundation, George Soros, Angelina Jolie, and Bono (among others). Research funding from philanthrocapitalism has increased substantially, and the sociopolitical role of philanthropic organizations in research endeavors has changed dramatically since 2008 (Reckhow 2013; Reckhow and Snyder 2014; Tompkins-Stange 2016a, b; Hess and Henig 2015).

This paper examines the Bill & Melinda Gates Foundation MET project and synthesizes current research on philanthrocapitalism to highlight some implications of current trends in funding for educational research. Issues of philanthrocapitalism

L. Fendler (✉)
Department of Teacher Education, Michigan State University, East Lansing, MI, USA
e-mail: fendler@msu.edu

© Springer International Publishing AG, part of Springer Nature 2018
P. Smeyers, M. Depaepe (eds.), *Educational Research: Ethics, Social Justice, and Funding Dynamics*, Educational Research 10,
https://doi.org/10.1007/978-3-319-73921-2_16

in educational research include the establishment of an incestuous plutocracy, the conduct of educational research in a shadow economy, the promotion of the special interests of private wealthy donors, and shifts in the terms of debate about educational issues for research in the public interest.

Overview of the Gates Foundation MET Research Project

"Measures of Effective Teaching" is actually the third major educational project funded this century by the Bill & Melinda Gates Foundation. The first was the 2000–2004 Small Schools Initiative, a $51 million grant to support the establishment of 67 small schools in New York City. It is widely agreed that the Small Schools Initiative failed to produce the desired results, and so it was abandoned by the Gates Foundation in 2006 (some say prematurely). The second major Gates-funded project in education is the Common Core State Standards [CCSS], which the Gates Foundation began funding in 2009. The $200 million budget was spent largely on funding research, working with Pearson Publications to develop materials, and lobbying state officials to support the adoption of the CCSS in individual states.[1] As of 2016, only seven (of 50) U.S. states have not adopted the CCSS, and so the project is generally regarded as successful, if not always popular.[2]

The Measures of Effective Teaching [MET] project was designed to create research instruments and protocols that would allow schools to identify "effective" teachers and distinguish them from "ineffective" teachers. According to a Bill & Melinda Gates Foundation Policy Brief:

> In fall 2009, the Bill & Melinda Gates Foundation launched the Measures of Effective Teaching (MET) project to test new approaches to recognizing effective teaching. The project's goal is to help build fair and reliable systems for teacher observation and feedback to help teachers improve and administrators make better personnel decisions. (Gates Foundation 2010 online)

The MET Project was directed by Steven M. Cantrell, Ph.D., an education research and policy executive who was the Chief Research Officer for the Bill & Melinda Gates Foundation and provided leadership during the years of the MET project. Other authors of the MET research reports included Principal Investigator Thomas J. Kane (Harvard Professor of Education and Economics; Brookings Institution fellow), Daniel F. McCaffrey (RAND Corporation), and Douglas O. Staiger (Dartmouth Professor of Economics). In its early years, the MET project claimed partnership with several universities (Dartmouth, Harvard, Stanford, University of Chicago, University

---

[1] According to the U.S. Constitution, education belongs in the jurisdiction of individual states, and so it is technically illegal to initiate or enforce educational reform at a national/federal level. The CCSS are meant to apply nationally, but (as the name implies) all educational policies must be adopted and implemented at the state level.

[2] Most objections to the CCSS come from the U.S. Right on the grounds that CCSS constitutes big government interference with education, which belongs rightfully to individual states. Some objections come from the U.S. Left on the grounds that education decision-making should not be driven by private money, but by elected officials.

of Michigan, University of Virginia, and University of Washington), nonprofit organizations (Educational Testing Service, RAND Corporation, the National Math and Science Initiative, and the New Teacher Center), and other consultants (Cambridge Education, Teachscape, Westat, and the Danielson Group).

At its outset, the MET project took a stand against the prevailing approach to teacher evaluation that uses only student test-score data to determine whether a teacher is effective. In the United States, the reliance on student test-score improvement as the basis for teacher evaluation is known as "Value Added Measures" or VAM.[3] Instead of a VAM-only approach to teacher evaluation, the MET project originally planned to investigate multiple measures in order to design a composite protocol to measure teacher effectiveness. In addition to student test scores, the researchers would also collect data from two other sources: classroom observations and student perception surveys. The research was conducted in 3000 classrooms (Mathematics and English Language Arts) in six urban school districts across the United States (New York City, Charlotte-Mecklenburg in North Carolina, Hillsborough County in Florida, Memphis in Tennessee, Dallas in Texas, and Denver in Colorado, plus a pilot study in Pittsburgh, Pennsylvania). The results of the MET research project were reported in four policy and practitioner briefs published between 2010 and 2013.

MET research project policy and practitioner reports:

1. First MET Report (2010) *Learning about Teaching: Initial Findings*. It examined correlations between student survey responses and value-added scores computed from state tests and from higher-order tests of conceptual understanding. The study found that the measures are related, but only modestly.
2. Second MET Report (2012). *Gathering Feedback for Teaching: Combining High-Quality Observation with Student Surveys and Achievement Gains*. It focused on classroom observation protocols as potential measures of teacher effectiveness. The report found that the observation instruments examined have fairly low reliability and are only weakly correlated with value-added measures.
3. Third MET Report (2012) *Asking Students about Teaching: Student Perception Surveys and Their Implementation*. It focused on student surveys as potential measure of teacher effectiveness. The report found that teachers' student survey results are predictive of student achievement gains.
4. Culminating MET Report (2013). *Ensuring Fair and Reliable Measures of Effective Teachers*. It summarized recent analyses from the MET project on identifying effective teaching while accounting for differences among teachers' students, on combining measures into composites, and on assuring reliable classroom observations.

---

[3] VAM is actually calculated by comparing the actual test score relative to the statistically predicted test score.

Year One: Learning About Teaching – Initial Findings

The MET study design was sophisticated and ambitious. In the first year researchers collected data from two different standardized tests, classroom observations, and student perception surveys across 13,000 classroom lessons with 3000 different teachers. The aim of the first phase was to set up an analysis protocol that would isolate the effects of the teacher from other variables that affect student achievement. In their efforts to isolate teacher effects, MET researchers analyzed the test scores of two different classes taught by the same teacher to see if the score changes in one class reliably predicted the score changes in another class. Researchers also compared test score changes for the same teacher in two different years. In this way, researchers worked to eliminate the possibility that test score gains were a function of a particular class or year rather than the teacher.

The research report from the first year of the MET project claimed four initial findings:

1. A teacher's past VAM results were the best predictors of subsequent VAM results.
2. Teachers with the highest VAM results on the (easier) standardized test tended to produce higher scores on the (more difficult) conceptual test.
3. Student evaluations of teaching tended to align with VAM scores.
4. Feedback from classroom observations have potential to help teachers improve their practice.

Year Two: Gathering Feedback for Teaching – Combining High-Quality Observation with Student Surveys and Achievement Gains

The second year of the MET project focused on investigations of instruments to be used to record classroom observations (Wood et al. 2014). The analysis of classroom observation instruments was based on 7491 videos of instruction by 1333 teachers in grades 4–8. MET researchers studied the validity and reliability of five established and widely implemented classroom-observation protocols:

- Framework for Teaching [FFT] developed by Charlotte Danielson of the Danielson Group.
- Classroom Assessment Scoring System [CLASS] developed by Robert Pianta, Karen La Paro, and Bridget Hamre at the University of Virginia.
- Protocol for Language Arts Teaching Observations [PLATO] developed by Pam Grossman at Stanford University.
- Mathematical Quality of Instruction [MQI] developed by Heather Hill of Harvard University.

- UTeach Teacher Observation Protocol [UTOP] developed by Michael Marder and Candace Walkington at the University of Texas-Austin.

  The policy report in year two claimed five major findings:

1. All five observation instruments were positively correlated with VAM results.
2. Reliability of the instruments required averaging scores across multiple raters and multiple observations.
3. Reliability across time was better when classroom observation ratings were combined with VAM and student perception surveys.
4. The combination of classroom observations with VAM and student perception surveys was more reliable than credentials or years of teaching experience for predictions of VAM across time.
5. The combination of classroom observations with VAM and student perception surveys was more reliable than credentials or years of teaching experience for predictions of scores on the more difficult conceptual tests.

Year Three: Asking Students About Teaching – Student Perception Surveys and Their Implementation

The third year of the MET project focused on the role of student perception surveys in teacher evaluation. The MET project analyzed the validity and reliability of four different student perception survey instruments:

- Tripod 7Cs, developed by Harvard researcher Ronald Ferguson (survey was distributed and administered by Cambridge Education)
- YouthTruth, developed and distributed by the Center for Effective Philanthropy
- My Student Survey, developed by Ryan Balch, Expert Fellow at Vanderbilt University
- iKnowMyclass, developed by Russell Quaglia at the Quaglia Institute for Student Aspirations in Portland, ME, as tool for teacher feedback.

To provide some idea of the sorts of questions included on the student surveys, here are the seven constructs the Tripod 7Cs instrument uses to operationalize students' perceptions of teaching:

Care: My teacher seems to know if something is bothering me.
Control: My classmates behave the way the teacher wants them to.
Clarify: My teacher knows when the class understands.
Challenge: In this class, we learn to correct our mistakes.
Captivate: I like the way we learn in this class.
Confer: My teacher wants us to share our thoughts.
Consolidate: The comments I get help me know how to improve.

In addition to those seven constructs, the survey also included "engagement items" in four other categories: academic goals and behaviors, academic beliefs and feelings, social goals and behaviors, social beliefs and feelings.

Most of this third MET policy report consists of methodological explanations of how validity and reliability were examined in the process of administering the student perception surveys. The report claimed to have established five benefits of student perception surveys for the evaluation of teaching:

1. Feedback. Results point to strengths and areas for improvement.
2. "Face validity." Items reflect what teachers value.
3. "Predictive validity." Results predict student outcomes.
4. Reliability. Results demonstrate relative consistency.
5. Low cost. Expense of administration is minimal.

Culminating Report: Ensuring Fair and Reliable Measures of Effective Teachers

The last MET report summarizes the three-year research project and sets priorities for the evaluation of teachers. The report claims that the MET project has provided answers to three big questions:

- Can measures of effective teaching identify teachers who better help students learn?
  Answer: Yes
- How much weight should be placed on each measure of effective teaching?
  Answer: 33–50% weight on VAM test scores
- How can teachers be assured trustworthy results from classroom observations?
  Answer: By having more than one observer complete evaluations.

After three years and $45 million of research funding, the culminating report announced five conclusions:

1. Student perception surveys and classroom observations can provide meaningful feedback to teachers.
2. Implementing specific procedures in evaluation systems can increase trust in the data and the results.
3. Each measure adds something of value.
4. A balanced approach is most sensible when assigning weights to form a composite measure.
5. There is great potential in using video for teacher feedback and for the training and assessment of observers.

Each of the four MET policy and practitioner reports has been critiqued and reviewed. Prominent critical reviews of the MET reports were written by researchers from the National Education Policy Center (NECP), which leans Left, and has been consistently critical of privatization agendas in educational research and policy. Several points of critique raised by NECP reviewers will be cited in the second part of this paper to develop the analysis.

Philanthrocapitalism As Exemplified by the MET Project

The term *philanthrocapitalism* was coined by Matthew Bishop in 2006 (Bishop and Green 2015, p. 541). In their book subtitled "How the Rich Can Save the World," Bishop and Greene (2008) explained this new approach to "giving" this way:

> As they apply their business methods to philanthropy, philanthrocapitalists are developing a new (if familiar-sounding) language to describe their businesslike approach. Their philanthropy is 'strategic,' 'market conscious,' 'impact oriented,' 'knowledge based,' often 'high engagement,' and always driven by the goal of maximizing the 'leverage' of the donor's money. Seeing themselves as social investors, not traditional donors, some of them engage in 'venture philanthropy.' As entrepreneurial 'philanthropreneurs,' they love to back social entrepreneurs who offer innovative solutions to society's problems. (Bishop and Greene 2008, p. 6)

By most accounts, philanthrocapitalism differs from previous versions of philanthropy in several ways. First, unlike earlier philanthropic tycoons, philanthrocapitalists do not "give away" money; they "invest" money in particular projects with the expectation of some kind of return on their investment. Eli Broad, for example, claims to be "not in the check writing charity business. We're in the venture philanthropy business" (quoted in Riley 2009). Second, philanthrocapitalists tie funding to particular policy outcomes; they are invested not only monetarily but also politically. Third, current philanthrocapitalist funding reflects the values and priorities of individual living donors who tend to work as hands-on directors of the projects they fund. By most accounts, compared to other philanthrocapitalist organizations, the Bill & Melinda Gates Foundation has been less interested in making a profit, and more interested in effecting social change, particularly in global health and education.

Philanthrocapitalism has garnered a fair amount of criticism in the United States. Most criticism comes from the U.S. political Left on the grounds that private funds, and the pro-privatization agendas of philanthrocapitalists do not serve the public good (Au and Ferrare 2014; Gabriel and Allington 2012; Garnett 2016; Reich 2013). The Gates Foundation, however, is also criticized by the political Right who object to Gates' promotion of the Common Core State Standards, which is regarded by the Right as too much big government interference in education (Porter-Magee and Stern 2013).

In this section, I synthesize commentaries by several researchers to suggest four broad features of philanthrocapitalist research funding in the United States as exemplified by the Gates MET project: incestuous plutocracy, shadow economy, advocacy over analysis, and business over education.

Incestuous Plutocracy

Plutocracy Since about 2008, funding patterns for educational research have changed in important ways. Research funding from U.S. government sources has declined, and funding from private foundations has increased steeply. Philanthropists have been funding educational research in the United States for decades. However, the bulk of research funding used to come from governmental sources such as the National Science Foundation. The NSF overview statement typifies the status and role of governmental funding sources for research:

> The National Science Foundation (NSF) is an independent federal agency created by Congress in 1950 'to promote the progress of science; to advance the national health, prosperity, and welfare; to secure the national defense...' With an annual budget of $7.5 billion (FY 2016), we are the funding source for approximately 24 percent of all federally supported basic research conducted by America's colleges and universities. In many fields such as mathematics, computer science and the social sciences, NSF is the major source of federal backing... NSF determines which research has the greatest potential and would be the most fruitful investment of taxpayer dollars. (National Science Foundation)

In this mission statement, we can see that the NSF holds itself accountable, at least in principle, to the general public – national health, prosperity, and welfare – and to taxpayers.

In contrast, funding for educational research now comes primarily from private donors who invest their money in the tradition of philanthrocapitalism: "The Gates Foundation has outfunded the U.S. Department of Education on studies of teacher effectiveness at a rate of about 40 to 1" (Gabriel and Allington 2012, p. 44). Michigan State University Professor of Political Science Reckhow (2013) describes changes in philanthropic involvement in education from the 1990s to the 2000s this way:

> Three key changes in the nature of philanthropy have allowed major education grant makers to play a more public role and have a greater policy influence: (1) major foundations are giving away more money, (2) individual philanthropists and education philanthropies have become more openly involved in policy advocacy, and (3) major foundations have tried to emulate business practices and develop more selective and targeted grant-making strategies. In combination, these changes mean that major foundations have more resources to promote their policy ideas, they are more openly political about supporting their ideas, and they are learning to be more effective in the ways they distribute funds to advance their ideas. (Reckhow 2013, pp. 27–28)

Because philanthrocapitalists are not only monetarily but also politically invested in the educational projects they fund, the choices of projects for support reflect the personal preferences of the individual donors. Since all philanthropists are rich, current funding for educational research has taken on characteristics of a plutocracy. As Reich (2013) noted: "A democratic society is committed, at least in principle, to the equality of citizens. But foundations are, virtually by definition, the voice of plutocracy."

It is perhaps worth noting that public school educational research and reform is now being directed and funded by people whose children do not attend public schools. All research for the MET project was conducted in U.S. public schools. Bill and Melinda Gates' own children attended the Lakeside School in Seattle, which is a private school and therefore not considered for inclusion in the MET project, and not subject to the reform initiatives advocated by the Bill & Melinda Gates Foundation.

Incestuousness Funding for educational research is coming from rich private donors; that's the plutocracy part. But equally remarkable is the degree to which the various philanthropic agencies are connected to each other, and how their respective reform agendas appear to be aligned. To begin with, nearly all philanthropists in the United States are White men. According to the BBC, as of 2015 there were only two Black billionaires in the United States (Michael Jordan and Oprah Winfrey), compared to 500 White billionaires (BBC News 2015), and so cultural homogeneity pertains even at demographic dimensions of philanthropy. Educational policy analyst Rogers (2015a, b) concurs: "There is, at the very least, a narrowing of voices in education reform. That pattern began around 2000 and has accelerated since 2005, as a result of big donor philanthropy" (p. 746).

One dimension of incestuousness reflected in the Gates project is that MET research appears to have relied almost exclusively on its own paid researchers for background, design, and analysis of the research. The critical reviews by Rothstein and Mathis (2013) and Guarino and Stacy (2012) note that the MET reports appear to have drawn their conclusions without making reference to previously published research that speaks directly to the questions posed by the MET project, and without submitting their research design or analyses to peer review.[4] In addition, critical reviews of the MET research reports were published after every MET report, but there is no indication that the specific methodological critiques in those reviews had any impact on the subsequent conduct of the research or reports of the MET findings.

Several researchers have documented the incestuous practices of philanthrocapitalist agendas for funding educational research. As Reckhow and Tompkins-Stange (2015) note in the title of their article, the Gates and Broad foundations are "Singing from the Same Hymnbook" when it comes to choosing and designing educational projects to fund. Similarly, Scott and Jabbar (2014) describe the trend toward inbreeding as "the hub and the spokes," in which there is one agenda for reform – the hub – around which various philanthrocapitalist organizations and foundations radiate like so many spokes. Garnett (2016) calls the homogeneity of philanthrocapitalism a "walled garden." Vogel (2016) notes that a homogeneity of agendas comprises a "tangled network" of (primarily right-wing) organizations including advocacy groups (e.g., StudentsFirst), media (e.g., Education Next), philanthropy (e.g.,

---

[4] Rothstein cites the following studies as pertinent to the MET research, but absent from the MET report: Kane and Staiger (2008); Rivkin et al. (2005); Rothstein (2010). Guarino and Stacy also mention Corcoran et al. (2012); Guarino et al. (2012).

Charles Koch Foundation), corporations (e.g., Pearson PLC), and think tanks (e.g., American Enterprise Institute). Vogel refers to the incestuousness of philanthrocapitalism as an "echo chamber," saying there are:

> many overlapping connections in this echo chamber of advocacy groups, think tanks, and media outlets that are increasingly funded by a handful of conservative billionaires and for-profit education companies—often without proper disclosure. These groups are driving the education privatization movement forward by co-opting the education reform mantle. (Vogel 2016 online)

The incestuous network of philanthrocapitalism extends to include even media outlets such as the U.S. National Public Radio that have traditionally been regarded as independent. Because of foundation advocacy funding for media coverage, there are very few opportunities for critique or external review of philanthrocapitalist agendas in education reform:

> In the field of education, where Gates' emphasis on teacher quality and small schools has been hotly debated, a $500,000 grant to the Brookings Institution aims to 're-engineer media coverage of secondary and postsecondary education.' *Education Week* magazine has received $4.5 million from the Gates Foundation. (Doughton and Heim 2011, online)

The Gates Foundation is directing the choices for school reform, the approach to research of those choices, the review of their own research, and the media coverage that publicizes their research.

Finally, the philanthrocapitalistic network has extended its reach into governmental offices. The activity and prominent visibility of big-money foundation work has led to the placement of former Gates Foundation staff members into positions of power in large urban school districts and in the U.S. Department of Education including Jim Shelton, U.S. Assistant Deputy Secretary for Innovation and Improvement, and Joanne Weiss, director of the Obama administration's Race to the Top.

Vogel's (2016) meticulous analysis shows that not only is philanthrocapitalism the exclusive domain of the richest people, but that among the primary players, there is apparently no disagreement about priorities; instead there is a blanket acceptance of the value of privatized schools and the use of VAM for teacher evaluation. Notably, there is no apparent acknowledgement or consideration of the viewpoints of people whose children attend the schools that are being studied and subjected to foundation-sponsored reforms.

"Incestuous practices" refers to an inbred network of think tanks, advocacy groups, university research units, and foundations – including Gates – that have established their legitimacy by referencing one another in a tight orbit of relations. Vogel's (2016) analysis shows that in one case, a member of The74 media group is married to a board member of the StudentsFirst advocacy group. In another example, the American Federation for Children/Alliance for School Choice shares board and/or staff members with the Foundation for Excellence in Education, the Policy Innovators in Education Network, and the American Center for School Choice (Vogel 2016). This "echo chamber" network provides mutually reinforcing research, lobbying, funding and policy-making by a small number of elite groups that are all "singing from the same hymnbook" (Reckhow and Tompkins-Stange 2015).

NECP reviews of the MET policy and practitioner reports:

1. NECP Review of First MET Report (Rothstein 2010)
2. NECP Review of Second Report (Guarino and Stacy 2012)
3. NECP Review of Third Report (Camburn 2012)
4. NECP Review of the two culminating reports (Rothstein and Mathis 2013)

Shadow Economy and the Problem of Accountability

The National Science Foundation funds a great deal of university research in the United States. As a government-sponsored organization, its agenda, priorities, and criteria are publicly available, and the NSF budgetary operations are accountable to taxpayers. However, private foundations are under no obligation to make their operations public or to subject their decision making to any kind of scrutiny (LA Times Editorial Board 2016). Lack of accountability is one of the strongest and most frequent criticisms of philanthrocapitalist involvement in education, which includes the Gates MET project (Buchanan 2008; Reckhow 2013; Reich 2013; Tompkins-Stange 2016a, b).

Scott and Jabbar (2014) use the term "Intermediary Organizations" to refer to the network of foundations, think tanks, media groups, and corporations that operate in a fuzzy, ill-defined shadow economy. Intermediary Organizations are neither fully public nor fully private; they "include a range of entities, including think tanks, advocacy groups, teachers' unions, research consortia, civil rights organizations, lobbyists, and parent coalitions … that operate between formal policymaking structures and schools" (Scott and Jabbar 2014, p. 237). There are neither formal laws that regulate nor civic mechanisms that restrain the operations of Intermediary Organizations including philanthrocapitalist foundations, which places philanthrocapitlist educational projects in a shadow economy.

Reich (2013) argues that philanthrocapitalist foundations lack electoral accountability – if you don't like it, you can't vote them out; they also lack market accountability – if you don't like it, you can't boycott the product, either. Referring to SAC Capital, owned by Connecticut charter-school promoter Steven A. Cohen, Singer (2016) wrote: "Maybe someone can explain to me why the CEO of a company that pleaded guilty to criminal fraud, a man who is barred from managing other people's money, is permitted to influence educational policy in the United States" (Singer 2016).

One may argue that foundation-funded educational research and reform is not so shadowy because they are ultimately accountable to local school districts that have the option of refusing to participate in foundation-sponsored research or reforms.[5] That would be true if there were no element of coercion in the relationship between the foundations and the schools. Tompkins-Stange (2016b) describes typical situa-

---

[5] Thanks to Ethan Hutt for raising this point.

tions of educational funding in which state money is not available or not sufficient for schools, especially those in poorer areas. In those strapped conditions, school districts often agree to accept the "golden handcuffs" of private donors in attempts to improve conditions in their local schools. Tompkins-Stange goes on to note that this pattern of foundation-backed funding exacerbates inequalities between rich and poor school districts. Children in poor school districts are disproportionately subjected to the experimental educational pet projects favored by rich philanthropists, which usually amounts to privatization, more frequent testing, and more corporately owned charter schools. Tompkins-Stange writes, "Foundations are notoriously insular institutions, which rarely welcome or seek out criticism, especially from the voices of affected communities" (Tompkins-Stange 2016b).

In support of foundations' rights to do as they please with their own money, Coyne (2013) argues, "If we are truly committed to a free society, we should embrace foundations as a manifestation of private citizens making their best judgments with their own property" (Coyne 2013). That would be reasonable if philanthrocapitalist foundations were entirely private, and if they restricted their involvement to private corporate ventures. However, projects such as Gates' MET have extended their reach and intensified their influence into *public* education. The MET project (and the Common Core State Standards) have had a profound impact on publicly supported schools, but without shouldering concomitant accountability to the public. As University of Michigan Public Policy Professor Tompkins-Stange (2016b) asks, "Why should Bill Gates decide how our children should be educated?"

In the United States, tax incentives for philanthropic gifts began with The War Revenue Act of 1917, which specified deductions for:

contributions or gifts actually made within the year to corporations or associations organized and operated exclusively for religious, charitable, scientific, or educational purposes, or to societies for the prevention of cruelty to children or animals, no part of the net income of which inures to the benefit of any private stockholder or individual, to an amount not in excess of fifteen per centum of the taxpayer's taxable net income as computed without the benefit of this paragraph. (War Revenue Act, ch. 63, section 1201[2], 1917)

Reich (2013) points out that since the enactment of this law, foundations have been publicly subsidized in two ways: "the donor makes the donation more or less tax-free, diminishing the tax burden she would face in the absence of the donation; and the assets that constitute a foundation's endowment, invested in the marketplace, are also mostly tax-free" (Reich 2013). Reich estimates that the loss to the U.S. treasury from these tax-sheltering arrangements for foundations has been approximately $53 billion. Based on the tax structure, it is not entirely true that foundation money is private money; foundations are themselves publicly subsidized at two levels of tax sheltering. Because foundations benefit greatly from public policy tax sheltering, it is not true that foundations function entirely in the private domain. Therefore, because they are subsidized by public money, foundations should not be exempted from accountability to the public interest.

The activities of foundations in the shadow economy have implications for educational policy at the national level. Rogers (2015a, b) wrote: "in 2003, 15 percent of experts testifying before Congress had received funding from the Gates or Broad foundations. By 2011, it was 60 percent" (p. 745). Reckhow and Tompkins-Stange (2015) analyzed testimony in front of the U.S. Congress to examine the effect of philanthrocapitalist networks on the legislative process:

> Our analysis of congressional testimony suggests that alternate perspectives did not share the same level of coherence and cross-referencing among a broad set of actors. Thus Gates and Broad were able to amplify a message regarding teacher performance evaluation that did not face a rigorous and coordinated critique at the federal level. (Reckhow and Tompkins-Stange 2015, p. 74)

The Gates MET project was privately directed and privately funded, it was in effect an experiment on school children. The project has had an irreversible effect on public schools in some U.S. districts: "In cities like Memphis, New Orleans, New York and Los Angeles the money and monopoly of Gates and his cohorts have fundamentally changed the landscape of education, children's school experience, and patterns of access to school" (Olmedo and Ball 2016). In spite of these fundamental impacts, foundations have not been held accountable for their effects on the educational experiences of thousands of schoolchildren.

Advocacy Overrides Analysis: The Case of VAM

The Bill & Melinda Gates Foundation, like most current philanthrocapitalist foundations today, is directed by living donors who advocate for specific research agendas. Unlike most Right wing foundations, however, the Gates Foundation has a reputation for being less interested in monetary gain and more interested in having an impact on society. The drive to have an impact seems to have had an effect on what counted as research in the MET project: advocacy for specific reforms appears to have overridden scientific analysis in the research design and reporting. This section focuses on the special case of VAM as an indication of how advocacy affected analysis in the MET research project (Resmovitz 2013).

The advocacy-driven research in the MET project is not unique. Several commentators have remarked on the tendency for philanthrocapitalism to replace scientific research with advocacy for particular kinds of school reforms. As Buchanan (2008) wrote: "The biggest mistake comes in equating all of this emphasis on 'impact' and 'strategic philanthropy' with 'business' and 'capitalism.' It's as if these words are all synonyms to the authors" (Buchanan 2008, online).

Reckhow and Tompkins-Stange (2015) quoted an unnamed Gates foundation official who basically admitted that the MET research process was a pro forma exercise:

> It's within [a] sort of fairly narrow orbit that you manufacture the [research] reports. You hire somebody to write a report. There's going to be a commission, there's going to be a lot of research, there's going to be a lot of vetting and so forth and so on, but you pretty much know what the report is going to say before you go through the exercise. (quoted in Reckhow and Tompkins-Stange 2015, p. 70)

Over the three years of the MET project, the construct of Value Added Measures morphed from a dependent variable (one of multiple measures of teaching effectiveness) to an independent variable (the standard against which all other measures were validated). Before the first research report was published, a Bill & Melinda Gates Foundation 2009 press release indicated that MET would investigate several measures of effective teaching:

> The Measures of Effective Teaching (MET) project … seeks to develop an array of measures that will be viewed by teachers, unions, administrators, and policymakers as reliable and credible indicators of a teacher's impact on student achievement. (Gates 2009)

In the first (2010) MET report, most of the conclusions were focused on VAM: "Teachers with the highest VAM results on the (easier) standardized test tended to produce higher scores on the (more difficult) conceptual test; Student evaluations of teaching tended to align with VAM scores." Across those conclusions, VAM was still portrayed as a dependent variable, one of several measures of effective teaching.

In his critique of the first MET report, NCEP reviewer Rothstein (2011) noted that the data actually do not support the MET conclusions that VAM on one test is a good predictor of VAM on a different test:

> The data suggest that more than 20% of teachers in the bottom quarter of the state test math distribution (and more than 30% of those in the bottom quarter for ELA) are in the top half of the alternative assessment distribution. … More than 40% of those whose actually available state exam scores place them in the bottom quarter are in the top half on the alternative assessment. (Rothstein 2011, p. 5)

In its treatment of VAM data, the MET report indicates that advocacy for VAM was clouding the analysis and driving what was publicized as educational research; Rothstein provided a compelling analysis that the MET claim about the reliability of VAM results is not justified. Education journalist and New America Foundation fellow Goldstein (2015) agrees. She summarized the two main critiques of MET this way:

> first… the study's data does not support the Gate Foundation's strong preference for value-added measurement as the 'privileged' tool in evaluating teachers, and second… the very questions the Gates Foundation sought to answer limit policy makers' conceptions of how to improve student achievement. (Goldstein 2015, pp. 118–119)

By the second (2012) MET report, however, the construct of VAM had shifted from dependent variable to independent variable. From the second report on, VAM was held as the standard against which other measures would be validated. NCEP reviewers of the second (2012) MET report Guarino and Stacy (2012) wrote: "The title of the last chapter, 'Validating Classroom Observations with Student Achievement Gains,' signals a point of view that considers value-added measures of teacher performance to be valid a priori, a view that is still disputed in the research literature" (Guarino and Stacy 2012, pp. 7–8). Gabriel and Allington (2012) concur:

> In 2009, the Bill and Melinda Gates Foundation funded the investigation of a $45 million question: How can we identify and develop effective teaching? Now that the findings from their Measures of Effective Teaching (MET) project have been released …, it's clear they asked a simpler question, namely, What other measures match up well with value-added data? (Gabriel and Allington 2012, p. 44)

By the third (2013a, b) MET report, the entire analysis was focused on the question of whether student perception surveys reliably predicted VAM results. By the close of the MET project, the only measure of effective teaching was VAM of effectiveness, and other measures were pushed to the sidelines as redundant and/or too time-consuming as mechanisms for evaluating teachers. At a rhetorical level, MET reports continued to make claims that we should use multiple measures to evaluate teachers. However, those claims come across as empty political rhetoric in view of the fact that VAM had become the independent variable against which other measures were validated.

In an apparent effort to finesse its mixed messages about VAM, the culminating MET report took the stand that different measures ought to be combined into a "composite index" of teacher effectiveness. The culminating MET report claimed that different measures serve different purposes for teacher evaluation:

> **Each measure adds something of value**. Classroom observations provide rich feedback on practice. Student perception surveys provide a reliable indicator of the learning environment and give voice to the intended beneficiaries of instruction. Student learning gains (adjusted to account for differences among students) can help identify groups of teachers who, by virtue of their instruction, are helping students learn more. (Gates 2013a, p. 20)

After 3 years and $45 million, the culminating MET report came to the astoundingly underwhelming conclusion that: "Teachers previously identified as more effective caused students to learn more. Groups of teachers who had been identified as less effective caused students to learn less" (Gates 2012, p. 6).

The Gates MET project, as one part of the intertwined network of the shadow economy has had a profound impact on assumptions about teacher evaluation in the United States. VAM has become almost universally regarded as *the* way to measure the effectiveness of teaching. There is no longer any debate among grant-funding agencies about which other characteristics might constitute good teaching, in spite of the fact that no scientific research exists that documents the validity or educational efficacy of VAM to evaluate teacher effectiveness.

Business Conversations Replace Education Conversations

It is not news that business practices and agendas have prevailed over political, cultural, and educational discourses in the United States. In the 2016 U.S. presidential campaign we can see evidence of the widespread assumption that: If you know how to run a successful business, then you know how to run a successful school (or country…). Several aspects of philanthrocapitalism contribute to the proliferation of businesslike thinking throughout all sectors, most basic of which is that philanthrocapitalists are themselves businesspeople – not educators, not scholars, not politicians, not artists, and not lawyers. In addition, philanthrocapitalist foundations are closely partnered with for-profit corporations such as Pearson and Educational Testing Services [ETS]; educational research and reform activities reflect the mutual agendas of philanthrocapitalism and profit-oriented corporations. Figueroa (2013) notes: "One of the best ways a standardized testing corporation can make more money is by coming up with new standards, which is why it's not surprising that Pearson has played a role in crafting the new Common Core State Standards" (Figueroa 2013).

In philanthrocapitalist educational grant-funding organizations, the parlance is no longer "educational research"; it is "educational R&D" (Sheekey 2013). With her critical response to the predominance of business practices in educational governance, Darling-Hammond's phrase has now become an internet meme: "We can't fire our way to Finland." Michigan State University notes with pride that Gates "uses the tools of business to improve educational systems" (MSU 2013). In social theory, these shifts are now being called the "foundationalization of social problems" and the "financialization of the public interest" (Social Finance 2017). The incestuous plutocracy of philanthrocapitalism circumscribes how it is possible to talk about education and educational research. This has resulted in an extreme narrowing of focus for any activity that can be called research; if the research does not test the implementation of an educational reform against VAM, it is not regarded as viable research for purposes of funding or policy considerations. That approach to educational research is a business conversation, not an educational conversation.

As an example of philanthrocapitalism, the Gates MET project participated in restricting the scope of what can legitimately be called educational research. Among policy makers for example, questions about the purpose of education are no longer taken seriously as research topics (Ladson-Billings and Tate 2006; Simon-McWilliams 2007). Educational research is now defined as implementation studies focused on whether schools operate in an efficient way as indicated by standardized tests that are developed by for-profit corporations. Test scores are euphemistically referred to as indicators of "student achievement," and research questions about other possibilities for educational achievement have been displaced. We can see this feature in the MET project's research construct of VAM as it morphed from one of many possible measures of effective teaching to the only measure of effective teaching. In addition to prioritizing technical efficiency, educational research is now dominated by questions of efficient scaling up. For example, in 2000 the Bill & Melinda Gates Foundation spent $2 billion advancing the Small Schools Initiative that established urban "learning communities" of fewer than 400 students. In this case, "scaling up" does not refer to building bigger schools; rather it refers to the assumption that there is a "silver bullet" that can be applied everywhere to solve whatever problems. A third aspect of the MET project influence on educational research is the shift of focus from long-term reform to short-term results. As in business ventures, success and failure of educational reform projects are declared almost immediately after a single – often experimental – intervention. Ventures that do not pay off within the initially established timeframe are abandoned, while philanthrocapitalists move on to launch the next experiment on children's education.

Closing: Educational Research in the Wake of the MET Project

The *We're Pretty Sure We Could Have Done More with $45 Million Award*
goes to the Gates Foundation and its Measures of Effective Teaching Project.
NEPC

The Gates Foundation has recently admitted the failure of their approach to educational research, including the MET project. In her open letter, Bill & Melinda Gates foundation CEO Sue Desmond-Hellman acknowledged that the MET project failed to accomplish what it set out to do:

> We're facing the fact that it is a real struggle to make system-wide change.... It is really tough to create more great public schools. ... This has been a challenging lesson for us to absorb, but we take it to heart. The mission of improving education in America is both vast and complicated, and the Gates Foundation doesn't have all the answers. (Desmond-Hellmann 2016)

The Gates Foundation laid out billions of dollars to pursue their vision of how to improve schooling in the United States. The MET project, along with the Small Schools Initiative and the Common Core State Standards have had profound impact on schoolchildren in the United States with disruptions in their school schedules and distraction of their teachers, with no detectable advantages for the children (Rogers 2013). I could find no evidence that children in the United States benefitted from Gates-funded educational reform projects. The ventures were experimental for the Gates Foundation, and as Olmedo and Ball (2016) wrote: "now we are being told 'sorry it was a mistake'" (Olmedo and Ball 2016). We will never know what effects a different $45 million investment might have had on the educational opportunities of the children in Pittsburgh, New York City, Charlotte-Mecklenburg, Hillsborough County, Memphis, Dallas, and Denver.

Even though the Small Schools Initiative and the MET project have been generally regarded as failures, the Gates Foundation and its Pearson partners have figured out how to monetize the failures for their own profit (Simon 2015a, b). In 2014 the Bill & Melinda Foundation published *Building trust in observations: A blueprint for improving systems to support great teaching,* which explicates in minute detail the protocol for setting up effective classroom observations. Schools interested in adopting these protocols for teacher evaluations may be interested to know that Pearson has developed and is now marketing digital instruments for scoring observations, as well as videotapes (used for calibrating scores), scoring rubrics, and workshops for training classroom observers (see, e.g., Fletcher et al. 2013).

There is one outcome of the MET project that has good potential for further educational research on effective teaching. The MET Longitudinal Database (videos and survey results) has been made publicly available to researchers outside the Gates Foundation through the Inter-University Consortium for Political and Social Research (Henig and Hess 2015). This is an enormous trove of data that is freely available to educational researchers. The available data could be used by those beyond the incestuous plutocracy for a variety of scientific research projects that would be shared under conditions of accountability and transparency. These possibilities would make it possible to challenge business conversations with more educational conversations that are inclusive of a broader spectrum of voices, not least of which are the voices of those whose lives are affected by the proposed school reforms.

Acknowledgements I am grateful to Samantha Caughlan and Sarah Reckhow for sharing their expertise with me in conversations about the MET Project. Thank you to Cori McKenzie for comments on writing. I assume responsibility for any errors and misrepresentations.

References

Au, W., & Ferrare, J. J. (2014). Sponsors of policy: A network analysis of wealthy elites, their affiliated philanthropies, and charter school reform in washington state. *Teachers College Record, 16*(8), 1–24. http://www.tcrecord.org. ID Number: 17387.

BBC News. (2015). *US race relations: Six surprising statistics.* Available: http://www.bbc.com/news/world-us-canada-30214825

Bishop, M., & Greene, M. (2008). *Philanthrocapitalism: How giving can save the world.* London: Bloomsbury

Bishop, M., & Green, M. (2015). Philanthrocapitalism rising. *Society, 52*(6), 541–548.

Buchanan, P. (2008, October 10). Book review: The strengths and weaknesses of "Philanthrocapitalism". *Chronicle of Philanthropy.*. Available: https://www.philanthropy.com/article/Book-Review-The-Strengths-and/162933

Camburn, E. M. (2012, November 15). *NEPC Review: Asking students about teaching: Student perception surveys and their implementation.* National Education Policy Center. Available: http://nepc.colorado.edu/thinktank/review-asking-students

Corcoran, S., Jennings, J., & Beveridge, A. (2012). *Teacher effectiveness on high- and low-stakes tests* (.Working Paper). http://www.nyu.edu/projects/corcoran/papers/Corcoran_Jennings_Houston_Teacher_Effects.pdf

Coyne, C. J. (2013). The rights of the wealthy. *Boston Review.*. Available: http://bostonreview.net/forum/what-are-foundations/rights-wealthy

Desmond-Hellmann, S. (2016). *What if...A letter from the CEO of the Bill & Melinda Gates Foundation.* Available: http://www.gatesfoundation.org/2016/ceo-letter

Doughton, S., & Heim, K. (2011, February 19). Does Gates funding of media taint objectivity? *Seattle Times.*. Available: http://www.seattletimes.com/seattle-news/does-gates-funding-of-media-taint-objectivity

Figueroa, A. (2013, August 6). 8 Things you should know about corporations like Pearson that make huge profits from standardized tests. *Alternet.*. http://www.alternet.org/education/corporations-profit-standardized-tests

Fletcher, P. R., Basset, K., Kirkland, J., & Bimler, D. (2013). *Teacher effectiveness card sort devices: Efficiently measuring educator effectiveness and informing teacher development.* Paper presented at NCME 2013 annual meeting in San Francisco, CA.Available: http://researchnetwork.pearson.com/wp-content/uploads/TeacherEffectivenessCardSortDevices-EfficientlyMeasuringEducatorEffectivenessandInformingTeacherDevelopment.pdf

Gabriel, R., & Allington, R. (2012). The MET project: the wrong $45 million question. *Educational Leadership, 70*(3), 44–49.

Garnett, D. (2016, October 16). The brilliant strategy of the philanthrocapitalists: The echo chamber. *Diane Ravitch's blog.* Available: https://dianeravitch.net/2016/10/13/doug-garner-the-brilliant-strategy-of-the-philanthrocapitalists-the-echo-chamber/

Gates Foundation. (2009). Press release. http://www.gatesfoundation.org/Media-Center/Press-Releases/2009/11/Foundation-Commits-$335-Million-to-Promote-Effective-Teaching-and-Raise-Student-Achievement

Gates Foundation MET Project. (2010). *Learning about teaching: Initial findings from the Measures of Effective Teaching Project.* Available: http://k12education.gatesfoundation.org/wp-content/uploads/2015/12/Preliminary_Finding-Policy_Brief.pdf

Gates Foundation MET Project. (2012). *Gathering feedback for teaching: Combining high-quality observations with student surveys and achievement gains.* Available: http://k12education.gatesfoundation.org/wp-content/uploads/2016/06/MET_Gathering_Feedback_for_Teaching_Summary1.pdf

Gates Foundation MET Project. (2013a). *Ensuring fair and reliable measures of effective teachers.* Available: http://www.edweek.org/media/17teach-met1.pdf

Gates Foundation MET Project. (2013b). *Feedback for better teaching: Nine principles for using measures of effective teaching..* Available: http://k12education.gatesfoundation.org/wp-content/uploads/2015/05/MET_Feedback-for-Better-Teaching_Principles-Paper.pdf

Goldstein, D. (2015). *The Gates Foundation MET project: Paying attention to pedagogy while 'privileging' test scores.* American Enterprise Institute 2015 conference proceedings. Available: https://www.aei.org/wp-content/uploads/2015/01/Goldstein.pdf

Guarino, S. & Stacy, B. (2012). *Review of "Gathering feedback for teaching: Combining high-quality observation with student surveys and achievement gains."* Boulder: National Education Policy Center. Retrieved October 1, 2016, from http://nepc.colorado.edu/thinktank/review-gathering-feedback

Guarino, C., Reckase, M., & Wooldridge, J. (2012). *Can value-added measures of teacher performance be trusted?* In *Working Paper.* Available: http://education.msu.edu/epc/library/documents/WP18Guarino-Reckase-Wooldridge-2012-Can-Value-Added-Measures-of-Teacher-Performance-Be-T_000.pdf.

Henig, J. R., & Hess, F. M. (2015). Conclusion: Philanthropies on a shifting landscape of policy and practice. In F. M. Hess & J. R. Henig (Eds.), *The New education philanthropy: Politics, policy, and reform* (pp. 181–192). Cambridge, MA: Oxford University Press.

Hess, F. M., & Henig, J. R. (2015). Introduction. In F. M. Hess & J. R. Henig (Eds.), *The new education philanthropy: Politics, policy, and reform* (pp. 1–10). Cambridge, MA: Oxford University Press.

Kane, T. J., & Staiger, D. O. (2008). *Estimating teacher impacts on student achievement: An experimental evaluation* (Working Paper #14607). National Bureau of Economic .Research. http://www.nber.org/papers/w14607

LA Times Editorial Board. (2016, June 1). Gates Foundation failures show philanthropists shouldn't be setting America's public school agenda. *Los Angeles Times..* Available: http://www.latimes.com/opinion/editorials/la-ed-gates-education-20160601-snap-story.html

Ladson-Billings, G., & Tate, W. F. (Eds.). (2006). *Education research in the public interest: Social justice, action, and policy.* New York: Teachers College Press.

Michigan State University, Corporate and Foundation Research. (2013). *Current trends in national foundation funding for education with a focus on ten national foundation.* East Lansing: Michigan State University. Available: https://education.msu.edu/irtl/pdf/Trends%20in%20National%20Foundation%20Funding%20for%20Education%202013.pdf.

National Science Foundation. Website available: https://www.nsf.gov/about/

Olmedo, A., & Ball, S. (2016). Philantrocapitalism: The new tyranny of giving. *Education International..* Available: https://www.unite4education.org/global-response/philantrocapitalism-the-new-tyranny-of-giving/

Porter-Magee, K., & Stern, S. (2013, April 3). The truth about Common Core. *National Review..* Available: http://www.nationalreview.com/article/344519/truth-about-common-core-kathleen-porter-magee-sol-stern

Reckhow, S. (2013). *Follow the money: How foundation dollars change public school politics.* Oxford: Oxford University Press.

Reckhow, S., & Snyder, J. W. (2014). The expanding role of philanthropy in education politics. *Educational Researcher, 20*(10), 1–10. https://doi.org/10.3102/0013189X14536607.

Reckhow, S., & Tompkins-Stange, M. (2015). Singing from the same hymnbook at Gates and Broad. In F. M. Hess & J. R. Henig (Eds.), *The new education philanthropy: Politics, policy, and reform* (pp. 55–77). Cambridge, MA: Oxford University Press.

Reich, R. (2013, March 1). What are foundations for? *Boston Review.*. http://bostonreview.net/forum/foundations-philanthropy-democracy

Resmovitz, J. (2013, January 8). Gates Foundation MET report: Teacher observation less reliable than test scores. *Huffington Post.* .Available: http://www.huffingtonpost.com/2013/01/08/gates-foundation-met-report-teacher-_n_2433348.html

Riley, N. S. (2009, August 28). We're in the venture philanthrophy business. *Wall Street Journal.* Available: https://www.wsj.com/articles/SB10001424052970204251404574342693329347698

Rivkin, S. G., Hanushek, E. A., & Kain, J. F. (2005, March). Teachers, schools, and academic achievement. *Econometrica, 73*(2), 417–458.

Rogers, R. (2013, July 14). The price of philanthropy. *Chronicle of Higher Education.*. Available: http://www.chronicle.com/article/The-Price-of-Philanthropy/140295/

Rogers, R. (2015a, September). Making public policy: The new philanthropists and American education. *American Journal of Economics and Sociology, 74*(4), 743–774.

Rogers, R. (2015b, October 20). Why the social sciences should take philanthropy seriously. *Society, 52*(6), 533–540.

Rothstein, J. (2010, February). Teacher quality in educational production: Tracking, decay, and student achievement. *Quarterly Journal of Economics, 125*(1), 175–214.

Rothstein, J. (2011). *Review of "Learning about teaching: Initial findings from the measures of effective teaching project".* Boulder: National Education Policy Center. Retrieved October 1, 2016, from http://nepc.colorado.edu/thinktank/review-learning-about-teaching

Rothstein, J., & Mathis, W. J. (2013). *Review of two culminating reports from the MET project.* Boulder: National Education Policy Center. Available: http://nepc.colorado.edu/thinktank/review-MET-final-2013.

Scott, J., & Jabbar, H. (2014). The hub and the spokes: Foundations, intermediary organizations, incentivist reforms, and the politics of research evidence. *Educational Policy, 28*(2), 233–257. https://doi.org/10.1177/0895904813515327.

Sheekey, A. D. (2013, July 9). Why we need state-based education R&D. *Education Week.* .Online available: http://www.edweek.org/ew/articles/2013/07/10/36sheekey.h32.htm

Simon, S. (2015a, February 10). No profit left behind. *Politico.*. http://www.politico.com/story/2015/02/pearson-education-115026

Simon, S. (2015b, September 15). Pearson's philanthropy entwined with business interests. *Politico.*. http://www.politico.com/story/2015/02/pearsons-philanthropy-entwined-with-business-interests-115034

Simon-McWilliams, E. (2007, Summer). Federal support for educational research and development: The history of research and development centers and regional educational laboratories. *The Journal of Negro Education, 76*(3), 391–401.

Singer, A. (2016, October 10). Keep Wall Street financiers and hedge fund billionaires out of schools. *Huffington Post.*. Available: http://www.huffingtonpost.com/entry/keep-wall-street-financiers-and-hedge-fund-billionaires_us_57fb6ea1e4b090dec0e717f7?timestamp=1476096233285

Social Finance, Impact Investing, and the Financialization of the Public Interest. (2017). *Academic conference call for papers.* Available.: https://www.ehess.fr/fr/node/9746

Sulzer, M. A. (2014). A critical discourse analysis of the Gates Foundation's MET project: Discursive representations of teaching and learning. *63rd Yearbook of the Literacy Research Association.*

Tompkins-Stange, M. E. (2016a). *Policy patrons: Philanthropy, education reform, and the politics of influence.* Cambridge, MA: Harvard University Press.

Tompkins-Stange, M. (2016b, September 14). Why should Bill Gates decide how our children should be educated? *Transformation Open Democracy*. .Available: https://www.opendemocracy.net/transformation/megan-tompkins-stange/why-should-bill-gates-decide-how-our-children-will-be-educated

Vogel, P. (2016, April 27). Here are the corporations and right-wing funders backing the education reform movement: A guide to the funders behind a tangled network of advocacy, research, media, and profiteering that's taking over public education. *Media Matters for America*. .Available: http://mediamatters.org/research/2016/04/27/here-are-corporations-and-right-wing-funders-backing-education-reform-movement/210054

Wood, J., Tocci, C. M., Joe, J. N., Holtzman, S. L., Cantrell, S., & Archer, J. (2014). *Building trust in observations: A blueprint for improving systems to support great teaching*. Available: http://k12education.gatesfoundation.org/wp-content/uploads/2015/12/MET_Observation_Blueprint.pdf

We're (Not) Only in It for the Money (Frank Zappa): The Financial Structure of STEM and STEAM Research

Karen François, Kathleen Coessens, and Jean Paul Van Bendegem

Introduction: The Social Framework of Funding Dynamics[1]

In a sense philosophy of science, if science is understood as a process that will generate knowledge of our surrounding world and of ourselves, is as old as philosophy itself. After all, both Plato and Aristotle dealt with the problem of knowledge. Mathematical knowledge, because of its inherent certainty (who can doubt that 2 + 2 = 4?), became the standard model, perhaps not available here and now, but surely present at a distance that was and is finite for the one and infinite for the other. But in another sense philosophy of science "as we know it today" is a recent phenomenon for the simple reason that one had to wait until science itself became an identifiable part of society. Take, as the most famous example, Isaac Newton who no doubt many would describe as a physicist or an astronomer. The title however of his 1687 *magnum opus* is: *Principia Mathematica Philosophiae Naturalis* or *Mathematical Principles of Natural Philosophy*, not *of Nature*. One has to wait until the last quarter of nineteenth century to see science clearly described as something separate from philosophy, from theology and other religious matters, and from politics. This not being a coincidence at all, it runs parallel with the Second Industrial Revolution, where links between "pure" and applied science became much stronger.

---

[1] This section and the first part of the next one -on the interest of research 'practices' – is a kind of general introduction that one of the authors, namely Jean Paul Van Bendegem, has used on a number of occasions. It is updated and adapted to the specific theme of this conference.

K. François (✉) · J. P. Van Bendegem
Vrije Universiteit Brussel (VUB), Brussels, Belgium
e-mail: Karen.Francois@vub.be; jpvbende@vub.ac.be

K. Coessens
Vrije Universiteit Brussel (VUB), Brussels, Belgium

Koninklijk Conservatorium Brussel, Bruxelles, Belgium
e-mail: kathleen.coessens@ehb.be

© Springer International Publishing AG, part of Springer Nature 2018   261
P. Smeyers, M. Depaepe (eds.), *Educational Research: Ethics, Social Justice, and Funding Dynamics*, Educational Research 10,
https://doi.org/10.1007/978-3-319-73921-2_17

Is it not striking then that a short time before that, 1834 to be precise, William Whewell, allegedly, proposed to introduce the term "scientist", to have a term comparable to "artist"? Being a scientist was on its way to become an independent and clearly recognizable profession.

Once the scientific undertaking became thus clearly identifiable, philosophers asked both methodological and systematic questions about scientific disciplines, often specific disciplines in particular. Up to the beginning of the twentieth century, their attention was typically drawn, almost exclusively, to the scientific output, i.e., mainly outcomes of experiments and scientific theories, including as most prominent ingredient, scientific laws. Predictions were seen as theoretical calculations or reasonings, deductively derived from accepted theories. This exclusivity view went well together with of a view of theory change that was linear and cumulative. The scientific process itself, i.e., how one arrives at such theories, was largely ignored. This only changed when Thomas Kuhn (1962) published his *The Structure of Scientific Revolutions*. Although now the complete scientific process was studied, it was still mostly an internal approach. External factors were usually not taken into account. This only happened when, among others, Robert K. Merton (1973) published his *Sociology of Science*, linking science to, e.g., economy and politics (and, perhaps surprisingly, to protestant ethics). Thus the field of social studies of science was created. By now philosophy of science sees science as part of society with both internal and external dynamics with radical differences from one discipline to another. This is most clearly visible in the recent development of the study of scientific practices.[2] An excellent reader is *Science as Practice and Culture*, edited by one of the leading figures, Andrew Pickering (1992).

The Interest of Research 'Practices': Unfolding Funding Dynamics

Why are practices so interesting and what is so specifically novel about them? The reasons are plentiful. We will list the most important ones in order to have a better understanding of the interrelation between funding dynamics and the research practices:

- *Practices have a material aspect*: it involves scientific instruments that need to be manufactured, maintained and improved, it involves performing experiments and their registration, it involves computing on often dedicated machines. The prototypical example is the laboratory. Do note that in today's terms the notion of laboratory includes large-scale enterprises involving thousands of scientific

---

[2] In another volume of this book series (Coessens et al. 2012) we have presented in more detail the practice turn as it took place specifically in mathematics. We believe it is better to make the distinction between the sciences on the one hand and mathematics on the other, if only for the simple and basic fact that the practice turn took some more time to catch on. More importantly of course, is that in mathematics different sets of practices are at play.

'workers'. Classic examples are pharmaceutical laboratories and the famous Large Hadron Collider (LHC) at CERN in Switzerland, the world's largest and most powerful particle accelerator employing more than twenty thousand people, technicians included. The material aspect of research practices has important consequences on the funding needed for doing research which is differing tremendously from one discipline to the other. With the example of the CERN, one can easily understand that elementary physics needs more funding than e.g. mathematics or philosophy.

- *Practices are related to learning*: a famous distinction made in philosophy is between "knowing that" and "knowing how". "Knowing that" is the theoretical notion of knowledge, as embodied in scientific theories and "knowing how" involves both explicit and implicit (or "tacit") knowledge. Furthermore it opens the possibility of learning "by doing". The classic example is learning how to ride a bike. Maintaining one's balance is not something that needs to be told but has to be experienced, very much like the skilled driver who is no longer capable of explaining what it is she is doing. STEM initiatives try to implement these practices into the (sometimes all too abstract) learning process of especially the 'hard' sciences.
- *Practices have a social nature*: from the two characteristics above it follows that a laboratory requires more than one researcher and that the learning process presupposes at least two persons, the learner and the teacher. There is at the same time a synchronic feature, corresponding to the networks that scientists form, and a diachronic feature, typically associated with different generations, which takes the form of education and training. This invites us to look at teaching practices not only within academia but outside of it as well and to keep the distinction between public and private enterprises not so much at the back of our minds but preferably deeply imbedded in it.
- *Practices are easily linked to other practices*: if one sees economical processes primarily as economical practices such as bargaining, negotiating, setting up enterprises, checking balances, and so forth then not only the comparison but also the interplay of such practices with scientific and teaching practices are almost straightforward. Needless to say, it is also at this level that technology enters or rather technologies enter into the picture.

As to the specific theme of funding dynamics, we argue that it can be a refreshing approach to look at funding from the practice(s) perspective. An important reason is that we need to take two things simultaneously into account, namely the social network wherein a practice is situated and that concrete practice itself. Just think of any scientist alone at her desk, filling in all the forms of a grant application. At the same time, it is a specific and isolated task but it is also an expression of a social, economic and political system. In addition sufficiently similar practices can occur in different social settings, as in the already mentioned example of bargaining and negotiating.

Given the above sketched framework, in the following section we will focus on a specific case of funding dynamics within the field of education sciences; the case of Science, Technology, Engineering and Mathematics (STEM) education and its variant in combination with the Arts, Science, Technology, Engineering and Mathematics with Art (STEAM) education. By comparing both initiatives as initiated by the government we will argue that the same logic is applicable. Quite some funds are invested in both initiatives. Two questions come up immediately: (a) have these initiatives been successful so far and (b) are there alternatives? As to (a) one can observe that an interesting discussion is going at present (Hacker 2016) In his *The math myth and other STEM delusions* he debunks the assertion about STEM education and the value of requiring secondary school pupils to master higher-level mathematics. Hacker (2016) demolishes unrealistic policies and uncritical celebration of school mathematics knowing that mathematics is the cause of many drop outs at secondary schools. As a teacher of mathematics and of political science Hacker is sensitive to the uncritical fervour of STEM. He connects the academic subjects of STEM to the broader context of the politics of the nation. It goes beyond promoting Science, Technology, Engineering and Mathematics. Rather, it is about the kind of nation and the people we are to be (Hacker 2016). This brings us to the second question (b) if there is an alternative to STEM literacy. Part of Hacker's (2016) critiques have to do with the fact that most of the high level mathematics are of no direct use in most jobs. Moreover we have to take into account that current and prospective jobs require rich STEM literacy. Based on the new job requirements and the broader focus on transferable skills, it becomes clear that STEM can benefit from interaction with art and humanities. This brings us to the dynamics within the cultural and epistemological domain of art in relation to science. Initiatives as STEAM (STEM with Art) or art-based methods, processes and practices can help develop and transmit science and knowledge as well as provoke innovation (Lafrenière and Cox 2012). We should be aware that the domain of arts and its modes of research is a big container having different loads. First, as a practice, art has interesting empirical ways of looking at and experimenting with materials and knowledge. Second, research concerning the arts is a broad field containing different approaches:

- *Research 'into' art*, referring to critical and theoretical views from the outside upon the artefact or artists mostly done by art scientists or musicologists.
- *Research 'for' art* where researchers develop new technologies, instruments or related practices and knowledge that help art to develop; the researchers can be both of the arts or from different disciplines
- *Research 'through' art*, in which the object of research is not only the artist's own art but, most importantly, the artistic process, the trajectory and methods of the artistic practice leading to an artistic output (Frayling 1993); the artist is here necessarily also the researcher.

The necessary combination of the art practice itself with the last domain – research through the arts – offers new methods or ways of investigation and understanding that can potentially be implemented in educational processes and knowledge transmission. The many art-based approaches of STEAM interested institutions as well as the institutionalisation of artistic research have led to a growth of funding dynamics concerning research in the domain of art, however in an ambiguous way and with the danger of copying other disciplines practices. Funds even risk to increase a division between artistic research and artistic practice – the last one being funded by the cultural domain and the first one accepted in science funding only if it fulfils the scientific discourse and aims. When real cross-over projects from art to science and vice versa bridge the gap, funding instances often decline to sustain them. Reflection on and implementation of artistic practices in scientific learning and communication would enhance a knowledge practice that takes into account Pickering's view. Not only for the money. Though we are in it.

We will first investigate the financial dynamics in the academic science subjects in education. In a following section we will argue that STEM as a practice has to be embedded in the broader context of humanities and the arts and vice versa to develop the full pictures of both practices.

STEM Initiatives

Our theoretical framework gives us an insight in the practical turn and the way how it opens up the possibility to study the broad political context of the research field of mathematics education, the mathematics curriculum and the way how classroom practices construct pupils' mathematical identity. This new framework with an emphasis on science-as-practice provides theoretical tools to better understand the socio-political mechanisms and the (funding) dynamics of educational research and of curriculum changes. We can now better understand the incentives of new initiatives that promote intensive collaboration between education and industry. The European policymakers are quite explicit about their international and national policy about education and recently about science and mathematics education. The European discourse is clearly framed within the neoliberal political economy as we will show with the example of STEM education. STEM is an example par excellence to illustrate the post-structuralism and Foucauldian concept of governmentality (Foucault 2004). The concept here is used as an analytical tool to analyse the (European) educational governments' policies. It is about the 'how' of educational governing, about the calculated means of directing how educational researchers, teachers and at the end, pupils should behave and act. This aspect is also emphasised by mathematician and political scientist Hacker (2016). Mathematics teachers are recommended to become STEM teachers who are teaching a STEM curriculum and who will set up STEM departments at school, modelled after international good practices of successful STEM centres. For sure, STEM is an international and intersectional project to enhance collaboration between education and industry. Mathematics teachers but also primary school teachers are governed into a STEM practice of normalization. The STEM curriculum is not implemented by authoritarian principles or a mandatory STEM curriculum, it is recommended and most of the principles are suggestions, recommendations, teachers should be encouraged and supported to adopt …, schools should strive and motivate … in order to install

STEM education at all levels; primary, secondary and higher education (Veretennicoff and Vandewalle 2015). Coessens et al. (2015) analysed the case of mathematics education to conclude that "It is not really about showing how interesting mathematics is for everyone but rather to find the next generation of brilliant mathematicians." (Coessens et al. 2015, p. 124). We then believed that many STEM-initiatives show the same tension, which we will argue for in the next section.

The STEM initiative goes back to the Lisbon presidency conclusions of the Lisbon Conference held at 23 and 24 March 2000. The European council agreed upon a new strategic goal for the European Union in order to strengthen employment, economic reform and social cohesion as part of a knowledge-based economy (European Council 2000, p. 1). The strategic goal for the next decade was to become the most competitive knowledge economy and knowledge society all over the world (Veretennicoff and Vandewalle 2015, p. 6). Therefore 'Europe's education and training systems need to adapt both to the demands of the knowledge society and to the need for an improved level and quality of employment' (European Council 2000, p. 5). The STEM initiative is a new approach towards learning practices, processes and outcomes in educational curricula building upon and integrating the four blocks of Science, Technology, Engineering and Mathematics (Hunter 2014). It often refers to the five E's Learning cycle: Engage, Explore, Expand or Elaborate, Explain and Evaluate to enhance science learning. Within the framework of 'European Schoolnet – Transforming education in Europe', many STEM initiatives were launched to improve educational research and science education in collaboration with industry to keep Europe growing. The economic incentive is clearly dominant. The more than 30 STEM initiatives are financed through European Schoolnet members, industry partners, or by European Union's funding programmes. Educational funding dynamics for STEM initiatives are at the national and international level coming from "Ministries of Education, schools, universities, industry, associations and federations, NGOs, government and intergovernmental institutions." (EU STEM Coalition 2015). The main goal is to keep Europe growing, to improve the competitiveness of Europe and to support the European knowledge for growth economy as formulated in the European Horizon 2020 framework.

Where are we now? We refer to the central questions 'if these initiatives have been successful so far' and if the project serves for the weak and for the strong thesis of the STEM project. The answer depends on the way we measure the outcome. The aims of the Lisbon council (2000) are implemented in the European governments' policies. Last year, on the 2nd of October 2015, the 'EU STEM Coalition' was launched "to create momentum for the development and implementation of national STEM strategies across Europe." (EU STEM Coalition 2015, p. 1). The main goal of the EU STEM Coalition is quite clear. In order to improve European competitiveness, the domains of governments, industry and education have to be intertwined, they have to collaborate and develop in the same direction. EU STEM Coalition uses the metaphor of the 'triple helix approach' as the idea of a strategy that implies a closely involvement of government, education and industry. The incentive of the governments is clearly economical and concerns the economic growth based on an increasing knowledge of the academic quartet Science,

Technology, Engineering and Mathematics. The individual life or the massive drop out of secondary school pupils is of less importance.

Flanders' STEM is one of the national partners. October 2016, the Flemish minister-president announced funding of 3.2 million euro for the promotion of STEM subjects to bridge the gap between classroom and workplace, with links formed between schools and businesses. The funding is allocated to 3 (out of 5) Flemish universities (universities of Leuven, Ghent and Brussels), as well as university colleges across Flanders. The 15 projects include "12-year-olds building their own Lego robots; screening STEM students for enterprise talent; helping teachers and school administrators with awareness of enterprise; holiday workshops aimed at encouraging girls to study STEM subjects ; and boot camps for the various disciplines involved in games development." (Flanders Today 2016).

The belief that Coessens et al. (2015) formulated, namely that STEM-initiatives show the same tension as mathematics education can now be formulated as follows. It is not really about showing how interesting Science, Technology, Engineering and Mathematics are for everyone but rather to find the next generation of brilliant entrepreneurs and engineers to build a strong and competitive economy. One of the above mentioned STEM projects is 'screening STEM students for enterprise talent'; this is the most clear pronunciation of the economic STEM incentives. We can now return to the questions we raised about the funds that are invested in STEM and the awareness of Science, Technology, Engineering, and Mathematics: (a) have these initiatives been successful so far and (b) are there alternatives? Based on the analysis of European and national educational policy we have to conclude that STEM governmentality is working; it is indeed successful, depending on how we measure the outcome. Despite some interesting and critical discussions that are going at present (Hacker 2016) STEM initiatives are a growing business. The alternatives to STEM governmentality are formulated by sociopolitical and post-structuralist paradigms. François et al. (2012) described the sociopolitical turn in mathematics education emphasizing the role of critical mathematics education and ethnomathematics. Besides these two critical sociopolitical paradigms, Gutierrez (2013) also mentions post-structuralism that focusses on identity and power relations and the way pupils mathematical identity is constructed within a discourse of hegemony.

These critical paradigms criticize the economic driven curriculum and they focus on the human right of education and the declarations of literacy for all pupils in order to enable them to participate our democracies as critical citizen. One stream within critical mathematics education raise a new question that should be settled. Pais et al. (2010) shifted the question from 'how' mathematics education to 'why' mathematics education. Pais (2015) takes criticism a step further by examining the social, cultural and political perspectives in mathematics education research to conclude that "mathematics is involved in processes of social selection, in excluding groups of people considered to be disadvantaged, or in providing a clear social mechanism of accountability and accreditation" (Pais 2015, p. 384). If there is alternative to the (re)production of the power relations and the way mathematics is used in schools as an accreditation instrument, we should investigate in the real practice of mathematics and of the sciences in general. This implies first and foremost slow mathematics, slow sciences, slow curricula in order to give pupils the possibility to experience mathematics and sciences and to give them to possibility to practice them. Back to practices in math and STEM education is (in the short run) not competitive, and it will not serve for the exponential growth of the European economy. We do believe that it serves for the exponential growth of a human being and a critical citizenship. With the following example of STEAM initiatives we will show the advantages and the risks of collating Science, Technology, Engineering and Mathematics with Art (STEAM). The inclusion of the arts in the science quartet is not to make them digestible or to strengthen the weak thesis of STEM in making the Science, Technology, Engineering and Mathematics more attractive. We will argue that methods, outcomes and empirical models of artistic research – as an investigation of the artistic practice itself, thus 'research through the arts', but also potentially in combination with 'research into the arts' and 'research for the arts' – become attractive in itself to enhance and develop the new demands from industry and non-academic partners. New competences and transferable skills are needed in a dynamic, international and intersectional global market and globalized world. Innovation, creativity, and out of the box thinking, are competences that go beyond the technical skills of a disciplinary expert. The funding of such artistic research is no step stone to reach higher levels at science education, it is a value in itself. In the following section we investigate the advantages and the risks of STEAM.

From STEM to STEAM, or Let's Move to STARTS

In the introduction we made the distinction between 'research through the arts', 'research into the arts' and 'research for the arts'. We also referred to the importance of artistic practice combined with its nearest kind of research, 'research through the arts', because of its focus on empirical, exploratory and holistic approaches to enhance understanding. When moving from STEM to STEAM or STARTS it will become clear that we move from research through the arts properly said, to the implementation of its practices, characteristics and outcomes into educational settings.

Let's first put the money aside and consider why art matters in a knowledge society, beyond art as art, beyond art for the art. This means questioning art-based knowledges and practices for broader/other aims than merely aesthetic experience, artistic value and entertainment; more specifically as educational, epistemic or innovative tools. As information and research is discipline-related, this kind of information is rarely available in art journals. We need to consult art education journals (like the *International Journal of Education and Arts* or *Art & Research – a Journal of Ideas Contexts and Methods*) or interdisciplinary journals to find some answers.

The added value or complementary add-ons to knowledge processes, developments and descriptions in scientific disciplines are present at the different levels of method, communication and process. Research in arts education or based upon artistic methods offers the following foci: an inductive and experience-based (phenomenological) method, a relational, discursive and collaborative approach, an explorative and creative process negotiating between practice and theory.

First, research through the arts demonstrates that artistic practices mainly use an inductive approach that starts from particular instances and opens up experiences, data and analysis that are usually ignored in deductive and confirmatory research. It is always research through first-hand experience, with the self as primary research instrument, drawing multiple insights from one specific (unique) account: the artist is, with her own mind and body, researching her own artistic practices and processes (Gaztambide-Fernández et al. 2011). While it seems to refer to the egocentric person of the artist, in the heart it is "the process of pushing something away from you far enough that it can be witnessed by others" (Gaztambide-Fernández et al. 2011, p. 19).

This leads to its second characteristic: an artistic approach is always relational and involves a triple negotiation with the self, the material and the other (public). It always negotiates the boundaries of relation and communication and as such promotes new questions, revealing parts and parcels of that what is beyond the visible and expressible. The process of communication of the arts often leads towards an attitude of discovery by the audience (Gaztambide-Fernández et al. 2011). Methods of artistic practices can thus be crucial to a transformation of knowledge discourses.

The third characteristic is its open-ended way of developing knowledge: by way of exploration, by the use of different senses, by dissolving the boundaries between knowledge and the unknown, between theory and practice, between constraints and the creative (Gaztambide-Fernández et al. 2011). Artistic practice always involves knowing, doing, making, without hierarchy or predefined order, but weaving in and out of these three verbs. As such, it can open the horizon of expectation and provoke both reflection and understanding.

The development of research through the arts has provided new and more profound insights on how artistic practices offer different ways of knowledge transmission through approaches that are of value in educational contexts. The *International Journal of Education & the Arts* is one of the important platforms where these insights are shared in an educational context, JAR (Journal of Artistic Research) offers a virtual publication platform where this is shared amongst artists and artist researchers.

Moving towards other discipline's journals, we find research on the importance of the arts for the knowledge society in interdisciplinary articles, mainly in the recently launched STEAM journals or articles. These articles start from new developments of knowledge and science education and consider the import of artistic processes as inescapable for innovation, creativity and knowledge production. Referring to the five E's Learning cycle: Engage, Explore, Expand or Elaborate, Explain and Evaluate, the first two E's, Engage and Explore, are rather actor-involved, open-ended and experience-based; and are thus actions that are more related to an inductive and artistic process than a deductive, confirmatory process of the sciences and its theory production. The three last ones relate more to the scientific process of theory confirmation or articulation out of certain hypotheses or experiments.

The aim of STEAM, a fast evolution after the move in science education towards STEM, is to add artistic skills into this learning and research process and to reveal how necessary artistic competencies are to enrich and to help the proficiency and benefits of the five E's (Rule 2016). STEAM defenders communicate the following values of integrating the arts in the curricula of STEM: (i) problem solving, exploration and adaptability – which relates to the first point of induction and self-experience; (ii) critical thinking, communication and collaboration – which refers to the second point of relationality and negotiation; and last but not least (iii) creativity, agility, divergent thinking and inventiveness – which brings us again to the third element of open-endedness and expectation (Henriksen 2014; Rule 2016; Kawasaki and Toyofuku 2013). All these competences are of great value in new job requirements.

The integration of arts-based methods and practices with research is a marginal but ongoing practice for example in the humanities, sciences, and education. One of these art-based methods is the use of performance for presenting knowledge and research. Various studies reveal that the use of the artistic format of a performance in pedagogical and research situations enhances understanding both for the performers and the audience (Lafrenière and Cox 2012; Lea et al. 2011). Artistically-framed formats generate "possibilities for fresh approaches to creating, translating, and exchanging knowledge" (Lea et al. 2011).

We will develop shortly one example for clarity: the study of Lafrenière and Cox (2012) described in *Means of Knowledge Dissemination: Are the* Café *Scientifique and the Artistic Performance Equally Effective?* (Lafrenière and Cox 2012). The researchers compared two formats of dissemination and communication of the same topic in health research to a wide audience: the scientific café and the artistic performance. The questions at the heart of this experiment concerned the effectiveness of transference of research knowledge. The first format, the research café involved the introduction of the topic 'being a human subject in health research' and three formal ten-minute oral presentations by experts, without visual aids. The public was then invited to engage in the discussion for 50 min. The second format, the artistic presentation, involved a performance by artists embedding the content of the same relevant themes on health research in different artistic forms – poetry, drama, song and visual arts (Lafrenière and Cox 2012, p. 192). Both formats were accompanied by a questionnaire the respondents (audience) were invited to fill in.

What comes out of this research offers insights into knowledge transfer and understanding at different levels which are some of the transferable skills that are required for interdisciplinary and intersectional jobs in our global economy.

A first reflection by the authors is that attention, credibility and trustworthiness as well as emotional response increase when experiential expertise is communicated first hand and thus from the own experience (Lafrenière and Cox 2012, p. 196). The presentation of research by experts when it involved their own experiences was received more positively than just the exposition of a theory. The means of conveying was also very important. In the performance situation the research findings were presented through artistic messengers, and responders could easily connect with them, as the situations expressed were close to their personal experiences.

A second reflection of the authors is that the transfer of the message by artistic means opens up multiple layers of interpretation and reflection. In contrast with the analytic format of research presentation in the café, offering factual and concise knowledge, artistic performance was more open and provoked aesthetic, ethic and emotional responses. Overall comparison of both formats revealed that the artistic tool of performance for disseminating research enhances a diversity of understandings as it appeals both to the creative and the theoretical, to emotion and intellect, to the linguistic and the non-linguistic:

> The artistic performance [...] triggers more emotions among audience members, generates more questions on the topic discussed, and influences a greater number of individuals to alter their opinion and initial understanding of an issue. The Café Scientifique and the artistic performance both help participants to better understand the topic examined. The arts, however, shine a different light on the issue. (Lafrenière and Cox 2012, p. 198)

We will not dig deeper into this example, but a short view upon the 5 E's pushes the artistic performance as the winner leaving more engagement, exploration, elaboration, explanation and potential evaluation on the side of the audience of the scientific topic and contributed to better understanding. This is one of the examples that shows us that reflection on and implementation of artistic practices in scientific learning and communication would enhance a knowledge practice that takes into account Pickering's (1992) view.[3]

But what about the money? Why is the government investing funding not only in research through the arts but also in arts related or interdisciplinary art-science research? There are some funding initiatives that point to positive directions. One of these is part of the big EU funding and named STARTS. Indeed, in Europe, a similar (but not identic) move as the American STEM to STEAM is the S&T&ARTS, or STARTS project line prepared in 2013–2014 and realized from 2016 on, for the Horizon 2020 research funding of the European Union. START means the following:

> STARTS – Science, Technology and the Arts brings together artists and researchers to creatively innovate in ICT. The study presents artists' critical but constructive approach to technology with close-to-market outputs, a strong common focus towards social innovation, linking research and science communication to new social and educational platforms. The multidisciplinary and hybrid approach with technology as common ground blends research and artistic practices into tangible outcomes and results. (European Commission 2015, p. 3)

This was followed up in 2016 by a funded project line 'ICT-36-2016: boost synergies between artists, creative people and technologists', fostering interaction and innovation by bringing artists and technologists/scientists together. The scope of the project is to establish:

> a structured dialogue between creative people and technology developers and encouraging artists' integration into research and innovation projects, providing visibility of good practices and rewarding them. (European Commission 2016, p. 92)

---

[3] Although we should leave open the possibility that, apart from enhancement, more types of interactions are imaginable, including negative cases where the practices counteract one another.

Looking at the origins of STEM and STEAM, as well as of the European STARTS, we can conclude a timid but interesting move towards research on and funding of inter- and trans-disciplinary projects that aim at the transmission and exploration of knowledge in engaged, both artistic and scientific, ways. We hope to see a future continuity and growth of these interactive, interdisciplinary and innovative formats of funding where knowing, doing and making are complementary assets of engaged explorative and negotiating learners.

From Funding Dynamics to Funding Human Dynamics

In this paper on the topic of funding dynamics and how they shape educational research we focussed on the disciplines of sciences (including mathematics) and its combination with the arts. In order to understand the complexity of how funding dynamics impact educational research we need a theoretical framework that goes back to the philosophy of sciences from the second half of the twentieth century. From the tradition of analytical philosophy we mentioned the practical turn in philosophy of science. With Kuhn (1962) it becomes clear that sciences are a human practice. Therefore a full study and philosophy of sciences has to reflect on the process of sciences and not only on the output or the final (consistent) theory. Kuhn's (1962) internal perspective on the social aspect of sciences was broaden by the work of Merton (1973) who emphasised the social embeddedness of sciences. From this perspective we have a first opening to take funding dynamics into account to study the practice of science. The work of Merton (1973) was elaborated on by Pickering (1992) who collected the research of sociologists, anthropologists, ethnographers and philosophers of sciences. He offered a rich pallet of how sciences as a human practice is embedded in the complexity of communities of researchers, material conditions of doing sciences, paradigms, institutions, funding bodies, communication canals, journals, indexes; but also sciences, politics, education and economy.

About the same period – during the second half of the twentieth century – the political aspect of sciences was unfold by post-structuralism and Foucauldian philosophers (Foucault, 2004). The concept of governmentality gives us a theoretical tool to analyse the impact of funding dynamics on scientific and philosophical research but also on the effects of the research on teachers and pupils individual life.

One concluding point we can draw based on the analysis of STEM, STEAM and STARTS is that our research practices (at least in Europe and USA) take place in a democratic context of neoliberal economy. Science practices are one of the pillars of our neoliberal economy as expressed in the EU 'Horizon 2020 Knowledge for growth'. As a result, sciences are monetised and have to serve for the growth of Europe and of the USA (as explicitly formulated in the sources we mentioned in our analysis). A second concluding point is that it is primordial to take into account the social and human component for developing knowledge growth. Science practices are and remain human practices, realized by the broad capacities of the human being that not only encompass analytical and logical thinking and know-that, but that also reveal the necessity of creativity, communication, tacit and embodied knowledge and know-how. A pendulum for such growth will always balance between these human complementarities. The result is that STEM always will need at a certain point STEAM or STARTS, and research funding will have to acknowledge this given.

A further interesting discussion for researchers, educators and philosophers but also for teachers who are expected to deal with STEM, STEAM and STARTS curricula, is then how we can make use of this governmentality research context, educational policy and curriculum to connect to the basic needs of human beings in their Lifeworld. Funding dynamics are basically human dynamics, or they will not survive.

Afterword

We're only in it for the money is an album released by Frank Zappa in 1968. The title tackles the commercial and economic value of everything, in this case of rock and pop music. The aesthetic and political intentions of a 'progressive' rock and pop music were of course dependent upon funding dynamics in the existing economic and political context:

> Within the overall relations of capitalism and under the conditions of an industry structured along monopolistic lines the relationships between goods and money is the foundation which makes the production and distribution of rock music possible, whether musicians admit this or not. (Wicke and Fogg 1990, p. 114)

All about funding dynamics, or about funding human dynamics?

References

Coessens, K., François, K., & Van Bendegem, J. P. (2012). Mirror neuron, mirror neuron in the brain, who's the cleverest of them all? From the attraction of psychology to the discovery of the social. In P. Smeyers & M. Depaepe (Eds.), *Educational research. The attraction of psychology* (pp. 91–104). Dordrecht: Springer.

Coessens, K., François, K., & Van Bendegem, J. P. (2015, November 12–14). Math and music: Not for profit. In P. Smeyers, & M. Depaepe (Eds.), Proceedings of the philosophy and history of the discipline of education – Purposes, projects and practices of educational research. Ethics and social justice (pp. 119–131). Leuven: Conference Proceeding.

EU STEM Coalition. (2015). *About the coalition*. Retrieved November 1, 2016 from http://www.stemcoalition.eu/

European Commission. (2015.) *ICT art connect – Activities linking ICT and art: Past experience – Future activities*. Retrieved November 3, 2016, from https://ec.europa.eu/digital-single-market/en/news/ict-art-connect-activities-linking-ict-and-art-past-experience-future-activities

European Commission. (2016). Horizon 2020 – *Work programme 2016–2017*. European Commission Decision C(2016)4614 of 25 July 2016.

European Council. (2000). *Presidency note on employment, economic reforms and social cohesion towards a Europe based on innovation and knowledge* (5256/00 + ADD1 COR 1). Retrieved

November 1, 2016, from. http://www.consilium.europa.eu/en/search/?q=5256%2F00+%2B+ADD1+COR+1&search=search

Flanders Today. (2016). *€3.2 million for science and maths projects. Initiatives bridge the gap between the classroom and workplace*. Retrieved November 1, 2016, from. http://www.flanderstoday.eu/education/%E2%82%AC32-million-science-and-maths-projects

Foucault, M. (2004.). *Sécurité, territoire, population*, Cours au Collège de France (1977–1978). Paris: Editions du Seuil.

François, K., Coessens, K., & Van Bendegem, J. P. (2012). The interplay of psychology and mathematics education: From the attraction of psychology to the discovery of the social. *Journal of Philosophy of Education, 46*(3), 370–385.

Frayling, C. (1993). Research in art and design. *Royal College of Art Research Papers Series, 1*(1), 1–5. London: Royal College of Art.

Gaztambide-Fernández, R., Cairns, K., Kawashima, Y., Menna, L., & VanderDussen, E. (2011). Portraiture as pedagogy: Learning research through the exploration of context and methodology. *International Journal of Education & the Arts, 12*(4). Retrieved November 2, 2016, from http://www.ijea.org/v12n4/

Gutierrez, D. (2013). The sociopolitical turn in mathematics education. *Journal for Research in Mathematics Education, 44*(1), 37–68.

Hacker, A. (2016). *The math myth and other STEM delusions*. New York: The New Press.

Henriksen, D. (2014). Full STEAM ahead: Creativity in excellent STEM teaching practices. *The STEAM Journal, 1*(2), art. 15. Retrieved November 3, 2016, from http://scholarship.claremont.edu/steam/vol1/iss2/15.

Hunter, W. J. F. (2014). Welcome back to the Journal of STEM Teacher Education. *Journal of STEM Teacher Education, 49*(1), 1–2. Retrieved November 2, 2016, from http://ir.library.illinoisstate.edu/jste/vol49/iss1/3.

Kawasaki, J., & Toyofuku, D. (2013). A distributed intelligence approach to multidisciplinarity: Encouraging divergent thinking in complex science issues in society. *The STEAM Journal, 1*(1), 1–8. Retrieved November 2, 2016, from http://scholarship.claremont.edu/steam/vol1/iss1/10.

Kuhn, T. [1962] (1970). *The structure of scientific revolutions* (2nd ed., enlarged). Chicago: The University of Chicago Press.

Lafrenière, D., & Cox, S. M. (2012). Means of knowledge dissemination: Are the *Café Scientifique* and the Artistic performance equally effective? *Sociology Mind, 2*(2), 191–199.

Lea, G. W., Belliveau, G., Wager, A., & Beck, J. L. (2011). A loud silence: Working with research-based theatre and a/r/tography. *International Journal of Education & the Arts, 12*(16), 1–18. Retrieved November 2, 2016, from http://www.ijea.org/v12n16/.

Merton, R. (1942/1973). The normative structure of science. In N. W. Storer (Ed.), The sociology of science. Theoretical and empirical investigations (pp. 267–278). Chicago: The University of Chicago Press.

Pais, A. (2015). Symbolising the real of mathematics education. *Educational Studies in Mathematics, 89*(3), 375–391.

Pais, A., Stentoff, D., & Valero, P. (2010). From questions of *how* to questions of *why* in mathematics education. In U. Gellert, E. Jablonka, & C. Morgan (Eds.), *Proceedings of the sixth international mathematics education and society conference* (pp. 398–407). Berlin: Freie Universität Berlin.

Pickering, P. (Ed.). (1992). *Science as practice and culture*. Chicago: The University of Chicago Press.

Rule, A. C. (2016). Editorial: Welcome to the Journal of STEM Arts, Crafts, and Constructions. *Journal of STEM Arts, Crafts, and Constructions, 1*(1), 1–9. Retrieved November 2, 2016, from http://scholarworks.uni.edu/journal-stem-arts/vol1/iss1/1.

Veretennicoff, I., & Vandewalle, J. (Eds.). (2015). *De STEM-leerkracht* [The STEM-teacher]. Brussels: WK KVAB Press.

Wicke, P., & Fogg, R. (1990). *Rock music: Culture, aesthetics and sociology*. Cambridge: Cambridge University Press.

Dynamising the Dynamics of Funding and Investment Conditions: Coaching Emerging Researchers for Publishing in Intercultural Settings

Edwin Keiner and Karin Karlics

Publication strategies gain in importance as crucial factors for academic advancement since several years. However, it is not only the quality of publication as assessed by peers, but also the quality of publication as indicated by quantitative measurement, e.g. by bibliometrics or journals' reputational ranking lists. The standardized use of such qualitative and quantitative instruments of evaluating and assessing research quality differ according to national research cultures as well as to academic disciplines.

It is of high interest for universities, to introduce emerging researchers into these new strategies of publishing and of performance assessment. They have a vital interest to support and coach researchers in order to produce 'visible excellence' and to get and administer third party funds. In these respects, coaching emerging researchers counts as a strategic investment not only into younger scholars, but also into the universities' reputation and, finally, into their budget. Coaching has to consider – in a diachronic perspective – changes and transitions of valuing and evaluating research quality and its criteria from the past to the future. In a synchronic perspective it has to consider multilayers of parallel changes and transitions as diverse contexts, when different research cultures, definitions of quality and evaluation cultures interact and compete.

Against this background emerging researchers are facing diverse, even contradicting, tasks, challenges, obligations and commitments within universities or projects. As novices they are placed at the lower levels of the traditional academic hierarchy, which they are expected to reproduce, even to transcend at the same time.

E. Keiner (✉)
Free University of Bozen-Bolzano, Faculty of Education, Bozen-Bolzano, Italy
e-mail: edwin.keiner@unibz.it

K. Karlics
Free University of Bozen-Bolzano, University Library, Bozen-Bolzano, Italy
e-mail: karin.karlics@unibz.it

© Springer International Publishing AG, part of Springer Nature 2018   275
P. Smeyers, M. Depaepe (eds.), *Educational Research: Ethics, Social Justice,
and Funding Dynamics*, Educational Research 10,
https://doi.org/10.1007/978-3-319-73921-2_18

Theories of modernisation, of individualisation and risk management as well as analyses about a 'reflexive modernity' (Beck et al. 1994) could serve as instruments to explain such contradictions, uncertainties, paradoxes, ambiguities and ambivalences.

Such conflicting strands and challenging aspects gain the more in importance, when universities and doctoral students are considered, who themselves are working in an intercultural and multilingual academic milieu – especially in the field of social sciences, arts and humanities or – here – in the field of education and educational research. These conflicts and challenges get a material basis, when this cultural and linguistic diversity at the same time is governed by standardised means and criteria, which do not consider such complex intertwined and intersecting intercultural and multilingual academic milieus.

The Free University of Bozen-Bolzano, South Tyrol, Italy, serves as our experiential background to reflect on the multifaceted paradoxes, challenges and conflicts arising from the problems mentioned beforehand. This institution is a small, multilingual, performance oriented university. It works under special legal and political conditions, it officially includes three different cultural language groups – German, Italian, Ladin –, and it expresses its international and multilingual orientation by the consistent use of three languages in teaching and research: German, Italian, English. Of special interest for our investigation is the faculty of education, especially the field of teacher education and educational research.

We use the field of educational research in this multicultural context to investigate the different definitions of quality and of quality assessment, as they are shown by a culturally heterogeneous research community, by different evaluation institutions and agencies, especially regarding the importance of educational research journals. We ask how criteria and strategies of publication influence 'funding governance' and strategies of investment. We, finally, reflect on coaching strategies for emerging researchers and on the ambivalences embedded in and resulting from such strategies. We interpret such strategies also as an investment into the development of competencies and academic performance of emerging researchers, which also will have both an individual and societal return, e.g. in the form of cultivating a reflexive academic entrepreneur, for whom getting funds is essential.

Our sources for these analyses are state evaluation guidelines and regulations, rankings, bibliometrical sources and databases and our own experiences and observations in the above sketched intercultural setting (Abramo and D'Angelo 2015a, b).

First, we expect to contribute to a more differentiated view of evaluation and assessment of educational research quality in complex intercultural settings. Secondly, and of special interest, we expect to find and develop tools and instruments for informing, supporting and coaching emerging researchers to adequately and innovatively enter the academic field and successfully contribute in constructing their own career and in being able to cope with and critically reflect upon such modern conditions of academic work.

Theoretical Aspects, 'Evidences', Contexts and Questions

New beliefs could enter the academic arena during the past years. Beliefs in management according to economy, beliefs in learning instead of education, beliefs in applied rather than basic research, beliefs in decoupling research and teaching, beliefs in market-driven competition according to benchmarks and performance indicators, and beliefs in high-quality and useful outcomes of research, measured by using de-contextualised organisational correlates. These new concepts and beliefs have generated new contexts for research in new alliances between universities and business, and new 'quasi-research institutions', sometimes linked to universities, which are mobilised by national EU funding policies.

Seen from a sociological perspective, educational research is based on such infrastructural conditions, social roles, status, staff etc. Seen from an epistemological perspective, educational research is based on the characteristics of scientific networks of communication, on the publication and reception of research processes and products (Stichweh 1984, 1994; Keiner 2010; Knaupp et al. 2014). Drawing on concepts of systems theory: the specific mode of disciplinary communication in the science system is publication; specialised journals significantly gained in importance as media of publication (and rating). This also means, that publication in the scientific system is equivalent to the function of money in the economic system. Considering the shifts sketched above one could conclude, that publication more and more turns to become a commodity instead a public good (Ball 2004). The so-called information or knowledge society serves as the modern ideology against which usefulness, innovativeness and accountability are to be legitimised (Stadler-Altmann and Keiner 2010).

From a historical point of view, however, we cannot ignore the emergence and persistence of different disciplinary research cultures, described e.g. as natural versus social sciences, hard versus soft sciences, insular versus porous sciences et cetera. And, we also cannot ignore the emergence and persistence of different national research cultures (e.g. Ambrose 2006; Wagner 2004; Wagner and Wittrock 1991; Galtung 1981). They affect educational research in particular due to its significant contribution to reflecting on education as an instrument of building the 'nation state' – e.g. described as a kind of reflection not on, but within the educational system (Luhmann and Schorr 2000).

In the recent contexts of an increasing impairment of an European identity and an increasing renationalisation we also can find that national research organisations gain in importance regarding monitoring and controlling performance as well as maintaining the power of definition and the application of criteria for research quality (Smeyers et al. 2013; Rees et al. 2007; Bridges 2006). These attempts to standardise and to homogenise criteria for research quality are also due to the fact of increasing knowledge production, which leads to the necessity of strategies to reduce the amount and the complexity through categorizing publication units according to quality criteria, bibliometrics or other indicators the big databases provide for retrieving information.[1] In addition, these attempts also have to face changing knowledge formats, e.g. described as shifts from mode I to mode II knowledge (including its criticism) (Gibbons et al. 1994; Nowotny et al. 2001) or described as a distinction between evidence based, cumulative, or hermeneutic, cyclic forms. These varying forms and formats, also driven by modern digital technologies, lead to the problem of constructing 'tables of knowledge value conversion', which – just like tables of currency conversion – value different knowledge formats, national or disciplinary backgrounds, diverse quality criteria etc. against a straightedge of a tertium comparationis – if possible ever (Depaepe 2002).

All these processes and changes indicate an increasing economisation of knowledge production; they show knowledge as a commodity and raise the question, whether research knowledge counts as a commercial or a public good, whether we should rate research knowledge as of use value or as of exchange value. In addition, we see, that not only production, but also reception and rating of research knowledge itself turned to become an industry and a market. Infrastructural conditions and loci, i.e. organisations, administration, budgets etc., play an increasingly important role and superpose, even instrumentalise, the relatively autonomous disciplinary communication (depending from 'national' research cultures) (Bourdieu 1998, p. 19). In this context national research and research governance organisations increasingly govern the knowledge market through defining criteria for free exchange and restricting protectionism of knowledge and respective quality criteria, but also of regulations regarding funding, investment, qualification and career steps of emerging researchers. Commodified evaluation and rating structures and processes define 'quality' and reputation more than e.g. 'open access' for everyone. The increasing dominance of particular competing universities led to a dominance of administration governing infrastructural conditions of the production of 'research quality' – often measured according to criteria and interests of public and private stakeholders (Lawn and Keiner 2006). As targeted publication strategies become a crucial factor for academic advancement, strategic investment in libraries, doctoral students, promising professors and themes necessarily affect the publication behavior of (emerging) researchers and produce new conflicts within the academics – diachronically (e.g. advise, supervision, speed of change) as well as synchronically (e.g. competition between different research cultures). Rapidly changing possibilities and limitations regarding competition, coaching and career raise increasing uncertainties for emerging researchers (Smeyers and Depaepe 2007), which open – in contrast to the logic of standardization and rationalization of quality criteria – the space for exercising new irrational and unjustified forms of power. Power, as to Crozier and Friedberg (1979), is control of uncertainty.

---

[1] Interesting to note the engaged attempts of the European Educational Research Association (EERA) to establish a particular European Social Science Citation Index, which should be driven by European research values, more sensitive and reliable than its American pendant. See Gogolin et al. (2003) and Gogolin (2016).

Such uncertainties are mirrored by questions emerging researchers raised:

- What counts for career?
- Quality of products or quality of networking?
- National or international recognition?
- How do I get access to relevant journals, and how do I identify low quality, predatory or fake journals?
- Who are the influential gatekeepers to the academic market?
- How is teaching and research quality balanced?
- Which standards and expectations do I have to follow?
- Which methodological profile offers best career opportunities?
- Who defines these standards?
- Who assesses my papers/proposals?
- How is inter-disciplinarity related to which discipline(s)?
- To what extent should I consider psychological, sociological, ethnographical, philosophical etc. references?

In view of the Free University of Bozen-Bolzano these questions are related

(a) to particular structures and instruments of the Italian research governance, which significantly affects university financial means,
(b) to the special political and legal situation of South Tyrol ('autonomy status'),
(c) to governance and strategic investment of the 'Free' University of Bozen-Bolzano,
(d) to difficulties and limitations arising from the political and cultural placement 'in between', and
(e) to inter-cultural and inter-lingual situation and career options and opportunities of emerging researchers.

The Free University of Bozen-Bolzano

The above mentioned questions of emerging researchers about their possibilities and limitations regarding competition, coaching and career are related to and depending from the particular academic milieu they are working in. They are related to particular structures and instruments of the Italian research governance structures, which also significantly affect university financial means and budget. They have to consider the special political and legal situation of South Tyrol ('autonomy status') as well as the governance and strategic investment of the Free University of Bozen-Bolzano. They depend on possibilities, difficulties and limitations arising from the placement 'in between' cultures and languages, and they are related to their inter-cultural and inter-lingual situation and career options and opportunities.

The Free University of Bozen-Bolzano, South Tyrol, Italy, especially the field of teacher education & educational research, serves as an example to show such conflicts arising from these changes. The Free University is a small, multilingual and performance oriented university, which is subject to special legal and political conditions due to historical contexts of the region. It officially covers three different cultural language groups, German, Italian, Ladin, and it is committed to an international and multilingual orientation regarding teaching and research: German, Italian, English. Founded in 1997 it is a very young university with a short academic tradition. According to its self description:

> *The Free University of Bozen-Bolzano was founded in 1997. Our university has a strong international outlook, as testified by its multilingual courses (German, Italian, English and Ladin) and the high number of students and teaching staff from abroad.*
>
> *The university has five faculties, and a high percentage of lecturers (35%) and students (17%) come from abroad and they study, teach and do research in the fields of Economics, Natural Sciences, Engineering, Social Sciences, Education and Design. We have 3,600 students registered to more than 30 undergraduate and postgraduate degree courses.*
>
> *The taught modules on offer and our research projects are linked to international and inter-regional networks. For example, within the Euregio project, we are partnered with the universities of Innsbruck and Trento, and we are committed to reaching top quality standards. (https://www.unibz.it/en/home/profile/)*

The Faculty of Education is located at Brixen-Bressanone, a town about 40 km in the north of Bozen-Bolzano and has 1.300 students registered in several bachelor and master programs, a PhD program, professional training and specialization courses. The largest and for the region most important study program is the five years Master in Primary Education, which serves as teacher training institution for educational professionals in Kindergarten and primary school of the region/province. In parallel to the administrative structure of the education system of the province, also the Master programme is divided into a German, an Italian and a Ladin section. (https://www.unibz.it/en/faculties/education/)

Of special relevance for our investigations is the full time PhD program on General Pedagogy, Social Pedagogy and General Education with courses taught in German, Italian and English. Although the program has only 16 places per year available (13 of which with scholarship), it serves as a good example to show frictions and problems arising from national regulations and academic structures, European and international academic profile, strategic investment and possibilities and limitations of emerging researchers aiming at a regional, national, foreign or international career.

The Italian Educational Research Structure

The Italian research structure in general is rather differentiated and follows strict disciplinary classifications, which regulate, reproduce and govern nearly everything regarding teaching and research, budgets and capacity planning, evaluation and assessment. The University structure is rather centralised, nearly everything is ruled, executed and controlled by MIUR, the 'Ministero dell'Istruzione, dell'Università e della Ricerca' and its subordinate agencies in Rome. It is characterised by a very

Functions	M-PED/01	M-PED/02	M-PED/03	M-PED/04	Total
Associato	27	11	26	13	77
Associato confermato	61	17	49	14	141
Associato non confermato	4			1	5
Ordinario	66	22	32	12	132
Ricercatore	96	24	44	22	186
Ricercatore non confermato	6	2	7	2	17
Straordinario	12	1	1		14
Total	272	77	159	64	572

Fig. 1 Disciplinary structure and functions in Italy (selected items, October 2016)

powerful administration, which sometimes acts rather bureaucratic, always being afraid of the legal possibility of getting a recourse against a decision. The university system has a lot, and also sometimes rather non-transparent and bureaucratic, ways of applying for funds, however, there are no independent and self-governed research organisation like the German DFG or the French CNRS. Regarding evaluation, assessment and governance the Italian administration and research policy to a large extent trusts in categories and numbers, which are assumed to guarantee objectivity and non-appealability. This fact also leads to trusting in instruments of structural 'rationalisation', especially to trusting in the useful help of ICT.

Regarding educational research the academic field traditionally is divided into particular theoretical and political 'camps', e.g. the laic, catholic, liberal, Marxists etc. groups. These camps usually are centred around universities; in combination with the disciplinary classification system (which also structures processes of filiation and disciplinary reproduction) one finds hierarchical, sometimes even 'dynastic' structures of the university staff composition. Insofar, the strict Italian disciplinary categorisation also has consequences for individual careers and university performance. This differentiated disciplinary categorisation system characterises the Italian academic field in a specific manner and is, therefore and at least regarding educational research, only to a smaller extent connected and related to academic fields outside Italy. This might also be one reason that the academic publication and presentation culture mainly remains locked into the national or linguistic realm.

Figure 1 shows a small part out of the highly differentiated disciplinary categories and the functions for Italy as well as the hierarchies with the 'ordinario' on the top. That means, that at the moment 572 scholars are working in these differentiated branches in Italy.

Regarding the disciplinary categories you find the following descriptions at http://sito.cineca.it:

M-PED/01 – PEDAGOGIA GENERALE E SOCIALE

Il settore include due ambiti di ricerca differenziabili per l'immediatezza delle implicazioni applicative. Il primo comprende l'area delle ricerche pedagogiche di carattere teoretico-fondativo ed epistemologico-metodologico; in particolare raccoglie le competenze che hanno una tradizione trattatistica e speculativa e che pongono le basi teoriche e procedurali per le competenze pedagogiche. Il secondo ambito di ricerca è caratterizzato dall'attenzione per i bisogni educativi e formativi nella società e nelle organizzazioni e dalle ricerche sulle attività educative connesse ai cambiamenti culturali e degli stili di vita e sulle implicazioni educative dei nuovi fenomeni sociali e interculturali. Comprende altresì l'educazione permanente e degli adulti.

M-PED/02 – STORIA DELLA PEDAGOGIA

Gli studi nel settore riguardano la ricostruzione dello sviluppo storico della riflessione e della ricerca pedagogica, lo sviluppo della scuola, delle istituzioni e delle pratiche educative viste nel contesto socio-culturale di appartenenza nonché la storia e la letteratura per l'infanzia.

M-PED/03 – DIDATTICA E PEDAGOGIA SPECIALE

Il settore raggruppa le ricerche a carattere applicativo e pragmatico che riguardano la didattica, le tecniche e le tecnologie educative sia in ambito scolastico sia nel più vasto contesto della formazione. Comprende inoltre le ricerche sulle forme didattiche applicate all'handicap, all'attività di sostegno e di recupero, all'inserimento e all'integrazione e, in generale, al trattamento pedagogico della differenza.

M-PED/04 – PEDAGOGIA SPERIMENTALE

Il settore comprende le ricerche a carattere applicativo ed empirico, con impostazione sperimentale, relative alla valutazione delle competenze e dei rendimenti scolastici e dei processi di formazione, nonché quelle relative alla progettazione e alla valutazione delle tecnologie e tecniche educative e degli interventi nei sistemi scolastici. Comprende altresì le competenze metodologiche necessarie alla ricerca didattica e docimologica.

Evaluation Systems and Bibliometrics As Important Tools for Monitoring and Governing (Educational) Research

Present-day bibliometrics is mainly targeted at three different interest groups with three different lines of applications (Glänzel 2003).

- Bibliometrics for scholars (scientific information): Researchers from scientific disciplines form the most heterogeneous interest group in order to get information about networks, access to information and hot topics in a discipline.
- Bibliometrics for bibliometricians (methodology): Basic bibliometric research is done in this interest group, which applies it methodologically.
- Bibliometrics for science policy and management (science policy): The large field of research evaluation is currently the most important aspect of bibliometrics. Comparative studies are done on research assessment, and methods to measure output and performance are developed.

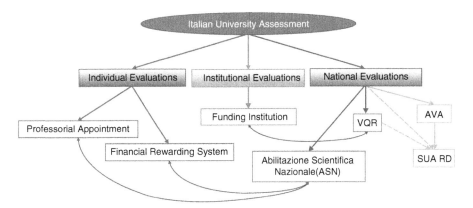

Fig. 2 An example for an Italian university evaluation and assessment system

Especially emerging researchers are confronted with numerous evaluation requests, often not being aware of the application, the output, the impact and the individual consequences of evaluation results, e.g. regarding career, funding, support, organisational investment.

As a consequence, a new line of occupation evolved for librarians and bibliometricians. The counselling or researchers regarding publication strategies and support of bureaucratic data submission procedures, has the aim to achieve the best outcome for both, universities and the individual researcher. In parallel to the Italian evaluation structure, Italian universities started to set up research support systems in order to feed the national Italian evaluation system best and most efficient (see e.g. Abramo and D'Angelo 2015a, b).

The Italian university assessment is carried out by the „Agenzia Nazionale di Valutazione del Sistema Universitario e della Ricerca" (ANVUR) and is supported by the national research database CINECA, managed by a non-profit-consortium of Italian universities and research institutions. University assessments usually address three different levels:

On the individual level evaluation refers to appointments and individual rewarding systems. Whenever parts of the salary depend on academic performance, an evaluation of research output is conducted. This also applies to professorial appointments, where assessment procedures usually include quantitative evaluation elements.

Evaluations on the institutional level are based on obligations to prove and to report its efficiency and performance to the funding body.

On the Italian national level several performance and quality assessment measures have been introduced in the past few years (Fig. 2).

(a) The Abilitazione Scientifica Nazionale (ASN), the national habilitation/qualification (see Marzolla 2015, 2016), is a prerequisite for applying for a professorship at an Italian public university. ASN regulations are well defined and used for individual assessments. In 2012 the ASN was introduced; in autumn 2016 a new round of the ASN cycle started. The ASN is of particular importance as quantitative thresholds are defined for each disciplinary category, which need to be reached by the individual scholar in order to pass the habilitation/qualification (two out of three thresholds).

In addition, the ASN highlights another interesting detail, which reveals the limits of such standardised and standardising systems, when they are confronted with different disciplinary cultures (see Chap. 5). Associated with the introduction of the ASN was the distinction of disciplines into 'hard' and 'soft' sciences. As bibliometric "hard" sciences are considered nine areas including natural sciences and technology.[2] Non-bibliometric or "soft" sciences comprise social science disciplines and humanities.[3] This distinction became widely accepted (DM 76 2012).

The terms bibliometric and non-bibliometric do not only relate to disciplinary categories, but also to indicators to be used for measuring performance. The calculation of bibliometric indicators for bibliometric (hard) disciplines is based on citation databases like Scopus and Web of Science (number of articles; number of citations; H-index). The calculation of non-bibliometric (soft) indicators is based on defined research products, which meet specific formal criteria (number of articles and book chapters; number of articles in class A journals; number of books).

Characteristic for the bibliometric sectors is the need of expensive commercial databases and a convertibility within and across disciplinary fields they are addressed to. Non-bibliometric analyses are less costly. There are no expenses for commercial databases; it is sufficient to use and retrieve institutional research information systems. There are no external and standardised selection procedures. The convertibility of research output within and across the disciplinary fields is rather limited. Although the non-bibliometric indicators look rather open for 'soft' sciences, they create additional problems in view of intercultural and multilingual settings.

(b) The Valutazione della Qualità della Ricerca (VQR) is a national ranking system to which the researchers can submit her/his the "best-of"-publications (see Ancaiani et al. 2015). Depending from position ranked, the universities get rewarded with financial resources, up to 20% of their budget. (The first VQR started in 2011 for the years 2004–2010; for the years 2011–2014 publications were submitted in spring 2016.)

---

[2] Bibliometric disciplines: Mathematics and Computer Sciences, Physics, Chemistry, Earth Sciences, Biology, Medical Sciences, Agricultural Sciences and Veterinary Medicine, Civil Engineering and Architecture and Industrial and Information Engineering, with the exception of Design and technological planning of architecture, Architectural design, Drawing, Architectural restoration and history and Urban and landscape planning and design, but including the whole macro sector of Psychology

[3] As non-bibliometric disciplines are considered: Antiquities, Philology, Literary Studies, Art History, History, Philosophy, Pedagogy, Law, Economics and Statistics and Political and Social Sciences

(c) The Autovalutazione, Valutazione e Accreditamento (AVA) is an accreditation and quality assurance system, based on self evaluation, monitoring of the whole output, periodic internal quality assurance and external assessment of the quality process with a subsequent accreditation.

(d) The Scheda Unica Annuale della Ricerca Dipartimentale" (SUA-RD) is part of the AVA, 2015 carried out the first time, and is designed to serve as the basis for quality assurance measures.

Consequences of the Research Assessment System

This complex and also somewhat transparent-non-transparent research assessment system has been introduced in the past few years to structure and to assess the quality of the Italian research system and, especially, to connect this system to European and international standards. However, some traditional elements remained, for example the differentiated disciplinary categories, which do not consider particular inter-cultural and multi-lingual situations, like the one in South Tyrol.

This system, now, raises several problems for (educational) researchers, here: especially for doctoral students. In addition, the problems significantly increase in complexity, when the particular situation in South Tyrol, here: the Free University of Bozen-Bolzano is considered.

We name the most significant problems:

Nearly the whole preconditions of evaluation and assessment depend on research databases and complex IT structures, a great part of which the researchers have to serve. The applications to enter the respective data are not always very intuitive and user-friendly; in some respects a high command of computer usability skills is required. In addition, the administrative procedures are rather complex and time-consuming resulting in a low acceptance of feeding the system with research information.

Furthermore, from the viewpoint of the traditional faculty member the 'technocratic' research assessment system significantly contrasts to classical 'romantic' ideas of autonomous and independent scholarly work. In this respect also an age factor comes into play, as older supervisors of doctoral students feel less familiar with the new obligations and procedures; this, however also holds true for foreign doctoral students and foreign professors with a lower command of the Italian language and the academic culture, who often have problems to understand details of complex regulations and of data management.

For Non-Italian mother-tongue doctoral student the situation is even more challenging. They usually lack detailed knowledge about the evaluation system, although they are obliged to serve this system. These problems especially apply to the intercultural region of South Tyrol, where German is the dominant language, and the German-speaking contexts in Austria, Germany and Switzerland are highly influential. For emerging researchers, therefore, it is the more challenging, that the Italian evaluation system is not fully compatible with international ones, especially with the (also emerging) systems in neighbouring countries, Austria, Germany or Switzerland.

This situation at a very practical level also means that projects only get funded if research proposals are written not only in English or German, but also in Italian, which additionally increases the bureaucratic work load. For these reasons, researchers follow national, 'domestic' rules and linguistic requirements due to pragmatic reasons using the Italian language. This, however, is a problem especially for researchers in South Tyrol coming from abroad, but also for emerging researchers and doctoral students, who want to keep the possibility of an international career open - due to several reasons in the field of education preferably in German speaking countries.

However, regarding publication in scholarly journals we find further limitations caused by the evaluation system itself. Due to linguistically imbalanced ranking of A-journals, the German research space tends to remain rather limited. A look at the language 'research currency converter' (see Fig. 3) shows that an educational researcher at the Free University of Bolzano could publish in 123 English and 24 Italian high ranked educational research journals, but only in 3 German journals (July 2016). This fact not only reduces linguistic diversity in general, which always means a loss of diversity of worldviews, but in particular reduces the opportunities of doctoral students to publish in other than these three German high ranked educational research journals, which would be of high importance for their academic career in the field of educational research.

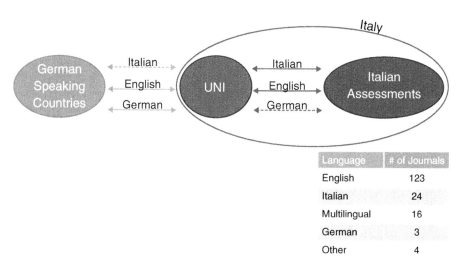

Fig. 3 Publication language relationships and language of educational research journals classified as class A journals in Italy

In more detail: From an Italian point of view, problems are not to be expected regarding publications in the national language. A range of 24 journals with Italian publishing language is offered. In view of respective English journals, the range gets even broader; 123 class A journals are at disposal. Regarding German education class A journals, researchers may choose only among three journals. However, changing the perspective to a German point of view, researchers are facing a different situation. In a German or Austrian context an Italian publication will not be easily considered as high class publication, as only a small number of scholars will know the journal or will be able to understand the language and the content. Therefore, the chances to rate an Italian class A journal in a German speaking country as high as in Italy, are rather small.

Although we have a 'publication market', the 'research publication currency converter' among countries for specific disciplines obviously does not work. What are the consequences? Is publishing in English the only adequate solution (although funds are obtained only with an Italian proposal)? What would a bibliometrician recommend to an emerging researcher? Just telling "these are the class A or Q1 journals" will not be sufficient. What can be done to improve the convertibility of high-quality research in social sciences and humanities, especially in educational research?

Consequences Regarding Coaching Doctoral Students

There is not very much literature about (positively connoted) 'strategic' or 'hybrid' forms of coaching and promoting publication strategies according to Excellence in Research.

In our specific multilingual context we find more questions than answers, here a selection of ideas:

- Try to increase the number of German class-A-journals at ANVUR?
- Recommend to publish only in English? Who is able to guide and supervise doctoral students within a rather national educational research system?
- Offer specific language courses in English or Italian or even a rather expensive translation service?
- Determine the distribution of publication languages in a curriculum vitae?
- Recommend non-Italian researchers with short-term contracts to play a challenging game on different cultural research grounds or to leave the country?
- Work on internationally accepted quality indicators to increase the convertibility of educational research output?
- Compare the situation with other multilingual regions and look for best-practice examples?

We, firstly, opt for better communication between the administrative and research support section and the scholarly production section in order to build strategic alliances. The right box (research view) in Fig. 4 is well known; the left box, however,

Research Output Life Cycle

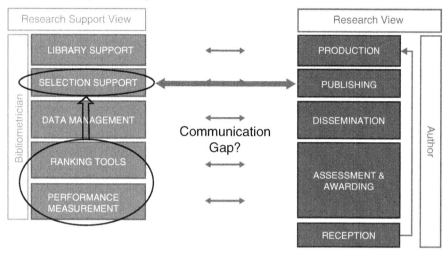

Fig. 4 Bibliometrician's and Author's different perspectives on the research output life cycle

remains often less recognised. Our situation encourages us to suggest to relate both boxes.

However, this measure is just a starting point and might not be enough, because it lacks the reflexive, critical elements. If, however, scholarly literature and educational research knowledge more and more get the character of a commodity instead of a public good, we more and more have to critically accept the Janus-headed character of the 'free' market.

We therefore suggest to teach and to coach students and researchers to use clever, hybrid strategies of research production, to disenchant the 'scientific' ideals, to learn to walk on the edge between the market, on which you have to sell yourself, and the scholarly and public responsibility, from which you draw your professional ethics and identity.

Appendix

Italian classification of 'science of education' (examples):

Scientific Area
11: History, Philosophy, Pedagogy and Psychology

Group of Academic Recruitment Fields (MSC)
11/D – Pedagogy and Educational Theories

Recruitment Field
11/D1 – Educational Theories and History of Educational Theories

Academic Discipline

M-PED/01 – PEDAGOGY, THEORIES OF EDUCATION AND SOCIAL EDUCATION

M-PED/02 – HISTORY OF PEDAGOGY AND EDUCATION

Recruitment Field

11/D2 – METHODOLOGIES OF TEACHING, SPECIAL EDUCATION AND EDUCATIONAL RESEARCH

Academic Disciplines

M-PED/03 – METHODOLOGIES OF TEACHING AND SPECIAL EDUCATION

M-PED/04 – EDUCATIONAL RESEARCH

M-EDF/01 – PHYSICAL TRAINING SCIENCES AND METHODOLOGY

M-EDF/02 – SPORT SCIENCES AND METHODOLOGY

References

Abramo, G., & D'Angelo, C. A. (2015a). The VQR, Italy's second national research assessment: Methodological failures and ranking distortions. *Journal of the Association for Information Science and Technology, 66*(11), 2202–2214.

Abramo, G., & D'Angelo, C. A. (2015b). A methodology to compute the territorial productivity of scientists: The case of Italy. *Journal of Informetrics, 9*(4), 675–685.

Ambrose, D. (2006). Large-scale contextual influences on creativity: Evolving academic disciplines and global value systems. *Creativity Research Journal, 18*, 75–85.

Ancaiani, A., Alberto, F., Barbara, A., et al. (2015). Evaluating scientific research in Italy. The 2004–10 research evaluation exercise. *Research Evaluation, 24*(3), 242–255. https://doi.org/10.1093/reseval/rvv008.

Ball, S. J. (2004). *Education for sale! The commodification of everything?* King's annual education lecture 2004. University of London, Institute of Education.

Beck, U., Giddens, A., & Lash, S. (1994). *Reflexive modernization. Politics, tradition and aesthetics in the modern social order*. Cambridge: Polity.

Bourdieu, P. (1998). *Vom Gebrauch der Wissenschaft. Für eine klinische Soziologie des wissenschaftlichen Feldes*. Konstanz: Universitätsverlag Konstanz.

Bridges, D. (2006). The international and the excellent in educational research In P. Smeyers & M. Depaepe (Eds.), *Educational research: Why, what works' doesn't work* (pp. 143–158). Dordrecht: Springer.

Crozier, M., & Friedberg, E. (1979). *Die Zwänge kollektiven Handelns. Über Macht und Organisation*. Königstein im Ts.: Athenäum.

Depaepe, M. (2002). A comparative history of educational sciences: The comparability of the incomparable? *European Educational Research Journal, 1*(1), 118–122.

DM 76. (2012). Criteria and parameters for evaluation of applicants for the national scientific qualification (Regolamento recante criteri e parametri per la valutazione dei candidati ai fini dell'attribuzione dell'Abilitazione Scientifica Nazionale), *Ministerial Decree 76*. http://attiministeriali.miur.it/anno-2012/giugno/dm-07062012.aspx. Accessed 15 Nov 2014.

Galtung, J. (1981). Structure, culture and intellectual style. An essay comparing saxonic, teutonic, gallic and nipponic approaches. *Social Science Information, 20*, 817–856.

Gibbons, M., Limoges, C., Nowotny, H., et al. (1994). *The new production of knowledge: The dynamics of science and research in contemporary societies*. London: Sage.

Glänzel, W. (2003). *Bibliometrics as a research field: A course on theory and application of bibliometric indicators*. Course material.

Gogolin, I. (2016). European educational research quality indicators (EERQI): An experiment. In M. Ochsner, S. E. Hug, & H.-D. Daniel (Eds.), *Research assessment in the humanities. Towards criteria and procedures* (pp. 103–111). Cham: Springer.

Gogolin, I., Smeyers, P., García Del Dujo, Á., & Rusch-Feja, D. (2003). European social science citation index: A chance for promoting European research? *European Educational Research Journal, 2*(4), 574–593.

Keiner, E. (2010). Disciplines of education. The value of disciplinary self-observation. In J. Furlong & M. Lawn (Eds.), *Disciplines of education. Their role in the future of education research* (pp. 159–172). London: Routledge.

Knaupp, M., Schaufler, S., Hofbauer, S., & Keiner, E. (2014). *Education research and educational psychology in Germany, Italy and the United Kingdom – An analysis of scholarly journals*. In Schweizerische Zeitschrift für Bildungswissenschaf-ten/Revue suisse des sciences de l'éducation/Rivista svizzera di scienze dell'educazione, *36*(1), S.83-106.

Lawn, M., & Keiner, E. (2006). The European University: Between governance, discipline and network (editorial). *European Journal of Education, 41*(2), 155–167.

Luhmann, N., & Schorr, K. E. (2000). *Problems of reflection in the system of education* (R. Neuworth, Trans.). Munster: Waxman.

Marzolla, M. (2015). Quantitative analysis of the Italian national scientific qualification. *Journal of Informetrics, 9*(2), 285–316. https://doi.org/10.1016/j.joi.2015.02.006.

Marzolla, M. (2016). Assessing evaluation procedures for individual researchers. The case of the Italian national scientific qualification. *Journal of Informetrics, 10*(2), 408–438. https://doi.org/10.1016/j.joi.2016.01.009.

Nowotny, H., Scott, P., & Gibbons, M. (2001). *Re-thinking science: Knowledge and the public in an age of uncertainty*. Cambridge: Polity Press.

Rees, G., Baron, S., Boyask, R., & Taylor, C. (2007). Research-capacity building, professional learning and the social practices of educational research. *British Educational Research Journal, 33*, 761–779.

Smeyers, P., & Depaepe, M. (Eds.). (2007). *Educational research: Networks and technologies* (S. 85–104). Dordrecht: Springer.

Smeyers, P., Depaepe, M., & Keiner, E. (Eds.). (2013). *Educational research: The importance and effects of institution*.

Stadler-Altmann, U., & Keiner, E. (2010). The persuasive power of figures and the aesthetics of the dirty backyards of statistics in educational research. In P. Smeyers & M. Depaepe (Eds.), *Educational research – The ethics and aesthetics of statistics* (pp. 129–144). Dordrecht: Springer.

Stichweh, R. (1984). *Zur Entstehung des modernen Systems wissenschaftlicher Disziplinen – Physik in Deutschland 1740 – 1890*. Frankfurt a. M.: Suhrkamp.

Stichweh, R. (1994). *Wissenschaft, Universität, Profession. Soziologische Analysen*. Frankfurt am Main: Transcript.

Wagner, P. (2004). Varieties of interpretations of modernity: On national traditions in sociology and other social sciences. In C. Charle, J. Schriewer, & P. Wagner (Eds.), *Transnational intellectual networks. Forms of academic knowledge and the search for cultural identities* (pp. 27–51). Frankfurt/New York: Campus.

Wagner, P., & Wittrock, B. (1991). States, institutions, and discourses: A comparative perspective on the structuration of the social sciences. In P. Wagner, B. Wittrock, & R. Whitley (Eds.), *Discourses on society. The shaping of the social science disciplines* (pp. 331–357). Dordrecht: Springer.

Name Index

© Springer International Publishing AG, part of Springer Nature 2018
P. Smeyers, M. Depaepe (eds.), *Educational Research: Ethics, Social Justice,
and Funding Dynamics*, Educational Research 10,
https://doi.org/10.1007/978-3-319-73921-2

Subject Index

A

Accountability, 7, 121, 156, 165, 168, 180, 192, 202, 249–251, 256, 267, 277
Action research, 6, 163
Alazony, 3, 34–36
Arts education, 87, 268
Assessment, 5, 11, 12, 25, 49, 74, 81, 86, 111, 114, 132, 143, 150, 156, 157, 171, 195, 201, 205, 210, 215, 242, 244, 252, 275, 280, 282, 283, 285–287

B

Berlin curriculum, 3, 11, 12, 15, 18–21
Bilingual education, 97–99, 101
Bill & Melinda Gates Foundation, 8, 239, 240, 245, 247, 251, 252, 254, 255
Biography, 59, 223, 225, 229, 235
Bologna, 85, 193
British Educational Research Association (BERA), 109, 112, 187

C

Case, 2, 25, 39, 56, 73, 96, 110, 131, 143, 166, 179, 194, 210, 226, 239, 263
Child care, 40, 44, 46, 48, 51
Coaching, 9, 275
Collectae, 193
Colonialism, 13, 15, 17, 45, 95, 104, 201
Commodification, 6, 178
Corruption, 7, 195, 218

D

Dehumanization, 6, 148, 152, 153
Democratic evaluation, 5, 115, 116
Determinism, 6, 148, 153, 154
Devaluation, 227
Dominicans, 193

E

Economic impact, 4, 32
Edinburgh, 196, 200
Education research, 4, 5, 60, 74, 83, 123, 124, 128, 130–132, 137, 138, 176, 240, 267
Education researcher, 133
Educational accountability, 157, 165, 168, 180, 192, 202, 249, 250, 255, 267, 277
Educational equity, 5, 123
Educational research, poetic conception of, 89, 270
El Sistema, 88
Emancipatory research, 59, 82, 83, 114
Emerging researchers, 9, 275
Epistemic drift, 6, 180, 185
Epistemology, 11, 56, 59–64, 68, 110
Ethical guidelines, 112
Ethics, 1, 2, 4, 5, 9, 11, 26–29, 31, 32, 39, 56, 80, 109, 151
Ethics of belief, 5, 116
Ethics of research, 1, 2, 4, 39, 55, 151
Evaluation, 2, 6, 25, 26, 30, 41, 47, 115, 130, 131, 152, 154, 176, 179, 180, 186, 210, 241–244, 248, 251–253, 255, 271, 275, 276, 278, 280, 282–286

© Springer International Publishing AG, part of Springer Nature 2018
P. Smeyers, M. Depaepe (eds.), *Educational Research: Ethics, Social Justice, and Funding Dynamics*, Educational Research 10,
https://doi.org/10.1007/978-3-319-73921-2

Printed by Printforce, the Netherlands